Sport, Culture, and Personality

Donald W. Calhoun, PhD
University of Miami

Second Edition

Human Kinetics Publishers, Inc.
Champaign, Illinois

Library of Congress Cataloging-in-Publication Data

Calhoun, Donald W.
  Sport, culture, and personality.

  Bibliography: p.
  Includes index.
  1. Sports—Social aspects. I. Title.
GV706.5.C34 1987   306.4   86-27196
ISBN 0-87322-094-3

Senior Editor: Gwen Steigelman, PhD
Production Director: Ernie Noa
Assistant Production Director: Lezli Harris
Copy Editors: John Edwards and Kathy Kane
Proofreader: Janet Ware
Typesetter: Sonnie Bowman
Text Design: Keith Blomberg
Text Layout: Craig Ronto
Cover Design: Jack Davis
Printed By: Braun-Brumfield, Inc.

Material quoted from Sydney J. Harris (p. 338) is reprinted by permission of Sydney J. Harris and Field Newspaper Syndicate.

Data from Loy (1969) and Webb (1969a) appearing on pages 211 to 214 are reprinted by permission of The Athletic Institute.

ISBN: 0-87322-094-3

Printed in the United States of America

10 9 8 7 6 5 4 3 2

Human Kinetics Publishers, Inc.
Box 5076, Champaign, IL 61825-5076
1-800-747-4HKP

FOR
ALFREDITO

*A*cknowledgments

I want to express my gratitude in particular to the following individuals: Gary Kusic, who as my student whetted my interest in the subject through his research on Monongahela Valley athletes who escaped the steel mills; Dr. Harry C. Mallios, who as Athletic Director at the University of Miami laid the groundwork for national baseball championships in 1982 and 1985 and a national football championship in 1983, meanwhile encouraging me to develop this course and encouraging intelligent and articulate athletes to take it; the student athletes and nonathletes from whom I have learned, some of whom are quoted in these pages; Vasiliki Toulu, who as a research assistant brought a personal cross-cultural background and imagination and perseverance in tracking down material; Esther Nedelman, who performed the miracle of translating my scribbling into a book for the fifth time in nine years; and Dr. Abraham D. Lavender, who gave extremely dedicated and competent service as my wheels (and brains) in running down inextricable references when I was "grounded" by surgery in the last stage of editing.

Contents

*P*reface

If you are or expect to be a player, coach, official, owner, athletic director, team physician, cheerleader, media person, or sports fan, this book was written with you in mind. Your behavior as a sport person is shaped by, and in turn shapes the society of which you are a part. The intent of *Sport, Culture, and Personality* is to lead you away from the provincialism and ethnocentrism that characterize many current texts on sport. In doing so, I hope to help you gain a cosmopolitan sense of sport as a dimension of the whole human enterprise.

The first edition of the text examined several themes. Significant changes in sport surfacing from the athletic revolution of the mid-60s were cast against a backdrop of sport history and cross-cultural variation. The relationship of sport to the pattern of social organization was analyzed as were topics in social psychology such as sport enculturation, dynamics of sport violence, self-actualization through sport, and player/spectator interactions. From this foundation, a substantial amount of revisions and additions have been made in the second edition.

First, more work has been done on the setting in which sport persons operate. To broaden the cross-cultural reach of the book, chapters have been added on sport in the Soviet Union, China, and Third World countries whose similarities and differences are compared and contrasted with sport in the United States. An additional new chapter focuses on the sport establishment in the U.S. and relates it to sport history and organization in the non-Western world. In the revised sport violence chapter, a wider sociological and historical sweep was added to the experimental social psychology discussion. Similarly broadened and enriched is the chapter analyzing the relationship of athlete to spectator. Finally, the general contents of this volume have been reorganized.

Sport, Culture, and Personality is organized in four parts. Part I, "Sport and Modern Society," begins with the commercialization and professionalization of what was once amateur play. Chapter 2 addresses the concerned reaction against this trend that occurred from the mid-60s to the present, particularly regarding the various liberation movements of the times. The third chapter continues with this theme by looking at basic concepts of play, game, and sport which are used throughout the book in analyzing sport in the United States and other countries.

Part II, "Sport in Space and Time," begins with a comparative study of games throughout the world. Then, in chapter 5, the tradition of the competitive contest is examined as it has developed in the Western world. Consideration is given to the origin of territorial games among the Egyptians, the omnipresent role of contest among the ancient Greeks, the Roman contribution of the brutal spectacle, and the origins of sportsmanship in the code of medieval chivalry. Puritanism's role in both promoting and inhibiting the development of modern Western society is discussed in chapter 6. Finally, sport in the USSR, the People's Republic of China, and in Third World countries is analyzed in chapters 7, 8, and 9 especially as they, like Americans, try to preserve a balance between mass fitness and elite sport.

Sport as a social institution is the topic of Part III, "Sport and Social Organization." First, the sport establishment is examined as a subculture with an organized structure, conflicts of interest, an ethos, and an ideology. Next, the relationship of organized sport to social stratification and social mobility is identified in chapter 11. The last chapter in this part establishes a typology of sport, analyzing how specific "major" and "minor" sports fit into the typology and general social structure.

Part IV, "The Social Psychology of Sport," treats sport as a system of symbolic interaction. Chapter 13 begins by addressing the roles of play, games, and sport as agents of socialization. Next, athlete and fan violence in sport are viewed, particularly as they relate to violence in society. Ways in which sport contributes to personal fulfillment and self-actualization is the topic of chapter 15, followed by the final chapter in the book, an examination of the meaning of the dramatic sport spectacle and the interaction between athlete and spectator.

The ideas for the first edition of *Sport, Culture, and Personality* grew out of my teaching a class on the subject at the University of Miami many years ago. Since then, many students have provided valuable comments which led to this second edition. Although the pages of the book contain discussion of sport persons ancient and modern from lands near and far, the focus of the book is primarily on you, the reader.

I hope as you read the book you will begin to see yourself in sport and become self-aware as a sport person, because it is by examining and better understanding your own sport experiences that you are able to enrich not only your own life, but those of your fellow human beings.

Donald W. Calhoun

Part I

*S*port and Modern Society

Chapter 1

From Fun to Business

The popularity of athletics, the growth of competition, and the rewards lavished on successful athletes completely changed the character of athletics. . . . It was a change . . . from spontaneous to organized sport. The change brought with it both good and evil: the standard of performance was greatly improved, but athletics ceased to be pure recreation and something of the old . . . joy was lost (Gardiner, 1970, p. 70).

These words were not written about the crisis in sport in America in the 1980s. They were written about a crisis of the Olympic spirit in Greece in the sixth century B.C., but they could have been written today. Excessive competition, excessive rewards, the change from spontaneity to organization, the gain of skill, and the loss of joy have again changed the character of athletics. History has repeated itself 25 centuries later. This is where we begin our book.

The history of sport is the story of transition from amateurism to professionalism. The *amateur* is a *lover*. The word is derived from the first and simplest verb many beginning Latin students learn—*amo* (I love). Although the transition away from amateurism has been taking place since the beginning of sport, it can be illustrated by a contrast that spans the recent period in which it has moved most rapidly.

The contrast begins in 1937, my last year as a college undergraduate in South Carolina. My school had a good small college football team, recruited for the most part from the regular student body. It was made up primarily of students who happened to play football, not of football players who happened to be registered for classes; that is, our players were genuine amateurs, not semiprofessionals. If an excellent football player chose our college, we were not unhappy, and our coaches and alumni did actively seek such athletes. There was an oc-

casional player from New York, New Jersey, or Pennsylvania, but our
roster listed mostly addresses in South Carolina or the immediately
adjoining states.

Not only were our players amateurs, but they were also fairly unspecialized. They played one-platoon football, with each man alternat-
ing between offense and defense. Eleven men ordinarily played most
of a game, with occasional individual spot substitutions to spell an injured or exhausted player or to let a benchwarmer get experience. If
a man was replaced by a substitute, the rules forbade him to return
again in the same quarter. The nearest thing to platooning might occur
when a new unit of 11 two-way players would start the second half
or come in toward the end of a lopsided victory. In several games that
year, 11 of our men played all 60 minutes. There were a few members
of the team who played through about half the games without substitution.

Lest we think this was just small-college stuff, in bigger time football 11 Yale men had in 1934 played all 60 minutes of their traditional
big game with Princeton. On the same level, the one-platoon system
produced such incidents as occurred in the sensational 1946 Notre
Dame tie with Army, when the great Irish offensive quarterback Johnny
Lujack saved the game in his role as defensive safety man by bringing
a touchdown-bent Army back down in an open field.

To illustrate the personal quality of this unspecialized amateurism
I can remember our tough, talented, no-nonsense all-state end who
several times wept openly when he ran to the sidelines in front of the
stands after being replaced because of injury or exhaustion.

Today, if football at my Alma Mater had been able (as it was not)
to survive the increasing specialization and professionalism that followed World War II, instead of a traveling squad of about 30 part-time
student athletes we would probably travel with at least 40 players from
many of the 50 states, a large number on athletic scholarship. Instead
of taking their classroom licks along with the rest of the student body,
these semipros would be kept eligible by tutors through specially arranged programs of not-too-demanding courses. Whereas my college
generation of athletes were kings of the campus, today's might be
looked down on as "dumb jocks" enjoying a free 4-year ride. Instead
of being ready to go both ways on offense and defense, these players
would be divided into offensive and defensive specialists and then sub-
divided into offensive running specialists, offensive passing specialists,
defensive specialists against the run and against the pass, specialists
in punting, placekicking, holding for the placekick, kicking off, returning kickoffs, covering punts, returning punts, and so on. If our all-
state end could return rejuvenated today, rather than starring and
weeping for old Erskine he would probably be calculating his chances
in the pro draft. If he could look back and compare the two situations

50 years apart, he might say, as do some of my students remembering their high school athletic years, That was fun, but now it's a business.

He would be commenting on the development of trends that had already been summarized during his sophomore year in high school, when the Carnegie Foundation published in 1929 a comprehensive report on American college athletics:

1. The extreme development of competitive games in the colleges has reached the secondary schools. The college athlete begins his athletic career before he goes to college.
2. Once in college, the student who goes in for competitive sports . . . finds himself under a pressure, hard to resist, to give his whole time and thought to his athletic career. No college boy training for a major team can have much time for thought or study.
3. The college athlete, often a boy from a modest home, finds himself suddenly a most important man in the college life. He begins to live on a scale never before imagined. . . . When he drops back to a scale of living such as his own means can afford, the result is sometimes disastrous.
4. He works (for it is work, not play) under paid professional coaches whose business it is to develop the boy to be an effective unit in a team.
5. Intercollegiate athletics are highly competitive. Each college or university longs for a winning team. A system of recruiting and subsidizing has grown up. . . . The system is demoralizing and corrupt, alike for the boy who takes the money and for the agent who arranges it.
6. In the matter of competitive athletics the college alumnus has in the main played a sorry role. It is one thing for the old grad to go back and coach the boys of his college as at Oxford or Cambridge. . . . It is quite another thing for an American college graduate to pay money to high school boys . . . in order to enlist their services for a college team.
7. There can be no doubt that athletics, if well conducted, may be made to contribute significantly to the physical health of students. . . . However . . . under the present system of conducting athletics, too few students benefit and too many incur positive harm. Moreover, certain widespread athletic practices . . . actually jeopardize the physical health of the participants. . . .
8. For many games the strict organization and the tendency to commercialize the sport have taken the joy out of the game. In football, great numbers of boys do not play football, as in English schools and colleges, for the fun of it. A few play in-

tensely. The great body of students are onlookers.
9. The blaze of publicity in which the college athlete lives is a
   demoralizing influence for the boy himself and no less so for
   his college. (Savage, 1929, pp. xiv, xv, 157)

A different example of the development of professionalized competitive sport—in this case without the extreme commercialism of
American sport—is the career of the martial art of judo, analyzed by
B. C. and J. M. Goodger. As developed in Japan under the influence
of Dr. Jigoro Kano in the late 19th century, judo was a "civilized" form
of the more violent jiu-jitsu, stressing *jita kyoei* (self-perfection and
mutual benefit and welfare) and *seiryoku-zenyo* (maximum efficiency).
Self-perfection was to be combined with an awareness of the benefit
of others; the individual was to be of service to the world while developing his or her own capacities, physical and spiritual. Judo was
primarily a middle-class art. It was Japanese. It was sometimes associated with the study of Zen. Foreigners would study in Japan, live there,
and even marry Japanese women while seeking to absorb its cultural
background.

After World War II, international competition became a major focal
concern in Judo. Before this time international matches tended to be
occasional, ad hoc friendly affairs, but European championships were
inaugurated in 1951, World championships and National Team Championships in 1956, and in 1964 judo was included in the Olympic
Games.

These developments meant the proliferation of rules and regulations administered by bureaucracies. In contrast to its original self-
improvement goals, successful judo became competitive medal
winning. It was taken up by the mass media, and rules were frequently
changed, as in other sports, to enhance spectator appeal. Successful
performance came to be thought of in terms of scientific analysis of
movement rather than of insight and special knowledge. Development
of judo as a sport led to the employment as coaches and referees of
a number of fairly low-grade players who were not thoroughly
grounded students of judo, but rather technicians. Recruitment of
working-class performers toughened judo. The judo specialist who
formerly went to Japan to soak up the judo culture was replaced by
the international star who visits Japan for a short period to sharpen
up or get a good hard practice for the European championships. Like
the senior British judo players, he may feel he could train as well at
home: Just because the Japanese take up rugby, I wouldn't encourage
their players to eat steak and kidney pudding.

In their 1977 study the Goodgers wrote:

The focal concern is almost exclusively national, and, even more, international competition. Whereas in previous stages most participants tended to view contests as an aspect of judo that contributed to the educational and developmental end of judo practice, competition would now appear to be an end in itself. Weight training and running have been incorporated into the schedules of most judo players. The esoteric and philosophical components of previous stages tend to be dismissed as mumbo-jumbo. . . . Thus, judo training and practice is now viewed in mainly instrumental terms, as a preparation for contest rather than as mental and physical training of essentially intrinsic value . . . and the moral significance of the training situation is more "secular" and more typical of Western amateur sport in general. (Goodger & Goodger, 1977, pp. 24–25)

Sydney Harris has given us excellent insights into the transition from amateurism to the new profession of sports. This, he tells us, is part of a transition in which the term "professional" has come to mean the opposite of what it originally meant. In the late Middle Ages, a professed person—a clergyman, physician, lawyer, or teacher (professor)—was a person who had sworn a religious vow professing that he would place human service above mere self-aggrandizement. This set the professional apart from the *tradesman,* who was motivated by profit alone. In the late 19th century, with the rise of industrial capitalism a new type of professional arose, a specialized individual who practiced a skill for money. Now the professional contrasted with the *amateur,* a nonspecialist who played out of love of the game or a sense of fun. Today's professional athlete, says Harris, is somewhere between the old-style professional and the modern high-class tradesman. Even though he has not professed a religious vow, he is dedicated to ideals of sportsmanship, fairness, and loyalty that make him a social role model. "When this model degenerates into total self-seeking, we are left without that sense of community on which every civilization must be nourished or die" (Harris, 1983, p. 58).

Very few people are really happy about the situation in sport today. There are, of course, some. In the semiprofessional athletics that are called amateur there are a few large winning schools whose players, coaches, students, athletic associations, public relations officers, and alumni are fairly content (except on the rare occasions when they lose). In the frankly professional sphere there are the fans (most of them powerless people) who get their thrills from identification with "our" Packers, Mets, Dodgers, Reds, Dolphins, Bruins, or 76ers. A small minority of very talented performers make it big with glory in the amateurs followed by dollars in the pros. TV networks enhance their public competitive image, if perhaps not their profit and loss accounts, by operating both amateur and professional sport as an entertainment business.

But dissent comes from more quarters than we would have at first imagined.

Jocks and Coaches

First, athletes themselves—more than 95% of whom will *not* make it big in fame or fortune—when they have time, energy, and inspiration enough to think of it, resent being recruited as valuable flesh by agents who have sometimes been rather accurately described as pimps. They resent the collusion of amateur and professional athletic bodies that results in their being paid much less than they could make in an open market. They resent that what began for them as play has become a business in which they must win at any cost to themselves or their opponents. They resent the routine acceptance of uppers, downers, anabolic steroids, and playing when medically incapacitated for this purpose. They resent being treated like children—being told where they can live and eat, how they can cut their hair, what they can do in their spare time, what their politics can be, when (and with whom) they can sleep. If they are black, they may feel that a white world that gives them no other significant opportunities has oversold and exploited them on the very long chance that they might reach the top in sports.

These are hard times for coaches, too. As Harry Edwards puts it, the coach's job combines limited control with complete liability (1973). That is, a coach can lose (or win) a game for any number of reasons about which he can do nothing, but when next year's contracts are written (and for many weeks before) he will get all the blame (or credit). Under these circumstances, he is under job pressure to keep things in hand by appearing decisive and authoritative. Thus his job situation makes him very sensitive when players question his authority, as they have increasingly since the mid-1960s.

The coach's personality and personal background are apt to make such challenges more threatening. As a group, coaches are, in the words of sport psychologists Bruce Ogilvie and Thomas Tutko, ''extremely conservative politically, socially, and attitudinally'' (1971). James Michener reports that of 60 prominent athletes he has known personally, 59 were Republicans and only Stan Musial was a Democrat. ''I have never so far heard of a coach who was a Democrat, although some of the Southwest Conference men may be so nominally'' (Michener, 1977, p. 264).

Job strains and personality may both make it very hard to live in the kind of atmosphere in which a Tennessee coach with a 46-12-2 record nearly lost his job one year for winning only 7 of 12 games; in which a small Ohio river town's high-school coach had a defeat by the archrival celebrated by a bullet that ripped through a window and lodged just above his baby's crib; in which University of Miami coach Charlie Tate in the middle of a fair season had garbage dumped on his lawn and his wife received obscene phone calls; or in which Oklahoma coach Barry Switzer, in an unbeaten season, experienced severe pressure because some games were *close*. Add to these pressures some other conflicts that Edwards suggests. As a church or temple goer, a coach may find it hard to play dirty in order to win. As an adult responsible for youth, he may have to risk their safety or health on the field in order to keep his job. He may also be uncomfortable when his intellectual colleagues, whose jobs are not on the line day by day as his is, stereotype him as a meathead who kicks dumb jocks around. Under such conditions, it is not surprising that as early as 1969, *Sports Illustrated* published an article entitled "The Desperate Coach" (Underwood, 1969). It may be that Ogilvie and Tutko were right in predicting that in the near future one third of our present coaches may not continue.

Profits and the Media

The promoters of amateur and pro sport aren't happy, either. They have been brought up against a hard fact: Spectator sports can no longer pay their own way locally. Because football ordinarily pays a large part of college athletic budgets, as football goes so go most other sport programs. Already in December, 1962, *Fortune* magazine announced to the business community that college football is a losing business (Jackson, 1962). Of 200 colleges playing marketable football, only 30 or 40 were clearly in the black financially. Two main causes cited were the expense of recruiting squads for the two-platoon system that came in after World War II and a loss of student interest (this was *before* the student unrest of the mid-1960s). A decade later things were worse. According to NCAA figures, the total athletic budget for colleges of over 4,000 students, which in 1960 was $60 million, in 1965 had risen to $115 million, and in 1971–72 was $195 million (Edwards, 1973, p. 288). The 1962 *Fortune* article estimated that it cost $400,000 to field a major football team. Today an estimate of $1 million would be conservative. Faced with these rising costs, in the 1960s 42 colleges dropped intercollegiate football.

In *Sports Illustrated* in 1971 Pat Ryan reported that two thirds of all college athletic programs were losing money; even Ohio State, though in the black, was hurting, and loss of the 10% of athletic income derived from student fees was a serious threat. He spoke of the strain of athletic "keeping up with the Joneses" as it was described by (then) Oregon State athletic director Jim Barrett: "If our major opponent hires another football assistant coach, we try to match them. If our major opponent has more football scholarships than we have, we try to catch up. If our major opponent has an athletic dormitory, we get out the hammer and nails. If our opponent shops for artificial turf, we start organizing a fund-raising campaign. This goes on and on" (Ryan, 1971, p. 19).

During the 1976 football season *Forbes* magazine described the state of the intercollegiate sport business:

> *College football as such has long been a powerful money-maker. . . . However, the margins are dropping and while many of the most powerful teams playing in big stadiums are still making money, there is less and less left over to cover the rest of the athletic department budget. Meanwhile, the cost of everything is rising. . . . The problem on everyone's mind is financing the red ink in the rest of the athletic budget . . . it looks like tough times ahead. (Forbes, November 15, 1976)*

Tough times were ahead for schools like the University of Miami, which normally expected the athletic budget to operate at only an $800,000 annual deficit. In 1977–78 the program was $1.1 million in the red, $1.5 million in both 1978–79 and 1979–80, $1.3 million in 1981–82, and $1.8 million in 1982–83. In 1983–84 a national championship football year, it was expected that "athletics will end the . . . year with a deficit under $1 million for the first time in at least eight years" (*Miami Herald*, April 28, 1984, p. 5D).

Writing in 1973, Edwards predicted that intercollegiate sports as we know it may eventually join panty raids among collegiate legends. It appeared highly unlikely that sport would survive even the 1970s in its present form. In the near future Edwards saw professional and big-time college sport continuing and interschool sport almost disappearing in the major high schools and being eliminated in favor of intramural programs in the non-big-time colleges. (I would guess this *may* happen by 2000.)

The professionals, whom Edwards sees as holding their own, are not doing so well, either. At the end of 1975 the World Football League had folded, and eight NFL teams finished in the red in spite of getting $1.2 million each for TV rights. Twenty-five of the 28 major basketball teams had lost money. So had half the teams in the National Hockey League, which had tabled plans for expansion and was talking about dropping teams instead.

If professional sport survives, along with big-league college programs, it will not be because it pays its own way as local spectator recreation. It will be as the tail of the kite of television entertainment. The TV industry, which played a large part in creating the crisis of organized sport, may bail it out.

The relationship between the television industry and the amateur and professional sport industry has been a mixed one. At first, in the 1940s and 1950s, TV undermined sport by posing this question: Why pay good money to sit in the sun at the ballpark to watch the Local Yokuls when I can sit at home for free with a bottle of beer and see the national Game of the Week? This question destroyed most of baseball's minor leagues, local boxing clubs, and small-college football. Even the big leagues were not immune. The Cleveland Indians, a really outstanding team who televised most of their home games, lost 67% in home attendance between 1948 and 1956. The Boston Braves, a good team who also televised most home games, dropped 81% between 1948 and 1952. They moved to Milwaukee and later moved again to Atlanta, in part because the virgin (to big-league ball) South seemed to offer a much better television market than the already saturated Chicago-Milwaukee-Minneapolis area.

On the other hand, TV has also helped the sports business. It has created a nationwide and worldwide market for major and minor sports. The role of TV in publicizing sport has been most dramatic in the economically less developed countries. The Polish sport sociologist Andrzej Wohl says,

> It is precisely television which in an unbelievably short time managed to transform people, who so far had been most indifferent in regard to sport, completely unaware of its role and significance, into its ardent adherents. Inhabitants of villages, who themselves had never practiced sport, express themselves, under the influence of television, in favor of their children going in for sport, fully approve the financing of the construction of sports facilities, declare their readiness to help with the building. These are not at all isolated statements, but have become a rule. (1975, p. 30)

Another Eastern European country, Hungary, illustrated the diversity of influence that television can bring. In the 1960s, according to Foldesi Támasné, the spread of television brought about a decrease in live attendance at sport competitions:

Involvement in sport did not decrease unambiguously; it merely took a different shape. Television increased the number of fans and widened sport related knowledge of the population. It made telecast of sports popular with such strata of society (women, children, the aged) that, for different reasons had not previously seen live sports competitions; and brought such sports into the orbit of involvement of TV viewers that previously had not been popular in mass dimensions (e.g., figure skating, ice hockey, car races, etc.). (Támasné, 1979, p. 62)

In America, ABC staged the championship tourney that revived boxing after the promoters had removed their biggest drawing card by dethroning Muhammed Ali. CBS has been the angel for the NFL; the AFL came of age with NBC support; ABC money has kept the NCAA football powers solvent; and ESPN shores up the USFL. Today most big-college athletic directors and owners of pro teams will agree that they would be helpless without TV contracts. However, he who pays the piper calls the tune: Game schedules are arranged, and timeouts are called not for the players, coaches, or spectators at hand, but for the convenience of network programming.

Who complains? The Minnesota Vikings, whose touchdown drive was stalled deep in Green Bay territory in 20°-below-zero weather by an official's timeout to allow a commercial. The players in the 1967 Super Bowl game who had to repeat the second-half kickoff because a commercial was on when the original kickoff took place. The fans who completely jammed NBC Broadcast Control in New York with protest calls when technicians mistakenly tuned off an NFL game and tuned in a children's program before the trailing team scored two touchdowns in the final minute to win. The churchgoers of Los Angeles when the National Basketball Association scheduled games at the church hour of 11 a.m. so that fans back east could see them at 2 in the afternoon.

Conversely, irate fans demonstrated at Belleview Baptist Church in Memphis when the local ABC station refused to cancel a weekly broadcast of services in order to carry the 1980 hockey game in which the American team won the Olympic gold medal. The admirers of basketball star John Havlicek complained in April, 1978, when CBS, to meet a commitment at the Augusta Masters golf tournament, cut off Hondo's 9-point scoring burst in the last 2 minutes of his final game in Boston Garden, and with it the standing, thundering ovation by 15,000 people that marked the end of his 16 years of stardom. Lee Trevino, on the 71st hole of a Florida golf tournament, was called to by a TV announcer from a booth above the putting surface: ''Hey, Lee, we're in a commercial break. If you wait 20 seconds you can get your putt live on television." Trevino looked up, stuck out his tongue at the announcer, went ahead and three-putted hole 71 and then bogied hole 72 with another three putts (Barkow, 1974, p. 277).

In the mid-1980s, even TV became disillusioned with the sport scene. As early as 1970 Tom Gallery, former sports director for NBC, complained: "The pro football people have been driving so damned hard for a buck, they've driven the sponsors right out of sight with those high fees. It's killing the networks too, and I for one don't know how long it can last" (Johnson, 1971, p. 143). In 1985 the three networks lost $45 million on the NFL. ABC sports fell from a $70 million profit in 1984 to a $30 million loss in 1985. Roone Arledge, who in 25 years as head of ABC sports had been the dominant mover of TV sports, was fired. The reasons for the trouble were boredom of TV viewers with incessant year-round sport programming and shifting of sponsors to other markets. In the first half of the 1980s the share of Miller Beer's TV budget going to sports fell from 95% to 70%. With more car-buying decisions being made by women, carmakers changed from sports to shows like Dan Rather or *Murder, She Wrote*. As a result, sport financing may shift back to the stadium, with rising ticket prices, which will be blamed on inflated salaries.

Apart from the objectors to television's handling of sport, a good many fans have the sense that they are being ripped off. Escalated admission prices are hard to pay in an era of inflation. As is usual with inflated consumer prices, the easy answer is to overlook business profits and blame it all on high wages. Professional athletes used to be semiliterate refugees from farming, mill, and mining communities who escaped more grinding poverty to become the legal and still poorly paid property of paternalistic sport owners who called the tune, financially and otherwise. Today's athletes may come from these communities plus the urban ghetto, but many have been attached to a college or university on the way up and some of it has rubbed off. The organization of labor that spread after the Depression has come to include professional athletes, who now bargain collectively. Legal changes have given them an increased power to bargain individually as free agents. Skilled lawyers help and encourage collective and individual bargaining. A 1980 sport column by Bob Rubin in the *Miami Herald* is fairly representative of fans' gripes at the excesses of this situation. Rubin sees a fuller and less one-sided picture than does the usual castigation of the greedy jock:

It's difficult to sleep at night knowing that Jim Palmer is forced to get along on $230,000 a year. . . . Do you realize that the pittance the Orioles pay Palmer amounts to . . . a lousy $26.25 an hour, 24 hours a day, 365 days a year?

The bizarre thing is that Palmer truly is underpaid by the incredibly inflated standards of baseball salaries today. Far lesser talents are paid more.

But that doesn't foster sympathy for Palmer. Instead it increases disgust over the excesses and inequities of an economic system that pays entertainers (including athletes) obscene amounts of money and it raises fundamental questions about the values of a society that created such a system. The more I hear of endless squabbling between whining owners and the athletes they have so badly spoiled, the less my interest in sports. It's insane for a man to earn millions to sing, dance, tell a joke, or pitch a baseball. . . . Entertainers serve a purpose as diversions from life's daily grind, but their contributions to society are trivial compared to those of teachers, cops, librarians, firemen, research scientists, hospital workers, soldiers, etc.

So pay the jesters a decent wage, but not a fortune that could be used in so many more important ways.

The owners merit no sympathy. Despite their constant complaining and doomsaying over the average player salary rising from $22,000 in 1970 to a current $120,900, they are not paying anything they cannot afford. If they did, they would go out of business.

They're crying all the way to the bank. I bleed for them as much as I do for the .250 hitters they sign for the gross national product of Bolivia. (Rubin, 1980a, p. D1)

Another unhappy group are some of the media personnel—sports writers and announcers with a journalistic conscience. As reporters, their job is theoretically to present an objective account of the events they cover. As media employees, they are actually housemen (and housewomen) for the local team and for the sport industry. In the face of this, a John R. Tunis or Red Smith can be a top-flight journalist and social critic. Bil Gilbert can expose the use of drugs in sport (1969). Jerry Izenberg can explode the myth that a sporting contest is the pursuit of the Holy Grail. Neil Amdur can argue the case for a maverick coach who practices democracy in football (1971). An editor like Dave Burgin can cover sport with fairness and honor in the San Francisco Bay area during the tumultuous era of the 1960s. Leonard Schecter, Robert Lipsyte, Joseph Durso, Sandy Padwe, and others may also dedicate their lives to telling the public the truth about the scene they report. But the strongest pressures, here as elsewhere, are to keep the boat unrocked.

Sport and Health

Also disturbed about the sport scene are those concerned with physical and emotional health—physicians, physical educators, psychiatrists, and the clergy. Few athletes, especially in contact sports, end their careers without some kind of permanent physical impairment. NCAA records show that an average of 28 players a year were directly killed in football from 1931 to 1975. In 1974, 86 out of 100 high school players could expect to be injured at least once during the season. (James Michener wonders what would be the reaction to high school physics if it were shown to have a record of killing 28 students a year and injuring 86% of its enrollees.) Similarly, in the pros in 1975 a Stanford University study for the NFL estimated that 90% of players could expect to be injured before the Super Bowl was over. One tenth of these injuries would finish the player for the season. The injury level is related to the way in which winning is put ahead of ordinary health standards. Under pressure from the medical community, there has been some relaxation in the brutal late summer practices where for some time it was routine to vomit and finally collapse into bed, unable to eat. However, seriously injured players are still "shot up" with Novocaine and sent back into action.

Neither health nor education is served by an experience like that of a senior football player who a few years ago explained to me why he had missed 2 weeks of my class. He had been sick with flu, which had not kept him from his daily spring practice. In the spring intrateam game he was so sick that he threw up at the half. His coach held him out of the second half but told him later that he could have done better if he had tried—presumably like another top player who had played the whole game with a severely congested chest.

Novocaine is not the only drug that concerns the health professions. Jim Bouton (1971) says that half the players in the American baseball league couldn't function without amphetamines (called greenies there) and Chip Oliver guesses that half the NFL would fall asleep in the third quarter if Pete Rozelle put a lock on the bottle of speed (called rat turds) (1971). In a class research project in the 1960s, Mike Mohler, a football player at the University of California, Berkeley, interviewed the whole team and found 48% using speed and 28% using weight-building anabolic steroids. In track, steroids are almost a must for success in the weight events and the decathlon. Commenting on the fact that one side effect of steroids is atrophy of the testicles, Paul Hoch sees an athletic future dominated by plastic Supermen with no balls (1972).

Broken bodies in sport are not only a physical concern. To some in the healing professions, they are a symptom of psychological and spiritual problems. Players will kill themselves, slowly or suddenly, to win. Such urgency to win is among other things a poor preparation for the hard realities of life. In every season, in every league, there must always be many more losers than winners. In the long run, for everyone, everything and everybody dear must be lost. How is a person brought up on the doctrine that winning is the only thing to contend with that?

To some in the healing professions the greatest problem in sport violence is that it dehumanizes both parties. Where violence is the name of the game—whether because one loves to hit or because one has to do it to carry out his assignment—one ceases to become a person, they say, and one's body becomes an instrument. The opponent also ceases to be a person and becomes an object to be removed. Both ways, people are turned into things.

The drug problem, from this standpoint, is similar. To "up" or "down" one's natural physiology, to stimulate muscle development artificially to win a game, turns one's body again into an instrument. As a human being one may wonder who, or what, it is that wins the coveted victory. One athlete told me, "I don't use drugs, because if I do great, I want to know that it was *I* that did it, and not bennies or steroids."

Beyond the effects on the athlete there is the problem of the impact of the sport system on the nonperformer. For a century sport has become increasingly a form of spectator entertainment. It has increasingly enlisted a minority of performers selected for very atypical height and weight (this is obvious in football and basketball, but *Sports Illustrated* noted in 1977 that it is also becoming true in baseball). The physically typical person sits and watches. In the TV age he or she doesn't even have to walk from the parking lot to the stadium. What happens to these spectators? Since Hans Kraus and Ruth Hirschland reported in 1954 that six times as many American as European school children from comparable urban and suburban backgrounds had failed a battery of very simple muscular fitness tests—and suggested that the American habit of spectating might be one of the reasons (Kraus & Hirschland, 1954)—this question has been of concern to many.

There is a stereotype of the athlete who overdevelops his heart, puts on weight after he ceases to be athletically active, and becomes a candidate for a heart attack. But a comparative study in 1956 did not show athletes to be significantly heavier than nonathletes in later life, although when active they had been. And strenuous athletic activity may develop alternative circulatory paths that can enable an ex-athlete to survive a blockage of normal blood flow to the heart muscle. The evidence is not all in, and many people have lived long with almost no exercise, but there is a good chance that the ex-jock with athlete's heart may outlive the spectator who watched him from the stands.

Another problem that bothers health professionals is the *kind* of sport that our athletic system encourages. It is the minor sport activities—walking, swimming, cycling, bowling, golf, and tennis doubles—that are most likely to help a person keep in shape over a long lifetime. Our emphasis on the major sports of baseball, football, basketball, and hockey stresses activities that do not ordinarily enlist the physically typical person, and for those who do participate will not continue beyond their youth. Relevant to this point is a 1970 study by Harvard anthropologists, who compared men who attended Harvard between 1880 and 1961 and had participated in major sports (baseball, football, crew, etc.) with those who had been in minor sports (fencing, golf, swimming, etc.). The minor sport athletes lived significantly longer than those in major sports (the difference was too large to have been due to chance factors) (Polednak and Damon, 1970).

"Sports, athletics, and games," says educator John Holt, "are too important to be just for the varsity. In fact, our professionalizing of sports, down to the high school level, is the greatest enemy of general health and fitness that we have" (Holt, 1970, p. 10). We shall see later that the problem of breeding an elite of top-caliber athletes at the expense of the physical health of the masses is a serious one in the U.S.S.R., Communist China, and some of the Third World, as well as in the U.S.

Sport and Education

The impact of sport on education has concerned many people—academically serious students (including some athletes), teachers, administrators, and alumni. Two events symbolize what bothers them. In the fall of 1975 a professor at North Carolina State University was arrested for jogging on his own university's running track, in violation of security regulations that had been set up to protect secrecy of football practice for a big game. In the same year Yale University, in the middle of a $370 million endowment drive, lost a $2-million bequest, among others, and a longtime recruiter resigned from the admissions committee because a certain quarterback didn't get admitted.

Most educationally serious people would agree with one of the irate Yale alumni that athletics has a proper place in a balanced educational experience, and that all work and no play makes Jack a dull boy. But they do not believe that such balance means making a university a base for mass spectacles performed by semiprofessionals who are students only secondarily and who generally don't graduate. They do not think balanced education requires turning the colleges into minor leagues that spare the professional promoters the salaries, recruiting costs, and other expenses of maintaining a farm system to secure and train players.

These critics applaud the fact that athletic ability enables some serious students, many from ethnic minorities, to go to college when they could otherwise not afford it. There are the Moe Bergs, Byron Whites, Bill Bradleys, Frank Ryans, Tom McMillens, Ted Hendrickses, and Pat Hadens, although in the total picture they are token scholars comparable to token blacks and token women in racial and chauvinistic settings. Although the critics may not agree that training for professional athletics is a proper function at college, they may be glad that some students with no conventional academic interests can use college as a stepping-stone to a professional sport career. But they are not pleased when money that could have given a genuine *scholarship* to a serious, able, and needy student is given to a nonstudent (however needy) to play ball.

Critics are also concerned about the possible damage to the career possibilities of students on athletic scholarships. Athletic departments pay lip service to academic requirements to keep their players eligible, and the more conscientious departments actually get them graduated. But in actual fact there is no doubt where the real priority lies. Athletic performance comes first. The player (whose preoccupation with sport in high school has usually left him short in academic preparation) is advised into a program of courses he can handle. If he still has time, energy, and motivation, he studies after practice, film sessions, and other athletic responsibilities have been met. Sometimes he can't—he is just too tired. He attends class enough to get by and maintain his eligibility. If he doesn't have time to write assigned papers, there are other students or off-campus professional services that will provide them for a fee. So this athlete leaves college, graduated or not, having learned little outside his sport. "By the time I graduated," says ex–St. Louis Cardinals' linebacker Dave Meggyesy, "I knew it was next to impossible to be a legitimate student and a football player too. There is a clear conflict, and it is always resolved on the side of the athletic program" (Meggyesy, 1970, p. 44). The athlete has been tracked on the basis of his athletic ability, out of the chance of realizing other possibilities to which college could open him. Who knows how many potential physicians, scientists, lawyers, and teachers have been lost to society (and to themselves) because their intelligence and skill were focused very early on the football or baseball field or the basketball or tennis court (Meggyesy, 1970)? This problem has persistently recurred in literally hundreds of class papers, written by both athletes and nonathletes, and in class discussions in my course in sport at the University of Miami.

During the 1930s one of the outstanding football ⟨
time, Robert C. Zuppke of the University of Illinois, pr⟨
the 1980s a more sophisticated and secure American p⟨
ject the linkage of education with high-powered semi⟨
and let coaches get back to their proper job of buildi₋₋ ⟨
ness and moral character (1975). (Again, we shall probably have ₋₋ ⟨
this prediction back to at least the year 2000.) Fifty years after Zuppke,
the educational critics of sport are not against school spirit, but they,
too, would rather have student group enthusiasm center around bona
fide student activities, not the activities of nonstudents to whom their
college's name happens to be attached.

Gender and Sport

In speaking of college semipros, I have used the pronoun *he*. This
is not entirely male chauvinism. As yet the *shes* in college sport have
not been professionalized like the males. Whether they will be is part
of another question.

Many members of both sexes are displeased with developments
in sport, but for opposite reasons. Female athletes, seeing women's
liberation gaining in other areas, cannot accept second-class citizenship in the world of athletics. In high school, they are put off by the
way in which girls are, for example, chased from gym floors when boys
come along. They are offended by the way in which the major athletic
events are dominated by males, whereas girls chosen as sex symbols
lead the cheers, "relegated to the position of worshiping at an altar
they can never really be part of" (Hoch, 1972, p. 154). In college they
are incensed when male teams routinely travel by plane, whereas
women have to scratch to get to their meets by car. They question the
appropriateness of using women students as bait in athletic
recruiting—the Gibson Girls (Kansas State), Gator Getters (University of Florida), Hurricane Honeys (University of Miami). In the pros,
women tennis players have sought equal pay for equal work by seced-
ing from the men's tournaments and forming their own. (These have,
incidentally, subsequently become as commercial as those for males.)
Socially aware women athletes are conscious that organized sport is
one of the strongholds of *machismo*. They are revolted by the kind of
infantile attitudes toward females described in Jim Bouton's account
of beaver shooting by big league baseball players: looking under
women's skirts from dugouts, or hanging from rooftops and fire escapes to play Peeping Tom (Bouton, 1971, pp. 36–38).

Women athletes must contend with the fact that for many people
sport does not fit their idea of a woman's role. The Polish sociologist

Barbara Krawczyk is right in describing as outdated a statement made in 1913 by a Harvard physics professor:

OTE

> *Sport, in the form it exists at present, is nothing but a loss of time and often a pretext for flirtations. The only sports which . . . could best serve to develop the female body are simple household chores, which put all the muscles into motion. There is nothing more useful for the strengthening of the leg muscles and to avoid obesity, than often to run up and down stairs. The best means to develop the muscles of the chest and the small of the back is washing floors with both hands and in a kneeling position. Sweeping floors strengthens the muscles of the shoulder blades, carrying buckets is an excellent athletic exercise. A woman who is baking bread and kneading the dough achieves magnificent development of her upper limbs. An exercise worth recommendation, too, is laundering—an hour at the wash tub means more than an afternoon of playing tennis. (Krawczyk, 1973, pp. 48–49)*

However, many people today might agree with the 1932 opinion of a physical educator from Krawczyk's own country, who does not consider housework to be great physical training, but who says that

> *The road of sport for women should not be completely the same as that of sport for men. The different physical structure, different psyche and finally a different activity in life requires that sport should cultivate different virtues in the case of women. While physical education for men and sport as its superstructure should prepare them for constant intensive motor activity and make them capable of frequent maximum effort, physical education for women should rather be treated as a neutralizer for lack of movement and a monotonous mode of life and should thus prepare not for a maximum, but should require a normal minimum of physical effort.*

There are still others everywhere who will be as bewildered and disturbed as the mother of a student at the Polish Academy of Physical Education, quoted by Krawczyk:

> *My mother was in principle against my going in for sport. . . . She was mainly concerned about the fact that sport is not the proper recreation for a girl. 'You are running around undressed on the sports field, together with boys, as if you had no shame at all.' . . . She would have preferred me sitting at home or being occupied with something else. . . . And suddenly she found out that (it was) not enough that I was practicing sport, I even wanted to start sports studies. That was too much for her. If at least it*

would have been under her eyes she could have accepted it but
to let me go to some other place, to live amidst athletes, far from
home—oh, no. She was afraid that I would get spoiled in the
world, that sport and freedom far from her maternal eye, would
destroy me completely. (Krawczyk, 1973, p. 53)

The sex issue in sport was brought to a head by Title IX of the Education Act of 1972, which forbids sex discrimination by federally funded organizations. The NCAA, the core of the male semipro sport establishment, put out practically a telephone book of argument against Title IX, contending that it would ruin college athletics. The NCAA was not concerned about women whose breasts might be injured if they came out for college football, which they are not likely to do. It was not worried about the possibility of mixed locker rooms, which for students used to co-ed dorms should pose no real problem, anyway. What did worry it was what might happen to amateur dollars. The male establishment was concerned that the cost of equalizing opportunities for women athletes might put an added drain on an already losing business. Underlying this anxiety was the fear that Title IX will undermine the male hero-female cheerleader syndrome and bring women as equals into a hitherto male world. The most recent blow to Title IX was the 1984 U.S. Supreme Court decision holding that only specific programs receiving federal aid are covered (and, wherever else college athletic programs get their money, they rarely receive direct federal grants).

Sex equality in sport raises another issue that bothers thoughtful women and men alike. Until recently, sex discrimination has kept women from profiting by, and being exploited and brutalized by, the commercialization of sport. Will equal opportunity bring to women the same competitive masculinization already satirized in the business world by Norman Lear's *All That Glitters?* On the bizarre fringe, there has already been in operation a semipro women's football league. In the mainstream (tennis especially) some very young women, like some very young men, are coming to take for granted the earning, in intense and widely publicized competition, of incomes that a few years ago were reserved for corporate executives: Along with the Boris Beckers we have the Mary Lou Rettons.

In the fall of 1978 an Association of American Colleges Study (Sports, 1978) reported that in 1974 only 60 colleges offered athletic scholarships to women. Today there are over 500. It also reported that the Department of Health, Education, and Welfare had set up a special task force to look into such matters as women's athletic scholarships, player recruitment, athletic association rules, contact sports, and coaches' pay, "problems that have plagued the men, but not the women, for years. . . . In a few short years the athletic scholarship has replaced the bake sale as the symbol of intercollegiate athletics for women. As a result, the nonfinancial problems of women's sports are now becoming harder to distinguish from those of the men's" (Hanford, 1979, p. 77).

Sport and Humanism

Another group who are unhappy about sport are people with humanistic values. This group includes some people from all the groups previously discussed. Humanists feel strongly the gap between sport as it might be and sport as it is. They object particularly to three things in sport as it is presently organized—competition, exploitation, and violence.

They regret that whereas sport could be a channel for release, for self-actualization, an oasis in the desert of real life, it instead reproduces and intensifies the merciless competition of a business civilization. In a world in which labor with hand and brain is technically a commodity to be bought, used, and sold (where a *person* is economically a *thing*), humanists see the sport and legal establishments repeatedly affirming that the athlete is the property of his employer, to be merchandised like a side of beef, subject to the command of whoever owns him at the moment.

The humanists see sport, which could be a respite from the violence of the everyday life of street, factory, and office, as in fact accentuating and glorifying this violence. (This is true not only of the contact sports—football, boxing, hockey—but also of the baseball pitcher throwing at the batter, the basketball player taking his opponent out under the basket, the power game that has taken over tennis.) Although sport has sometimes been a vehicle for bringing ethnic minorities a success elsewhere denied them, it has, in the eyes of some spokesmen for these minorities, made use of their social and economic powerlessness to exploit them as a source of eager and underpaid labor.

When the competitive urge expresses itself internationally in the struggle for national power and domination, the humanists see sport—which could bring people together as people to test their skills nonviolently against one another—serving instead as an arm of that national power. For example, they see President Ford's Commission on Olympic Sports asserting that winning is a reflection of our national spirit and purpose and calling for a national sports authority, for which Cuba suggested a model, that would improve United States medal winning in the Olympics.

In this first chapter, we started with the proposition that nobody is really happy about sport as it exists today. We have surveyed the feelings of players, of coaches, of sport promoters, of media people,

"Winning is a reflection of national purpose." President Carter embraces speed skater Eric Heiden, winner of five Olympic gold medals. Photo courtesy of UPE/Bettman.

of the healing professions, of educators, of women, of men, and of humanists. What we have seen is a social system in a crisis that can't be blamed on individual villains, but in which all (or almost all) participants are at this point victims. The social system of sport is in turn part of a larger social system (our society) that is also in crisis. Chapter 2 deals with this relationship.

Jock Liberation and the Counterculture

In May 1970 at Notre Dame University, the football bastion of Middle America, 10 football players petitioned Coach Ara Parseghian for permission to issue a statement registering concern about the murder of students at Kent State. That they should have asked an athletic coach before exercising their First Amendment rights said something about the athletic system. That they even dared to ask indicated that times were changing: Five years before, said sportswriter Sandy Padwe, such a request would have been unthinkable (1970). No statement was issued, but concerned players were allowed to skip—and later make up—a spring practice session to attend a campus demonstration. These events at Notre Dame were one expression of a growing dissatisfaction with the athletic establishment and, beyond it, with the social and political establishment.

The historic position of athletes was concisely put by sociologist Willard Waller: "Athletes have the inevitable conservatism of the privileged classes, and they can be brought to take a stand for the established order" (Waller, 1961, p. 116). Such a stand led Wisconsin football players in the 1930s to throw anti-ROTC protesters into Lake Mendota and Columbia crewmen in 1968 to beat up student demonstrators. It made it possible for Paul Brechler, the Berkeley athletic director during the agitated mid-1960s, to boast that California athletes had never been involved in political demonstrations—meaning, says Jack Scott, that they had never participated except by attacking their demonstrating fellow students. The typical attitude of the athletic establishment toward its employees was capsulized in the reply of Texas coach Darrell Royal when Gary Shaw told him he had decided to quit football: "Don't you think that's our decision to make? I'll decide whether there's any need or not. . . . We didn't put all that money into you to have you come tell me what you're going to do. *I* make those decisions. I expect you suited up tomorrow afternoon" (Shaw, 1972, p. 267).

But as the 1960s moved toward the 1970s, the traditional stance of jocks began to change. The defiant gesture of Tommie Smith and John Carlos on the victory stand at Mexico City in 1968 capped the Olympic Project for Human Rights. Shortly before this the Philadelphia Phillies baseball team, by threatening to forfeit, had forced cancellation of a game that league officials were determined to play on the day of Martin Luther King's funeral. In the fall of 1969 Harvard quarterback Frank Champi quit football after the second game of the season, protesting that players were treated like pieces of machinery. In the same fall 14 members of the Wyoming football team faced—and got—suspension over the issue of wearing black armbands on the field to protest what they saw as racism at Brigham Young University. In 1970 Carlos Alvarez, all-American and pre-law honor student at the University of Florida, was instrumental in organizing an athletes' union. At a campus rally after Kent State, he said of football: "If the sport doesn't change or bend a little, it might not last. I think the coaches will be made to change by kids coming up and not wanting to play under a lot of restrictions, where everything has to be done by the rules and you can't change the rules" (Padwe, 1970, p. 67). His quarterback John Reaves, the nation's top passer in 1969, protested in 1970 that he felt like a robot because Coach Doug Dickey called all the plays. Alvarez and Reaves reflected the feeling expressed by Jim Calkins, computer science major and 1969 football captain at Berkeley: "The most degrading thing is being treated like a child. . . . The attitude is that you're getting paid to play football, so you can't gripe. If that's the way they want it, fine. *But I say to them, you don't pay enough"* (Scott, 1971, 165n). The University of Pennsylvania's leading ground gainer quit in the middle of the 1970 season. The wages for winning at any cost displeased 1970 Ohio State quarterback Rex Kern: "We probably make less than a dollar an hour. There are days when you simply don't want to do it" (Padwe, 1970, p. 69).

While the semiprofessional amateurs were asserting themselves as persons, the open professionals began to pull the rug out from under a century-old system that made them economic chattels—the word chosen by Senator Sam Ervin in 1971 to describe the relationship of baseball, football, basketball, and hockey players to the giant sports trusts. Since baseball emerged as the first modern professionalized game, the athlete has typically worked for a monopoly subject to no external control. He has had no freedom to choose who shall be his employer through either individual or collective bargaining. He has characteristically entered his profession through a draft in which competing employers collaborate. Under a reserve clause his employer has had an indefinitely renewable option on his services. Thus the player has been subject to the arbitrary whims of coaches, managers, club owners, and sport commissioners. As Edward R. Garvey, former executive director of the National Football League Players' Association, put it, "Because a player cannot quit but can be suspended without pay by the club owner or the Commissioner, he must obey all the rules and regulations of the club and the league, whether they be reasonable or unreasonable, or be denied employment in his profession" (Garvey, 1979, p. 93).

This monopolistic system has been challenged unsuccessfully in the courts since 1922. But in 1975 the United States Supreme Court, in *Radovich v. NFL,* held that all team sports except baseball were subject to the antitrust laws. In the late 1960s and early 1970s, player unions were organized. In 1972 major league baseball players went on strike; in 1974 the football players, in 1977 the NFL referees, and in 1978 the baseball umpires followed suit. In 1975 a federal arbitrator (who wouldn't have been there except for the strength of the players' union) invalidated the baseball reserve clause and released a large number of veteran players as *free agents,* able to sell their services to the highest bidder just like any other employee in a capitalist economy. One outcome was that the average major league salary rose from $51,500 in 1975 to $96,000 in 1978, $144,000 in 1980, and $432,000 in 1986. Whereas in 1972, $125,000 was a huge salary for a baseball player (more than Ted Williams, Joe Di Maggio, or Babe Ruth ever made), in 1986 there were 525 players making over $108,000 (1986 figures from *USA Today,* 1986). At the same time, professional athletes in all sports got more control over their daily conditions of work.

Rise and Sweep of the Counterculture

The athletic revolution that peaked about 1970 was part of a cultural change described much earlier by the great Swiss psychologist Jean Piaget. Summarizing his empirical study of how children learn the rules of marbles, Piaget saw in individual development a transition from the very young child's unquestioning acceptance of parental authority to the later give-and-take of equal peers. In society, as in the individual, Piaget saw the same transition from constraint (exemplified in Darrell Royal's statement to Gary Shaw) to reciprocity (exemplified in Alvarez's prediction of a time when the kids would make their own rules):

Society is nothing but a series . . . of generations, each exercising pressure upon the one which follows it. Now when we think of the part played by gerontocracy [rule by the old] in primitive com-

munities, when we think of the decreasing power of the family in the course of social evolution, and of all the social features that characterize modern civilization, we cannot help seeing in the history of societies a sort of gradual emancipation of individuals; in other words a leveling up of the different generations in relation to each other. . . . The more complex the society, the more autonomous is the personality and the more important are the relations of cooperation between equal individuals. (Piaget, 1948, pp. 335–336)

In the 20th century the long-run change described by Piaget has taken the form of conflict between an old, authoritarian culture and a new, democratic counterculture, depicted by Theodore Roszak and Philip Slater.

This counterculture is working against the authoritarian pattern described by Jules Henry:

The work-a-day life in factory and office, the growing rigidity of our class structure, the disparity between existent goals and the individual's ability to achieve them; the vastly pyramiding structure of authority that ranges from parents through the hierarchies of church and government, make it imperative that the individual learn to discipline himself for a life of relatively restricted freedom. (Henry, 1949, p. 93)

Although the fever of change reached its crisis in the 1960s, the countercultural revolution began much earlier. In *The Professional Soldier* (1960) military sociologist Morris Janowitz spelled out a gradual democratization during the 20th century in the most authoritarian of human organizations (the military):

A change from authoritarian domination to greater reliance on manipulation, persuasion, and group consensus.

A tendency of professional military men to develop more and more of the skills and orientations common to civilian administrators and civilian leaders.

Recruitment of officers from a broader base, more representative of the population as a whole.

A tendency to select more creative and innovative, even unconventional people for top positions (not the ranks).

A weakening of traditional military images and concepts of honor. (Summary from Calhoun, 1976, p. 297)

In the factory, the heart of modern bureaucratic centralization, we have heard since the middle of the century that authoritarian methods are less efficient (as well as less humane) than participation by workers in decision making. A classic research in the 1930s by Fritz Roethlisberger and William J. Dickson showed that the most important element in factory productivity was not formal authority but workgroup morale (Roethlisberger & Dickson, 1947). In *The Human Problems of an Industrial Civilization* (1946), Elton Mayo made the case for human relations in industry. Under the leadership of behavioral scientists like Rensis Likert (1967), more and more businessmen have tried human relations as a way of increasing profits. In 1968 Warren Bennis and Philip Slater proclaimed that democracy is inevitable because it is the form of organization best suited to advanced industry. A result for sport is pointed out by Jay Coakley: "As expectations for management-level positions have changed, so have the evaluations of the tough, discipline-oriented coach" (Coakley, 1983, p. 190).

Changes in the army and the factory have been long-run trends of reform within our cultural establishment, but the counterculture has challenged that establishment head-on. It has been a movement by two majorities and a number of minorities.

The first majority is the previously colonial peoples of the world. The South (primarily Latin America and Africa) has confronted the North (primarily Europe and North America). The South is also called the Third World, and is predominantly nonwhite (or at least non–Anglo Saxon). The liberation of the Third World began around the beginning of the 20th century with the final breakup of the Spanish empire. It continued with the dissolution, in two World Wars and later, of the German, Dutch, and British empires. Since World War II, the Third World has become a powerful force in international politics, so the South has become a factor to be contended with along with the East and West. For the first time in history the majority of the human race now has a voice.

The other majority cuts another way. Throughout history, in the dominant civilizations of East and West, women have been second-class citizens. Females have been subordinate in economic and political life, in the home, in school, church, and temple, and in every branch of experience. The French and American revolutions, proclaiming the rights of man, opened the door for insistence on the rights of women. The Industrial Revolution brought the possibility of economic independence. Machinery made the sheer physical strength of males less important. Contraceptive techniques promised to give women, for the first time, control over their own bodies. The collapse of empire before the onslaught of Third World forces added momentum to the erosion of masculine chauvinism everywhere.

Women's liberation has reached a peak since about 1960, but it had vocal advocates like Mary Wollstonecraft in the early 19th century and John and Harriet Mill in the Victorian era. It has followed a general upward curve since the time of the Mills, two high points being the passage of female suffrage in 1920 and the Civil Rights Act of 1964. Passage of the Equal Rights Amendment, though now bitterly fought, is in the long run (by 2000 at the very latest) inevitable.

Around 1960 the Third World revolution erupted in the United States in the form of an uprising of the black minority. The linkage was expressed in a complaint I used to hear at the time around the black college where I then taught: All Africa will be freed before I can get a lousy cup of coffee. Sparked primarily by the active nonviolence of Martin Luther King, Jr., and his followers, the black movement so revolutionized the American scene that things that were unbelievable in the 1950s (such as blacks eating in "respectable" Southern restaurants) were taken for granted by the generation coming of age in the 1970s. (Directly on the jock lib scene, in 1977 one could see black football players at the University of Mississippi—which they could not have even entered 15 years earlier—hugging each other on the field while predominantly white spectators cheered them to an upset of Notre Dame.)

Four centuries of genocidal policy toward America's worst-treated racial minority, which began with the philosophy that the only good Indian is a dead Indian and continued with concentration on reservations, led in the countercultural period to refusal to accept second-class status for the red man (and woman). The oil crisis beginning in 1973 revealed, ironically, that location of large reserves of oil on Indian lands might give American Indians the kind of economic power wielded internationally by the OPEC nations—provided the historic pattern of robbing them of their resources is not repeated once more.

On one more forefront of cultural change, another exponent of nonviolent direct action, Cesar Chavez, during the 1960s organized and gave voice to the last unorganized mass of American laborers, the predominantly Latin migrant and stationary farm workers. As was King in his attitude toward certain black power leaders, Chavez was countercultural in discouraging anti-Anglo racism.

The cause of these minorities had much appeal for a generation of youth raised under a nuclear umbrella constructed by their parents, resentful of being processed in educational factories into raw material for vast bureaucracies or, as an alternative, being conscripted to fight a Third World nation in a jungle. All these things made the 1960s a decade of resistance to the educational, military, and economic machines and of support for rising minorities at home and the rising majority abroad.

The counterculture has embraced three other self-conscious and militant minorities: the elderly, the handicapped, and the gay. The Social Security Act of 1935 recognized the fact that in an urban industrial society older people can no longer expect to contribute to and be supported economically by their children's families. As the population boom that began with World War II tapered off and the percentage of senior citizens in the population increased, the elderly became another militant pressure group. In 1978 we were on the way to eliminating mandatory retirement. As health measures have increasingly made possible the survival of physically handicapped people, and as the Vietnam war added visible and vocal young people to their numbers, the less-than-able-bodied became another effective minority. In 1973 the Rehabilitation Act extended to physically and emotionally disabled people the protection granted to women and racial minorities under the Civil Rights Act.

Gays and lesbians, despite their distinguished achievements throughout history, are like women and blacks and the disabled in having been denied equal rights in employment and otherwise. Gays suffered a severe local defeat in 1977 when Miami citizens refused to guarantee their civil rights, and the AIDS scare of the 1980s has given gays a very bad press. Gay rights have not been written into national law, as have those of women, ethnic minorities, and the handicapped. However, in general the 1960s, 1970s, and 1980s have brought growing recognition of the right of sexual preference.

As I suggested earlier, the whole counterculture is much more than a matter of certain militant interest groups. It goes back to the basic trend from authoritarianism to reciprocity described by Piaget. It involves a fundamental questioning of the whole foundation of bureaucratic industrial society. We need to understand this to understand jock liberation as well as to understand any other part of the counterculture. The basic question raised by the counterculture is one of human exploitation. This is not a loaded dirty word, but simply refers to the situation in which people are regarded as mere instruments for the profit, power, or physical gratification of others rather than as persons with value in themselves. Who is guilty of this exploitation? Exploiters are white, black, yellow, Gentile, Jew, male, female, young, old, middle-aged, athletes, intellectuals, physically disabled, and physically able-bodied people. The counterculture opposes exploitation of, or by, any of these.

Slater has outlined in detail how the counterculture differs from our traditional culture (Slater, 1970, p. 170). I shall illustrate in the field of sport.

- **The counterculture gives preference to human rights over property rights.** In sport, this has led to challenge of the sport law that has made an athlete a piece of property, to be sold at will or depreciated on a corporate tax return.
- **The counterculture puts human needs above technical requirements.** If artificial turf is, for example, easier to maintain at the

cost of more injuries to players, the counterculture will opt for natural grass.

- **The counterculture stresses cooperation over competition.** For the philosophy of winning at any cost it substitutes the joy of group effort regardless of the final score.
- **For the counterculture, sexuality has priority over violence.** In sport, for example, it would prefer to see players spending the night before a game with their wives or girlfriends rather than in psyching up masculine group hatred for the "enemy."
- **The counterculture favors distribution over concentration.** For this reason, it would favor the suggestions of football players Dave Meggyesy (1970) and Bernie Parrish (1972) that sport franchises should be owned by players and fans rather than by businessmen.
- **The counterculture puts the consumer ahead of the producer.** Here, for example, it would oppose dragging baseball players and spectators out in Arctic clothing on October nights to fit the World Series to the requirements of TV sponsors.
- **For the counterculture, means are more important than ends.** It would concur with Grantland Rice's familiar slogan: It's not whether you won or lost but how you played the game.
- **The counterculture prefers openness to secrecy.** If it became dominant, there would be no practice sessions protected by armed guards at Ohio State and perhaps other big time athletic factories.
- **In the world of counterculture, personal expression is more important than social reforms.** It would recognize the need for fundamental changes in the sport establishment, but they would always be aimed at the personal growth and development of participants.
- **The counterculture stresses gratification over striving.** Here again, it would try to make sport fun for players and spectators rather than a device for becoming number one.
- **It puts communal love above Oedipal love.** Here it would favor the democracy through which football coach George Davis had his players pick their starting line-ups over the love-hate father-fixation manipulated by coaches like Vince Lombardi.

The athletic revolution is part of the long-run historical movement from constraint to reciprocity. More immediately, it is an expression of the specific countercultural movements that are struggling for their identity.

Jock Lib and the Black Movement

More than anything else, jock liberation is an outgrowth of the black liberation movement. In 1970, white California football captain Jim Calkins, previously quoted, said, "You see so many black athletes speaking out now. But the white players are gutless. They don't want to take a stand. They are so entrenched in the system and so full of all this super-patriotic stuff" (Scott, 1971, p. 165n). Whereas other careers were barred to blacks, athletics became an area in which it was possible for a black to get ahead in money and recognition. Black hopes for upward mobility still are to a large extent tracked into the sport and entertainment business. As always, rising expectations lead to discontent: Revolutions occur not when people are at rock bottom, but rather when they are on their way up—*but not fast enough.* Contrary to popular stereotypes, most black athletes are generally more disciplined, more punctual, more organized, and more respectful of authority than their white brothers. The main reason is that all their eggs are in one basket, so they have more to lose. But when they have suffered discrimination in this one avenue to success, or even the same kind of mistreatment accorded white athletes, the more perceptive blacks have been more likely to rebel. Leaders among black athletes have taken care of their own personal interests and struggled for those of black athletes in general, but the outstanding personalities among them—the Jackie Robinsons, the Bill Russells, the Curt Floods, the Arthur Ashes, the Abdul-Jabbars, the Roberto Clementes, and the Pelés—have been humanists identified with all athletes and with all people.

Jock Lib and the Third World

The athletic revolution has been clearly related to the rise of the Third World. The threatened Olympic boycott of 1968 (against South Africa and Rhodesia) and the actual boycott of 1976 (against New Zealand) had focused a protest against three forces that are actually one: (a) the international, big-power-dominated military-political establishment (mainly the U.S.S.R. and the U.S.A.), (b) the international big-power-dominated athletic establishment (mainly the national and international Olympic committees), and (c) the intranational and international racism of both.

The 1968 Olympic Project for Human Rights began as a black American protest, spread to other non-white teams and, especially after the suspension of John Carlos and Tommie Smith for their "black power" gesture on the victor's stand, drew in white competitors. Martin Jellinghaus, after winning a bronze medal in the 1600 meter relay race, said of the Olympic Project for Human Rights insignia that he wore, "I am wearing this medal because I feel solidarity not only for them as persons, but for the movement, the human rights move-

Racial protest in sports. The racial protest of the decade also reached the athletic fields. American Olympic medalists in 200-meter run, Tommie Smith (center) and Juan Carlos (right), register their protest during playing of Star Spangled Banner in Mexico City. World Wide Photos.

ment" (Hoch, 1972, p. 173). Veteran Olympic hammer thrower Hal Connolly threatened to withdraw from the games after the suspension of Carlos and Smith, and the white Harvard crew supported the human rights movement throughout.

The 1976 boycott in which 18 black nations, led by Tanzania, actually withdrew from the games was, as Erich Segal put it, an effort to dramatize racism by leaving the games a white Olympics. The issue was again South Africa, although the immediate target was New Zealand, which had sent a rugby team to play in the blacklisted land of apartheid. The African athletes seemed to feel that New Zealand should have followed the lead of India, which in 1974 had withdrawn from Davis Cup tennis competition in protest against the presence of South Africa and of Mexico, which had withdrawn in 1975 and 1976. That New Zealand played rugby in South Africa is not surprising in view of the fact that the two countries had long-standing athletic ties and that New Zealand practiced her own variety of apartheid against her native Maori minority, barring them from rugby, cricket, track and field, golf, tennis, weight lifting, and volleyball. The 18 teams left in protest against the refusal of the International Olympic Committee to bar New Zealand from the games. As Segal suggested, their departure, which made them *in*conspicuous by their absence, was probably less effective than another Smith-Carlos-type gesture might have been.

The 1976 Games also brought up the question of Taiwan, whose relationship to the counterculture is ambiguous. Established by Chiang Kai-shek as an anticommunist stronghold after his 1949 defeat by Mao Tse-tung, for 3-1/2 decades Taiwan has been used by, and has used, the Western powers in the Cold War game. Thus it was strange that in the world of international sport it should have been Taiwanese boys who came to Williamsport, Pennsylvania, for the Little League baseball championship and from 1971 through 1974 virtually annihilated the American opposition at their own national game. Following this, in a typical establishment-type gesture the Little League board announced that the Little League world series would henceforth be a United States series. The decision was, however, revoked before the 1976 championship, and the Taiwanese came back to win again.

Although the official national sympathies of the Third World powers have been Maoist and anti-Taiwan, it is hard to imagine that the ordinary people of the developing nations, if they knew of some of these events, did not feel some of the same kind of glee with which they greeted an "uppity" black man's domination of heavyweight boxing. Whatever the common people of the world may have felt, in 1976 the Taiwanese Olympic team was barely permitted to appear, but only under the banner of Taiwan, not as the representative of China—which they, and probably most of the Western political and athletic establishment, wished.

Jock Lib and Women's Lib

In sport as elsewhere, the greatest victims of discrimination are women. This is best exemplified in the colleges. Intercollegiate sport is almost entirely male-provided mass entertainment, sold in a market that demands the three Vs—violence, velocity, and victory. Even in noncontact sports like baseball, tennis, and golf, women can't throw a ball 95 miles an hour, blast the big serve, or whale the ball off the tee like men do. Here, as in track and field, their smaller size and lighter musculature make their product less salable to the old culture. Even when a contest between women may be more skillful, the blasting males will generally get the audience. In any sport, on a 1 to 10 scale the males are likely to rank closer toward 10 in power-speed-skill, and the women to rank closer toward 1. In the old culture, with its emphasis on top performance and its impatience with anything less, a one-sided tensionless match between a 9 and a 10 on the power-speed-skill scale is likely to outdraw a tensely contested match between a 2 and a 3. Thus Arthur Ashe, who knew race discrimination, could defend lower pay for touring women tennis pros: "Only three or four women draw fans to a tourney, so why do we have to split our money with them?" (Hoch, 1972, p. 159)

In the colleges, emphasis on violence, velocity, and victory leaves women's athletic budgets only a small fraction of the budgets for men. At the University of Miami in 1977 the total women's athletic budget—for softball, volleyball, basketball, tennis, swimming, and golf—equaled the salary of the male football coach. James Michener describes a state university with a student body 50% female in which less than .8 of 1% of a $3,900,000 athletic budget was spent for women. Under such circumstances it is not surprising that women athletes who are aware of what is going on are not very friendly toward the athletic establishment.

In 1970, the year with which I began this chapter, women players threatened to boycott Jack Kramer's Pacific Southwest tennis tournament because of the discrimination in allocation of prize money defended by Ashe. In considerable part because of Billie Jean King, an activist in the women's movement, they were successful in organizing their own tournaments. Ironically, soon the women's tournies became every bit as commercialized as the men's. The makers of Virginia Slims cigarettes capitalized by sponsoring five of the tournaments and were able to cash in on women's liberationist sentiment by marketing a cigarette created especially for women with the slogan, "You've come a long way baby."

In the same year, Patricia Palinkas, as a placekick holder for her husband, became the first woman in pro football. In the early 1970s a women's semipro football league was formed. Women broke in as horse race jockeys and ran in the Boston Marathon. A woman became a minor league baseball umpire in spite of fears that a female umpire might be subjected to unladylike language. By court order a young woman was placed on high school ski and cross country teams in Hopkins, Minnesota. The state of New Jersey ruled that sexual segregation must be eliminated in public schools in football, baseball, basketball, and wrestling (traditionally boys' sports) and also in the traditionally female sports of softball, field hockey, and lacrosse. The United States government revised the Little League charter to allow girls to play and replaced the stated goal of "manhood" with "citizenship and sportsmanship."

Title IX of the Education Act of 1972, which abolished sex discrimination in federally funded institutions, brought women into a basic collision with the athletic establishment. Although athletic programs are only one aspect of Title IX, the most intense opposition came from the NCAA, which claimed that equal athletic rights in colleges would destroy the intercollegiate athletic entertainment industry, which it represents. In 1981 it hedged against this loss by taking over intercollegiate women's sports from the Association for Intercollegiate Athletics for Women (AIAW). By 1982 that largely female-controlled body had disappeared.

To understand the intensity of the collision we must understand that not only profit, but also *machismo*, is at stake. As everyone knows who is aware of how little girls and little boys are brought up, playing physical games to win is the core of virility in our society. Thus sport is a no-woman's land and should, it is felt, be kept that way. The emotional collision is even wider than this. Extensive psychological testing has shown that those with machismo are likely to be politically conservative, rigid, dogmatic, and authoritarian—with antipathy to everything for which the counterculture stands.

So great is the economic and psychological stake of the athletic establishment that it is unlikely that we shall see real athletic equality for college women during the 20th century. The central rationalization will be the fact that college athletics is not primarily either for fun or student health but for a profit. A straw in the wind: Michener, after describing a 1% allocation for women as outrageous, says he would find acceptable a university athletic budget split of 77% for men and 23% for women (1977).

Jock Lib and the Youth Culture

Most athletes, amateur and professional, of whatever race, sex, or nationality, are under 30; thus they belong to the youth culture.

At a time when that culture has changed—in lifestyle, hair, dress, speech, and politics—this is a very important fact, one that sociologist Harry Edwards has analyzed well (1973, pp. 179–182).

Like all people, the athlete wishes to be thought well of by his peers. Traditionally he has been highly regarded, while at the same time his career and personal identity have been tied up with the social and political status quo. All this was possible as long as there was no serious conflict between the youth culture and the establishment. However, as the apathetic generation of the 1950s became the involved generation of the 1960s and gave rise to significant numbers of hippies, yippies, zippies, and New Leftists, things became more difficult for the athlete. Although the followers of the counterculture were a minority of youth, they were a vocal one and received a great deal of media coverage. When dissenters were an insignificant and powerless minority the athlete could simply ignore them or dismiss them as unrealistic, fanatical, and subversive. In an extreme, he might attack them verbally or physically. But when counterculture hair styles, dress, lifestyle, and political views began to be admired and imitated by large numbers of young people, the athlete could no longer ignore, dismiss, or attack them. Neither could he be comfortable as the crewcut, square, uncritical jock. He began to look at his culture, at himself, and at his role in his culture. As a result, even some of the descriptions of the athlete offered by people as knowledgeable as Jack Scott and Harry Edwards as late as the early 1970s are today regarded by some of my students as outdated stereotypes. Coach Woody Hayes, as far to the right athletically as Edwards is to the left, agreed in 1973: "Players living in dorms are exposed to the attitudes of other students. It's bound to rub off. They'll listen to their peer group. They've done it with long hair and in other dress areas. There will be influence in time in discipline, too" (ISSS Newsletter, December, 1973, p. 9).

Interesting in this connection is a study reported by Brian M. Petrie in 1977 comparing the social and political attitudes of jocks and nonathletes at the University of Western Ontario. Although this is a Canadian school, all three major U.S. TV networks are received there, and the campus newspaper used material from the U.S. student underground. So Petrie hypothesized that "there would be little variation in patterns of political orientations among students of the two societies" (1977, p. 53). The result: There were no significant differences in attitudes between athletes and nonathletes at Western Ontario. "The athletes, however, were more liberal than their nonathletic peers in their rejection of the idea that physical attacks against radical demonstrators were justified (only 3% of the athletes agreed with the item as against 13% of the nonathletes)" (Petrie, 1977, p. 57).

Whither the Counterculture?

What will happen in the future to the counterculture and to the athletic revolution as a part of it? Some people see the decade of the 1960s as an explosion that has run its course, a temporary outburst of utopian idealism by people who a decade later had mellowed and come to their senses. They anticipate that in a longer run things will return to normal. In the light of our overview in this chapter, this does not seem likely to me.

Evidence that the countercultural aspects of the athletic revolution did not quite end with the 1960s was the forced withdrawal of South Africa from the Davis Cup Tennis play in April, 1978, following major protests at Newport Beach and Forest Hills in 1976 and a March 1978 demonstration at the Vanderbilt University gym that reduced attendance for the matches between the United States and South Africa to 75 people, a number smaller than that of the protesters outside. Of this Al Campora, wounded in 1970 at Kent State, said, "I thought that State had the most hated gym in the world, but now I guess Vanderbilt does" (*Seven Days*, April 12, 1978, p. 10).

The counterculture has roots at least as old as our bicentennial. In the 1960s many different areas of rising expectations came to maturity simultaneously and became too much for the old culture to contain or satisfy. In the pattern by which societies change, peaks like this do not continue forever. They are followed by periods in which social gains born in the fever of crisis are slowly consolidated and expanded. In the counterculture in general, and in the athletic revolution in particular, this is what I think happened in the 1970s and will continue to happen at least until the end of the century.

Chapter 3

*P*lay, Games, and Sport

To understand the athletic revolution, we will need to examine critically the role of sport in the whole program of human activity. In any scientific investigation we must first stake out the areas of behavior we are going to study (the technical word is to *delimit*—establish the limits). In this book we are going to analyze *play*, *games*, and *sport*—their relationship to each other and their part in the total pattern of culture.

There is no absolutely right definition for anything. What we must ask of a definition is that it (a) delimit clearly what we are going to talk about, (b) be consistent with the way people have staked out the area in the past, and (c) be stated so as to indicate the kind of observation and manipulations that will test whatever statements we may make about the phenomena.

Play

The athletic revolution asks pointed questions about the meaning of human play. To think about these questions we will need to ask what play is. Most people who study the subject these days refer to the book *Homo Ludens* (man, the player) by the Dutch cultural historian Johan Huizinga (1964), which his colleague Roger Caillois has praised as the most important work in the philosophy of history yet produced in the 20th century. Play is, to Huizinga, not a domain of behavior sharply set apart from all other human activity. It is, rather, a way in which we can follow any kind of human interest. To use a metaphor from music that Huizinga does not employ, play is a key in which we can perform any kind of activity—art, music, business, politics, religion, science, love, or even war.

What then, is the key of play? The clue is *fun*. "It is precisely this fun-element that characterizes the essence of play" (p. 3). Huizinga said that "the fun of playing resists all analysis and logical interpretation" (p. 3). However, Brian Sutton-Smith, a psychologist of child development, in 1972 pointed to two elements in fun: When people play, they set aside the pressure of the ordinary rules that govern their nonplay life. At the same time they set up a new set of guidelines for their play. They substitute a more attractive *play order* for the *natural order* of life:

> *The player substitutes his own conventions and his own urgencies for those of society and nature. . . . This mixture of lowered tension in external relations and induced arousal within the novel restraints is probably the emphoric state we call fun. . . . What the player experiences is a sense of being possessed. He is under the control of forces that at times he himself can scarcely control, yet the pretense quality of the game means that he can control them. (Avedon & Sutton-Smith, 1971, p. 439; Sutton-Smith, 1972, pp. xiii, xv)*

The very complex interplay between the natural order and the play order may be clarified by three game situations in which the two conflict. These are suggested by Bernard Suits (1967):

1. *Given an oval running track surrounding an infield, the commonsense way to reach the finish line is to cut across the infield. But the runner in a track meet, in order to win, follows the rules of the race around the oval. The play order supersedes the natural order.*
2. *Given a long mowed strip with eighteen metal holes, the commonsense way to get the ball successively into the holes would be to walk and drop it in each turn. But the golfer instead hits the ball with a set of headed sticks made to specifications. The play order again supersedes the natural order.*
3. *A driver in a cross-country race sees a child wander on to the road ahead of him. Everyday commonsense tells him to leave the road. The rules of the game tell him to keep going. He goes into the ditch, the child is saved, and he loses the race. The natural order has superseded the play order.*

Or consider an example suggested by the Soviet sport sociologist I. N. Ponomarev: A high jumper who can clear 7 feet in competition (play order) might have trouble going over a 5' 6'' solid wall or barbed fence when pursued by a maniac (natural order).

In distinguishing between the demands of everyday life and the special demands set up by the rules of play, Sutton-Smith was follow-

ing the lead given by Huizinga's earlier analysis in which he had outlined the characteristics of play:

- *Play is a voluntary activity. . . . By this quality of freedom alone,
  play marks itself off from the course of the natural process. It
  is something added thereto and spread over it like a flowering,
  an ornament, a garment.*

- *Play is . . . a stepping out of real life into a temporary sphere
  of activity with a disposition all of its own. It stands outside the
  immediate satisfaction of wants and appetites, as a temporary
  activity satisfying in itself and ending there . . . an intermezzo,
  an interlude in our daily lives.*

- *Play is distinct from ordinary life both as to locality and duration.
  . . . It is played out within certain limits of time and place. It
  contains its own course and meaning. The arena, the card-table,
  the magic circle, the temple, the stage, the screen, the tennis-
  court, the court of justice . . . all are temporary worlds within
  the ordinary world, dedicated to the performances of an act
  apart.*

- *Inside the play-ground, an absolute and peculiar order reigns.
  . . . Into an imperfect world and into the confusion of life, play
  brings a temporary, a limited, perfection.*

- *Play is tense . . . a testing of the player's prowess: his courage,
  tenacity, resources, and last but not least, his spiritual powers—
  his fairness; because, despite his ardent desire to win, he must
  still stick to the rules of the game. [Also: Prestige for past victories counts for naught; the need for proving oneself is ever
  demanded anew. The attractiveness of sport lies in its genuine
  element of surprise, which can be capitalized on but not twist-
  ed out of shape by political demands. (Morton, 1963, p. 26)]*

- *All play has rules. They determine what holds in the temporary
  world circumscribed by play. The rules of a game are absolutely binding and allow no doubt. . . . Indeed, as soon as the rules
  are transgressed the whole play-world collapses. The game is
  over.*

- *A play-community generally tends to become permanent. . . .
  The feeling of being apart together in an exceptional situation
  . . . of mutually withdrawing from the rest of the world and
  rejecting the usual norms, retains its magic beyond the duration of the individual game. The club pertains to play as the hat
  to the head. (Huizinga, 1964, pp. 7, 8–9, 9–10, 11, 11–12)*

In summary, "play is a voluntary activity or occupation exercised within certain fixed rules of time and place, according to rules freely accepted but absolutely binding, having its aim in itself, and accompanied by a feeling of tension, joy, and the consciousness that this is different from ordinary life" (Huizinga, 1964, p. 28).

Jean Piaget, the Swiss psychologist whose studies of children's games are world-famous, agrees with Huizinga that play is not an isolated function, but is in reality one of the aspects of any activity (like imagination in respect to thought) (1960, pp. 147–150). Like Sutton-Smith he finds play to be "distinguishable by a modification of the conditions of equilibrium between reality and the ego" (1960, pp. 147–150). He also names the characteristics that are generally said to distinguish play from non-play:

- *"Play is an end in itself [autotelic], whereas work and other non-ludic behaviors involve an aim not contained in the activity as such."*
- *Ludic activity is distinguished by "the spontaneity of play, as opposed to the compulsion of work."*
- *"Play is an activity 'for pleasure,' while serious activity is directed towards a useful result irrespective of its pleasurable character."*
- *"Play is considered to be devoid of organized structure."*
- *In play, the inescapable real-life conflict between individual freedom and social restrictions is either absent or transposed so as to give an acceptable solution.*
- *Play is characterized by "overmotivation"—an extra unnecessary "twist," such as drawing figures with the broom while sweeping a floor. (Piaget, 1960, pp. 147–150)*

Piaget's extra twist leads to what anthropologist Stephen Miller thinks is the essence of play—galumphing (1973, p. 42). The word may not sound very coldly scientific, but it conveys the spirit of fun. In ordinary life, we are under pressure to behave efficiently and economically, to seek the shortest and easiest means to our goals. Galumphing, on the other hand, is a patterned, voluntary elaboration or complication . . . where the pattern is not under the dominant control of goals. Play, as compared with ordinary life, is a crooked line to the end. The most economical route from first to third base would take one through the pitcher's mound, but the rules of the game require that one detour by way of second base. One wastes time and energy to avoid stepping on the cracks in the sidewalk, but that is the nature of galumphing. Miller would suggest that in a world where we get tired of being structured to take the shortest route to our goals we deliberately structure activities that take the long way around—and here is the fun.

Another important dissection of play, which is useful to our understanding of sport, is performed by the French sociologist Roger

Caillois in his book, *Man, Play, and Games* (1961). Caillois distinguishes four main categories of play.

The first is *contest*, or struggle. To this Caillois gives the Greek name *agon* (related to the English word agony). Forms of agon are competitive games, economic competition, competitive advertising, and competitive examinations. The adjective describing such activities is *agonistic*.

The second form is *chance* or luck (which Caillois calls *alea*, after the Latin word for dice). Here the player, instead of summoning his energies for an agonistic struggle, lets go and submits to fate, chance, the Universe, God. Examples are craps, poker, bingo, roulette, parimutuel betting, state lotteries.

A third major type of play Caillois calls *mimicry*. This includes the imitative behavior of animals, role taking by children, drama, hero worship, the wearing of uniforms, and ceremonial etiquette.

Here we find ritual, which uses regularly repeated dramatic performances to portray and symbolize wider group experiences and conflicts of which the individual's life is a part. It is important that throughout history spectator sport has often been, and today still often is, a ritual dramatic spectacle, a morality play in which the athletes represent the forces of good clashing with the forces of evil.

The fourth form is *vertigo* (which Caillois names *ilinx*, from the Latin word for whirlpool). It includes swinging; ecstatic dancing; speed on skis, in cars, motorcycles, and boats; carnival rides; mountain climbing; alcohol and drugs; and tightrope walking. Today we might add such activities as rock music and skydiving.

Caillois summarizes his four forms of play in this way:

> In agon, *the player relies only on himself and bends all his efforts to do his best; in* alea, *he relies on everything except himself and he surrenders to forces that elude him; in* mimicry, *he imagines that he is other than he really is and invents a fictitious universe;* ilinx, *the fourth fundamental tendency, is an answer to one's need to feel the body's stability and equilibrium momentarily destroyed, to escape the tyranny of perception, and to overcome awareness. (1955, p. 74)*

Caillois' analysis of play contains another distinction relevant to the questions raised by the athletic revolution. This is the difference between impulse and control—between the kind of spontaneous unreflective turbulence and self-expression found in the play of children, for which he uses the word *paidiá* (child's play) and the tendency to formalize and conventionalize play which he describes by the Latin word for play, *ludus* (adjective, *ludic*).

The distinction between the two modes of play is so central to the basic issues raised in this book that it may be well to illustrate each mode very specifically with examples that are close enough to everyone's experience to ring a bell. First, *ludus* as delineated in Harold Garfinkel's statement of the basic rules of ticktacktoe:

Play is conducted on a three by three matrix by two players who move alternatively. The first player makes a mark in one of the unoccupied cells. The second player, in his turn, places his mark in one of the remaining cells. And so on. The term "ticktacktoe player" refers to a person who seeks to act in compliance. (Bowman, 1978, p. 272)

Then, John Bowman's description of adult *paidiá:*

Five women are walking along the edge of a large embankment. They stop momentarily and look at one another. One person remarks: "I used to love to roll down hills." Without comment, one of the other persons in the group flings herself to the ground and rolls down the hill. Everyone begins to laugh and three of the remaining four roll down the hill also. Upon reaching the bottom all laugh hysterically for several minutes with tears coming to several of the women's eyes. (Bowman, 1978, p. 144)

Bowman's illustration suggests what may be the most important thing in distinguishing *paidiá* (just fun) from *ludus* (organized play): the presence of smiling and laughter in *paidiá*, their absence in *ludus*.

Any act of play falls somewhere on a continuum (a continuous gradation) between spontaneity (*paidiá*) and conventionality (*ludus*). This continuum runs through all four forms of play.

Some students of play have emphasized that it is a form of communication through group make-believe related to metaphor in language (Bateson, 1972; Schwartzman, 1979). An example of a metaphor is "Richard is a lion." This is a paradoxical statement: "A is like B and is also not like B." Richard is courageous like a lion, but unlike a lion he has no tail. Similarly, in children's play a broom ridden by a child is like a horse but known not to be a horse. A piece of clay is molded like a cake but not eaten because it is known not really to be a cake. Linda, as her mother, talks to Linda, who is not her mother, and as not-mother-Linda, she also talks back. Much of the importance of play comes from the paradox of play as a metaphor of life: The play order is and is not the natural order. The ball game is just a game, but when my team wins on the field I feel myself more of a champion in real life. The ugly witch that I, as a child, destroy vicariously in a fairy tale is not my frustrating mother, and yet in removing a menacing parent figure I reduce some of the pain of being a mere child.

Games

Play is defined as a cooperative interaction that has no stated goal, no end point, and no winners; formal games, in contrast, are competitive interactions, aimed at achieving a recognized goal (e.g., touchdown, checkmate). . . . Formal games have a predetermined end point . . . that is simultaneous with the declaration of a winner or winners. (Lever, 1978, p. 473)

When we move from play in general to games and then to sport, the organized, ludic element becomes more prominent. The unorganized amusements, pastimes, and hobbies of children and adults contain much of the unstructured, spontaneous turbulence and self-expression of *paidiá*. Examples of such pastimes and amusements are bicycle riding, horseback riding, climbing, swimming, fishing, kite flying, throwing snowballs, skiing, tobogganing, hiking, and ice and roller skating. Hobbies include such early rural activities as play with leaves, flowers, grass, and nuts and cooking, sewing, knitting, playing with tools, machinery, model airplanes, and stamp and coin collecting. Also among the pregame play activities—especially of young girls—are central person games (chasing games with an "It" figure) in which "a central player has an arbitrarily game-granted status that allows her to dictate the course of the action, while the other players attempt to escape, or dispossess the central person of her power." (Avedon & Sutton-Smith, 1971, p. 404).

Compared with these less structured play activities—out of which it may have grown—a game is "a play activity which has explicit rules, specified or understood goals. . . , the element of opposition or contest, recognizable boundaries in time and sometimes in space, and a sequence of actions which is essentially 'repeatable' every time the game is played" (Ager, 1976, p. 80).

The contest may be between two individuals, between two teams, between an individual and a group, as in central person games, between an individual or team and inanimate nature (as in running rapids or mountain climbing), between a person or group and animate nature (as in hunting, fishing, or bull fighting), or between an individual or team and an ideal standard. As well as between or among people, contest may take place within an individual, as between a child and an imaginary companion, or between one's present and past performance. It may also be a struggle between two animals (as in a horse race or cockfight) or between a real and an artificial animal (as in a greyhound race against a mechanical rabbit).

In their anthropological study of games in different cultures, John M. Roberts and his colleagues have distinguished three major forms of games: games of *physical skill,* whose outcome depends on the physical abilities of the players; games of *strategy,* which involve a series of moves each representing a choice among alternatives; and games of *chance,* which are determined by either nonrational guesses or the behavior of a mechanical device (Roberts, 1959, 1966, 1970). Pure examples of the three types are weight lifting, chess, and craps. A prize fight or a marathon race is also a fairly pure example of a physical skill game. Chess, the Japanese board game *go,* or the simple, universal game ticktacktoe are fairly pure strategy games. High card win and roulette are other examples of pure chance. There are important combinations of the three types—physical skill with secondary reliance on strategy (as in baseball, football, basketball, and tennis); physical skill combined with chance (as in musical chairs); games of strategy and chance (such as bridge and poker); combinations of physical skill, strategy, and chance (e.g., the child's game of steal the bacon).

Of the three major forms of games, physical skill games are the most widespread among the human race and were probably the first to develop historically. For illustration, in her study of a simple Eskimo hunting people, anthropologist Lynn Ager reports that of 39 games played by children, 25 were games of physical skill (1976, p. 82).

Roberts has also found that the three types of games are related to different kinds of cultural problems. Physical skill games are in part training for mastery of the natural environment. Chance games are ways of mastering uncertainty; they are most common among peoples who have a hazardous and unpredictable existence. They are almost absent among the simplest peoples and grow in number and complexity as societies become more complex economically and technically and more stratified socially. We shall examine this and related research in chapter 4.

A distinction fundamental to the problems raised by the athletic revolution comes from the mathematical study of games of strategy, which we know as game theory. The distinction is between zero-sum games and positive-sum games. In zero-sum games, the winner's gains are equal to the loser's losses. It is impossible for both to win or for both to lose. Examples are ticktacktoe, checkers, chess, bridge, most competitive sports as now organized, war, a ratings contest between two networks, and a price war between two corporations. In positive-sum games, everybody can win or lose. An example of an everybody wins situation is the unique way in which basketball is played by some Navaho Indians, who enjoy the game intensely but don't keep score.

There have been attempts to develop noncompetitive forms of the major sports, which would really make them positive-sum games.

A zero-sum view of athletic competition is Vince Lombardi's famous slogan: Winning is not the most important thing—it's the only thing. An example of a positive-sum view is Grantland Rice's equally famous slogan: It's not whether you won or lost, but how you played the game. A good deal of the disappointment of some athletes with the current sport scene lies in the fact that they have a positive-sum view of athletic competition, whereas many coaches, fans, and alumni have a zero-sum view. The question at issue is whether there can be positive-sum competition. It is the same issue as is involved when businessmen caught in a cutthroat, competitive rat race long for a brotherly competition that would not be to the death.

Sport

With the rise of sport we reach the ultimate in the organization and formalization of play. A game, says philosopher Paul Weiss, is an occurrence; a sport is a pattern.

Sport in modern history has meant two essentially different things: a badge of status for rural gentlemen and professionalized entertainment for mass leisure in an urban industrial society.

Thomas Jefferson, a political democrat but still a Virginia aristocrat, expressed the difference when he said that games played with a ball stamp no character on the mind. Only a horse and gun, he felt, can do that. The directors of the 19th-century British Henley Regatta expressed the same distinction when they excluded from participation any person who was "by trade or employment a mechanic, artisan, or labourer" (McIntosh, 1971b, p. 36).

Sport as a gentleman's activity is primarily British. Neither Jefferson nor most British gentlemen would have approved the cruder of the blood sports that appealed to many Englishmen—"setting dogs to bait and kill chained bears . . . and pitting against one another gamecocks whose spurs were shod with steel" (Gabriel, 1929, p. 2). But British gentlemen did approve and practice a related blood sport, "pursuing with hounds the lone fox until he forfeited his life to the snarling pack." And Jefferson "thoroughly enjoyed . . . being in at the death of a fox" (Dulles, 1940, p. 61). Transplanted to the United States, sport took such forms as horse racing, fox hunting, horse shows, the breeding of dogs, polo, and yacht racing (cricket did not quite transplant). These survived to some extent into the 20th century, as sport historian John Rickards Betts tells us:

Even at the turn of the century society still remained in control
of the leading tennis and golf associations; fox hunting prevailed
among eastern and southern families; many continued to flock to
Newport, Saratoga, and other resorts; horse shows remained a
notable event on the social calendar; . . . yachting remained essen-
tially an aristocratic monopoly; racquets and squash were played
only by the metropolitan elite; and polo showed no signs of be-
ing vulgarized by the masses. (1974, p. 61)

However, with the shortening of the work week from about 70
hours to about 35 in the past 100 years, gentlemen's sport has given
way to commercial sport. This is a fairly modern development that
originated in England. Its main characteristics are (a) continuity, (b)
division of roles, (c) dynamic interaction with an audience, and (d) a
supporting sport establishment. Commercial sport usually involves
pure physical games or games of physical skill mixed with strategy.

Huizinga, we will remember, spoke of how play activity tends to
establish the playing group as a permanent community. "The great
ball-games require the existence of permanent teams, and herein lies
the starting point of modern sport" (Huizinga, 1964, p. 196). English
football legendarily grew out of the kicking of the skulls of dead Viking enemies. This led before the 12th century to the game of Dane's
Head, in which an inflated pig bladder was kicked between two towns
with the village greens as goals. It was in the 19th century that rugby
and cricket became organized sports involving permanent teams.
Huizinga names conditions in English life that made it the scene for
the development of modern sport:

Local self-government encouraged the spirit of association and
solidarity. The absence of obligatory military training favored the
occasion for, and the need of, physical exercise. The peculiar form
of education tended to work in the same direction and finally the
geography of the country and the nature of the terrain, on the
whole flat and, in the ubiquitous commons, offering the most per-
fect playing-fields that could be devised, were of the greatest im-
portance. Thus England became the cradle and focus of modern
sporting life. (1964, p. 197)

Organized sport was first a creation of the British middle class. This
class, says Peter McIntosh, "rose to a position of political power and
social influence on the crest of the Industrial Revolution. They shaped
their games and sports to a large extent at the Public Schools (1971a,
p. 36). These were railway schools like Marlborough College, where
middle-class young men came via the new railway system, hoping to

emulate the upper-class boys who went by horse and coach to Eton, Harrow, and Winchester.

Writing of the drive to power of the business classes in 19th-century England, Peter McIntosh says,

> *Team games encouraged just those qualities of cooperation and conformity to the needs of the herd which were so much prized by a middle class which was establishing its power and influence throughout the world. . . . The great acceleration of athleticism and the growth of competitive games in the nineteenth century, with their supposed potential for training character, was an intrinsic part of the intensely competitive commercial development and imperial expansion of that era. (McIntosh, 1972, pp. 71–72, 106)*

Sport came to the working class when the work week was reduced, as by the introduction of the Saturday half-holiday in industrial Birmingham, and the introduction of the 9-hour day between 1869 and 1873.

The next development of sport occurred across the Atlantic as part of American industrialism. In Allen Sack's very interesting study of the professionalization of American football in the late 19th century, he emphasizes that this was part of the revolution by which the manufacturing class came to power in the United States (Sack, 1973). The first ruling class was the seafaring New England commercial aristocracy. Harvard was their college. After independence from Britain, the urban industrial bourgeoisie gained power. From 1861 to 1865, in the Civil War, it broke the back of the planter aristocracy of the South. But the old aristocratic ideals of the merchant seamen lived on in New England, especially at Harvard, which was a symbol of contempt for the win-at-all-costs ethic in both athletics and business. Sack quotes a fictional Yale athletic hero, "Harvard is more status conscious; aristocracy is not important at Yale" (1973, p. 28). The 33-year string in which Yale beat Harvard 29 times represented in sport the rise to power of the business ethic and its Social Darwinist code of survival of the fittest. Yale's coach Walter Camp, the father of modern football, spoke the ideology of the successful business class. His biographer says of Camp: "He could not possibly have been described as a good loser. . . . His spirit hated defeat, and he planned systematically with all his wits for victory." Camp himself said, "When you lose a match against a man in your own class, shake hands with him; do not excuse your defeat, do not forget it, and do not let it happen again if there is any way to prepare yourself for the next match" (Powel, 1926, pp. 112–113). Camp also said, "There were two things for which we were noted, our toughness and our tackling. No wonder we were tough, for [our practice] had been a general survival of the fittest'' (Sack, 1973, p. 30). It was no coincidence that Camp was the brother-in-law of the great Yale professor William Graham Sumner, author of *Folkways* and an outspoken and uncritical admirer of the successful business class:

> *The law of the survival of the fittest was not made by man and cannot be abrogated by man. We can only, by interfering with it, produce the survival of the unfittest. . . . The strong and the weak are terms which admit of no definition unless they are made equivalent to the industrious and the idle, the frugal and the unfrugal. . . . All the achievements of the plutocrats which are denounced prove that they are men of transcendent ability, more powerful than thousands of other men put together simply by force of brains (Sumner, 1885, p. 85; Keller & Davie, 1934 (vol. 2), p. 96; Sumner, 1933, p. 752).*

Organized sport, like the industrial society that gave it birth, involves a sharply marked specialization of roles. There are team games without this differentiation—for instance, the children's games of cowboys and Indians and cops and robbers. The team game of buzkashi, a kind of mounted football played in Afghanistan by riders with the carcass of a beheaded calf on a quarter-mile field, has teams up to 100 in number but without the assignment of roles that appears in soccer, rugby, or polo. The early English Dane's Head, although played by teams from town to town, apparently did not have positions and roles allocated as in modern English football.

Sport also includes dynamic interaction between players and spectators who identify with their efforts. The great cultural historian Lewis Mumford defines sport as organized play in which the spectator is more important than the performer and in which the game loses a large part of its meaning if there is no audience.

Finally, the players are related not only to the audience but to an institutionalized sport order that includes sporting goods manufacturers, sport clubs, national and international governing bodies for amateurs and professionals, publishers of sport magazines, and the personnel of the media that cover sports.

Play, Sport, and Work

The complex technical organization of sport as an establishment led Huizinga to ask a fundamental question that many athletes are asking: Is sport play? Reviewing a century of modern sport, Huizinga said, "In the case of sport we have an activity nominally known as play but

raised to such a pitch of technical organization and scientific thoroughness that the play-spirit is threatened with extinction" (Huizinga, 1964,
p. 199).

In this chapter we have analyzed play as an area of behavior that
includes games, which in turn include sport. We have treated sport
as a subdivision of play. Three sociologists of sport question whether
this is the case. Heinz Meyer says the following:

> *Sport is to be seen as a phenomenon that, although it started its*
> *development from play, contrasts with play, especially because*
> *of the regulations set up for competitions and of the control of*
> *records; these accents are of course, . . . already there in play; but*
> *they got a new stress in the British movement of sport and they*
> *dominate sport of nowadays in such a way that the relationship*
> *to play is no longer to be seen (1973, pp. 48–49).*

Harry Edwards lists a number of characteristics in which sport differs
from pure play (1973, p. 59). Sport is less spontaneous and less under
the individual participant's control. Formal roles and responsibilities
play a larger part. Sport is less separated from the pressures of daily
life. The participant's goals are no longer derived from the activity but
from outside it. Sport's extreme seriousness demands a greater proportion of his time and attention. He is required to exert himself beyond
the point where his activity is interesting or refreshing. Edwards says
that there is *no* overlap at all between play and sport. Allen Sack (1977)
is less dogmatic, but he does ask whether sport is really play or work.
He points out that commercial sport fails to meet three of Huizinga's
main standards for play. "Professional games . . . inasmuch as they
(1) involve activity that participants are obliged to perform, (2) are
oriented to the pragmatic concerns of everyday life, and (3) are pursued for profit or material gain, share almost nothing in common with
play." He suggests that "upon hearing the final gun that ends his game
the professional athlete is likely to experience feelings of relief as is
any other worker when a whistle ends his working day" (Sack, 1977,
pp. 190–191).

Reality requires us, Sack feels, to locate different activities on a continuum from play to work. Dancing, riding a bicycle, sexual intercourse,
riding a merry-go-round, camping, mountain climbing, when not competitive or institutionalized, are non-sport play. Small-college football
may be close to the play end of the continuum. Big-time college football is close to work. Pro football is work. A related continuum is put
forward by Michael Salter (1980). At one end is play, which involves
a message "this is play," is voluntary in nature, has rewards that are
intrinsic rather than extrinsic, and is fun. In the center of the continuum

are three kinds of games: the ludic game, in which the spirit of play prevails; the sport, in which the spirit of play and the will to win are in balance; and athletics, in which winning is paramount. At the far end from play is the *terminal contest*, in which winning is *all* that counts and any means are justifiable (see Figure 3.1). The pure terminal contest is war; among sports, the gladiatorial games were as good an example as any, and boxing is close.

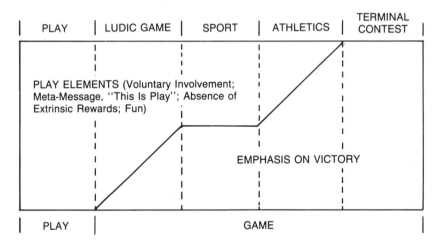

Figure 3.1 Play-Game Continuum. *Note.* Modified from Figure 2 in "Play in Ritual: An Ethnohistorical Overview of Native North America" by M. A. Salter. In H. B. Schwartzman (Ed.), *Play and Culture* (p. 72), 1980, Champaign, IL: Leisure Press. Copyright 1980 by Leisure Press. Reprinted by permission.

Kent Pearson (1979), an Australian sociologist, has made a helpful distinction between two stages in what he calls the athleticization of play—play-sport and athletic-sport. Play-sport remains essentially informal. Athletic-sport is more competitive, has more systematic techniques for developing skill, and tends to become bureaucratically organized like big business, big government, and the military. In Australia Pearson finds a contrast between surf lifesaving (an organized athletic-sport) and surfboard riding (still essentially a noncompetitive, informal play form). Surf lifesaving is a highly organized competitive sport covering four main areas of competition: (1) rescue and resuscitation, (2) beach events (including sprint running, beach flags, etc.), (3) boat events, and (4) small craft events (board and ski racing). On the contrary, although surfboard riding has developed as a competitive sport, for the vast majority in Australia and New Zealand surf board riding is a sport providing challenge in a natural environment and the opportunity for self-expression (Pearson, 1979).

Pearson outlines the conditions that promote one form or the other. Athletic-sport is more likely to develop when participants must cooperate in order for the event to take place; when there are clear-cut criteria for victory by individuals or teams; when artificial sport settings (field arenas, tracks, swimming pools, etc.) are important and require organization for building and management and regulation of sport activity; when science and technology are applied to the development of game skills; and when there are commercial sponsors. On the contrary, activities are likely to remain play-sports when organization is not necessary, competition is not important, the sport can be pursued in areas (like the ocean) that are easily accessible and don't have to be fabricated, improvements in equipment are worked out by enthusiasts themselves rather than by commercial equipment-makers, and when the participants value informal fun and resist organization.

Surfboard riding is a play-sport providing challenge in a natural environment and the opportunity for self-expression. Photo by Dick Kassan.

Ordinary fishing and hunting, I would think, are still essentially play-sports (despite the presence of the gun lobby); organized fox hunting, long central to British upper-class recreation, is more of an athletic-sport. Volleyball, when I was a boy, was almost always a pick-up play-sport. Today it has been organized as an athletic sport—a half-mile from my home, Miami-Dade Community College has organized competitive volleyball teams, as does the University of Miami. Frisbee, which would seem a natural play-sport is today in transition—there are already organized competitive contests. Skydiving, mountain climbing, hang gliding, hot-air ballooning, and surf swimming are, I think, still play-sports. Pearson's example of a play-sport—surfboard riding—is no longer play, as he suggests, when it is sponsored by soft drink companies or when it is organized for TV production and beamed around the globe by *Wide World of Sports.*

Figure 3.2 may furnish a final basis for discussion of this chapter.

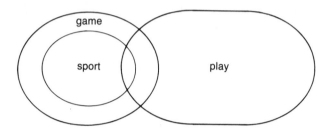

Figure 3.2   Play, Game, and Sport. *Note.*   From "On the Inadequacies of Sociological Definitions of Sport" by K. V. Meier, 1981, *International Review of Sport Sociology,* **16,** p. 96. Reprinted by permission.

The diagram, says Klaus Meier (1981, p. 96), tells us these things:

All sports are games,
Not all games are sports,
Sports and games may or may not be play,
Sports and games are play if voluntarily pursued for intrinsic rewards,
Sports and games are non-play if involuntarily pursued or participated in for extrinsic rewards,
Play may take forms other than sport or games.

We will examine the sport establishment at length in chapter 10.

Part II

Sport in Space and Time

Chapter 4

Games and Culture

In this chapter we shall expand what we said in chapter 3 about the types and functions of games as they have been studied by anthropologists.

Anthropology has contributed in many ways to our understanding of technically advanced societies, but its distinctive contribution has been through study of preliterate (sometimes called primitive) cultures. Although play, games, and sport have not been given as much attention by anthropologists as have other aspects of preliterate cultures, some researchers have always held with the great Robert Lowie that an accurate account of a boys' game on stilts is as significant as a report of Tahitian priests' explanation of the origin of the world. For example, as early as 1829, although some scholars, then as now, believed that primitive man was too busy for games and that only with leisure and civilization were games invented, William Ellis reported in the Society and Sandwich Islands of Polynesia, that many diverse games were of national importance (1829). In 1879 the British anthropologist Edward B. Tylor wrote for the *Fortnightly Review* an article on "The History of Games." One of the biggest controversies in anthropology at that time centered around the close similarity between the backgammon-type game *patolli,* played by the Aztecs of Mexico, and the Hindu Indian game of *pachisi.* Tylor held that two games with so many similarities could not have been invented independently by Hindus and Aztecs, but that *pachisi* must at some early time have been carried across the Pacific, then to become *patolli* (Tylor, 1878). Other anthropologists supported the idea of independent invention against the diffusion theory. One of them was Stewart Culin, who around the beginning of the 20th century published a book on games in Korea, China, and Japan, studied the play of boys in Brooklyn, and prepared for the Bureau of American Ethnology an 800-page study of the games of the North American Indians. In this last book, published in 1907, a colleague said that Culin's thorough studies had completely disposed of the idea that games are trivial matters.

Research in Mexico also brought to light the fascinating story of *pok-ta-pok*, the longest-surviving game in the history of the western hemisphere. During and after the great Mayan civilization, from about 700 to 1765 A.D., this team game was played on stone courts from Guatemala to Arizona. The objective of pok-ta-pok was to put through a fixed stone ring one of the first rubber balls known to sport. Because of the ring, pok-ta-pok has been called a forerunner of basketball, but the ball could be struck only with buttocks and knees, not with hands or with feet (as in soccer). William A. Goellner, who visited archaeological sites in Mexico and Guatemala to research pok-ta-pok while a graduate student in physical education, points out that the game was very central to the cultural and religious life of the Mayan civilization. He also relates how pok-ta-pok, first a game for amateurs, became so popular that it underwent the same professionalization and corruption that have visited ancient Greek and contemporary American sport (Goellner, 1953).

In the later years of the 20th century there has been a revival of interest in the anthropology of play. Physical educators Frederick Cozens and Florence Stumpf Frederickson have reported anthropological findings to their colleagues, urging them to see their work as an aspect of culture (Cozens & Frederickson, 1953). Developmental psychologist Brian Sutton-Smith has performed extensive field research on games in his native New Zealand and elsewhere and has also edited collections of studies by other scientists. John M. Roberts and others have used modern statistical techniques to interpret the data on play, games, and sport as reported in anthropological field work. In the 1970s research on play was officially recognized as a specialty in the field of anthropology, and there was formed an Association for the Anthropological Study of Play. What does the anthropology of games tell us? The main premise of anthropology is that the nature and meaning of anything depends on the total cultural situation in which it occurs.

Three illustrations may clarify this. One is the play of the Tununak villagers of Nelson Island, Alaska. Struggling to keep alive in a harsh environment, these Eskimos learned early that everyone's survival depended on everyone else. Thus they developed a very strong, noncompetitive group morale. This affected the games they borrowed from the outside world. Lynn Ager, the first anthropologist to visit Nelson Island, says, ''The kind of competition I saw was one in which everyone tried to do his best but not at anyone else's expense'' (1976, p. 82). Specifically, these Eskimos enjoyed a nonwinning game of marbles, a test of skill in which each player came with one marble and left with the same marble. The children tried the winning game in which one player takes all the marbles but didn't seem to care for it.

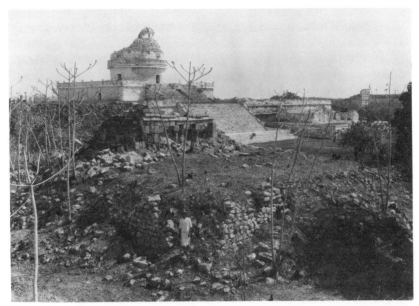

Mayan ball court at Chichén Itzá, Yucatan. *Note.* From *The Caracot at Chichén Itzá: Yucatan, Mexico* by K. Ruppert, 1935, Washington, DC: Carnegie Institution of Washington. Courtesy of Peabody Museum, Harvard University. Photography by Carnegie Institution of Washington. Reprinted by permission.

Stone ring fallen from the wall of the Chichén Itzá pok-ta-pok court. *Note.* From *The Caracot at Chichén Itzá: Yucatan, Mexico* by K. Ruppert, 1935, Washington, DC: Carnegie Institution of Washington. Courtesy of Peabody Museum, Harvard University. Photograph by Carnegie Institution of Washington. Reprinted by permission.

A similar case of a nonwinning game is *paro paro* (little fish), a water game played by young girls among the Motu people of New Guinea. The game involves two circles of players in the water, one inside the other. The inner group tries to penetrate the outer circle by swimming underwater, and the outer group sings, beats the water, and uses body blocks to prevent them. The cultural background is that the Motu, like the Tunanak villagers, have very hard conditions of survival. For them, too, it is urgent to cooperate to survive, and this fact colors their games. Annette Rosensteil, an anthropologist who has studied the Motu, points out that in paro paro excellence is sought and admired, and thus swimming skill is developed, but nobody wins. "The games are non-competitive. . . . No prizes are awarded" (Rosensteil, 1976, p. 55).

A third illustration is the game of tag as played by the Mescalero Apache Indians of New Mexico. Claire Farrer (1976) distinguishes two characteristics of the Apache culture. People spontaneously have much more body contact than do Anglo-Americans. Also, circles are a very basic feature of the culture. Houses are circular. Meetings are circular. Tribal decisions are made by consensus. In a circle, Farrer says, there are no obvious leaders. Dances are circular. And tag games are circular, played by three to eight children while they circle clockwise on a jungle gym. Farrer says she has never seen tag played on the ground. The circling tag players are also in close physical contact, very unlike those in the Anglo-American game, in which each person runs on the ground in a straight line by himself or herself and is apart in his own private space until he or she is tagged.

The Functions of Games

Games must be understood in terms of the *function* they perform for people in their particular cultural setting. We can make two general statements about the games of children and of adults that anthropologists have studied. First, games are a form of what Sutton-Smith calls buffered cultural learning. That is, in games children model and adults reinforce in symbolic, and therefore safe, form the activities and attitudes important in their cultures. These may be patterns now existing or patterns that existed in the past. For example, chess is a buffered model of war in the classic sense. Murray (1913), in his history of chess, dissects the elements: (a) two armies on (b) a limited field of battle with (c) no advantage of ground to either army. Second, games are also a form of emotional expression similar to folk tales, music, drama, and painting. They are *fun*, as we saw it defined by Huizinga and Sutton-Smith in chapter 3, and they are also *catharsis* in the two senses of the word as used by Aristotle: They are a safe theater for discharging the tensions developed by living in a culture and also a way of lifting depression and stimulating excitement. As sociologists Pearton and Gaskell say of these two forms of catharsis, "People might be thus drawn down from the dizzy and dangerous heights; they could also be brought up from the dismal and equally dangerous depths" (Pearton & Gaskell, 1981, p. 63).

Thus games have both a modeling and an expressive function. Let us look at some concrete examples from anthropological research.

In the historic culture of Samoa, physical educator Helen Dunlap (1951) reported to her colleagues that games, sports, dancing, and other vigorous recreational activities had these functions:

- They were forms of social intercourse that strengthened group unity.
- They were socially approved ways of expressing rivalry and gaining prestige and honor.
- They provided outlets for the emotions generated by such life crises as birth, marriage, and death.
- They strengthened people's relationships to their gods. For example, through symbolic fights tribal members could display devotion to their deities. Also, erotic dancing might stimulate and please the gods as it stimulated humans.
- Games trained for participation in adult society. Rivalry in fishing and pigeon netting were preparation for very important economic activities.
- In games people learned such war skills as disc and stick throwing, spear throwing and parrying, and fighting with clubs. They also developed strength and endurance that served them well in war.

Maxwell Howell, Charles Dodge, and Robert Howell generalized for sport historians in a 1975 article about the function of play in four preliterate societies: Melanesians, Polynesians, Eskimos, and the aborigines (blackfellows) of Australia.

- *Economic* training, as in the Australian game of spearing the disc, Polynesian games of stilts, Melanesian canoe contests, and Eskimo sealing games.
- A *political* (or military) function, exemplified by boomerang tourneys in Australia, boxing matches in Polynesia, the Melanesian game of crossing the bridge, and the Eskimo tug-of-war.
- *Domestic* functions, as in playing at marriage among the Australians, Melanesian courting games, and Eskimo doll play.
- A function of unification through *ceremony*—examples, the corroboree among the Australian aborigines, pitching discs among the Polynesians, Melanesian dancing, and Eskimo drum playing.

- *Social* gratifications (fun?): mud sliding in Australia, juggling in Polynesia, finger games in Melanesia, Eskimo ball games.

Summarizing the functions of games among the Maori of New Zealand, who were until recently in the Stone Age, Frederickson and Cozens (1947) see them playing such roles in that culture as (a) training for war, (b) acquiring skill and grace, (c) contributing to economic efficiency, (d) a fundamental part of recreational life, (e) a means of promoting tribal loyalty and solidarity, and (f) an outlet for healthy competitive urges in a culture organized for cooperation rather than competition. Frederickson (1960) gives a dramatic example of the range of functions a single sport activity can have. Wrestling competition, one of the oldest sports, can be:

- a way of settling the boundaries of rice fields (Philippines) or villages (Cook Islands).
- a part of the tribal initiation rites at puberty (Cook Islands).
- a way of selecting a mate (Nigeria).
- a demonstration of a chief's power and prestige (Hawaii).
- a way of securing a successful harvest (ancient Japan).

An important treatment of the role of games in culture is Michael Salter's (1980) discussion of the part played by games in rituals connected with crucial events in the lives of the northeast American Indians from the Saint Lawrence River to Louisiana at the time of settlement by the white man. The main critical events Salter discusses are fertility of crops, control of weather, illness, and death. The rituals were related to supernatural beings who were thanked or supplicated by feasts, dances, taboos, and ceremonies of purification. Associated with these rites were games—archery contests, pole climbing, foot races, wrestling, handball, football, lacrosse, dice games, guessing games, hide-and-seek, and tug-of-war. Each game was a contest symbolizing a struggle between elemental forces—good and bad weather, fertility and famine, illness and health, or life and death. The successful playing out of the athletic contest was supposed to win the favor of, or give help to, supernatural forces or beings in these very life-important natural struggles—for the falling of needed rain, the fertility of crops or game, the healing of an illness, or the freeing of a dead person's spirit. Thus, on the principle of like begets like, the successful playing of the game was believed to give a homeopathic reinforcement to the forces favorable to human beings. With issues so central to the very life of a people at stake, it is not surprising that intense competition was encouraged by gambling and prizes and that in terms of Salter's play-game continuum (see Figure 3.1) these ritual games were often much closer to terminal contest than to fun. Salter (1980) says that it is hard to imagine people having fun warding off an epidemic of small-pox. We shall return to this homeopathic function of games in chapter 5.

Latitude, Maintenance, and Cultural Complexity

These examples of the cultural function of games will give us background for examining the studies conducted by Roberts and others, using cross-cultural data collected under the direction of John Peter Murdock (Roberts, Arth, & Bush, 1959). In the mid-20th century Yale anthropologists, under Murdock's leadership, gathered together and classified data on a number of topics gathered by major anthropological investigations up to that time. These were collected in the Cross-Cultural Survey Files, the Ethnographic Index, and the Human Relations Area files. Using these files, Roberts, Sutton-Smith, and other colleagues proceeded to correlate different kinds of game behavior with different environmental and cultural conditions. They asked how the type and frequency of games played by different peoples have been related to favorableness or harshness of surroundings, to geography and climate, to methods of food getting, to levels of technical development and political organization, to ways of bringing up children, and to concepts of the supernatural.

Roberts defines games as organized play involving (a) competition, (b) two or more sides, (c) criteria for determining an outcome, and (d) agreed-upon rules. A basis for this research was the distinction, which we saw in chapter 3, of three kinds of games: games of physical skill (pure examples, weight lifting and a marathon race), games of chance (pure examples, craps and roulette), and games of strategy (pure examples, chess and the Japanese board game Go). Other games are mixtures of types; our major sports—baseball, football, basketball, hockey—for example, mix sheer physical skill with strategy and some luck. (For an excellent account of football as strategy that makes it sound much like chess, see Kyle Rote and Jack Winter's *The Language of Pro Football* [1966]).

Which types of games occur most frequently? In a sample of 50 cultures selected from the files, 44 had games of physical skill, 19 had games of chance, 19 had games of strategy, and 5, surprisingly, had no games at all. Roberts feels that, historically, physical skill games, being the simplest type, generally originated first, followed by games of chance, and then, in more complex societies, by the more involved games of strategy.

We have looked at some of the general functions that games perform in culture. How do the functions performed by the three types of games differ? Each is primarily concerned with mastery of a certain aspect of the environment. Physical skill games are concerned with mastering the physical world and oneself. Games of chance involve mastery of the supernatural. Games of strategy train for, and express, mastery of the social order.

How is each type of game shaped by the physical and social environment? To answer, we must establish a framework for looking at this environment. We shall prepare to locate societies and their games on a geographical and on a maintenance axis (see Figure 4.1). Physically, all societies that exist and have existed are situated somewhere on the surface of the globe. Let us establish some points of reference. In the northern hemisphere, 20° from the equator is approximately the latitude of the island of Jamaica, 30° the latitude of Jacksonville, Florida, and New York City is about 40° north. South of the equator, Rio de Janeiro is about 20° south, Cape Town, South Africa and Santiago, Chile about 30°, and Buenos Aires about 40°.

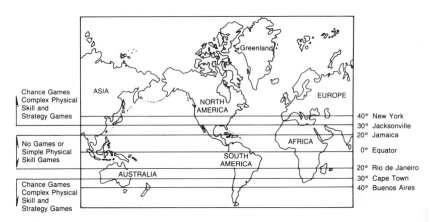

Figure 4.1 Distribution of games of physical skill, chance, and strategy is related to distance from the equator.

Culturally, all societies now and in the past have maintained themselves in one of several ways. The earliest stage, which still exists in some part of the world, is *hunting and gathering*. Among now-living peoples, the Bushmen of South Africa, the aborigines of Australia, the Tierra del Fuegans of Patagonia, and some Eskimos are still hunters and gatherers. Having no metal tools, they are still classified as Stone Age people. Around 7000 B.C. a revolution in food getting took place. Since then it has occurred all over the world and is still taking place. The collection of wild plants and animals gave way to their domestication in *agricultural* and *pastoral* societies. The Old Testament Hebrews are a classic example of a pastoral people. The Pueblo Indians of the southwestern United States are a typical settled agricultural society. The transition from hunting and gathering to settlement was accompanied by a number of changes. Metal tools, such as the plow, replaced stone implements, thereby making possible more productive technology. Whereas hunting and gathering tribes usually had no sharp social distinctions and very simple government, settled peoples developed social classes and a political state. They developed slavery, war, industry, art, philosophy, science, leisure for the classes and eventually for the masses, and conspicuous consumption.

How, now, are the three types of games related to the geographic and maintenance axes? In terms of latitude, as we move from the tropics toward the poles we find greater cultural complexity. In historic times (approximately from the agricultural revolution on) scholars have noted that, beginning in areas with an annual mean temperature of about 70°, the center of civilization has moved to areas with an annual mean of about 50°. This coldward course of civilization may be related to lower tropical and subtropical energy levels due to heat and poorer protein in the diet. In keeping with this, it is in the cooler areas of the earth that we find the more complex games.

Within 20° of the equator are located cultures with no games or with a few simple physical skill games (hitting, throwing and catching, hopping, jumping, running, swimming, and sailing). Cultures farther away are likely to have a wider variety of physical skill games. Of 23 cultures within 20° of the equator, only 5 had as many as 5 different physical skill games. Of 24 cultures beyond the 20th parallel (north of Jamaica or south of Rio) 16 had 5 or more physical skill games. I must emphasize here that we are dealing primarily with native, independently invented games, not with games that have diffused from elsewhere. This was brought sharply to my attention by a student from Trinidad who objected that, according to the findings of Roberts and Sutton-Smith, a complex physical skill-strategy game like soccer would be impossible in his country, where it is in fact a favorite sport.

As the climate gets cooler, there are also likely to be more games of chance. Chance games typically occur beyond the 30th parallel (north of Jacksonville and south of Santiago). This fits with the correlation between physical skill and chance games—where there are few games of physical skill there are also few games of chance, and vice versa. Of 30 cultures with fewer than 5 physical skill games, only 4 had games of chance. Of 19 cultures possessing 5 or more games of physical skill, 15 did have chance games. In the northerly areas we are also likely to find the most advanced form of game—games of strategy—and especially those games of physical skill and strategy that carry us toward modern sport.

The coldward course of civilization suggests that latitude and maintenance are not unrelated independent variables. However, let us now shift our focus to the relationship between game types and maintenance patterns.

First, the rare cultures without games. We must remember that these have no games as game was defined earlier. This in no way means that these people do not play or that they have no individual or group pastimes for their unoccupied moments. The no-game cultures are tropical, mainly in South America and Australia. They have a fairly undeveloped political organization and no stratification into classes (Roberts & Sutton-Smith, 1970).

The cultures with only simple physical games are quite similar to the no-game cultures. They differ in that women and men are more likely to be segregated, and separate nuclear families of mother, father, and children appear along with the three-generation extended family. This separation may require more individual male self-reliance in hunting and fighting, for which games like spear throwing and archery are a preparation.

Games of chance, which are a symbolic way of handling supernatural forces, are likely to occur where the environment is harsh and anxiety-provoking and there is a great deal of personal and social uncertainty. As compared with the no-game and the simple physical game cultures, chance game cultures are farther from the equator, are colder, and have greater seasonal change. People typically live in small nomadic groups without fixed settlements and maintain themselves by hunting, fishing, and gathering. Their food supply is insecure and food shortages are common. Warfare is frequent. Premarital sexuality is typically tabooed, and people are likely to experience sexual anxiety and personal self-doubt. With such environmental, social, and personal uncertainty, it is not surprising that people will welcome supernatural help. The cross-cultural files show that people with chance games are likely to believe that the gods are friendly and easily influenced. In short, people play chance games where life is too hard for their scientific and technical skills and they believe that it can be managed by playing games with the fates. Chance games are practice in a way of making up one's mind with the help of a benevolent Fate. Also, success in games of chance may strengthen people to endure hardship in hope of a more fortunate future.

Games of strategy, symbolizing mastery of the social environment, are related to social complexity—large agriculturally based settlement, advanced technology, stratification of social classes, and political complexity.

Of the societies with strategy games that were studied, 4 were classified as nomadic (wandering), seminomadic or semisedentary; 35

were sedentary (settled). The relationship between strategy games and maintenance patterns is spelled out in greater detail in Table 4.1. It is clear that the development of intensive farming is the point at which games of strategy become prominent.

Table 4.1   Games of Strategy and Intensity of Cultivation

Method of Maintenance	Strategy Present	Strategy Absent
No agriculture	2	32
Gardens	0	14
Casual agriculture	1	6
Extensive agriculture	13	33
Intensive agriculture with irrigation	13	7
Permanent intensively cultivated fields	12	3

Note. From "Strategy in Games and Folk Tales" by J.M. Roberts, B. Sutton-Smith, and A. Kendon, 1963, *Journal of Social Psychology,* **61,** p. 186 (Table 1). Copyright 1963 by Journal of Social Psychology, a publication of the Helen Dwight Reid Education Foundation. Reprinted by permission.

Technical development in agriculture is likely to be accompanied by other kinds of technical maturity. Only three cultures with strategy games were without pottery, and most had weaving and leather work. Working in metal was highly correlated: Of 42 cultures with metal work, 31 had strategy games and 11 did not; of 59 who did not work in metal, only 1 had games of strategy. All of these factors are highly related to size of community, which is shown in Table 4.2 as being directly correlated with strategy games.

Of cultures with high political integration and social stratification, 12 had strategy games and 3 did not; of cultures where both political integration and social stratification were low, 3 had strategy games and 13 had none. Anthropological examples of high political integration are the Hottentots and Dahomians of Africa, the Aztecs of Central America, the Kwakiutl Indians of the Pacific Northwest, and the Polynesians. All of these, although preliterate, developed a political state. Examples of low political organization are the Melanesians, the Samoans, the Hopi Indians, and the African Bushmen. All have simple, more informal methods of group control.

Table 4.2 Games of Strategy and Mean Size of Local Community

Mean Size of Local Community	Games of Strategy Present	Absent
50 or less	1	18
50–59	1	10
100–199	7	10
200–399	5	3
400–1000	3	4
1000+	2	0
Towns up to 50,000	5	1
Towns of more than 50,000	11	0

Note. From "Strategy in Games and Folk Tales" by J.M. Roberts, B. Sutton-Smith, and A. Kendon, 1963, *Journal of Social Psychology,* **61**, p. 188 (Table 3). Copyright 1963 by Journal of Social Psychology, a publication of the Helen Dwight Reid Education Foundation. Reprinted by permission.

What is meant by political integration should be made clearer by Table 4.3, which deals with the number of political levels above the local community. (Example: the resident of Coral Gables, Florida is subject, beyond the city of Coral Gables, to the governments of metropolitan Dade county, the state of Florida, the United States, and the United Nations, a total of four jurisdictions beyond the local community.) The table shows dramatically that the greater the number of jurisdictional levels the more likely it is that the community will have games of strategy.

Table 4.3 Jurisdictional Levels and Strategy Games

Level Beyond Local Community	0	1	2	3	4
Games of Strategy Absent	66	26	2	0	0
Games of Strategy Present	5	10	14	9	4

Note. From "Strategy in Games and Folk Tales" by J.M. Roberts, B. Sutton-Smith, and A. Kendon, 1963, *Journal of Social Psychology,* **61**, p. 188. Copyright 1963 by Journal of Social Psychology, a publication of the Helen Dwight Reid Education Foundation. Reprinted by permission.

Societies with complex technical and political development are likely to believe in strong (often monotheistic) supernatural beings (high gods). (An example would be the contrast between the Old Testament

Hebrews and the Canaanite tribes they displaced in their conquest of Israel.) So it is in keeping with the other correlates of games that of 36 tribes with games of strategy, 29 had high gods.

These findings on the relationship of game complexity to cultural complexity are paralleled by the work in which anthropologist Alan Lomax has related dance forms to levels of cultural development. Through choreometrics Lomax has identified three forms of dance in terms of their dominant pattern of movement—linear (one-dimensional), curvilinear (two-dimensional), and spiral (three-dimensional). The simplest linear dances are found in the economically simplest Stone Age hunting-gathering cultures. Dances become circular with the use of metal tools. Dance pattern follows work pattern: Stone and wood tools are too breakable for any but the simplest straight-line stroke, but metal edges make possible sweeping cutting movements. Spiral dances are typical of preindustrial states with irrigation and social stratification. (Eighty percent of the cultures with metal have two-dimensional dances; 80 percent of the irrigation cultures have spiral dances.)

Lomax has found a similar relationship between cultural complexity and another element in dance—use of the torso as a single unit or as multiple units. The American square dance, most American Indian dances, and the folk dances of Scotland and Ireland typically move the torso as one piece. The hula, the twist, and the belly dance are examples of a multi-unit dance. As with forms of games, single- and multiunit dance are distributed according to both geography and cultural characteristics. Single-unit dances are typically found among hunters and gatherers, multiunit forms among people who practice agriculture and keep herds. Dances in cold climates tend to be single-unit. Multiunit dance is generally tropical—African, Polynesian, or Caribbean. (An exception Lomax found is some Hungarian folk dances where the women swing their hips. This is explained by another principle: Multiunit dance is correlated with the status of women, and among these Hungarians the woman typically shares work in the fields with men, rather than staying in the house.)

Returning to the geography of games, we find two kinds of cultural situations with physical skill games: very simple societies that have only games of physical skill and very complex societies that combine physical skill with strategy. The complex societies are also likely to have other games of chance and strategy.

Simple achievement societies are those in which survival depends on the mastery of basic physical skills necessary for food getting. Physical skill games are practice for survival. Those who succeed in this practice are honored by their peers; those who fail tend to lose status.

We touched earlier on the Alaskan Eskimo village of Tununak. Because this village existed before 1945, out of 39 recorded games, 25 were games of physical skill. There were no chance or strategy games. The only nonphysical games were those that Eifermann, the Israeli student of children's play, has called memory-attention games. To understand all this, we must know of these Tununak Eskimos that "the overwhelming fact of their lives, that their very survival depends on a hunter's ability to find, kill, and retrieve game, has dominated every aspect of their culture" (Ager, 1976, p. 81). Lynn Ager's explanation of the function of the memory-attention games describes also the main function of achievement in the physical skill games: "A good memory . . . was a valuable personal asset in a hunting culture, for it is of positive survival value to remember one's own experiences in emergencies, the experiences of others in similar situations, to remember landmarks on an almost featureless terrain, to remember animal habits which enable one to predict their behavior. Remembering helps the hunter and may even save his life" (Ager, 1976, p. 82). Skills achieved in physical skill games may do the same.

The Motu of New Guinea, also mentioned earlier, live under equally hard conditions. The rainfall is low, the soil shallow and infertile. Thus the Motu depend on hunting and fishing, which are done on a cooperative, communitywide basis, with established rules for distributing the catch so that everyone eats. Of greatest importance is the annual *hiri*, a trading expedition of several hundred miles to exchange thousands of pots made by the Motu for sago, a starch food, and wood, which is essential for the outrigger canoes (lakatoi) that are their main source of water transportation.

Under these conditions, it is not surprising that the Motu children can swim before they can walk, that the girls begin to play *paro paro* (the two-circle swimming game previously described), and the boys early in life build and race miniature outrigger canoes. Also, "at eight to twelve years of age, boys are already adept at handling the fish spear, using a toy spear about two-thirds the size of the adult spear. Thus, when they are ready to accompany their fathers on hunting and fishing expeditions, the small boys have already acquired those characteristics of fearlessness, poise, and visual and muscular coordination which will be necessary during their entire adult life" (Rosensteil, 1976, p. 55).

These purely physical skill games of simple achievement societies are quite different from the competitive sports into which games of physical skill and strategy often turn in the more complex achievement cultures. There, instead of learning skills for the common welfare, children of the same age may be trained by their elders to throw baseballs at each other's heads and how to hold opponents in football without being detected. These complex physical skill-strategy games are the culmination of the tradition of *agon* that we shall now examine.

Chapter 5

The Agonistic Tradition

In *Homo Ludens* Johan Huizinga contends that the competitive striving for excellence has been a central factor in the development of civilization:

> *From the life of childhood right up to the highest achievements of civilization, one of the strongest incentives to perfection, both individual and social, is the desire to be praised and honored for one's excellence. . . . We want to be honored for our virtues. We want the satisfaction of having done something well. Doing some-thing well means doing it better than others. . . . Competition serves to give proof of superiority. (1964, p. 63)*

In this chapter we shall examine how the drive to surpass others has laid the foundation for modern sport. We begin with examples of three types of human rivalry.

Three Forms of Rivalry

First, let us look at the role of *emulation* (the striving to equal or surpass) in the life of the preliterate Trobriand islanders of southwest Melanesia as reported in Malinowski's famous 1922 study (1950). Along with fish they caught in the bays and open sea, the chief source of food for the Trobrianders was grown in their yam gardens. Here healthy competition was strong and played an important part in economic and social life:

> *A good garden worker in the Trobriands derives a direct prestige from the amount of labour he can do, and the size of the garden he can till. . . . Men vie with one another in their speed, in their*

thoroughness, and in the weights they can lift, when bringing big
poles to the garden, or carrying away the harvested yams.
(Malinowski, 1950, pp. 60–61)

After the harvest, each worker piled his yams for display under a small shelter of yam vine. Parties of natives would walk around comparing, criticizing, and praising the best yields. In years when a good yield was likely, the chief might proclaim a competitive ceremonial *kayasa* display of yams, thereby increasing the straining to confirm one's status as a good gardener. Trobriand competition was an altruistic competition in the sense that three fourths of the crop for which one worked so hard, and was honored, went to his relatives and to his chief. It was also part of a lifestyle that—compared with the aloofness and hostility of some neighboring people—was so open, friendly, cooperative, and in the best sense civilized as to come to Malinowski almost as a shock.

Malinowski's mention of "straining" in the special kayasa competitions suggests another kind of competitive display that was not so friendly and relaxed as that of the Trobriand islanders. This is the *potlatch phenomenon* traditionally found among the also preliterate Kwakiutl Indians of the Vancouver Island, British Columbia, and other Northwest Indian tribes from Puget Sound to Alaska.

Social position among the Kwakiutl was highly competitive, depending on great wealth: the shells and etched copper sheets that served as money, cedar bark blankets, canoes, candlefish oil. It was not mere possession that counted, but competitive display. "We do not fight with weapons. We fight with property" (Benedict, 1934, p. 189). Every person of possible tribal importance, female or male, entered this competition as a child. Women made mats, baskets, and blankets for their men. There were two ways of claiming superiority over others. One could give lavishly of one's wealth, and if the receiver could not return with excessive interest (up to 100%) he was shamed. Or one could destroy one's property—burn one's candlefish oil or one's blankets, break up one's canoes or coppers, or kill his slaves. "The whole economic system of the Northwest Indians," says anthropologist Ruth Benedict, "was bent to the service of this obsession" (p. 193). The most dramatic competitions were the potlatches, ceremonies offered by a tribal chief on the occasion of a marriage, birth, or death, a tatooing ceremony, a house raising, the coming to adolescence of a female, or as a challenge to the chief of another tribe. At the potlatch, the host chief was glorified by hymns sung by his retainers, which Benedict calls "unabashed megalomania":

I am the great chief who makes people ashamed. . . .
Our chief makes people cover their faces by what he is continu-

ally doing in this world, giving again and again oil feasts to all
the tribes.

• • • • • • •

Bring your counter of property, tribes, that he may try in vain to
count the property that is to be given away by the great copper-
maker, the chief. (1934, p. 190)

In the potlatch, the chiefs vied in exhibiting their wealth through
gifts of blankets, shells and coppers. The ultimate way of demonstrating superiority was to destroy one's wealth by fire. In one potlatch
described to Benedict, the rival chief threw 7 canoes and 400 blankets
on the host chief's fire in an attempt to put it out while his host poured
valuable candlefish oil on the blaze to keep it alive. The roof of the
host's house caught fire and the house was almost completely destroyed, while the host and his rival kept their cool, continuing to throw
more coppers, blankets and oil on the flame (pp. 199–200).

Trobriand rivalry is not an agon; the potlatch is. Whereas I used
the term "healthy competition" to describe the Trobrianders' ritual
display of yams, I think Benedict's terms "megalomania" and "obsession" better characterize the potlatch syndrome. Except for the
name, the potlatch is not peculiar to the Northwest Indians. Like the
Trobriand striving to excel in work, competitive display and destruction of possessions is a core type of human contest found in many cultures. Huizinga says, "Such competitions in unbridled liberality, with
the frivolous destruction of one's own goods as the climax, are to be
found all over the world." He believes that we should "regard the
potlatch proper as the most highly developed form of a fundamental
human need, which I would call playing for honor and glory"
(Huizinga, 1964, pp. 59, 82). Comparable customs have been found
in Greece, Rome, the old German culture, and in ancient China and
India. There are similarities in the behavior of Cleopatra, going Mark
Antony one better by dissolving her pearl in vinegar, and Philip of
Burgundy, crowning a series of banquets given by his nobles by throwing a Gargantuan feast at which students ceremonially smashed the
glassware (Huizinga, 1964, p. 62).

In this chapter on contest it is significant that the Mahabharata,
one of two great Asiatic Indian epics, depicts the world as a great dice
game between the god Siva and his queen, and that Marcel Mauss,
in his study of ritual gifts, says that the Mahabharata is the story of
a gigantic potlatch (Mauss, 1923–1924).

The derivation of the word for the pre-Mohammedan Arabic
equivalent of the potlatch, *mu'agára*, shows the similarity: "to rival in
glory by cutting up the feet of camels." Huizinga thinks that this incident, recorded in an Egyptian newspaper, expresses the tradition of
mu'agára:

Two gypsies had a quarrel. In order to settle it they solemnly called the whole tribe together and then proceeded each one to kill his own sheep, after which they burned all the bank-notes they possessed. Finally, the man who saw that he was going to lose, immediately sold his six asses, so as to become victor after all by the proceeds. When he came home to fetch the asses his wife opposed the sale, whereupon he stabbed her (Huizinga, 1964, p. 61).

Nor is the potlatch-mu'agára syndrome found only in faraway times and places. "The manipulation of wealth on the Northwest Coast," says Benedict, "is clearly enough in many ways a parody of our own economic arrangements" (1934, p. 188). With probably no knowledge of the Kwakiutl, in 1899 the American sociologist Thorstein Veblen had described the conspicuous consumption and conspicuous waste that he saw making up so much of the life of the leisure class in western civilization. Writing in the middle of the United States' drive to affluence, Veblen spoke of how this conspicuous consumption and waste, which began with the leisure classes, was now being imitated by the rest of the people. Today we see, inside and outside organized sport, the obsessive drive to be Number One.

A third core experience in the agonistic tradition, is *human participation in divine struggles.* To a person without modern scientific knowledge (and even to one with it) life and the world are mysterious and unpredictable. One mystery that is of life-and-death importance is the rotation of the seasons. Trees and plants bud into life in the spring and are at their greenest and fullest in the summer. With autumn they begin to brown and die. The days get increasingly shorter, leaving the question: Will they ever get longer again? Will life return? In late December in the northern hemisphere (late June in the southern) the days are at their shortest and the nights their longest. The turning point has been reached. No wonder that this is the occasion for myths and rituals of rebirth. (We celebrate the birthday of Jesus on December 25 not because it is so recorded in the bureau of vital statistics at Bethlehem but because this was the time of the pagan celebration of the winter solstice.)

For the study of sport and culture, the next turning point is the most important—the arrival of spring, with the return of fertility. With it comes the hard and uncertain task of bringing the year's food supply through to harvest. It is not strange that human beings, with limited powers, should project this as a struggle in which the gods are involved. The best known example is from the time and area where an economic surplus was first developed. The Egyptian sun god Osiris, who promoted fertility in plants and animals, was opposed by the god Set, who tried to block and undo his work, even to the point of murdering Osiris' son Horus. Preliterate peoples generally believe that by imitating or participating in the struggles of the gods they can influence the outcome and thereby help themselves. So, at the festivals of spring, while the "good" gods were struggling to maintain fertility, the people would engage in contests—between villages, between subtribes, between women and men, between the married and the unmarried. "All these forms of contest," says Huizinga, "betray the connection with ritual over and over again by the constant belief that they are indispensable for the smooth running of the seasons, the ripening of crops, the prosperity of the whole year. . . . Every victory represents, that is, realizes for the victor the triumph of the good powers over the bad, and at the same time the salvation of the group that effects it" (1964, p. 56). We can see the similarity to Michael Salter's discussion of American Indian games, reported in chapter 4.

A specific example of this homeopathic reinforcement will bring us to the threshold of sport. At the Egyptian Temple of Papremis, more than a thousand followers of Osiris would line up some distance from the temple with an image of Osiris in a gilded box on a four-wheeled cart. Each man had a heavy wooden club. The object of the ceremony was to rush Osiris to and through the gates and door of the temple. In the way stood an opposing array of priests, also armed with clubs. "There was hard fighting with clubs and heads were broken," but no lives lost (Henderson, 1947, pp. 8–9).

Here is a model of the territorial type of game—soccer, American football, hockey, lacrosse, basketball—with movement by a group, against opposition, toward a distant goal. First, we have the team. H.I. Massingham suggests that peaceful conflict between teams arose in the ritual opposition of two parties who dramatized the conflict between departing winter and oncoming spring:

> *No sooner are we back in antiquity than we find it was the teams that made the game. Whenever it was played among peoples who . . . retained traces of the archaic culture which once overspread the world, we are made aware that it was a formal and sacred rite, conducted between two sections of the community. . . . Out of this dualism rose the ball game which . . . was a ritualistic, spectacular exhibition of this dual grouping in action. (Massingham, 1929, cited in Henderson, 1947, p. 15)*

We have the teams, but what about the ball? In the fertility rite at the Temple of Papremus there was no ball, but an object that served the purpose—the image of Osiris. In an earlier chapter I referred to the Afghan game of buzkashi, a polo-like contest in which the ball was the carcass of a calf or sheep. So a body, or an image of one, can suffice. But it is an awkward object of contention. If one is going to play a territorial game, a head-shaped object is more practical than a whole body. Robert Henderson, in his book *Ball, Bat and Bishop* (1947), feels that the ball originally represented the head of Osiris, or the sun (also a fertility symbol), or both. In a fertility rite which was often associated with a Saturnalia—a period of sexual license—it could also have symbolized a testicle (note the double meaning of ball).

I have introduced three core elements that appear in human rivalry. Not all three are agonistic, especially if by *agon* we mean something close to *agonia* (agony). Trobriand-type emulation is the humane striving for excellence that underlies all contest. The potlach and the territorial contest are the typically civilized forms of rivalry. The potlatch spirit is, as Huizinga says, the striving for honor, glory, and the sense of superiority. The territorial fertility ritual is the root of all those contests that mobilize intense group rivalry in what is conceived as a confrontation between light and darkness.

Let us now turn to the society that gave us the word *agon*.

The Agonistic Society: Greece

Just after the 1984 Olympics it is hard to forget that one of the sources of contemporary sport lies in the agonistic tradition of ancient Greece—in "the serious contests that formed the core of [Greek] social life" (Huizinga, 1964, p. 48). Homer, in the early days of Greece, memorialized the urge to be always the best and to excel others. The beginnings of the agonistic tradition, over 1,000 years before Christ, are described by Huizinga in this way:

> Our point of departure must be an almost childlike play-sense expressing itself in various play-forms, some serious, some playful, but all allowing the innate human need of rhythm, harmony, change, alternating contrast and climax, etc., to unfold in full richness. Coupled with this play-sense is a spirit that strives for honor, dignity, superiority, and beauty. Magic and mystery, heroic longing, the forebodings of music, sculpture and logic all seek form and expression in noble play. A later generation will call the age that knew such aspirations "heroic." (1964, p. 73)

Aristotle, a member of this later generation, said, "Men crave honor in order to persuade themselves of their own worth, their virtue. They aspire to be honored by persons of judgment and in virtue of their real value" (*Aristotle* 1095/1911).

Central to the way of life of Greece were *agon* (contest) and *agonia* (death struggle or fear), both related to *agora* (a gathering—the name of the central meeting-ground in Athens and other Greek cities). In these public events one sought to express or establish his *arete* (personal virtue or excellence), a concept related to *aristos* (superior), the quality of aristocracy.

Huizinga says the Greeks staged contests in anything that offered the bare possibility of a fight. Alexander the Great celebrated the death of a hero by a musical and gymnastic agon in which prizes were given to the heaviest drinkers. Thirty-five of the contestants died during this agon. The winner, along with five others, survived, only to die shortly afterward. The Greeks, whose sculpture preserves their admiration for the male body, also held beauty contests for men at their festivals, along with competitions in singing and in keeping awake. There were slanging matches in which people would strive to insult and put down one another. One of the outcomes of these slanging matches was political satire—Greek political life, like ours, rested to a large extent on ability to put down an opponent. As with us, the courts of law had the same agonistic quality—courtroom eloquence was a more sophisticated slanging match. Another outcome of these slanging matches may have been poetry (*iambos*, the root of the word *iambic* for one of the basic verse forms, originally meant derision). Greek philosophy may have originated in competitions in solving riddles. Greek drama, both tragic and comic, was composed for public competitions, especially the feast of Dionysius. "The whole public reacted to the subtleties of style and expression, sharing the tension of the contest like a crowd at a football match" (Huizinga, 1964, p. 145).

In the Greek quest for excellence, the most admired figure was the athlete (from the word *athlos*—prize—which united the concepts of contest, struggle, exercise, exertion, endurance, and suffering). In the *Odyssey*, Homer said, "There is no greater glory for a man as long as he lives than that which he wins by his own hands and feet" (1919, Pt. 8, p. 146). "We must not," says the cultural historian Will Durant, "think of the average Greek as a student and lover of Aeschylus or Plato; rather, like the typical Briton, or American, he was interested in sport, and his favored athletes were his earthly gods" (1939, p. 211).

On one occasion the record shows that a general returning from a military triumph was welcomed home "like an athlete." Even military invasion could not stop athletic competition. On the history-making day when a handful of Greeks turned back Xerxes' army at Thermopylae, thousands watched the games at Olympia. A Persian exclaimed to his general, "Good heavens! What manner of men are these against whom you have brought us to fight?—men who contend with one another not for money but for honor!" (Herodotus, date unknown/1862)

Greek games were private, municipal, and national (Panhellenic). A relief (flat) sculpture in Athens shows a wrestling match on one side, a field hockey game on the other. Bareback riding, swimming, and throwing and dodging missiles when mounted were not only specta- tor sports but common activities. The Greeks, like us, had ball games— in Sparta the word for *youth* also meant *ballplayer*. A short description by Antiphanes of a star player in a game 4 centuries before Christ reads like a modern sports page. In this game a team tried to throw the ball over or through the other team until one side was driven back over its goal line. Here is the star: "When he got the ball, he delighted to give it to one player while dodging another; he knocked it away from one and urged on another with noisy cries. Outside, a long pass, be- yond him, overhead, a short pass" (Gardiner, 1930, p. 234).

The oldest of the Panhellenic games began at Olympia in 776 B.C. (the first definite date in Greek history) and took place every 4 years.

We have seen Durant describe Greek athletes as earthly gods. This could, in a way, be said of the feeling of many people today about their sports heroes. But there is a difference. The Olympic games were a formally religious festival for all of Greece. The Olympic enclosure was a sacred area with shrines that were open all year and in which the fires were never allowed to die out. Although Greek towns and states were almost constantly quarreling, hostilities were suspended during the month when athletes and spectators traveled to and from Olympia "under the protection of tradition and the watchful eyes of the gods" (Kieran & Daley, 1973, p. 14). For these religious rites the participants were required to dedicate themselves intensely. All had to swear that they had been in training during the 10 months before coming to Olympia. Once there, they followed strict programs of exercise and diet. "There were hot and cold baths; steam and vapor baths . . . dry- ing rooms, restrooms and luxuries that few modern athletic plants can boast" (Kieran & Daley, 1973, pp. 14–15). At one time in the early Olympics the training table diet consisted entirely of fresh cheese and water.

Durant paints graphically the color of the Grecian Olympics, ob- viously a scene of both fun and business, something like an ancient Disney World:

We picture the pilgrims and athletes starting out from distant cities, a month ahead of time, to come together at the games. It was a fair as well as a festival; the plain was covered not only with the tents that sheltered the visitors from the July heat, but with the booths where a thousand concessionaries exposed for sale every- thing from wine and fruit to horses and statuary, while acrobats and conjurers performed their tricks for the crowd. Some juggled balls in the air, others performed marvels of agility and skill, others ate fire or swallowed swords: modes of amusement, like forms of superstition, enjoy a reverend antiquity. Famous orators like

*Gorgias, famous sophists like Hippias, perhaps famous writers
like Herodotus, delivered addresses or recitations from the porti-
coes of the temple of Zeus. It was a special holiday for men, since
married women were not allowed to attend the festival; these had
their own games at the feast of Hera. Manander summed up such
a scene in five words: crowd, market, aerobats, amusements,
thieves. (1934, p. 213)*

The competition lasted 5 days. Forty-five thousand spectators typically stayed in the stadium all day, battling heat, thirst, and insects.
Hats were forbidden and the water was usually bad. All contestants,
who had to be freeborn Greeks, were naked, except sometimes for a
loincloth.

One of the featured events was boxing, with blows confined to
the head, no rule against hitting a man when he was down, and no
classification of boxers by weight. There were no rounds and no rests,
and bouts lasted until one gave up or was beaten down. Eventually
boxing was combined with wrestling in a game called *pankration* (contest of all powers). Here biting and gouging and even kicking in the
stomach were allowed. The brutality is suggested by the case of one
winner who "struck so ferociously with straight extended fingers and
strong sharp nails that he pierced the flesh of his adversary and dragged
out his bowels" (Pausanias, 1918, Pt. 8, p. 40). One footrace went for
400 yards, another for 2 2/3 miles, and a third was an armed race in
which the runners carried heavy shields.

The main Olympic contest was the pentathlon—five events
designed to test a man's all-around skill. The victor had to win three
events out of the five: a long jump, holding weights, from a standing
start; throwing a 12-pound discus of stone or iron; the javelin throw;
wrestling; and a final sprint race the length of the stadium—about 200
yards.

The culminating event of the games was the chariot races in the
hippodrome below the stadium. In a typical race 10 chariots, each
drawn by four horses, had to run 23 laps of a course with posts that
had to be rounded at each end. So, as in a modern auto speedway
race, "accidents were the chief thrill of the game" (Durant, 1939, p.
215). In one race, out of 40 chariots that started, one finished the race.

In the sixth century B.C. Greek athletics was at its peak. There were
established also the Pythian games at Delphi, in honor of Apollo, the
Isthmian games at Corinth, and games in honor of Zeus at Nemea.
In these later games contests were added in music, pottery, poetry,
sculpture, painting, choral singing, oratory, and drama. These influenced the whole development of the arts in Greece.

Together, the games formed a *periodos*, or cycle: Every Greek athlete's ambition was to win the quadruple crown at Olympia, Delphi,
Corinth, and Nemea.

The contrast between the early magnificent discus thrower (Discobolos by Myron) and the later paunchy Olympic performer (Farnese Heracles by Glycon, after original by Lysippus) dramatizes the degeneration of the Greek athletic idea. Courtesy of The Bettmann Archive.

Victorious athletes were intensely popular. Cities voted them substantial sums of money on their return. Some became generals. So idolized were they that the philosophers complained jealously. Their names were written into history: By the later Greek historians, time was designated by Olympiads, each named after the victor in the stadium sprint.

Although the Olympics were an all-Greek festival, they did not include *all* Greeks. Women were not allowed in the early games as participants, and married women were excluded from the stadium. At one time a dramatic event occurred when the father of a runner, Pisodorous, died during the training period. The runner's mother took over the training and attended the games in disguise. When Pisodorus won, she was understandably so elated that she could no longer conceal herself. The penalty for such an invasion of a male event called for her to be thrown off a huge rock to her death, but the penalty was not enforced. Finally, women were admitted as spectators and eventually as contestants. In the 128th games in 264 B.C. the chariot race for pairs of colts was won by Belisiche, a Macedonian woman.

Within 4 centuries after the beginning of the Olympics in 776 B.C., Greek athletics went through the same kind of change that modern sport has undergone. Writing in 1910 in the most thorough book researched on the Greek Olympics, E. Norman Gardiner saw this lesson in Greek sport: "The nemesis of excess in athletics is specialization, specialization begets professionalism and professionalism is the death of true sport" (1970, p. 122).

The original Olympic ideal had been the well-rounded development of the body, primarily as a preparation for national self-defense; this included *aidos*, the disciplined self-control of the sportsman. The early Olympic athlete was an amateur. He ate the simple nourishing vegetarian diet of the Greek farmer or villager; figs, cheese, porridge, and meal cakes.

In the sixth century B.C., however, amateur athletes began to be professionalized. Gardiner (1970) explains this process:

> *There is a point in any sport or game where it becomes overdeveloped, and competition too severe for it to serve the true purpose of providing exercise or recreation for the many. It becomes the monopoly of the few who can afford the time or money to acquire excellence, while the rest, despairing of any true measure of success, prefer the role of spectators. When the rewards of success are sufficient, there arises a professional class, and when professionalism is once established, the amateur can no longer compete with the professional. (p. 130)*

If we want a specific date, we might place the beginning of professionalism in the year 594 B.C., when Solon promised that any Athenian winning at Olympia would receive 100 drachma (the value of 100 oxen).

By the fifth century B.C. the amateur sportsman had been replaced by the specialist, in the hands of a professional trainer. The well-rounded development of the body gave way to intensive preparation to win a particular event. In the 80th Olympiad (456 B.C.) a meat diet was introduced to provide bulk for the boxing and wrestling that were highly favored. This change, says Gardiner, created "an artificial distinction . . . between the life of the athlete and the life of the ordinary citizen" (1930, p. 102). Thucydides reported that the ordinary man had become a passive spectator. Hippocrates of Cos, whose oath is now taken by all physicians, lamented that specialization was creating an unhealthy one-sided development. Plato, who himself had won in wrestling at Delphi, Corinth, Nemea, and possibly at Olympia, in his *Republic* did not include athletics in the preparation of youth to defend his ideal state. Euripides in the play *Autolycus* said: "Of all the countless evils throughout Hellas, there is none worse than the race of athletes. . . . I blame the custom of the Hellenes who gather together to watch these men, honoring a useless pleasure" (Gardiner, 1930, p. 103). In 388 B.C. a low point in commercialization was reached when Eulopos was caught bribing opponents to lose to him in the 98th Olympic boxing competition.

Bread and Circuses: Rome

As the Panhellenic games expressed and symbolized the glory that was Greece, says Durant, so the spectacles in her Colosseum expressed and symbolized the vainglory that was Rome.

For almost 500 years following the assassination of Julius Caesar in 44 B.C., the Roman empire extended, over the larger part of the known world that Caesar had conquered, the largest and most widespread period of peace and affluence that the world had known. Rome preserved the solid culture of the Greek poets, philosophers, and sculptors, and added to it. But her talent was engineering and administration, her chief qualities affluence and power. Public spectacles and games were a central part of the life of the Empire. Anxious to spread the power and affluence of Rome, emperors built cities to the very edge of the desert, and each one of them had an amphitheater for the entertainment of the people. As the Empire declined, this public entertainment became more important to its life.

Let us look at sport in Rome in the first century after the birth of Christ. There were in the Roman year 76 religious festival days celebrated by *ludi*—about two thirds by plays and other shows (Caillois' mimicry) and the other third by games in the circus, stadium, or amphitheater (*agon*).

In a stadium, wrestling and boxing matches and foot races, mainly by professionals and aliens, typically took place. The masses of people found simple athletics dull compared to the boxing matches in which huge Greeks fought with gloves reinforced at the knuckles by a thick iron band. The Roman populace was turned on by action like that described by Virgil:

> *Then the son of Anchises brought out hide gloves of equal weight, and bound the hands of the antagonists. . . . Each took his stand, poised on tiptoe and raising one arm. . . . Drawing their heads back from the blows they spar, hand against hand. They aim many hard blows, pummeling each other's sides and chests, ears and brows and cheeks, making the air resound with their strokes. . . . Entellus puts forth his right, Dares slips aside in a nimble dodge. . . . Entellus furiously drives Dares headlong over the arena, redoubling his blows, now with the right hand, now with the left. . . . Then Aeneas put an end to the fray, Dares' mates led him to the ships with his knees shaking, his head swaying from side to side, his mouth spitting teeth and blood. (Virgil, 1934, Pt. 10, pp. 362–63)*

At the Circus Maximus there were races, either by horses and jockeys or chariot races such as we saw at Olympia.

The most colossal Roman sport was the *naumachia*, a sham naval battle in a flooded area or artificial lake in which captives or condemned criminals reenacted historical naval engagements until they had killed off each other. The victors, if they pleased the audience, might be granted freedom.

The most famous Roman games were the fights involving animals and gladiators in the Colosseum. There were events such as a contest between a bull and a man. But what really turned on the Roman audiences were the fights by pairs or masses of armed men. Augustus gave eight spectacles in which a total of 10,000 men took part. Attendants prodded fallen gladiators with iron rods to make sure they were dead and, if they were not, killed them with mallet blows on the head (Durant, 1944, p. 387).

The combatants were war captives, disobedient slaves, or condemned criminals. The criminals came from all parts of the Empire: Murder, robbery, arson, sacrilege, or mutiny might lead one to be sentenced to a gladiatorial career. This could happen even to knights and senators. The gladiators were trained in gladiatorial schools, of which there were four in Rome, several others in Italy, and one in Alexandria. On entering a school one swore "to suffer himself to be whipped with rock, burned with fire, and killed with steel" (Friedlander, 1928, ii, p. 49).

A gladiator who fought very hard might be freed immediately. If he just survived, he might have to fight again and again on other holidays.

It is hard to believe that not all the athletes were displeased with their work:

Some were elated with victories and thought of their prowess rather than their peril; some complained that they were not allowed to fight often enough. . . . They had the stimulus and consolation of fame; their names were daubed by admirers on public walls; women fell in love with them, poets sang of them, painters portrayed them, sculptors carved for posterity their iron biceps and terrifying frowns. (Durant, 1944, p. 386)

Prominent Romans found many justifications for the gladiatorial spectacles. The gladiators' crimes had been serious, they said, and the spectacles would deter the audience from making the same mistakes. And was not the chance of life in the Colosseum more merciful than sure and sudden execution? In any case, what was shed was only *vilis sanguis*—the blood of common men.

Others, like the philosopher Seneca, were not impressed by such arguments. He dropped into the games one day at noon when most of the spectators had gone to lunch and reported:

I came home more greedy, more cruel and inhuman, because I have been among human beings. By chance I attended a midday exhibition, expecting some fun, wit, and relaxation . . . whereby men's eyes may have respite from the slaughter of their fellow men. But it was quite the contrary. . . . These noon fighters are sent out with no armor of any kind; they are exposed to blows at all points, and no one ever strikes in vain. . . . In the morning they throw men to the lions; at noon they throw them to the spectators. The crowd demands that the victor who has slain his opponent shall face the man who will slay him in turn; and the last conqueror is reserved for another butchering. . . . This sort of thing goes on while the stands are nearly empty. . . . Man, a sacred thing to man, is killed for sport and merriment. (Seneca, 1970, pp. 8, 95)

Seneca's reaction reminds us of the way some people feel about the brutality and violence of some of our contemporary sports. By examining why these spectacles were important to Rome, we may throw some light on our own times. (Whether they are right or not, some people think that we are now living in a period similar to the decline and fall of Rome. Also, some of my football players refer to themselves as gladiators.)

For one thing, Roman sport was a way of keeping the masses of people busy and amused and thereby keeping down rebellion. In the affluent society, the Roman working class called for a share of *panem et circenses*—bread and circuses: free food and engrossing spectacles in the circular arena in which they could forget their own suffering by seeing others suffer.

Furthermore, for the upper classes in an affluent society, sponsorship of sport was a form of conspicuous consumption. "During the first centuries of the Empire thousands of citizens from all quarters competed in the funding and donating of halls, baths, and theaters, in the

---

At the Hippodrome

On the appointed day 180,000 men and women moved in festive colors to the enormous hippodrome. Enthusiasm rose to a mania. Excited partisans smelled the dung of the animals to assure themselves that the horses of their favorite drivers had been properly fed. The spectators passed by the shops and brothels that lined the outer walls; they filed through hundreds of entrances and sorted themselves out with the sweat of anxiety into the great horseshoe of seats. Vendors sold them cushions, for the seats were mostly of hard wood, and the program would last all day. Senators and other dignitaries had special seats of marble, ornamented with bronze. Behind the imperial box was a suite of luxurious rooms, where the emperor and his family might eat, drink, rest, bathe, and sleep. Gambling was feverish and fortunes passed from hand to hand as the day advanced. . . . The usual length of a chariot race was seven circuits, about five miles. The test of skill lay in making the turns at the goals as swiftly and sharply as safety would allow; collisions were frequent there, and chariots, and animals mingled in fascinated tragedy. As the horses or chariots clattered to the final post the hypnotized audience rose like a swelling sea, gesticulated, waved handkerchiefs, shouted and prayed, groaned and cursed, or exalted in almost supernatural ecstasy. The applause that greeted the winner could be heard far beyond the limits of the city.

(From *Caesar and Christ* Pt. 3 of *The Story of Civilization*, pp. 382–383 by W. Durant, 1944, New York: Simon and Schuster. Copyright 1944 by W. Durant. Reprinted by permission.)

mass distribution of food, and in the institution or equipping of new games, all of which was recorded for posterity in boastful inscriptions'' (Huizinga, 1964, p. 178). Huizinga calls this the potlatch spirit.

More than this, the sporting festivals gave meaning to life and fostered a patriotic identification with the Roman state:

> *A modern ear is inclined to detect in this cry (for panem et circenses) little more than the demand of the unemployed proletariat for the dole and free cinema tickets. But it had a deeper significance. Roman society could not live without games. They were as necessary to its existence as bread—for they were holy games and the people's right to them was a holy right. Their basic function lay not merely in celebrating such prosperity as the community had already won for itself, but in fortifying it and ensuring future prosperity by means of ritual. (Huizinga, 1964, p. 177)*

Another outstanding cultural historian, Lewis Mumford, related Roman sport to a broader setting that includes us:

> *Play in one form or another is found in every human society and among a great many animal species: but sport in the sense of a mass spectacle, with death to add to the underlying excitement, comes into existence when a population has been drilled and regimented and depressed to such an extent that it needs at least a vicarious participation in difficult feats of strength or skill or heroism in order to sustain its waning life sense. The demand for circuses, and when the milder spectacles are insufficiently life-arousing, the demand for sadistic exploits and finally for blood is characteristic of civilizations that are losing their grip: Rome under the Caesars, Mexico at the time of Montezuma, Germany under the Nazis. These forms of surrogate manliness and bravado are the surest sign of a collective impotence and a pervasive death wish. The dangerous symptoms of that ultimate decay one finds everywhere today in machine civilization under the guise of mass sport. (1934, p. 303)*

The World of Camelot: The Middle Ages

Those who saw one of the most popular musical movies of our time (*Camelot*, with Vanessa Redgrave, Richard Harris, and Franco Nero) will know what the veteran sportswriter Jerry Izenberg meant when he wrote in 1972 of his ex-semipro baseball player father:

*Sports were the biggest single thing in my old man's life, because
everything was always clear-cut. There were good guys and bad
guys, and sometimes the bad guys played dirty, but that was part
of it, too. That's the way I grew up, and when I became a sports
writer for money. . . , I still thought of the whole thing as a kind
of wall-to-wall Camelot. . . . Well, it's not, and it never really was.
(1972, p. 2)*

To pick up our continuity: The period from the fall of Rome to about
1300 we call the Middle Ages, its way of life medieval. In 455 A.D.
Rome, the center of the most developed urban culture yet known, was
sacked for 10 days by Vandals from the north. The next 5 centuries
saw the European remnants of the Graeco-Roman-Christian civilization repeatedly overswept by invading Arabs, Germans, Vikings, and
Hungarians from the north and east. Beginning about the year 1000,
Europe finally stabilized around a new type of political and economic
organization called feudalism, of which the Camelot myth was an important part.

The work of feudalism was twofold. First, it was to master nature.
"At the beginning of the Middle Ages," Durant says, "the greater part
of Europe's soil was untilled and unpeopled forest and waste, at their
end the Continent had been won for civilization" (1950, pp. 559–560).
The peasants of Europe had "drained marshes, raised dykes, cleared
woods and canals, cut roads, built homes, advanced the frontier of
civilization, and won the battle between jungle and man." To do this
it was necessary that order be maintained—against invading hordes
and against fighting among neighbors. For these purposes there was
no longer the Roman government that had built aqueducts and amphi-
theaters, no longer the imperial army that had enforced the *pax Romana*
(Roman peace). So there arose a new form of structure based not on
the sovereignty of a central state but upon private contracts between
individuals. A powerful person would grant land to another as a fief
or *feudum* (note the origin of feudal) and agree to protect his vassal
in exchange for the vassal's military service. "Imagine," says an historian writing of the period, "a society in which the governmental
authority of the state, as we know it, has almost completely disappeared. . . . There, instead of one central government that all must
answer to, hundreds of little 'governmental' organizations come into
being, each virtually an independent territory, though vaguely connected by a kind of feudal hierarchy or network of personal agreements
among the local 'governments'" (Geanakoplos, 1968, pp. 359–390).
Each fief was organized economically in the form of a manor, an agricultural estate, on which worked a peasantry composed of serfs, free land-
holders, and semifree people called villeins. Everyone's station in life,

from the lord of the manor down to the serf, was ascribed by his birth. Each had hereditary rights and obligations. In the absence of central government the widest unifying force was the church. This saw the feudal arrangement as part of a larger plan:

> *Society, like the human body, is an organism composed of different members. Each member has his own function, prayer, or defense or merchandizing, or tilling the soil. Within classes there must be equality. . . . Between classes there must be inequality, for otherwise a class cannot perform its function or . . . enjoy its rights. Peasants must not encroach on those above them. Lords must not despoil peasants. (Tawney, 1947, pp. 27–28)*

A central part of the medieval pattern, very important to the traditions of sport, was *chivalry*—the code of conduct for the mounted vassal warrior, called the knight, toward his lord, toward his fellow-knights, toward women, and toward the church. The term comes from the Latin word for horse, *caballus* (related to the French *cheval* and the English *cavalry* and *cavalier*). The chivalric code was extremely important to security in the society I have described. The knight did not attack a wounded man. He kept his word (*parole*), which was good enough to free him when he was captured in battle and held for ransom. In a world where men were often away at war and left women at home, the knight was pledged to honor and protect them. Out of this idealized protectiveness grew the concept of romantic love—which was more often for a mistress than for a wife. The knight was to fight when necessary in defense of the church and of the needy. All this was the Camelot ideal, although in fact "more knights looked for damsels *to* [italics added] distress than *in* [italics added] distress and churches to raid than to aid" (Geanokoplos, 1968, p. 603).

Chivalry was very important in maintaining the class structure of society. It set the lords and knights off from the peasants, who had no obligation to be chivalrous, and also from the merchants of the towns that had survived the decline of the Roman empire. By the late 13th century, chivalry had solidified into a very elaborate system of ideals and rituals. The chivalric code and way of life distinguished the nobility from the upstart merchant *bourgeoisie*. There is a parallel in the way in which the Southern landed aristocracy in the United States preserved a medieval code of chivalry against a rising urban and industrial society before and after the Civil War.

> *Behind the formal structure of feudalism, the feudal picture is not merely one of serfdom, illiteracy, exploitation, and violence, but as truly a scene of lusty peasants clearing the wilderness; of men colorful and vigorous in language, love, and war; of knights*

pledged to honor and service, seeking adventure and fame rather than comfort and security, and scorning danger, death, and hell; women patiently toiling and breeding in peasant cottages, and titled ladies mingling the tenderest prayers to the virgin with the bold freedom of a sensuous poetry and courtly love. (Durant, 1950, pp. 578-579)

Where did sport, what Huizinga calls the "joyous and unbuttoned play of the people," come in? On Sundays and holidays, after Mass,

the peasant sang and danced, and forgot in hearty rustic laughter the dour burden of sermon and farm. Ale was cheap, speech was free and profane, and love tales of womankind mingled with the awesome legends of the saints. Rough games of football, hockey, and wrestling, and weight throwing pitted man against man, and village against village. Cock fighting and bull baiting flourished, and hilarity reached its height when, within a closed circle, two blindfolded men, armed with cudgels, tried to kill a goose or a pig. Sometimes of an evening, peasants visited one another, played indoor games and drank. (Durant, 1950, p. 559)

Almost everybody swam. In the north, in the winter, skating was about as common. All classes practiced archery, although later it became an upper-class pastime. Hunting had its practical as well as its sportive aspects: Medieval Paris, for example, was sometimes invaded by wolves. The fields of peasants would sometimes be trampled down by hunting nobles, who had no doubt about their right to enter. Only the working classes fished—this had not yet become a leisure class game. Ice hockey is recorded in Ireland as early as the second century A.D. Tennis (named for the cry, *tenez!* [hold!], of server to receiver) was introduced from Moslem areas and was popular in France. In England it attracted large crowds in theaters and in the open air. A Turkish historian of the 12th century describes a form of polo played with corded racquets that resembled lacrosse. A medieval writer tells of football as "an abominable game wherein young people propel a huge ball not by throwing it into the air but by striking and rolling it along the ground, not with their hands but with their feet" (Coulton, 1974, p. 83). Gardiner believes that the game came to England from China by way of Italy.

"Planned spectacles," says Durant, "were a vital part of medieval life: church processions, political parades, guild celebrations, filled the streets with banners, floats, wax saints, fat merchants, and military bands" (1950, p. 839). One of the distinctive public spectacles central to the Camelot myth was the tournament. Tournaments had their highest popularity in France (the original home of Lancelot du Lac, the successful suitor for the favor of Queen Guenivere at Camelot), beginning about the 10th century. They were held in connection with an important symbolic public event such as the ordination of a knight, a royal marriage, or the visit of a king.

Heralds would be sent around to announce the tournament. Knights would come to the tournament town, hang their armor in their windows, and post their coat of arms in public places where they could be examined. Anyone who challenged a knight's participation could lodge his protest with the tournament officials. If the challenge was upheld, the knight was disqualified and thereafter had a "blot on his scutcheon" (shield). The tournament town had some of the carnival quality of Olympia (and Disneyland):

> To the excited gathering came horse dealers to equip the knight, haberdashers to clothe him and his horse in fit array, money-lenders to ransom the fallen, fortunetellers, acrobats, mimes, troubadors and trouvéres, wandering scholars, women of loose morals, ladies of high degree. The whole occasion was a festival of song and dance, trysts and brawls, and wild betting on the contests. (Durant, 1950, p. 573)

The event itself might last about 1 day or as long as about a week. It took place in the "lists": The town square would be partly enclosed by stands and balconies for the richer spectators. The commoners would stand on foot around the field. All the knights would enter, to the fanfare of opening music, before the first engagement.

In a man-to-man event, the *joust* or tilt, the mounted knights would approach each other with their lances extended, at top speed. When one or both were knocked off their mounts, the tilt would continue on foot until one was *hors de combat* (disabled or killed), or one quit, or the king or lord called a halt. A tournament consisted of a large number of such tilts in which the knights vied for the favor of the lords and ladies.

The feature of the tournament was the *tourney*, a mock battle by masses of knights, usually with blunted weapons. This might be very bloody: In a tourney at Neuss in 1240 about 60 knights were killed. The tourney was a miniature war. Prisoners were taken and could be held for ransom. At the end of the tournament the victors and the nobles celebrated by feasting, singing, and dancing. The successful knights heard songs and poems composed in their honor and were kissed by beautiful ladies.

The Church tried repeatedly to ban tournaments but, along with the feasts and poems and kisses, the knights loved money even more than war. We are reminded of professional athletes in Greece and Rome, and today, by the legend of a knight who "protested the Church's condemnation of tournaments on the ground that if effective, it would end his only means of livelihood." (Prestage, 1928, p. 75)

Chapter 6

Puritanism and the Achievement Ethic

On August 22, 1926, at Shibe Park, the Philadelphia Athletics beat the Chicago White Sox 3-2 behind the pitching of the great Lefty Grove. The game was a memorable event, not particularly because of the brilliance of Grove but because it was the first Sunday baseball game in the history of Philadelphia (Information courtesy of Tom Danazo, *Philadelphia Bulletin*).

"The Puritan Sabbath," says Winton Solberg, "exerted a powerful influence on the life of the American people from the time of the initial settlements until well into the twentieth century. . . . At stake was not simply the religious observance of a stated day of the week, but a whole way of life involving man's relations with God and the entire realm of work and play" (Solberg, 1977, pp. ix, 3).

The roots of the Puritan way of life take us back to 16th-century Europe, and especially England.

Between the 14th and the 18th centuries the Middle Ages became the modern world. Much as the landed aristocracy tried to hold on with the myth of Camelot, power nevertheless moved to the craftsmen, merchants, and bankers of the towns and cities. An economy based on land gave way to one based on money. Science began to replace traditional faith as the method for handling reality. First in Italy and later in western Europe, economic power shifted to the *bourgeoisie*, the townsmen or burghers (note the French suffix—*bourg* and the English—*burg,—berg,—burgh,* and—*bergh*). Voyages of discovery expanded the known world and the market for trade. The feudal system was replaced by new national states. Political power shifted from the lords to the commoners (again, mainly the townsmen) in England in 16th- and 17th-century political revolutions and in France in the 18th century.

Preserved Smith, the historian of the Reformation, summed up how this began:

Such a change in man's environment and habits as the world has rarely seen took place in the generation that reached early manhood in the year 1500. In the span of a single life . . . men discovered not in metaphor but in sober fact, a new heaven and a new earth. In those days masses of men began to read many books, multiplied by the new art of printing. In those days immortal artists shot the world through with a matchless radiance of color and meaning. In those days Vasco da Gama and Columbus and Magellan opened the watery ways to new lands beyond the seven seas. In those days Copernicus established the momentous truth that the earth was but a tiny planet spinning around a vastly greater sun. In those days was in large part accomplished the economic shift from medieval guild to modern production by capital and wages. In those days wealth was piled up in the coffers of the merchants, and a new power was given to the life of the individual, of the nation, and of the third estate (the bourgeoisie). In those days the monarchy of the Roman church was broken, and large portions of her dominions seceded to form new organizations governed by other powers and animated by a different spirit. (1920, pp. 3–4)

Of all the revolutionary developments that ushered in the modern era, none was more important for society and for sport than was the last change named by Smith—the Protestant Reformation. We shall need to examine the different spirit that it brought to the world.

The Reformation was a religious revolution within the church that had grown up in the centuries after the life of Jesus. It was a protest (hence the name Protestant) against a power organization that had made itself the sole authority in religious matters and insisted that only through it could a person be related to God. The main thrust of Protestantism was its insistence on the direct relationship and responsibility of the individual to God.

The spirit that animated Protestantism was most clearly expressed in the 16th century by John Calvin in Geneva, by the Reformed church in the Netherlands, by the Presbyterians in Scotland, and by the Puritans in England and later in New England. It was the spirit of the self-conscious, dedicated individual who felt a personal responsibility to live righteously before his God and to persuade and if necessary to force others to live the same way. As Mrs. Storm Jameson says in her book *The Decline of Merry England*, "Every form of human activity should be dedicated to one single end, the self-perfection of man, whereby he purges himself of sin and may win Paradise" (1930, p. 18).

In England the intensity and single-mindedness of this dedication led their enemies to label such Protestants by the mocking term Puritan. The Puritan tended to regard himself as an instrument for doing God's work in the world and to see only two proper activities—work and worship. In this Puritan ethic there was no place for activity that did not have a high purpose but was just enjoyable in itself. The Puritan felt bound to keep under control his strong desires for fun and pleasure.

The Two Faces of Puritanism

Puritanism was an intensely controlled channeling of human energies that had two sides. It was repressive. The Puritan era began with an attack on sport. Weber says, "Sport was accepted if it served a rational purpose, that of recreation necessary for physical efficiency. But as a means for the spontaneous expression of undisciplined impulses, it was under suspicion" (1958, p. 167). In the agon for God and for political and economic individualism there is no place for agon in the pagan Greek sense or in the romantic Camelot sense.

Let us look at the world into which the Protestant ethic came and how it changed that world. The 16th-century poet Edmund Spenser spoke of pre-Puritan England in this way:

Then our age was in its prime . . .
A very merry, dancing, drinking,
Laughing, quaffing, and unthinking
Time. (The Faerie Queene, cited in Jameson, 1930, p. 15)

Describing England in the 15th century, Durant says:

Amusements ranged from checkers and chess, backgammon and dice, to fishing and hunting, archery and jousts. Playing cards reached England toward the end of the fifteenth century. . . . Dancing and music were as popular as gambling. . . . Men played tennis, handball, bowls, quoits; they wrestled and boxed, set cocks to fighting, baited bears and bulls. . . . Kings and nobles kept jugglers, jesters, and buffoons; and a Lord of Misrule, appointed by the king or queen, superintended the sports and revels of Christmas tide. . . . Women moved freely among men everywhere: drank in taverns, rode to the hounds, hunted with falcons, and distracted the spectators from the contestants at tournaments. (1957, p. 114)

In France Francois Rabelais filled a whole chapter listing games, and in the Netherlands Bruegel showed about a hundred games in a single painting. "Never," says Preserved Smith, "has the theater been more popular" (1920, p. 500). In Paris alone there were 250 tennis courts. Even the Protestant reformer Martin Luther approved of dancing as a way of bringing young people together, and the Protestant leader Melancthon still danced when he was in his 40s. Calvin himself, from whom Puritanism sprang, "bade his followers play harmonious games like bowling or quoits, and enjoy wine in moderation" (Durant, 1957, p. 477). The Scottish Calvinist John Knox once found Calvin himself bowling on the Sabbath (Dulles, 1940).

But when Protestantism came to power—as it did under the dictatorships of Calvin at Geneva in the mid-1500s and Oliver Cromwell in England in the mid-1600s—it "turned with all its force against one thing: the spontaneous enjoyment of life and all that it had to offer" (Weber, 1958, p. 166).

The Council at Geneva arranged yearly visits to every home to question the members on whether they had engaged in any forbidden activities: gambling, card playing, profanity, drunkenness, dancing; whether they had sung irreligious or indecent songs, or been excessive in their dress or entertainment; whether they had worn colors of clothes prohibited by law, used more than the legal number of dishes at a meal, worn jewelry or lace, or piled their hair too high. They were not questioned about their habits at the theater because eventually even religious plays were forbidden.

In England, "dancing, profane singing, wakes, revels, wrestling, shootings, leapings, ringings of bells, church-ales, may-poles, all . . . were thrown . . . upon the rubbish heap" (Jameson, 1930, pp. 20–21). The Puritans illegalized betting, made adultery a capital crime, ordered all maypoles cut down, attacked both plays in the palaces of nobles and wrestling matches and dancing by ordinary people on village greens. They attacked puppet shows, horseracing, and bearbaiting. The historian Macaulay, who was too anti-Puritan to be a fair judge, claimed "the Puritan hated bearbaiting, not because it gave pain to the bear, but because it gave pleasure to the spectators" (Macaulay, 1871, p. 80). The theater was closed. "The playhouses were to be dismantled, the spectators fined, the actors whipped" (Macaulay, 1871, p. 80). In Stratford-on-Avon the Puritan town government closed the theater while Shakespeare was still living there during his last years. Greek statues were to be "cleaned up" by the chisels of Puritan stonemasons. Even pictures of Jesus and the Virgin Mary in the royal collection were to be burned, presumably as a protest against Catholic Virgin-worship.

Very important for the future development of sport was the way in which the Puritans discouraged any spontaneous or free activity on

Sundays or holidays. "They were strict observers of the Sabbath," says Brinton, "because they felt strongly that the Catholics from whom they were revolting had profaned the Sabbath by letting all sorts of worldly activities go on then, making it what in English is now called a holiday, instead of making it what God intended it to be, a holy day" (Brinton, 1959, p. 225). Before Charles I lost his throne and his head to the Puritans, he and his father James I had specifically fought them on this issue by issuing *Book of Sports*, which legalized a number of Sunday amusements outside of church hours. "When shall the common people," James had argued, "have leave to exercise, if not upon the Sundays and Holy-Days, seeing that they must apply their labour and win their living in their working days? . . . If these times were taken from them, the meaner sort who labour hard all the week should have no recreations at all to refresh their spirits" (*The King's Majesties Declaration*, 1906, pp. 99, 101).

"The feudal and monarchical forces," says Weber, "protected the pleasure seekers against the rising middle-class morality" (1958, p. 167). In his history of sport from Elizabeth to Anne, Dennis Brailsford spelled this relationship out a little more:

> *Much of the early Stuart encouragement of popular sporting activities was not given on account of the benefits seen in the sports themselves, but for social, religious, or political motives, associated with the fact that those whom the crown increasingly recognized as its opponents had become identified with a negative, restrictive attitude towards games. The simple principle of opposition suggested encouragement to the people's play, while this encouragement seemed, at the same time, a useful means of propaganda on behalf of the established order. (1969, p. 107)*

One example may have been Robert Dover's organization of the Cotswold Games in the western English hills in 1612 in an effort to blend upper-class sport and rural folk games in an anti-Puritan revival of the Olympics. It was a deliberate attempt, says Peter McIntosh, to "bring together two patterns of sporting activity, the popular and the courtly, and thereby to preserve the existing social system against Puritan attack." When the Puritans won militarily and politically, the "Cotswold Games survived only as a local and unimportant celebration" (1971b, p. 10).

The other side of this may have been, as Foster Dulles suggests, that "the Puritans resented the amusements of the wealthy, leisured classes, making a moral issue of their discontent. These two influences, spiritual reform and economic envy, can never be disentangled" (1940, p. 3). In power, the Puritans had the *Book of Sports* publicly burned by the common hangman.

Solberg has analyzed the reasons behind the Puritan aversion to sport. Some non-Puritans would have accepted some of them. (James I, who issued the *Book of Sports*, held that football was more likely to lame its players than to make them more capable.)

First, to the Puritan sport was essentially frivolous. A person's chief duty was to glorify God through work in a chosen calling. "Work was serious, earnest, a material necessity. . . . Play was entirely different" (Solberg, 1977, p. 49).

Second, sports and games had to take place outside the full 6-day working week that was then customary, so they fell on the Sabbath. "Even innocent diversions such as running, jumping, stoolball [an ancestor of baseball], . . . marbles, archery, hunting, and fishing were devilish pastimes because they lured people away from church and kept them from spending the entire day in spiritual edification. . . . The player ran the risk of forgetting his religious duties by abandoning himself to the rapture generated by exhilarating physical exercise and sportive competition" (pp. 49–50).

Third, some sports were brutal. Brailsford says, "If Puritanism often allied itself with those forces that were restricting leisure activities, it also . . . supported the gradual civilizing of many sporting pursuits. . . . The Puritan tradition has been a considerable force in reducing barbarity and crudity in sport" (1969, p. 156). Cockfighting and the baiting of bears and bulls were widely popular sports that cruelly exploited animals. Of the Sunday game of football, a critic wrote during the reign of Queen Elizabeth:

> For as concerning football playing: I protest with you, it may rather be called a friendly kind of fight, than a play or recreation. A bloody and murdering practice, than a fellowly sport or pastime. For, doth not everyone lie in wait for his adversary, seeking to overthrow him and to [pitch] him on his nose, though it be upon hard stones, in ditch or dale, in valley or hill, or whatever place it be, he careth not so he have him down. By this means, sometimes their necks are broken, sometimes their backs, sometimes one part thrust out of joint, sometimes another, sometimes the nose guts out with blood, sometimes their eyes start out. . . . Is this murdering play an exercise for the Sabbath day; is this a Christian dealing for one brother to maim and hurt another? (Stubbes, 1583/1972).

The football described is not modern soccer, rugby, or American football (which the description might conceivably fit fairly well), but a mass struggle like the ancient Dane's Head, played by hordes of young men who sought to propel an inflated bladder across country from one village green to another.

A Puritan tract laments the supposedly true story of eight young men who fell through the ice and drowned after a scuffle in a Sabbath football game. Reprinted by permission of Houghton Library, Harvard University.

Fourth, sport encouraged gambling, a way of getting something for nothing that was contrary to the Puritan ethic of hard and serious work. Elizabethans enjoyed betting on athletic contests—bowling, pitching the bar, and the like.

Finally, sporting events attracted crowds whose behavior violated the Puritan's ideal of how a person should behave on the Sabbath, or any other day. "Sunday recreations provided an opportunity for rogues and ruffians to practice trickery and deceit. Permit Sabbath recreations, and what followed was sexual immorality, crime, drinking and gambling, brutal sports, quarreling and brawling, scenes of wild disorder" (Solberg, 1977, p. 51).

Heinz Meyer, a West German sport sociologist, insists further that sport and the Puritan religion are two total and incompatible ways of life. Although Puritanism supported physical training as a way of keeping the body fit for work, its real goal was not the happiness and well-being of the body but the salvation of the soul. Not so with sport:

Sport . . . has a certain demand and totality of its own, it is a way of life with its own horizon of values. Sportsmanship, a mingling

of healthy and beautiful corporeality, acceptance of life, moderni-
ty, and a bit of fairness has been established as an important value
in our culture. Sportsmanship understood that way is a genuine-
ly profane phenomenon, an unreligious form of mastering and
widening existence and of enjoying it. Seen from a Christian point
of view this activates shallow worldliness. The demand to use the
time meaningfully to reach salvation is not obeyed, time is spent
in self-sufficient distraction. And the Christian demands of
modesty and altruism are antagonistic to the striving for success,
a maximum of proficiency and beating other competitors. About
sport there is something essentially heathen. (1973, p. 49)

Thus, says Meyer, the emperor Theodosius was logical in A.D. 395
when he banned the Olympic games along with other heathen sports
3 years after making Christianity the state religion. So also were the
Puritans consistent.

In 1644 the Puritan Parliament declared December 25th a day of
fasting in which people would do penance for their previous celebrations on Christmas. The Puritans not only thought the Catholics had
allowed holy days to be misused, but they also felt that they had had
too many of them, and reduced the number. Karl Marx once observed
that by eliminating many Catholic holidays the Protestants made is possible to do more work and make more profit. According to the calculations of one speaker in Parliament in 1715, it cost Catholic France 6
million pounds a year (at today's exchange rates about $12 million dol-
lars) to have 50 more holy days than did Protestant England (Jameson,
1930, p. 22).

As well as being repressive, Puritanism was also liberating.
Preserved Smith says that "politically, it favored the growth of self-
reliance, self-control and a sense of personal worth that made democracy possible and necessary" (1920, p. 345). It also favored economic
individualism. Crane Brinton, in *A History of Western Morals*, says that
the Protestant ethic took the agon (formal contest, combat) into the
world of business, where it "began to take economic channels that were
to lead to the Napoleon of Industry" (1959, p. 222). It stimulated scientific progress: Two thirds of the original Royal Society of scientists were
Puritans.

A Dutch Protestant writer, Abraham Kuyper, interprets what happened in the Netherlands:

Scarcely had Calvinism been firmly established in the Netherlands
for a quarter of a century when there was a rustling of life in all
directions, and an indomitable energy was fermenting in every
department of human activity, and their commerce and trade, their
handicrafts and industry, their agriculture and horticulture, their

art and science flourished with a brilliancy previously unknown, and imparted a new impulse for an entirely new development of life, to the whole of Western Europe. (1931; p. 73)

In his 1906 work, *The Protestant Ethic and The Spirit of Capitalism* (1958), Max Weber contended that the spirit of the individual dedicating himself to God without intercession by the church was also the spirit of capitalist individualism breaking free of feudal restrictions. He gave evidence that capitalism in its early days had grown most successfully in Protestant areas. Fifty years later a psychologist, David C. McClelland, showed statistically that in the 20th century Protestant nations led Catholic nations in economic development, measured in terms of per capita consumption of electric power (see Table 6.1).

Table 6.1   Electric Power Consumption by Protestant and Catholic Countries Outside the Tropics of Cancer and Capricorn

Protestant countries	Consumption of electricity kwh/cap (1950)	Catholic countries	Consumption of electricity kwh/cap (1950)
Norway	5,310	Belgium	986
Canada	4,120	Austria	900
Sweden	2,580	France	790
United States	2,560	Czechoslovakia	730
Switzerland	2,230	Italy	535
New Zealand	1,600	Chile	484
Australia	1,160	Poland	375
United Kingdom	1,115	Hungary	304
Finland	1,000	Ireland	300
Union S. Africa	890	Argentina	255
Holland	725	Spain	225
Denmark	500	Uruguay	165
AVERAGE	1,983	Portugal	110
		AVERAGE	474

Note. From *World Population and Production: Trends and Outlook* (Table 415, p. 972) by W.S. Woytinsky and E.S. Woytinsky. Copyright © 1953 by the Twentieth Century Fund. Further arrangement and statistical treatment from *The Achieving Society* (Table 2.2, p. 51) by D.C. McClelland, 1976, New York: Irvington. Reprinted by permission.

That the impact of the work ethic need not be totally antisport is suggested by cross-cultural studies of John Roberts and Brian Sutton-Smith on how the training of children is related to the kind of games a society prefers (Roberts & Sutton-Smith, 1962). They found that societies that reward their children for individual achievement (performance that is distinctive and outstanding) usually have a large number of physical games (see Table 6.2). How all this fits the culture of Puritanism I have diagrammed in Figure 6.1. This shows positively that Puritanism produced a workaholic mentality that increased production and created leisure and affluence, thus generating a market for commercial sport. It also shows how this development was resisted by the Puritan opposition to fun and games.

Figure 6.1 Puritanism and Sport.

Table 6.2 Physical Skill Games (including combined Physical Skill and Strategy) and Frequency of Reward for Achievement

Achievement Score	9 or more Games of Physical Skill	8 or fewer Games of Physical Skill
Above median	14	4
Below median	7	19

Note. From "Child Training and Game Involvement" by J.M. Roberts and B. Sutton-Smith, 1962, *Ethnology*, **1** (April), p. 174 (Table 4). Reprinted by permission.

Puritanism and American Sport

The Puritan attitude toward sport crossed the Atlantic with the settlement of America. Solberg sums up this attitude thus:

While the Puritans were not always opposed to sports and recreation as such, for all practical purposes this appeared to be the case, because they feared and prohibited recreations and entertainments that touched the irrational springs of man's nature, those that catered to the sensual appetites, and those that took place on the Lord's Day. Hence Sabbatarianism suppressed the sportive, playful, and aesthetic element in American culture in the formative years. (1977, p. 301)

The *Book of Sports* (1618) was a main factor behind the emigration of Puritans like John Cotton and Thomas Hooker. The settlement at Plymouth (1620) followed James' declaration by 2 years. Historian John Allen Krout says, "Dancing, running, jumping, and kindred sports of the village green were associated with profanation of the Sabbath. . . . Had the leaders of Plymouth, Salem, and Boston been in Parliament in 1643 they would have voted with the majority that all copies of the *Book of Sports* be seized and burned" (1929, p. 10). There was more to this than transplanted English prejudices. "Fighting Indians, clearing new lands, and building towns," says John Rickards Betts, historian of American sport, "allowed little time for most colonists to devote to merry-making. Only after two centuries of settlement in the New World was sport to emerge as an important institution in American life" (1974, p. 5).

Puritanism was strongest on the rural frontier and among the Anglo-Saxon population and began to weaken with the development of towns and cities and their settlement by non-WASP immigrants (like the Germans, with their tradition of Sunday picnicking and beer drinking). Although Betts says that in the 1820s and 1850s "in both the frontier town and the eastern city there was a decline in religious restraint and in Puritan orthodoxy,"(1974, p. 28) as late as the 1900 Olympics these feelings were still so strong that 8 of 13 University of Pennsylvania athletes refused to participate on the Sabbath. In 1906, when the Chicago White Sox beat the Cubs in the World Series, a local minister who was a baseball fan lamented: "It is a shame and disgrace to any community as enlightened and civilized as Chicago that Sunday baseball should be tolerated and indulged in, not only by professionals, but by boys and young men in general, many of the better classes" (*Chicago Daily Tribune*, October 15, 1906). Blue laws against Sunday sport were on the statute books of all states except California as late as 1915. Pennsylvania, in spite of being a strongly urban state with a large immigrant population, tried to enforce into the 1930s the 1794 statute against worldly employment on the Sabbath. In 1927 in *Commonwealth v. the American Baseball Club of Philadelphia*, the judge declared in support of the blue law: "We cannot imagine . . . anything more worldly and irreligious in the way of employment than the playing of professional baseball as it is played today. Christianity is part of the common law of Pennsylvania, and its people are Christian people. Sunday is the holy day among Christians. No one, we think, would contend that professional baseball partakes in any way of the nature of holiness" (Schaffer, 1927, p. 28).

How the Puritan ethic wavered in the balance with other forces is illustrated by the fact that at about the same time, whereas the very conservative churchman Daniel Poling and the liberal John Haynes Holmes both opposed commercialized sport, Bishop Manning planned a Sport Bay (window) in the Episcopal Cathedral of St. John the Divine in New York City, saying, "Not only does religion not frown upon sport, but encourages and sympathizes with it and gives it an important place in the temple of God" (*New York Times*, January 7, 1926, p. 27). Similarly, in their famous community study of Muncie, Indiana, in 1925, Robert and Helen Lynd (1963) found Sunday baseball still condemned by the churches and many other people, whereas golf courses and gun clubs were open. Several states, including Pennsylvania and Alabama, solved the rural-urban conflict by laws that left Sunday codes up to local option. Thus Philadelphia got legal baseball, and Birmingham, Montgomery, and Mobile got Sunday movies, baseball, and tennis, all in strongly Sabbatarian states.

Takeoff and the Leisure Masses

On the last lap of our historical journey, it will be helpful to look at one of our most important tools for understanding how our modern world has developed. This is Walt Rostow's analysis of the stages of economic growth (1962).

Looking back at how we have arrived at our contemporary urban industrial world, Rostow outlines five phases of development:

1. *The traditional society,* in which one generation essentially repeats the last. Feudal society is an example. Most of the primitive cultures studied by anthropologists also are. Ancient Greece is perhaps another case: In his book *The Idea of Progress* (1955) J. E. Bury tells us that the Greeks did not have the idea of progressive growth.
2. *The preconditions for takeoff,* in which a traditional society is changing in ways that will make it ready for economic progress. The sixteenth century as described earlier by Preserved Smith was such a period.

3. *Economic takeoff,* in which the conditions for economic growth, especially investment in machinery, accelerate strongly. This happened in England about 1775, in the United States after 1850, in Japan and Russia about 1880 to 1890.
4. *The drive to maturity,* in which investment in capital equipment, at first confined to a small part of the economy, spreads to include all activities. This happened in the United States in the three generations following the Civil War.
5. *The age of high mass consumption,* where the earlier investment in productive equipment pays off in a spread of consumer affluence. The United States was the first country to reach this stage, in the 1920s, followed by Japan and western Europe in the 1950s, and the Soviet Union in the 1960s.

These five stages begin with dire need, of the kind which has gripped most human beings since the beginning of history, and still does. Then there is a period of intense hard work and saving, dominated by a Puritan ethic, which builds up the equipment for mastering need. Finally concentration on production gives way to an emphasis on consumption of goods and services, including sport.

The rise of sport in the modern sense coincided, in time and place, with the world's most spectacular burst of industrial takeoff, in the late 19th-century United States. John Rickards Betts summarizes concisely what happened:

Manufacturers, seeking cheap labor, encouraged immigration; factories were most efficiently run in larger towns and cities; urban masses, missing the rural pleasures of hunting and fishing, were won to the support of commercialized entertainment and spectator sports; the emergence of a commercial aristocracy and a laboring class resulted in distinctions every bit as strong in sport as in other social matters; and the urgency of physical exercise as life became more sedentary was easily recognized. (Betts, 1953, p. 146)

"Only when the first fierce struggle against the wilderness was won," says John Allen Krout, "did a few in the older communities find wealth and leisure which enabled them to introduce to the New World such sports and pastimes as intrigued the nobility and gentry of Europe (Krout, 1929, p. 9). But sport also had roots in the struggle itself. Hunting was a necessary way of getting a living, but a cooperative venture with elements of a game. Also, Krout reports the following:

On each successive frontier barn raisings, log rollings, plowing bees and corn huskings were ventures which developed into sport-

ing tests of strength and skill so dear to the heart of the pioneer. In them were matured those elements of competition and cooperation essential in the development of modern organized sport. . . . One can see the settlers . . . testing marksmanship with bow and arrow as well as matchlock, comparing strength in wrestling and throwing the bar and competing with each other for supremacy in running and jumping. (1929, pp. 9, 11)

Before 1950, the leisure classes had followed the traditional upper-class pastimes of fox hunting and horseracing. There has been some general interest in rowing, running, prizefighting, cricket, and fencing, but horseracing was the only organized sport that really turned people on. After the middle of the century, masses of city dwellers needed escape or diversion from the routine of factory and office. They also had time and income to afford it. "During the years which passed from the close of the Civil War to the end of the century were laid in America the foundations of the new era of sport. . . . British sport was primarily a phase of the life of the upper classes; in America the appearance of baseball at the very beginning of the athletic era signified a mass movement affecting all groups of the population" (1929, p. 3).

City dwellers, with workday hours cut, a half-Saturday holiday, and sometimes 2-week summer vacations, were trapped in the city with as yet no parks and no access to the country. They found a substitute for the activity of pioneers: "A people whose attitude was greatly influenced by the traditions of a pioneering frontier life felt restless under city restraints. Until they found the escape value of sports for themselves, they eagerly took the next best thing. If they could not play or compete, they could at least get the thrill of vicarious participation by cheering on their favorites from a grandstand" (Dulles, 1940, p. 137).

Table 6.3 shows the transition from play to work in seven American sports. R.T. Furst (1971) points out that five of the sports were professionalized in the years from 1895 to 1903. This commercialization coincided, he says, with a burst in the application of new bureaucratic methods for maximizing industrial profit. (It was, for example, the period when industrial and financial concentration was colliding with antitrust laws that sought to check it.)

I cannot stress too much how new a thing is leisure for the majority of people. Life for most human beings has always been work, work, work to survive—and still is in most places. Before America's mid-19th-century takeoff we could speak of the leisured minority and their sports, as did Thorstein Veblen in his famous classic, *The Theory of the Leisure Class* (1899). But it was only with industrialism that there arose, as Gregory Stone points out, alongside the leisure class the leisure masses, who furnish the market for spectator sport (1972).

Table 6.3 Commercialization of Major American Sports

	Baseball	Football	Hockey	Basketball	Golf	Tennis	Bowling
Play	1831–1945 (14 years)	1874–1882 (8 years)	1855–1875 (20 years)	————	1779–1786 (7 years)	1874–1881 (7 years)	1825–1875 (50 years)
Game	1845–1869 (24 years)	1882–1895 (13 years)	1875–1903 (28 years)	1891–1898 (7 years)	1786–1894 (108 years)	1881–1926 (45 years)	1875–1895 (20 years)
Work	1869–1970 (101 years)	1895–1970 (75 years)	1903–1970 (67 years)	1898–1970 (72 years)	1894–1970 (76 years)	1926–1970 (44 years)	1895–1970 (75 years)

Note. From "Social Change and the Commercialization of Professional Sports" by R.T. Furst, 1971, *International Review of Sport Sociology,* **6**, p. 157. Reprinted by permission.

This leisure was accompanied by the fact that from the 17th century to the 19th the Puritan ethic had weakened. This made it possible for Sunday in the industrial cities to be again a day of games.

Another way in which industrialism fostered mass sport was by advances in transportation and communication. Before 1860 the railroad and steamboat began to bring spectators long distances to horse and trotting races, regattas, cycling races, track and field events, and prizefights. The first intercollegiate rowing race, between Harvard and Yale in 1852, was sponsored by the Boston, Concord, and Montreal railway (Kelley, 1932). In 1869 a jerky little engine steamed out of Princeton to Rutgers for the first intercollegiate football game. The outstanding 1870 Harvard baseball team went by rail on an extended tour, winning a majority of games against both amateurs and professionals. After the formation of the National Baseball League, an advertisement in the 1886 Spalding Official Baseball Guide told dramatically of the role of the railroad in the development of organized baseball: "The cities that have representative clubs contesting for the championship pennant this year are Chicago, Boston, New York, Washington, Kansas City, Detroit, Saint Louis, and Philadelphia. All of these cities are joined together by the Michigan Central Railroad. This road has enjoyed almost a monopoly of Baseball travel in former years" (Betts, 1953, p. 149).

The technology of communication vastly expanded the number of people involved in sporting events. "The expansion of sporting news . . . ," says Betts, "was directly related to the more general use of telegraphy, which made possible instantaneous reporting of ball games, horse races, prize fights, yachting regattas, and other events. Box scores, betting odds, and all kinds of messages were relayed from one city to another, and by 1870 daily reports were published in many metropolitan papers" (1953, p. 152).

A popular magazine of the time tells graphically what telegraph communication meant to the American sport lover. When Harvard rowed in England against Oxford in a famous 1869 race, "the result was flashed through the Atlantic cable to reach New York about a quarter past one, while the news reached the Pacific Coast about nine o'clock, enabling many of the San Franciscans to . . . swallow defeat with their coffee" (*Frank Leslie's Illustrated Newspaper*, Sept. 28, 1869, p. 2). The Sullivan-Kilrain fight in New Orleans in 1889 was covered by reporters from every prominent journal in the Union, and Western Union had 50 operators to handle 208,000 words of special news dispatches (Betts, 1953, p. 240).

In 1887 big league baseball scores were wired to every large city inning by inning and were often posted on a board by telegraph operators at saloons as a special attraction. Before TV or even radio transmission had become familiar, the Associated Press wired the 1916 Brooklyn-Boston World Series on a single 26,000-mile circuit to all of its lease wire members.

These developments foreshadowed the changes in the sporting market that the sociologically oriented jurist Jerome Frank dramatized in the 1948 Gardella case testing the reserve clause in baseball contracts. The federal court refused jurisdiction in the case on the ground that baseball had been held by the Supreme Court in 1922 not to be interstate commerce because a game and its audience were always confined to a single state. This might have been true in 1922, said Frank, but in 1948 this precedent had been sociologically outdated by radio and television, which had created an audience that knew no state lines (*Gardella v. Chandler*, Second Federal Circuit Court of Appeals, 1948).

Another technological advance central to sport as we now know it was the electric light. In 1883, although Madison Square Garden had installed some electric lights, fans at the Sullivan-Slade heavyweight boxing championship had to battle both cigar smoke and gaslight fumes. Ten years later the Chicago *Daily Tribune* reported, "Now men travel to great boxing contests in vestibule limited trains. They sleep at the best hotels . . . and when the time for the contest arrives, they find themselves in a grand, brilliantly lighted arena" (Sept. 8, 1882). The late 19th century made indoor night sport possible. A third of the way through the 20th century the outdoor night game began to become commonplace, thus expanding the range of the sport business.

In 1905 James Bryce, the British historian of America, said of the "passion for looking at and reading about the athletic scene":

It occupies the minds not only of the youth at the universities but also of their parents and of the general public. Baseball matches and football matches elicit an interest greater than any other public events except the Presidential election and that comes only once in four years. The interest in one of the great contests, such as those which draw forty thousand spectators to the great "Stadium" recently erected at Cambridge, Massachusetts, appears to pervade nearly all classes more than does any "sportive event" in Great Britain. The American love of excitement and love of competition has seized upon these games. (pp. 738–739)

Sport and the Achieving Society

Now let us analyze some of the characteristics of modern sport as it has developed since our industrial takeoff.

Sport is at the same time an escape from modern industrialism and an expression of it. In the words of Adriano Tilgher's history of work, "Not only has modern sport been called into existence as a corrective by labor, our master and our god, but labor has stamped upon sport every one of its own traits" (1965, pp. 186–187). First of all, team sports are a part of the industrial society. Frontiersmen (and women) and settled farmers practiced spontaneous cooperation in barn raisings and husking bees, but these did not involve a continuous assignment of specialized roles, as do organized team sports. These reflect the organization of industry. Historian Ralph Gabriel says of early 19th-century sport, "The few sports of the time were those emphasizing individual skill (hunting, fishing, and horse racing). Americans were not ready to submit to the discipline of team play" (Gabriel, 1929, p. 3).

The fan who crowds into a stadium or sits glued to his TV set is experiencing a release from the stress of his daily factory or office job and is at the same time the consumer of a commodity mass-produced for profit. What does it do for him? Obviously, it satisfies to some degree his desire for fun, as defined in chapter 3. Also, it provides catharsis in two senses. As Sutton-Smith pointed out, the world of sport can upset the hierarchy of ordinary life, so that the chronic loser becomes a winner. Also, especially in the violent sports, the fan, through his team, can discharge some of the hostility built up by social frustration. Even in a noncontact sport like tennis, he can identify with the overpowering big game that has taken over the sport in recent years.

Furthermore, in a mobile urban world where most people have few close, long-standing ties, sport gives a sense of roots:

The sports pages provide some confirmation that there is a continuity in the events and affairs of the larger society . . . reassurance that is not possible from following currrent events, the

continuity of which is not readily discernible for many readers.
. . . Team loyalties formed in adolescence and maintained through
adulthood may serve to remind one, in a nostalgic way, that there
are areas of comfortable stability in life—that some things are per-
manent amid the harassing interruptions and transitions of daily
experience. (Stone, 1972, p. 73)

James Reston says, "Sports in America are a unifying force, and a counter to the confusion about the vagueness and the complexity of our
cities, our races, and in this long-haired age, even the confusion between our sexes" (1966, p. 6).

But there are those who see these as misleading escapes. Writing
of the relationship of Japanese sport to business enterprise, Takaaki
Niwa says that for two reasons the typical modern worker feels alie-
nated from his work. First, in advanced capitalism he works for a large
business enterprise whose profits go to someone else. Second, mass
technology and industrial organization are so vast that he feels over-
whelmed. Sport partially relieves the problem, and at the same time
intensifies it:

We can discover many worthy and significant aspects in sport to-
day, as a leisure activity connected with the healthy body and
mind, etc., but sport is in fact performing the role of channeling
a person's attention away from the solution of these alienation
problems. When the masses become enthusiastic about sport and
its basic appeal, they gradually forget their uneasiness and dis-
satisfaction which is based on the condition of society. This means
that the greater the effect of sport on the unhappy psychological
condition of the individuals, the more the individual is divorced
from the solution of the problems of social reality. (1973, p. 55)

As Stone has put it, *play has tended to give way to display, the game*
to the spectacle. The spectacle is distinguished from the game by the
overwhelming way in which the spectators outnumber the players.
It is also distinguished by the predictability of the outcome. Related
to this is the degree of personal expression by the player. The purest
example of the predictable spectacle is the staged drama of professional
wrestling, with its good guys and bad buys, each playing his or her
part. A pure example of the unpredictability of the game is the spectacular play in which the player outdoes himself, makes the impossible
catch. Another example of the contrast: The Super Bowl, which reached
stature with the startling 1969 upset of the Colts by the Jets, has in
the opinion of many people degenerated into a much-ballyhooed but
unexciting and predictable spectacle. Stone feels that the trend toward
display is unhealthy. He would probably agree with Lewis Mumford:

Sport, which began originally, perhaps, as a spontaneous reaction against the machine, has become one of the mass duties of the machine age. It is part of that universal regimentation of life— for the sake of private profit or nationalistic exploit—from which its excitement provides a temporary and only a superficial release. Sport has turned out, in short, to be one of the least effective reactions against the machine. (1934, pp. 303–305, 307)

Spectatoritis has not taken over completely. "In the first forty years of the twentieth century," says Dulles, "there was a far greater increase in the number who played than in those who watched" (1940, p. 349). The early years of the century brought a progressive movement, from Theodore Roosevelt to Woodrow Wilson, that shifted some of the benefits of industrialism from the few to the masses. A part of this was the development of city parks and playgrounds. Religious organizations, schools, and ethnic athletic clubs promoted games for youth as an antidote to crime and delinquency. There was another surge in opportunities for participant play during the 1920s. The automobile took people to urban and suburban recreational facilities and national parks. Under the New Deal of the Depression years, the federal Works Progress Administration (WPA) spent half a billion dollars constructing 3,700 recreational buildings, 881 parks, 1,500 athletic fields, 440 swimming pools, 3,500 tennis courts, 123 golf courses, and 28 miles of ski trails. In 1940 Dulles estimated that the number of people swimming annually at municipal beaches and pools (200 million) was almost as large as the total yearly attendance at all spectator sports (1940, p. 349). An observation in the 1950s by social historian Frederick Lewis Allen suggests the democratization of a traditionally elite sport: "A street was being torn up for repairs and while the workmen were standing waiting for the arrival of new equipment, one of them, who had in his hands an iron rod presumably used for prying off manhole covers, was enjoying a little relaxation. I looked twice to see what he was doing with that rod. He was practising a graceful golf stroke" (1950, p. 159). After the 1954 study by Hans Kraus showing American children trailing Europeans shockingly in basic physical skills (Kraus & Hirschland, 1954), there was a wide surge of concern for physical fitness. Jogging was one of the outcomes. A 1978 survey of TV sport viewers by Opinion Research Corporation showed that three fourths had played organized sports at some time in their lives, and nine tenths had engaged in unorganized sports (*TV Guide*, Aug. 19, 1978, p. 3). Other surveys reported in the late 1970s showed 60 million roller skaters, 30 million tennis players, 14 million skiers, a million or more gymnasts, 22 million bowlers, 15 million bicyclists, 20 million joggers, and 40 million walking for exercise (Eldridge, 1978).

Modern sport embraces three classes of participants: the genuine amateur, the formal amateur, and the frank professional. It arose, as we have seen, from two sources—the stylized activity of the leisure classes and the occasional unbuttoned play of the laboring class which, as Paul Hoch says, was "most of the time worked so brutally that it simply would not have had the time or energy to engage in sports activity" (1972, p. 32). With the rise of the leisure masses we continued to have some people, rich and poor, doing their own thing for fun (genuine amateurs). We also developed a class of specialists who played for the entertainment of others. In addition there arose a group of people who were nominally amateurs but actually were unpaid or underpaid professionals. This included the players of the gentlemen's sports like tennis and golf, the college athlete, and Olympic performers and aspirants. Stone points out some important and paradoxical facts about these three groups. The sports that are played are professional (baseball, football, hockey, tennis, golf). Precisely those sports that are "played" have become work in America. Here is the matrix of professional athletics. The sports that are amateur (hunting, fishing, archery, bowling, skiing, yachting) are not "played" and are not work. They are mostly upper-class pastimes with the exception of bowling, which is mainly lower class. Summarizing the paradoxical situation, Stone says, "In the United States, sports that were once work are never played, but these engage the "players"—the amateurs. Sports that were never work are always played, and these engage the workers—the professionals" (Talamini & Page, 1973, p. 72). The formally amateur sports—intercollegiate athletics and the gentlemen's games—are mainly feeders for frank professionalism.

The Japanese sociologist Sadao Morikawa has analyzed systematically the self-contradiction of amateur sport:

First of all, amateur sport can exist only by relying upon the results of other people's labor, because it cannot be used as means for earning one's livelihood. . . .

Secondly, the emphasis on amateur sport gives rise to a contradiction that works against (its) development . . . because of the difficulty in combining sports life and work to earn a livelihood.

This contradiction, thirdly, creates a tendency that amateur athletes either abandon amateur sport or turn into professionals.

Fourthly, under such circumstances, the efforts to maintain amateur sport strengthen the "parasitic" character of amateur sport. . . . (We can easily understand this phenomenon by observing the present conditions of the so-called amateur sportsmen belonging to companies and universities.)

Fifthly, universal characteristics of modern sport promote the popularization of sport, but for the working people who are lack-

ing in physical and economic conditions, amateur sport transforms itself into the sport to "be seen." Consequently, the growing popularity of amateur sport paves the way to professional sport.

Sixthly, the unbalanced development and dual structure of sport . . . brings about too much emphasis on rewards and victory on the one hand, while prize money and reward as its compensation become a problem. This narrows the distinction between amateur and professional sport, bringing the crisis of the existence of amateurism to the surface. (1977, pp. 64–65)

As a business, professional sport exercises an influence far beyond its actual size. All of the people employed in amusement, recreation, and related services in 1960 made up eight tenths of 1% of the whole labor force. In 1964 only one worker in 10,000 was a professional athlete. Roger Noll, a Brookings Institution economist who is sometimes called the Ralph Nader of the sports industry, says that professional sports is about half the size of the canned soup industry. Senator Sam Ervin, in Senate hearings on the industry, said that it is about equal in size to pork and beans. Harry Edwards calculates that in 1970 there were 500 industrial corporations, each of which had gross sales greater than all 24 major league baseball clubs combined (1973, p. 277). Paul Hoch, who stresses the domination of sport by the power elite, estimates the total American sports budget at $25 billion a year (which is only about 2% of the gross national product). (Hoch, 1972, p. 48)

Yet we would be way off base if we took these cold statistics as a measure of the importance of sport on the American scene. About a third of the population of the United States (63 million) saw one game of the 1971 World Series on television and a third (65 million) again saw the 1972 Super Bowl Game. "Intercollegiate athletics," said George Hanford, Senior Vice President of the College Board, in 1979, "are big business." He continued with the following statistics:

Five years ago it was estimated that inter-collegiate athletics consumed about 1% of the [$30 billion] budget for higher education in the United States. That came to $300 million or so, at a time when $3 million was a high sports budget. Today, with the budgets for athletic programs at some institutions approaching $5 million, the intercollegiate athletic enterprise could be approaching the half billion dollar mark. (1979, p. 73)

These figures bring us closer to the remarkable proportion of space the 1971 *New York Times Encyclopedic Almanac* gave to sport among other American activities: religion, 21 pages; science, 18 pages; education, 27 pages; medicine and public health, 21 pages; foreign affairs and national security, 37 pages; *and sport, 93 pages* (Talamini & Page, 1973, p. 4).

Sport trains youth for a competitive society. Introducing a research project investigating the development in sport of attitudes central to the achievement culture, sociologist Harry Webb says:

> In the transition from communal-agrarian to urban-industrialized society, "achievement" criteria are presumed to replace "ascription" ones as a basis for the allocation of positions and the distribution of rewards. The urban-industrialized society, based as it is on technological knowledge and a consequent division of labor, presumably requires a distribution of roles, at least in the economic and political institutions, based on qualifications of training and ability, and not necessarily on family background. "To the swift goes the prize," goes the saying indicating not only the constant connection between sport values and those of the economy, but the emphasis on individual differences in ability, training, and desire, and their consequences for influencing excellence presumably rewarded in a free competitive atmosphere. (1969, p. 161)

In the ideology of the achievement culture, says Webb, there is a "trinity of values"—equity, skill, and victory (fair play, doing your best, and winning). Sport reflects and reinforces these general cultural values. The three are given different emphasis by different people in different situations. Webb's problem was, How, in attitudes toward sport, are these three values rated in importance at different stages of a person's growing up from jacks to linebacker?

In 1967 Webb was able to ask 920 public school and 354 parochial school pupils in grades 3, 6, 8, 10, and 12 in Battle Creek, Michigan, to rate the importance of these three values in sport. The question, as asked to grades 8, 10, and 12, was this:

> What do you think is most important in playing a game?
> Number the items below from 1 to 3, starting with the one you think is MOST important (1) and finishing with the one you think is LEAST important (3)
> _____ to play as well as you are able
> _____ to beat your opponent
> _____ to play it fairly (1969, p. 166).

A simpler form was employed for grades 3 and 6.

There are six different ways in which the three values (hereafter abbreviated play [skillfully], beat, and fair) can be ranked. Webb scored the six combinations on a continuum from play to professionalism. Figure 6.2 is an adaptation of Webb's ranking. You can see that as we move from left to right, from 1 to 6, play orientation to professional orientation, fair (equity) becomes less important and play well (skill) and best (winning) becomes more important.

	Rank Orders						
	1. Fair	1. Fair	1. Play	1. Play	1. Beat	1. Beat	
Play	2. Play	2. Beat	2. Fair	2. Beat	2. Fair	2. Play	Professional
Orientation	3. Beat	3. Play	3. Beat	3. Fair	3. Play	3. Fair	Orientation
	1	2	3	4	5	6	

Degree of Professionalism

Figure 6.2   Play-Professional Continuum. *Note.*   Adapted from ''Professionalization of Attitudes Toward Play Among Adolescents'' by H. Webb in *Aspects of Contemporary Sport Sociology* (p. 166, Table 1) by G.S. Kenyon (Ed.), 1969, Chicago: Athletic Institute. Copyright 1969 by the Athletic Institute. Reprinted by permission.

What we find, in general, is that as children grow older, from grade 3 through high school, fairness loses in importance and skill and winning take its place. The play orientation, with emphasis on fairness, is strongest in sixth grade (age 11), which is about where Piaget found the morality of reciprocity (cooperation) entering. But in Webb's study, it does not continue. From sixth to eighth grade (age 11-13) is the time at which professionalism enters in. Webb suggests that this is the time when the child moves from the elementary school, which is typically a neighborhood school, to the more impersonal junior high school, from a single classroom situation to a succession of rooms for different subjects. In the child's play and other life of the neighborhood, admission to participation was based on such qualities as likability, neighborhood residence, and so forth. In the more impersonal environment of the junior high school, one is rated less according to who he or she is as a whole individual person and more according to observable achievement—ability to perform skillfully and compete successfully. At this point the child is moving out of the communal situation in which he or she grew up and into the achievement society in which he or she will spend the rest of life. Play and sport are a model of the outside rat race and are so presented by coaches and fans. Also, because age keeps the child or adolescent from winning his or her mark in the adult world, sport is the one area where his or her skill can be competitively rewarded. (Here I am expanding points that Webb discusses.)

Differences between girls and boys tell us more about sport in the achieving culture and about the roles of the sexes in that culture. From 6th to 10th grade both sexes become more professionally oriented (emphasis on playing skillfully and winning). In the last two high-school years, however, the girls move away from the skill-win orientation. The big factor in this seems to be the drop in the ''beat'' emphasis.

Another difference that appears in Webb's research is between Protestants and Catholics. Until the eighth grade Protestants placed more emphasis on winning than do Catholics, but from then on Catholics rated it higher. By 12th grade, Catholic boys *and girls* ranked fairness lower than did both Protestant groups. Historically, the achievement ethic was originally Protestant, as described in Weber's *The Protestant Ethic and the Spirit of Capitalism* (1958). McClelland has impressively demonstrated that Protestant countries are more economically advanced than Catholic countries (see Table 6.1). Why, then, are the Catholic kids more Protestant than the Protestants? Webb thinks that it is because they are a minority. At about the eighth grade, when boys and girls settle down to what their respective roles are to be, there also comes the moment of truth at which Catholic youths realize that they are going to have to mobilize all their skills to survive or get ahead in a predominantly WASP culture.

In conclusion, Webb says this:

Sport and economic structure are related not only on the basis of shared values, but sport experience additionally makes an important contribution . . . by providing a basis for attitudes and beliefs appropriate to adult participation in politics as well as the economy. . . . This investigation demonstrates that participation in the play world is substantially influential in producing that final result, the urban-industrial man. (1969, pp. 163, 177)

Somewhat later, Brian Petrie (1977) used Webb's play-professionalism scale with 306 males and 318 females who represented American citizen undergraduates at Michigan State University. Petrie found males, as we would expect, rating skill and competition as values of sport much higher than did females, who were more interested in social interaction, fun, and aesthetic pleasure. But he found neither college group showing results on the play-professionalism scale reported by Webb at the high-school level. "It became apparent that both the male and female respondents were more strongly committed to the play, rather than the professional orientation, than had been the case among the children in the upper levels of high school studied by Webb. Specifically, 87.8% of the Michigan State men and 98.4% of the women had the play orientation" (Petrie, 1977, p. 96).

In a study of attitudes toward winning among young Canadian hockey players, Edward Vaz found results that were also different from Webb's. About his hypothesis and his findings Vaz says,

In an earlier paper we wrote, ". . . at the higher team levels the value of success, i.e., winning the game, rapidly takes precedence over other considerations among coaches and managers as well

as players.'' However our research findings do not substantiate this statement. . . . In general, the importance of winning to the players decreases noticeably as one advances from the lowest (youngest) to the highest level teams. (Vaz, 1973, p. 40)

Both the Petrie and Vaz studies seem to show that as one matures agewise and sportwise Webb's findings with school children tend to be reversed.

Sport is intimately related to social stratification and social mobility. For one thing, athletics has been a way for minority group members to get up in the world. The idea that first interested me in the sociology of sport was the 1948 analysis by George Saxon of young men of southern and eastern European extraction who used athletics to escape the coal mines and steel mills of the Monongahela Valley (1953). David Riesman and Reuel Denney (1951) have traced the democratization of American football. Before 1890, All-America teams were almost entirely Anglo-Saxon. Gradually the German, Irish, Jews, and Poles began to break in. By 1927, names like Casey, Kipke, Oosterbaan, Koppisch, Garbisch, and Friedman were appearing with as much frequency as names like Channing, Adams, and Ames in the 1890s. My 1937 college team, with which I started chapter 4, was still about 90% WASP. Since the Riesman-Denney and Saxon studies, the whole All-America picture has been changed by the rising prominence of black athletes. How prominent blacks have become is indicated by the fact that in 1979, whereas blacks made up only 1 1/2% of college enrollments, they received 6% of athletic grant money.

However, opportunity is for only a minority. For every Joe Namath rising to fame from Beaver Falls, Pennsylvania, Jack Scott suggests, there are hundreds of ex-athletes drowning their faded hopes in the taverns of the Monongahela Valley. Dr. Roscoe Brown of the New York University Institute of Afro-American Affairs says, ''Black youngsters pour too much time and energy into sports. They're deluded and seduced by the athletic flesh peddlers, used for public amusement—and discarded'' (1975, p. 85).

Also, at the same time that new ethnic groups have entered the lower echelons of sport, control has continuously passed to a minority with capital. Professional baseball teams were first run by the players. But then financial promoters took over. College athletics were also first run by the athletes. But early in the 20th century control passed to professional coaches, athletic administration, and alumni.

A dramatic statistical illustration of how money speaks in professional sport is the history of the Boston Red Sox after they were taken over by millionaire Tom Yawkey. In my boyhood, the Red Sox were habitually eighth in an eight-team league. Then this happened, as reported by two economists: From 1922 to 1932, before Yawkey, the

Sox had a winning average of .359, and their average place in the eight-team league was 7.66. From 1933 to 1970, after Yawkey, their winning average was .522, their average place-finish 4.39 (Quirk & El Hodiri, 1974, p. 42n).

The concentration of control in sport is enhanced by what economist Walter Nolte has called its peculiar economics. Organized management has generally fought labor organization by glorifying the right of the worker to bargain freely as an individual (as in so-called right to work laws), but in organized sport neither collective bargaining nor free individual bargaining is really legitimate.

As Gary Shaw implied in the title of his book on Texas football, the athlete in our culture is meat on the hoof, a piece of property. The capitalist society, in theory, is a system in which one sells his assets, including his labor power, on a competitive market to the highest bidder. But organized sport has not been this kind of competitive market. Rather than competing freely for athletic labor power, the businessmen in the different sports have combined to establish procedures that prevent free competition for players. One such procedure is the draft, whereby prospective professionals are assigned to teams. Another is the reserve clause, which binds an athlete, once he signs a professional contract, to play for his team until he retires or his services are traded or sold to another team.

The reserve clause, in one form or another, has been the basis for all major professional sport in the United States. As early as 1922, in the case of the upstart Federal baseball league, such restriction of competition was attacked as a violation of the Sherman Antitrust Act. The Federal league charged the American and National leagues with moving into Federal league towns and buying up teams so as to kill off competition. Players Gardella in the 1940s, Toolson in 1953, and Flood in 1971 charged the major baseball leagues with conspiracy in restraint of trade. In 1962 the American Football league sued the National Football League for monopolizing the player pool. But in 1966 both leagues saw the advantage of combining and secured a special act of Congress protecting them against possible antitrust suits. In 1971 the National Basketball Association and the American Basketball Association tried to do the same thing, but players got a special Senate hearing and finally won damages in court for the harm done them by the reserve clause. These basketball players, football player Yazoo Smith in 1968, and baseball pitcher Andy Messersmith in 1975 were instrumental in breaking down the reserve clause and leaving players free, under stipulated conditions, to sell their services as free agents to the highest bidder. So, about 60 years after the Federal league suit, 30 years after Danny Gardella's challenge of commissioner Happy Chandler, and a decade after Curt Flood's historic suit, jocks have succeeded in bringing a measure of free competition into the athletic marketplace. A free agent is not meat on the hoof, but those athletes who cannot qualify still remain subject to drafts and reserve clauses.

Restriction of competition is not limited to frankly professional sport. The administrative limitations by the NCAA on athlete recruitment, says Bil Gilbert, "are essentially for the benefit of NCAA members, not the athlete. Substantially, they are monopolistic in intent, designed to minimize competition for the services of athletes. It is a 'restraint of trade' arrangement" (1974, p. 124). Gilbert says that if the NCAA were serious about abuses in recruiting athletes, perhaps the simplest answer would be to "abolish all the restraining regulations, and permit schools to select athletes on a highest-bidder basis." He thinks that such free enterprise would leave only a few schools able to hire athletes and force the rest to use student walk-ons.

The status of the athlete as property is dramatically reflected in the fact that his or her value can be depreciated by an employer for tax purposes. An individual or corporation with property that loses value over time can deduct in any year the value lost by that property in that year. Bill Veeck (1965) cites the case of the transfer of the Milwaukee Braves to Atlanta as an example of how depreciation works. The cost of the Braves to their new owners was $6 million, of which $50,000 was the price of the franchise. The rest, more than 99%, was the value of the players held as property. Assuming that they had an average life of 10 years in baseball (an optimistic assumption), the owners could claim $600,000 depreciation annually over a 10-year period. If the club made money, this could reduce its taxable net earnings. If it did not earn money, the depreciation could be used to reduce taxable net earnings from any other enterprises owned by the management. Veeck says that when one buys an athletic team, what he buys is essentially *the right to depreciate.* Clearly, one can depreciate only property that he owns, not the services of freely contracting persons.

The position of the run-of-the-mill professional athlete is still that of a property in the entertainment business where one is usually, as Phil Donahue put it in citing his own history, at the arbitrary power of people who can terminate you with a pregnant wife and an overdue car payment on a whim that comes to them while shaving (*Today Show*, February 29, 1980).

Another aspect that counteracts democracy in sport is the fact, pointed out by Stone, that the occupational structure of sport is an inverted pyramid, narrower at its base than at the top. "Those engaged first hand in the production of the . . . game or the match constitute a minority within the industrial complex, while those engaged in the administration, promotion, and servicing of the production constitute a sizeable majority" (1973, p. 69). This inverted pyramid is similar to the situation on college campuses: A major complaint of organized university teachers is the way in which the upper administrative levels have expanded at the expense of the teaching base.

Finally, the structure of organized athletics may not only raise false hopes of climbing to affluence and glory, it may also positively keep down young people who might climb the ladder. In an interview about why he quit football, former all-pro wide receiver George Sauer suggests that the concentration of energy and attention on a sport career that is encouraged by athletic scholarships may actually narrow the opportunity of young athletes of working class origin by putting all their eggs in the basket of athletic ambition (Scott & Sauer, 1971). Thus a bright and athletically gifted student who could become a doctor, lawyer, businessman, or scientist may be prevented by his athletic scholarship from really exploring these possibilities. "If you are black and can play some ball," says Harry Edwards, "your chances are infinitely greater of gaining access to a college education than if you have only limited athletic ability, but have the potential for a significant intellectual contribution to society" (1979, p. 122). Our elementary and secondary schools have been criticized for tracking working-class students into repeating the careers of their parents, whereas their middle- and upper-class peers are tracked into college preparatory programs. Athletic scholarships may continue this tracking on the college and university level.

We shall explore the whole relationship of sport to social stratification at greater length in chapters 10 and 11.

Chapter 7

Sport in the Soviet Union

In chapter 1, I suggested that in the Communist world, especially the Soviet Union and China, we find the same struggle in sport between the old culture and the counterculture that surfaced in the United States in the 1960s. Both nations, following Marxist sociology, view sport as a weapon in the struggle of classes—an instrument of exploitation before the revolution, an instrument of mass development afterward. In both, capitalist sport is seen as a degenerate example of greedy competitiveness in which athletes are used for profit and to provide shows that divert the masses of people from realizing their misery under capitalism. Communist sport, on the other hand, they see as an instrument to develop mass health for better production and defense of the nation. However, in different forms sport in both Communist countries has shown the same conflict between the psychology of winning and the psychology of popular physical development and self-realization that we find in the United States. In this chapter and the next we shall look at how this conflict has worked itself out, first in the U.S.S.R. and then in the China of Mao Tse-tung and his successors.

In his introduction to Henry W. Morton's classic work *Soviet Sport*, Michael Florinsky compares sport in the capitalist and Soviet worlds:

> *In the West, sport has been tinged with commercialism and in fact is at times big business. There are no identical developments in the Soviet Union, but the harnessing of athletes in the service of Communist politics has produced a similar and probably even more dreary form of professionalism. . . . The Soviet authoritarian system has advantages over the West in making the most effective use of native star performers, but there is no evidence that the Kremlin is equally successful in teaching the average youth the subtle art of "playing the game" which is the real object of organized sports. (Morton, 1963, p. 11)*

To understand the organization of Soviet sport, we must relate it to the political and economic situation in the Soviet Union since 1917 and to the ideology of Marxism. The 1917 revolution overthrew an authoritarian regime in which all institutions, including family, school, and church, supported the autocratic rule of the tsar and the nobility that surrounded him. During the 10 years following the revolution (until about 1930) the new Communist government tried to modernize a peasant nation and at the same time to promote revolution around the globe. During this period the U.S.S.R. was ostracized by the rest of the world and in fact was invaded by Western forces. The U.S.S.R. was not diplomatically recognized by the United States until 1934. Following this (about 1930–41), under Stalin, the U.S.S.R. tried to build socialism in one country through comprehensive 5-year plans of forced industrialization. In World War II (1941–45) the Soviet Union was invaded by the Nazis, with massive loss of property and life. After the war, her forced industrialization paid off as the Soviet Union reached the age of high mass consumption, with consumer goods and leisure beyond any previously known. During this last period, the U.S.S.R. has lived in a state of Cold War, modified by a decade of detente, in which she has striven to promote her way of life in competition with the capitalist world.

Performing on the balance beam, Olga Korbut of the U.S.S.R. finishes a backward somersault during an exhibition by the U.S.S.R. Women's Olympic gymnastics team. Korbut won three gold medals and a silver medal during the Munich Olympics. World Wide Photos.

Ideology

In the Marxist ideology, all social institutions are seen as part of a struggle of classes. After human beings had lived for 1 to 3 million years in the primitive communism of hunting and gathering peoples, for whom the rewards of the hunt and search for food were distributed almost equally (see chapter 4), there came an agricultural revolution that gave rise, about 10,000 years ago, to the domination of the majority of the people by a ruling-class minority. The most recent minority has been the capitalist class, which was displaced in Russia by the 1917 revolution. Marxists hold that all social institutions, including family, religion, education, *and sport*, have supported the interests of ruling classes. For example, mass spectator sports under capitalism are regarded as an opiate that, like religion, dulls people to their exploitation. Contact sports are seen as training the masses for war. The great writer Maxim Gorky summarized the Marxist view in this way in *Pravda* in 1928: "Bourgeois sport has a single clear-cut purpose: to make men even more stupid than they are. . . . In bourgeois states, sport is employed to produce cannon fodder for imperialist wars." Soviet sport, on the contrary, is looked upon as part of the revolution that replaces class domination. Its function is to keep the mass of Soviet citizens healthy and ready for labor and defense of the revolution (*massovost*, mass participation). Secondarily, it produces skilled athletes who can compete with the capitalist world in international sporting events (*masterstvo*, mastery).

Tsarist Sport

Soviet sports had their origin under tsarism. Before the revolution, winter sports, aquatic sports, cycling, fencing, and riding were enjoyed. Wrestling, boxing, weightlifting, and gymnastics had some popularity. In 1889 a Russian won the world speed skating championship. A Russian team (totally male) participated in the 1912 Olympic Games. The traditionally upper-class sport of tennis was popular; in 1913 there were 115 lawn tennis courts in Moscow and St. Petersburg.

In the British tradition, sport activity was for the upper and middle classes. James Riordan, a British authority on Soviet sport, suggests that sport among the common people was not encouraged because if they could have organized and played their own games the tsarist regime would have been threatened. He quotes a British diplomat who saw the connection between sport and politics. Before the revolution, soccer (now the most popular Soviet sport) was introduced by British residents. Alluding to the traditional saying that Britain's wars were won on the playing fields of the upper-class public schools this diplomat suggested that "had British entrepreneurs been able to spread the passion for playing soccer more quickly in Russia, the Whites [pro-tsarist forces] might have won on the playing fields of Moscow what they lost in the Reading Room of the British Museum [where Karl Marx wrote *Das Kapital*]" (Riordan, 1977, p. 40).

Early Soviet Sport

Sport in the Soviet Union today can be seen as a pyramid (see Figure 7.1) in which a base of physical culture and training for the masses (*massovost*) supports a pinnacle of elite and actually professional international sport (*masterstvo*). It has not always been so. Until World War II the U.S.S.R. participated in no international sport organizations. Their isolation from the capitalist world was symbolized when at Helsinki in 1952 Soviet athletes participated in their first Olympics, living behind barbed wire fences (at Rome in 1956 they joined the Olympic Village). In the first years after the 1917 revolution, emphasis was on the *massovost* (mass physical culture) aspect.

Lenin's view of sport was similar to that of the British upper-class schools—character building. It should be integrated with a variety of intellectual interests, study, and investigation. The immediate goal of *massovost*, in a rapidly industrializing country surrounded by enemies, was efficiency in work and military preparedness. Riordan believes that the young Soviet regime so easily adopted the bourgeois ideas of a sound mind in a sound body because they were consistent with socialist ideology and, more significantly, because they were needed to prepare a peasant population to build an industrial society.

The *masterstvo* aspect, sport competition, was looked down on during the 1920s as a form of capitalist decadence. According to Riordan, in the 1920s the Young Communists' criticism of sports sounded like the Puritans. In 1927 it was complained that "in a number of trade union sports organizations . . . all attention is now being concentrated on a leading group of athletes who show top-class results: the physical education of the vast mass of young people is becoming secondary" (Riordan, 1977, p. 92). In 1929 the Central Committee of the Communist Party deplored an overemphasis on setting records.

However, in the 1930s Stalin, having disposed of Trotsky's idea of world revolution, began building socialism in one country, and sport became an important aspect. It became important for Russia to catch up with the capitalist world, both industrially and with regard to sport. In 1935 the sport newspaper *Krasnyisport* urged, ''Young physical culturists! Remember that from you must come our new Masters of Sport who will surpass bourgeois sports records and will raise the banner of Soviet physical culture to new unprecedented heights.'' All this was very important for a country that was moving peasants to the city and regimenting them into industrial 5-year plans. What Morton says of industrializing societies began to be true for the Soviet Union in the 1930s:

Mass sport and organized competition in clubs, societies, leagues are an important by-product of modern industrial society. Urbanization, increase in population; technological advancement, leisure time; modern transportation, making interarea and international competition possible; modern communication, television, the sport page, improved equipment and sport structures—all have contributed toward focusing millions of eyes upon sport arenas large and small. (Morton, 1963, p. 26)

Sport in the Stalinist and post-Stalinist days served a number of functions. U.S.S.R.-wide events like the Spartakiads (named after a revolutionary Roman gladiator) brought a sense of unity to the multitude of nationalities. Also the successful sportsman, like the Stakhanovites who set high norms in industry, was a successful model for rank-and-file workers. Identification with athletes gave a vicarious sense of achievement. No doubt many a Russian could say with Khrushchev ''Whenever a [soccer] player kicks the ball, it is Khrushchev who kicks it, and whenever a player gets kicked in the shins, it is Khrushchev who gets kicked'' (Morton, 1963, p. 17).

Riordan suggests another function that, strangely, comes close to the Marxian view of sport as an opiate of the people. He sees the big sport spectacles in the Russian cities in the 1930s as serving, like the Grecian Olympic games, the Roman circuses, and bullfights in the modern Hispanic world, to distract the masses from the hard realities of everyday life. Another function was indicated by the dissident Dr. Matveyev, former medical advisor to the All-Union Physical Culture Council, writing from a labor camp in 1954:

The average Russian thinks, ''If Dinamo [the most famous sport society] can beat a French team, obviously the French have even less bread and meat than we do.'' This is exactly what the Soviets want the people to think, as a sort of gratification for their hunger and a consolation for the evils of the system. (Ekart, 1954, p. 207)

Up to Number One

World War II, in which the Soviet Union was involved from 1941 to 1945, had several results for the development of sport. Along with destruction of other physical property, which it was estimated set industrialization back by two 5-year plans, sport facilities suffered tremendous destruction just at a time when they were beginning to catch up with the rest of the world. A comparison between sport facilities in 1940 and in 1945 is made in Table 7.1. Furthermore, the usefulness, to soldiers at the front and partisans behind enemy lines, of sport and physical culture training in grenade throwing, combat sports, running, hurdling, skiing, and shooting convinced people of the practical social significance of the *massovost* program. Moreover, in a situation in which nearly everybody had lost a close relative, sporting events with prizes dedicated to the memory of war heroes had a powerful drawing power. Finally, victory in the war spurred the people and gave them confidence that they could take on the world in sport as well. On top of all these developments, it is not surprising that in 1948 the Communist Central Committee reversed its 1929 position and decided "to spread physical culture and sport to every corner of the land and to raise the level of skill, so that Soviet sportsmen might win world supremacy in the major sports in the immediate future" (Riordan, 1977, p. 165). As Morton put it, "the record mania, denounced by the Party in the resolution of 1929, was loudly trumpeted as the guiding party line in sport" (1963, p. 37).

By the beginning of the Cold War the emphasis had shifted from *massovost* to *mastervsto*—or mass physical culture continued to exist primarily as the basis for competitive sport. After the party line shifted in 1934, "it took the Russians just eighteen years of concentrated effort

Table 7.1 Sports Facilities During the War

Facility	1940	1945
Sports centers	7,858	6,401
Gymnasiums	6,684	4,694
Soccer pitches	9,172	3,741
Volleyball courts	25,137	23,725
Basketball courts	5,439	2,744
Tennis courts	1,270	272

Note. From *Sport in Soviet Society* (p. 158, Table 3) by J. Riordan, 1977, Cambridge: Cambridge University Press. Copyright 1977 by J. Riordan. Reprinted by permission.

to achieve world prominence—despite the interference of the Great Purge, a devastating war, and downright inefficiency'' (Morton, 1963, p. 36).

In 1948 the U.S.S.R. held 18 world records, compared to 56 for the United States. Although invited, the Soviets skipped the 1948 Olympics because, as these figures indicated, they could not expect at that time to sweep the Olympics as propaganda required that a superior Communist country should. In the 1952 Olympics at Helsinki the U.S.S.R. took 22 gold medals, compared to 41 for the United States; in 1956 at Rome it was U.S.S.R. 37, United States 32; and at Melbourne in 1960 the Soviets led by 43 to 34. In 1959 the U.S.S.R. held 81 world records, the United States 52. In terms of the point-scoring system used in the *Olympic Bulletin,* the U.S.S.R. was first in all Olympic Games, summer and winter, from 1952 through 1976, except in 1968, when it was second in both (Riordan, 1977, Table 21, p. 368).

All this sport development was related to the growth of consumption and leisure. Whereas the U.S.S.R. had been 11% urban in 1870 and 18% in 1913 and 1926, by 1958 half the population lived in cities, and in 1976 over 60% did. Although far behind those of Western countries, consumer standards rose significantly, as did leisure. Urbanization contributed to mass involvement on the part of both participants and spectators (to both *massovost* and *masterstvo*). In 1965 a 5-day week was introduced. This gave rise to weekenditis and tourism, much as in the Western world, especially for elites. By the 1970s it was the norm for city dwellers to live within 5 to 20 minutes of an athletic complex that provided for gymnastics, basketball, table tennis, volleyball, and figure skating. All this in spite of a 1970 criticism that ''the Soviets as a rule act as passive onlookers instead of following a concerted policy in building sports facilities corresponding to the needs of town planning'' (cited in Riordan, 1977, p. 195n); and of the fact that by the mid-1970s studies showed that the most time-consuming leisure activity in the U.S.S.R. was television watching.

The conflict between ideal and reality is indicated by comparing a 1972 statement by Brezhnev with a statement in the same year by two Soviet sport sociologists:

But free time can only be considered genuine public wealth when it is used in the interests of the all-round development of the individual, of his capabilities, and thereby, for an ever greater increase in the material and spiritual potential of our society. (Brezhnev, cited in Riordan, 1977, p. 197)

Eighty percent of the manual workers and 70 percent of the employees revealed that they have absolutely nothing to do with physical culture and sport. Even among young people, not more *than 10 percent take a regular and active part in sports. (L. A. Gordon & N. M. Rimashevskaya, 1972, cited in Riordan, 1977, p. 232).*

Riordan suggests that this lack of interest may be due to the tendency to focus attention on stars and to ignore less talented performers. Americans will see a parallel here.

Massovost and Masterstvo

Let us look now at the system of sport that has developed in the Soviet Union over the past 70 years. As a starting point let's take Figure 7.1 and spell out the details of the pyramidal structure that it shows. After this we can examine the role and status of the athlete in Soviet society, looking for comparisons with athletes in capitalist countries. We can look here at how sport is related to the position of women in the U.S.S.R. Then it will be appropriate for us to explore how sport is differently received in urban and rural areas and the place it plays in a country made up of many diverse nationalities. We can then observe the part played by sport in relations between the U.S.S.R. and other Communist nations, with Third World countries, and with the United States.

The base of Figure 7.1 is composed of active sportsmen who have engaged in physical exercise or sport under an instructor's supervision at least twice a week for not less than 6 months. In 1975, the official Soviet estimate put the number of these active sportsmen at nearly one third of the population between the ages of 10 and 60 (51 million people). More conservative estimates by Soviet sociologists put the number at about a third of this figure.

What are these active sportsmen doing? The youngest are taking physical education in the schools. Employed workers engage in organized on-the-job calisthenics. Beyond this, there were in the Soviet Union, in the early 1970s, 103,000 soccer fields, 401,000 basketball, volleyball, and tennis courts, 59,000 sport gymnasiums, 1,057 swimming pools, and 3,176 stadiums with a capacity of at least 1,500 each (Shneidman, 1978, p. 51). The range of sports that interest Soviet citizens is indicated indirectly by Table 7.2, which shows the growing variety of international sport involvements during the Cold War era, 1946–73.

For the mass of the Soviet people sport activities are organized mainly through sport collectives at the work site, which compete with other collectives. The biggest and most active collectives are called sport clubs. The collectives are affiliated with 34 voluntary sport societies

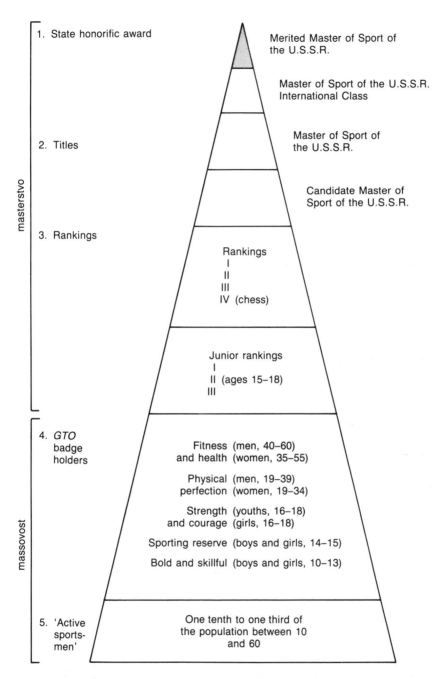

Figure 7.1 The U.S.S.R.'s Sport Pyramid, 1976. *Note.* From *Sport in Soviet Society* (p. 230, Figure 4) by J. Riordan, 1977, Cambridge: Cambridge University Press. Copyright 1977 by J. Riordan. Reprinted by permission.

Table 7.2   Affiliation to International Federations, by Sports: 1946–1973

Year	Sports federations affiliated to in given year	Cumulative total sports affiliated (no.)
1946	Basketball, soccer, skiing, weight lifting	4
1947	Athletics, chess, speed and ice skating, swimming (including diving and water polo), wrestling	9
1948	Gymnastics, volleyball	11
1949	Boxing	12
1951	(Soviet Olympic Committee formed and affiliated to the IOC)	12
1952	Cycling, canoeing, equestrianism, fencing, ice hockey, modern pentathlon and biathlon, pistol shooting, rifle shooting, rowing, yachting	22
1954	Table tennis	23
1955	*Bandy*	24
1956	Draughts, lawn tennis, motorcycle racing, motor racing	28
1958	Gliding, handball	30
1962	Judo, radio sport	32
1965	Subaqua sport	33
1966	Model boatcraft sport	34
1967	Archery, mountaineering, orienteering	37
1969	Motor boat sport	38
1970	Field hockey	39
1971	Tobogganing	40
1973	Trampoline, rugby	42

Note. From *Sport in Soviet Society* (p. 365, Table 19) by J. Riordan, 1977, Cambridge: Cambridge University Press. Copyright 1977 by J. Riordan. Reprinted by permission.

that are in turn affiliated with labor unions. The security police and technical students also have voluntary sport societies and clubs.

The next level of sportpersons above the base (Level 4 of Figure 7.1) is holders of GTO badges (GTO is the Soviet acronym for Ready for Labor and Defense). The GTO skills that qualify for badges are in such activities as cross-country skiing, obstacle climbing, gliding, parachuting, grenade throwing, and rifle shooting. Teaching of these begins in the schools.

As we move up into the *masterstvo* level, especially the upper eche-lons, we are dealing with semiprofessional athletes attending techni-cal sport institutes or attached to Dinamo (the sport society of the security forces), the Central Army Sport Club, or one of the union sport clubs. They are systematically recruited from the population base through specialized sport schools. Some of these take place after regular academic school hours, in cases in which students are involved. Some of them are boarding schools. A recent development has been the or-ganization in the ordinary academic schools of specialist classes of stu-dents in a particular sport who work together both athletically and academically (Jefferies, 1984, pp. 172–174). In 1983 there were 6,700 sport schools in the Soviet Union, with an attendance of from 4 to 6 million youngsters (*Sovietsky Sport*, September 1, 1983) who were pur-suing the rankings, titles, and honorific awards shown in the three top layers of the pyramid. Occasionally the workers' collectives, in ad-dition to keeping workers and their families in shape, produce an ath-lete of championship caliber, but this happens rarely. The sport schools are the main road up (Jefferies, 1984, pp. 184–185n).

The international-level athlete at the top of the pyramid is a very privileged person. Let us begin with two specific cases. The first is re-lated by Zhores Medvedev, a famous Soviet dissident. Relating how he was denied permission to lecture abroad on his specialty of geron-tology, Medvedev compared the experience of an athlete:

> *I knew of a case of a soccer player who was suddenly required for an international match and was summoned and rushed by air from the resort where he was on holiday, approved by all depart-ments, including the visa section, delivered from Moscow to En-gland, driven straight from the airport to the stadium, and all this within twenty-four hours. . . . But this, of course, was a special case; soccer, the sport glamor, the prestige! It was not a lecture on gerontology. (1971, pp. 160–161)*

The second example is the great hockey goalie Vladislaw Tretiak, who established himself as one of a kind when the Soviet team routed the National Hockey League All Stars. In a *Sports Illustrated* profile writ-ten when Tretiak was considering playing in the NHL, E. M. Swift (1983) described Tretiak as playing for the Central Army Club of Moscow, which can attract the country's finest athletes by the promise of a life career as an army officer. Tretiak, then a major, was also a member of the Central Committee of the Komsomols (Young Com-munist League). Like other Army Club players, he was paid $300–400 a month, twice the salary of the average citizen, plus bonuses for in-ternational championships, Olympic medals, etc. In a country where cars are almost a rarity, Tretiak drove a new Volga, shopped at stores that have clothing, meat, and dairy products unavailable to the ordinary Russian, and owned a two-story *dacha* outside the city. As a star in the most popular Soviet winter sport, Tretiak is a strong party spokesman and also a powerful role model for youth like the 5,000 youngsters over age 5 in the Army Club's sport programs. His fame has had liabilities, however; Tretiak lamented that although New Year's Eve is the biggest Russian holiday, he had not spent one at home in 15 years. Of the report that he might sign in the NHL, he said, "I am 20 years playing hockey. . . . Also, I am a military man, . . . I cannot dispose of myself as I wish." On this Swift commented, "When I first heard Tretiak say that, I thought he meant he was trapped. I was confusing politics with something bigger. He meant, I believe, that he now belongs to the Russian people" (1983, p. 46). His final decision not to join the Canadiens was predictable.

Generalizing about the top Soviet athlete in 1963, Morton said, "Once 'having arrived,' an athlete will most likely be given a nominal job, be a student, hold a commission in the armed forces or security police, and will be afforded opportunity to compete as often as necessary and [despite the subarctic climate] to practice the year round" (p. 57). An important prerequisite at the top of the *mastervsto* scale is travel. In Alexandr Solzhenitzyn's *The Cancer Ward* a young cancer victim says, "Anyone can be a sportsman. You've only got to train a lot. And it pays! You travel for nothing. You get thirty rubles a day for food and free hotels, and bonuses on top! And think of the places you see! (1971, p. 142). "Poor Asya could boast that she had been to Leningrad and Voronezh, but others can travel to Los Angeles, Montreal, and London" (Riordan, 1977, p. 234). As in the West, being an athlete is a good way to get to the city and avoid farm and industrial work. Although some dissident athletes have been in labor camps, Morton feels that the athlete, compared with other professionals, "is helped to realize his potential with maximum aid and with minimum interference" (1963, p. 57). Thus, he has politically a fairly safe career. Like athletic heroes everywhere, the top Soviet sportsman will have the attention of women, although the party line is that a suggestion that this interests him is "insulting to our athletes, who are aloof from the pursuit of wealth and spectator recognition, which sports leaders of bourgeois countries cultivate intensively" (*Pravda*, August 10, 1956; cited in Morton, 1963).

Riordan discusses one similarity, and one difference, between Russian and American athletes. Russians may spend as many as 10 or 15 years at a sport institute. Riordon recognizes a similarity to the athletic scholarships held by American athletes. There is, he says, an important difference: Many Soviet masters take their academic work seriously, as a way of preparing for life after sport when their brief careers are over. Riordan describes a trip he took in 1971 with a Russian friend, who was an international soccer player, to the athlete's Alma Mater, the Central State Institute of Physical Culture in Moscow. He said it became evident that his friend had really studied there for 5 years. He was told that nobody is allowed to play league soccer unless he has finished 10 years of schooling. Among the subjects listed at the Central State Institute in 1975 in the undergraduate curriculum for teacher-coaches were Sports Coaching, Sports Massage, Theory and Method of Physical Education, History of Sport, Biometrics, Statistics, Human Anatomy, Sports Medicine, Biochemistry, Political Economy, Marxist-Leninist Philosophy, and Scientific Atheism (Riordan, 1977, Appendix V, pp. 416–417).

Whereas there were no women in competitive sport under the tsar, Lenin saw sport as an important way in which women could be brought into public activity, and Soviet sportswomen have been prominent since then, except in the major sport of soccer, where there are no women's teams as a matter of policy. (It will be interesting to see if this exclusion continues now that a World Cup for Women has been initiated.) In Moslem areas of the U.S.S.R. sport has been a deliberate method for liberating women from historic Islamic male domination. In areas like Uzbek, where parents traditionally forbid their daughters to bare their arms and legs, sport is really revolutionary (we can compare American women athletes today with their counterparts in the 1920s or 1890s). As Riordan says, "It is an enormous step forward for girls from Central Asia to reach the top in a sport [like gymnastics] where they wear nothing but a leotard" (1977, p. 320). A Russian author said in 1973, "I would call our first sports women real heroines. They accomplished real feats of valor, in liberating women from the age-old yoke of religion and the feudal order" (cited in Riordan, 1977, p. 320).

Probably because they have been active in industry and the military, Soviet women don't seem to have the fear of losing their femininity that plagues many American athletes. The Soviet press gives equal attention to women's sports. Interestingly, a 1973 poll of *male* sportswriters choosing the Sportsperson of the Year gave the five top places to women. If we look at how the Soviet Union achieved the Olympic supremacy noted earlier, it was the women's teams that topped the balance, as it was in dual meets between the U.S.S.R. and the United States. This is in spite of the fact that the official line holds that females have only 70 to 80% of the performance level of males (a figure that Americans probably wouldn't argue) (*Sovietsky Sport,* January 25, 1973, p. 3) and that a 1972 study showed men giving five times as much time to sport as did women. Married Russian women typically work a job and come home to do housework, of which Russian males do notoriously little. So it is hard to be a sportswoman unless one is single.

Sport and the Multinational Society

In the U.S.S.R., as elsewhere, sport has developed as part of the transition from an agrarian to an urban-industrial society. The political form has been different, but the basic experience has been the same as in the West. It should come as no surprise that the sport pyramid (both *massovost* and *masterstvo*) is more developed in the city. A study by Artemov (1981) showed that about 6% of rural adults, as compared with 28% of urban adults, were regularly engaged in sport. Of students, 12% in the country and 30% in the city were regularly active. Another study of the rural population in one area of the Soviet Union concluded that "physical culture and sport occupy relatively little place in the system of cultural values and social activity in rural areas" (Bonsov, 1981, p. 45). Riordan analyzes the reasons for this rural lag: (a) hard-working peasants disdain extra physical effort; (b) subarctic weather limits sport in the winter as does hard summer work in the fields; (c) many rural areas lack gas, electricity, and transportation as well as physical sport facilities; (d) since Stalin's forced elimination of the independent peasantry (kulaks) in 1949 there has been a general rural opposition to urban ways; (d) sport and physical culture is less organized in the country; and (e) urban sponsorship of rural sport organization—as when sport clubs in the city are required to sponsor a rural sport collective as a requirement of being chartered—triggers rural resistance.

The U.S.S.R. is a multinational state that includes 15 republics stretching across two continents (of which the highly urban republic of Russia is only the most prominent republic). These have a wide variety of ethnic and cultural backgrounds. Riordan points out how, in the earliest days of the Soviet Union, sport was deliberately used as an instrument to create the supernational, Unionwide sense of unity and commitment necessary to motivate the people to make the personal sacrifices necessary to carry through a social revolution. In the 1920s sport festivals were deliberately held in remote areas like Central Asia and the Transcaucasus so as to break down national animosities by bringing these areas into athletic contact with Russia, the Ukraine, and Byelorussia.

The most dramatic example of unification through sport is the Spartakiads, Unionwide games modeled on the Olympics at a time when the U.S.S.R. was barred from them. The first Spartakiad was held in 1928. The finals of the 1956 Spartakiad, described by Morton as an Olympic dragnet, were held in Moscow's Lenin Stadium and involved over 9,000 athletes from 15 republics. They were attended by the Party Presidium and 100,000 spectators who had managed to secure very scarce seats. The fifth Spartakiad, in 1971, was accompanied by a cultural festival linking sport and the arts. At the sixth Spartakiad, in 1975, the Olympic symbolism was clear: A torchbearer started from the Moscow Tomb of the Unknown Warrior, passing the torch on to other bearers, each of whom ran a 1-kilometer lap, the last to the stadium.

How modern sport is related to the traditional ways is hard to unravel. Rivers says of the more primitive republics: "These highly tradition-bound people cannot grasp the abstractness of modern sports. They lack the enterprise, in their fatalistic village cultures, to see why people want to knock themselves out for sportsmanship's remote ideals; they cannot link such rituals, even remotely, with their own" (1965, p. 127). On the other hand, Wright Miller sees the older cultures as having a very positive element to contribute: "The old communal ways are still the most powerful element in Soviet manners and morals. They show themselves vigorously, for example, in that most spontaneous and recent Soviet development, the sense of sportsmanship" (1963, p. 148). For the most part, traditional games have been pushed into the background by urban sports. But some, such as the Central Asian games of chasing a maiden or wrestling on horseback, and a pololike game in the republic of Georgia, have continued and have in fact been legitimized by the sport authorities.

There is intense and sometimes violent support of national sport teams (throughout the U.S.S.R. soccer fields are routinely separated from spectators by a ring of soldiers). In 1973 the paper *Sovietsky Sport* complained that "the Azerbaidzhan soccer team [from a remote republic] carries with it a whole suite of 'fans' who consider it their duty to support their team by fair means or "foul" (May 16, 1973, p. 4 [cited by Riordan, 1977]). With the free time released by the 5-day week, fans can more easily do this. In 1975 a large group of supporters from the Kazakh republic told Riordan that they had gone 5 hours by jet to see their team play in Moscow. In Armenia, on a commercial flight, when flight attendants announced that the local team had beaten the hated Russians in Moscow, "the passengers, who were mostly Armenian, hugged and kissed one another as though a great war victory had been proclaimed" (Riordan, 1977, p. 314).

Until about the mid-1960s the Spartakiads, like Soviet sport in general, were dominated by Moscow and Leningrad. However, in the 1971 and 1975 games they ranked fourth and fifth instead of first or second. In 1972 Soviet world sport champions lived in 10 different cities. Riordan says that the provincial centers seem to be catching up with the metropolitan areas and predicts that in the fairly near future superiority may be taken over by areas that have only recently been introduced to organized sport programs. This would be part of the fulfillment of the revolution that Khrushchev tried to implement in 1959 when he decentralized sport as part of the "withering away of the state."

Sport and International Communism

Soviet sport is not only a binding force among nationalities within the U.S.S.R. but is also a deliberate and effective form of outreach toward the other Communist nations. This was symbolized when the 50th anniversary of the Soviet Union was celebrated by 87 climbers who ascended Peak Communism (formerly Peak Stalin), at 7,495 meters the highest point in the U.S.S.R., and planted flags of 15 Soviet republics and of Bulgaria, Czechoslovakia, East Germany, Hungary, Mongolia, Poland, Rumania, and Yugoslavia. The magazine *Sport in the USSR* described this event as "a symbol of unshakeable friendship and inspired by the ideal of proletarian peace and friendship between peoples" (*Sport v. USSR*, 1972, No. 9, p. 2 [cited by Riordan, 1977]). There has been a two-way exchange of coaches and athletes between the U.S.S.R. and other Communist nations. Between 1967 and 1972 more than 50 Soviet coaches trained Cuban athletes for the Pan-American and Olympic games. In 1972 East German coaches worked with Soviet bobsled teams; Cuban sprinters were working out in Minsk; Hungarian coaches were working with Soviet athletes in swimming, fencing, and the pentathlon; Czech coaches were advising Russian hockey players; and Soviet athletes were at training camps in East Germany, Czechoslovakia, Bulgaria, and Poland. China, Albania and North Vietnam did not participate in this kind of collaboration. There had, in 1977, been no Soviet-Chinese sport contacts since 1971.

Because the Soviet Union is itself a mix of fairly advanced modernization with economically very underdeveloped areas, Soviet sport feels that it has much to say to the Third World. "The Soviet Olympic delegation of 1972," said *Sport in the USSR*, "was a mirror of Soviet multinational sport (*Sport v. USSR*, 1973, No. 7, p. 19 [cited by Riordan, 1977]).

"Since the early 1960s," according to Riordan, "Soviet authorities have paid increasing attention to aid to the 'Third World' in the field of sport as well as in the economic [and] other culture spheres" (1977, p. 384). This aid has taken the form of sending coaches and instructors, building facilities, training administrators, sponsoring tours by Soviet athletes, and holding sports friendship weeks. "Sporting ties," said *Sovietsky Sport* in 1973, "are one way of establishing contacts between states even when diplomatic relations are absent" (April 22, 1973, p. 4 [cited by Riordan, 1977]). In 1972, there were more than 200 Soviet sport instructors in 28 foreign states. Sports treaties were concluded with Egypt in 1969, Nigeria and the Sudan in 1970, Algeria, Iraq, and Syria in 1972, and Lebanon in 1973. Nigeria, in 1972, had a sport friendship week dedicated to the 50th anniversary of the U.S.S.R. In 1970 Nigeria, Egypt, and the Sudan celebrated the 100th anniversary of the birth of Lenin. The U.S.S.R. had built sport centers in Afghanistan. Algeria, Cambodia, the Congo, Indonesia, Iraq, Senegal, and Togo have supported Third World boycotts of racist nations. In 1973 the Soviets refused to play World Cup soccer after the murder of the socialist premier Allende. Soviet sportsmen from the outlying republics are considered especially important ambassadors to the Third World. An example is the regular exchanges of Uzbek and Afghan athletes before the Soviet invasion of Afghanistan. Soviet media often cite the success of athletes from Azerbaidzhan in competition with Turkey as an example of what socialism has done for minorities.

In a way, sport relations with the United States were summarized by UNESCO in 1957, after the Rome Olympics: "The Olympic Games are now regarded by many as merely a testing ground for two great political units" (UNESCO, 1957, p. 57). This was borne out 16 years later when a United States-U.S.S.R. match in Minsk was covered by over 200 journalists, half of them from the West. BBC broadcast two half-hour programs in prime time, *although no British athletes were involved.* The low point is probably the rigged Russian basketball victory at Munich in 1972. There are, however, other trends. Current Russian supremacy in weightlifting probably dates back to 1955 when, in the middle of the Cold War, on a trip by American weightlifters to the Soviet Union, American Paul Anderson made an international debut so superior to that of U.S.S.R. weightlifters that the crowd was plunged into stunned silence. From that point Soviet performance was spurred, whereas that of Americans declined to the point that in 1983 the Moscow audience was left "sitting in embarrassed silence while the Americans displayed ineptitude" (*Sports Illustrated,* November 14, 1983, p. 80).

Another dramatic meeting was during the Nixon period of detente, which extended to sport. In the 1972 Soviet-American games that followed the detente agreement the Soviet athletes clearly beat the Americans. Afterward, the winners and losers together symbolized detente by linking arms, doing a lap together, and waving to spectators. Riordan comments on how far removed this symbolic camaraderie was from the hostile and paranoid relations typical of U.S. and U.S.S.R. politicians in the years before and after World War II.

Tretiak's 1983 reflection on the 1980 American hockey victory at Lake Placid is a thought from which politicians both Russian and American could well learn: "Our fans regarded it as a defeat for us to win the silver medal, but it's very hard to be always first" (Swift, 1983, p. 44).

Now let's draw up a balance sheet for Soviet sport, with special reference to sport in the United States. First of all, Morton and Riordan agree that spectator sport is the most enjoyed form of entertainment in the U.S.S.R. Excellence in ballet and the other arts is appreciated by sophisticated urban dwellers, but for a land of active and transplanted peasants, competitive sport is number one. It provides a catharsis, in terms of both of Aristotle's senses of the word, as we discussed them in chapter 4: It is a channel for letting off aggressions, and it provides intense meaningful excitement in the midst of a sometimes drab world. Morton says that in sport there is an essential element that transcends politics; and in Sutton-Smith's language Soviet sport enables the ever-controlled Soviet citizen to pass periodically into a separate realm more under his own control. The athlete is like the scientist, less immediately and directly under political control. Unlike the system in American universities, in which semiprofessional athletes are, for the only time in history, attached to otherwise academic institutions, Soviet athletic scholarships are an intellectually and ethically demanding means of preparing for a socially useful life after sport. Although physiological differences in performance level are recognized, sport in the U.S.S.R., especially in the underdeveloped republics, is a genuine avenue for liberation of women. Sport is a way up in the world for people of humble origins, as it is in the United States. As here, sociologists claim (although without finally convincing evidence) that athletes are less likely to be delinquent. In spite of some excesses of the "number one" psychology, Soviet sport, like sport elsewhere, does seem to teach a bottom line of sportsmanship and respect for opponents. On the international scene, with the same qualifications, it does furnish an oasis of international human interaction in a nuclear world.

On the negative side, whereas American sport's chief shortcoming is commercialism, that of Soviet sport is politicization. Whereas the American jock is "meat on the hoof" for corporate business, the Russian athlete is a pawn of the state. (This is true in spite of the presence in the U.S.S.R. of athletes who will sell their talents to the highest bidder and sport businessmen who will arrange their connections.) There are the same complaints in the U.S.S.R. as in the West about spectator hooliganism and violence (although in a police state it is less likely to get out of hand) and about spectator passivity. Along with pressures for world supremacy, there have been criticisms of the "number one" psychology *within* the Soviet Union. Educational and health authorities in the Soviet Union, as in the United States have been concerned about the slighting of the average citizen's welfare in order to produce a breed of superjocks, the sacrificing of mass physical culture in the interest of elite sport. Along with concern about eroding mass health and readiness for labor and defense, there must be awareness of the point made by Morton: The physical culture base is necessary for recruiting top record makers, but overstress on winning robs the mass base.

Chapter 8

Sport in the People's Republic of China

Sport in Communist China has an entirely different flavor from sport in the United States, the U.S.S.R., Western Europe, or even Communist Europe. China is still an economically backward country. Her revolution was primarily a peasant revolution, led by a peasant with the consciousness of a peasant (Mao Tse-tung). In the People's Republic the *massovost* (mass culture) aspect is emphasized far more than the element of *masterstvo* (competitive mastery). The slogans of personal fitness for revolutionary production and defense are the same as those of the Soviets, but (as we shall see) they are verbalized with an unself-consciousness and simplicity that befits a peasant state. Whereas the Soviets (like the Americans) are occasionally distressed by the excesses of the "number one" psychology, the Chinese, with the same unreflective peasant naiveté, repeat the sayings of Chairman Mao that in sport it is the friendship, not the victory, that really counts!

Friendship First

In 1973 William Johnson, a Minnesota-born staff writer for *Sports Illustrated*, toured the People's Republic with a visiting American basketball team and Peter Cooke, a photographer, and brought back a report on the state of sport under that version of Communism (Johnson, 1973a, 1973b). He was curious about how Chinese sport would compare with that of the Soviet Union, Japan, and East Germany. He found people, as he would have in the Soviet Union, doing their calisthenics at school, the office, and the factory. He found people of all ages, even up into their 90s, practicing individually and in groups the ancient ritual exercise called *wu shu*. At Tang Wang, the Swimming Village, where official statistics tell us that 70% of the population can swim, as compared with 10% before the revolution, he found 30,000 people simultaneously and patriotically in the swim in the Yangtse River.

But it was the skilled athletes, most of them the product of selection for spare-time sport schools, in whom Johnson was primarily interested. He wanted to ask them why they played their sports. He interviewed athletes like Chien Soong-yao, a chemistry major and basketball star at Tsinghua University, China's MIT; Huang Ying-min, a 13-year-old girl backstroke swimmer; and a local table tennis champion who was a stamp press operator. The answer was, invariably, that they were in sport to become healthier and more efficient instruments for production and defense of the motherland according to the precepts of Chairman Mao.

Johnson was particularly interested in finding out whether the number one psychology prevailed in the People's Republic. A good test was how the Chinese felt about the basketball series between the U.S. and Chinese teams that Johnson was accompanying. He queried Li Chi-yuin, his translator and almost constant companion, and also Kuo Lei of the All-China Sports Federation. From both he got the answer that the Chinese did not expect to win, but that they would learn much from the Americans and that the games would make the two nations closer friends.

At one point in the tour Johnson realized that he had never in any school seen a trophy or pennant (whereas, of course, the athletic trophy case is about the first thing one encounters in any American school). When he asked a middle-school principal in Shanghai where the trophies were he was told that the school had won a few but that the principal didn't really know where they were. Then the principal laid down the official priority line of the People's Republic: "We consider friendship first, learning good technique second, victory banners third or perhaps even less" (Johnson, 1973a, p. 86).

Chinese spectators Johnson found to be as cool and low-key as the athletes. They were turned on by quality performance. Slipping onto the floor at Peking's 5,000-seat Capital Arena for a practice session of the American team, Johnson and Cooke were surprised, when a 7-footer slam-dunked the ball, to hear from above them the collective gasp of 5,000 Chinese fans who had come to watch the workout. Johnson and Cooke had thought they were alone in the arena. Every morning before a game with the United States there were long lines at the box office, but when the game was on there were no cheers, boos, whistles, or leaps out of seats. Sometimes, Johnson said, they acted like a Western opera audience, applauding politely when either team made a good play. What was going on inside them is, of course, a question. Johnson's interpreter Li, an avid basketball fan, often seemed lost in Confucian thought at the games but admitted that the knots in his stomach were not good for his ulcer.

Although the Chinese lined up for the games with the U.S., sheer lack of facilities keeps mass spectatoritis from being a serious threat in the People's Republic. Peking (with a population of 4 million) in 1973 had two indoor arenas with 33,000 seats between them and an outdoor stadium for 100,000. Shanghai, with over 8 million people, had one indoor arena with 5,500 seats. Hangchow, a city of 750,000, had one with 5,000 seats. Canton, with a population of 2 million, had one 5,500-seat indoor arena. For all of China's 800 million people, Johnson calculated, there were fewer than 1 million stadium seats. Twenty-six NFL cities in the U.S., he reminded us, had 1.68 million seats (Johnson, 1973a, p. 100).

The Sociology of Chinese Noncompetitiveness

How do we explain the absence in China of the win psychology that is so pervasive in the rest of the Communist world, as in the capitalist nations? Could it be that everybody is just parroting the party line when they repeatedly insist, in action as well as word, that self-development for motherland, and the widening of friendships, are more important than victory? Johnson thought at one point that it might be just the dry rot of totalitarianism that makes responses so stereotyped. (I told my class once that I wasn't sure that these Chinese responses are any more predictable than the clichés routinely dropped by American coaches, players, and sport bureaucrats about God, country, and sportsmanship.)

Rather than passing everything off as stereotypes, we need to see it in the perspective of the economic and cultural situation of the People's Republic. First of all, contemporary Chinese sport is part of a society emerging from centuries of desperate poverty.

Kuo Lei, the sport bureaucrat previously quoted, expressed a hope that Chinese sport will very soon attain international caliber, but reminded Johnson that in sport, as in industry and agriculture, China is still a backward country. She will, he believes, overcome this backwardness in industry, in agriculture, *and* in sport, but it will be a hard task to overcome the burden of centuries of feudalism and bureaucracy and western imperialism (Johnson, 1973b, pp. 45–56).

I think we will be helped in understanding the sociology of Chinese attitudes toward winning if we recall the Tununak Eskimos, of whom we heard anthropologist Lynn Ager say, "The only competition I saw was one in which everyone tried to do his best but not at anyone else's expense (1976, p. 82). We saw that among the Tununak, Western games such as marbles became noncompetitive. The reason is that the Tununak live in a harsh subarctic environment where they must work together in order to survive. Competition is seen as a threat to the group unity that they must preserve in order (literally) to live. Chinese who remember the conditions before communism and see the revolution as having rescued them may be understood if, like the Tununak, they are afraid of anything that might split their group effort.

An older sociological reason for the Chinese lack of enthusiasm for winning may lie in the fact that the Eastern cultures of China, India, and Japan do not traditionally have the Western emphasis on individual achievement. This is actually an ecological question: Instead of standing apart from and above his or her environment, a person is ideally expected to live in a relationship of oneness with nature and fellow humans. In spite of the fact that *Time* magazine once referred to Japan as the best example of the Western work ethic, this sense of group identification has been held responsible by some for much of the competitive international success of Japanese industry. In China, this sense of ecological oneness goes far back beyond Mao Tse-tung to Confucius and Lao Tse; in fact, Mao himself quoted these sages as readily as he quoted Karl Marx.

T'i Yü and Chinese History

As in the Soviet Union, Chinese sport can be divided into mass physical fitness training (based on the military skills of archery, fencing, use of clubs, swords and spears, wrestling, and boxing) and competitive sports (mainly track and field, swimming, soccer, table tennis, and basketball). The Chinese do not distinguish the two: *t'i yü*, the Chinese word for sport, means both. More than in the U.S.S.R., sport in the People's Republic has deep pre-Communist roots. China was a monarchy for over 2,000 years before 1912. Then she was a semi-democratic republic for 15 years under Sun Yat-sen and his successors and a centralized dictatorship for 22 years under Chiang Kai-shek's Kuomintang before the Maoist takeover of 1949. Mass physical culture in the Empire went back well before 1000 A.D., followed by a period from the 14th century to the end of the Empire in 1912 when military prowess was downplayed in favor of intellectual skills. During the republican period and the Kuomintang dictatorship there was a stronger development of competitive sport than there had been before or than there has been since the 1949 revolution.

Let us trace the elements of mass and competitive sport back to their origins in the Empire. The history is discussed very well in

Jonathan Kolatch's book *Sports, Politics, and Ideology in China* (1972). In the Chou dynasty (1122–255 B.C.), archery, obviously a military skill, was a regular festival game for both nobles and the masses; along with charioteering, music, writing, and math, it was part of the education of the feudal nobility. In the third century B.C. precursors of our current weight room aficianados were lifting huge bronze cauldrons. Before the birth of Christ, soldiers trained for water fighting were skilled in diving, treading water, and the backstroke. In the first centuries A.D. boxing was introduced from India along with Buddhism. Its military and political significance is indicated by the proverb:

If one has neither boxing ability nor courage
Such may usually be the cause of uprisings and disturbances.

After the sixth century, polo was brought in by the Tartars. (Twentieth-century problems, and their solution, were foreshadowed in 1163 by the introduction of the first field covering—an oiled cloth.) In 1267 football (World Cup type, not American) was introduced in the training of soldiers for promoting team unity, which it was hoped would transfer to the battlefield. As I indicated earlier, from 1368 to 1912, under the Ch'ing and Ming dynasties, physical exercise fell into disrepute. A person of character was expected to stress the intellectual attainment that would enable him to pass the rigorous examinations for a place in the civil service bureaucracy.

This review shows that a basis was laid under the Empire for both mass and competitive sport. Just before the social democratic revolution of 1912 specific developments took place that led to sport under the republic. Military physical training was introduced into the schools. In 1888 Western sports were introduced. In 1904 a Chinese physical training school was set up in Shanghai. In 1905 a physical education school for women was founded. Western sports had a strong influence on China. In fact, the two most popular Chinese sports, table tennis and basketball, are American inventions. In sport organization the most prominent factor was the YMCA, which saw sport as a vehicle for Christian propaganda. Robert R. Bailey, a missionary who had been an All-American in football at Princeton, started a sport program in Tientsin in 1898. Baseball was introduced in 1907 in Peking. From 1896 on, Tientsin stressed athletic competition in the schools. In 1910 a national athletic meet was held that included track and field, tennis, soccer, and basketball. The average daily attendance was 40,000.

In 1912 the new social democratic republic laid down its position on sport: "The essentials of physical exercise are to cause all parts of the body to develop equally, to strengthen the body, to enliven the spirit, and to cultivate the habits of discipline and harmony" (Kolatch,

1972, p. 7). Internationally, from 1913 to 1934 China participated in the Far Eastern Championship Games with Japan and the Philippines (these may have been a model for the Pan-American Games). In 1915 the Games were held in Shanghai, with 350 athletes and 100,000 spectators. At Osaka in 1923, women participated in the games for the first time. In the 1927 games China won in soccer for the seventh straight time. In 1932, 1936, and 1948 Chinese teams went to the Olympic Games. By the 1920s sports had been secularized: Local people took over their operation from the YMCA. Sport also was playing a part in welding a loose confederation of rural areas into a nation. In 1919 an educator, speaking of the games, put it this way: "This is a great leveling force which cannot fail to be felt in future society. I have seen students cheering for their school and even for their city, but never before for China" (Siler, 1919). Although this happened in the cities, Kolatch says that an active sportsman of the 1930s told him that "it is highly probably that most of the people living in China at the time never even heard of the Far Eastern Championship Games" (Kolatch, 1972, p. 69).

As for the 22-year rule of Chiang Kai-shek and his Nationalists that preceded Mao's rise to power, Kolatch says, "It is difficult to pass judgments on the achievements of the Nationalist government in physical education" (1972, p. 507). All he can conclude is that sport suffered "stunted growth" under Chiang. Originally a Communist himself, Chiang started in union with the Communists then tried unsuccessfully to unify a country in which control was shared from time to time and place to place by the Nationalists, the Japanese, and Mao's Communists. His efforts deteriorated into a brutal and bitterly anti-Communist dictatorship. Chiang tried for a unified national sport program modeled on that of the early social democratic republic, but in a chaotic situation in which "the vast majority of Chinese had not only never participated in sports, but had never even been to schools," (Kolatch, 1972, p. 50) his efforts rarely got far beyond formal resolutions and formal bureaucratic structures.

Prerevolutionary Communist Sport

When the revolution of 1949 came, the background had already been laid for a sport ideology and program. The only article by Mao Tse-tung written before 1923 for which we still have the entire Chinese text is "A Study of Physical Culture," written in 1917. This treatise on *t'i yü* set out the Chinese Communist view of sport that now prevails. In contrast to the downgrading of sport in the last 6 centuries of the Empire, Mao the young revolutionary took the same view as had the social democrats (essentially, the old Roman slogan, "A sound mind in a sound body"):

The only misfortune of man is not to have a body. Otherwise, he has nothing to fear. If one finds a method to improve the body, the rest will improve automatically. To put the body in condition, there is nothing better than physical culture. Physical culture occupies a position of first priority in our life; when the body is strong one can advance rapidly in his studies and in his [level of] virtue and attain the potential of his great ability. (Schram, 1962, pp. 44–46)

In the pockets in the provinces of Hunau, Kiangsi, and Yenan that were controlled by the Communists at times from 1927 to 1945 under Chiang's Nationalist government, practice followed theory. Kolatch says that "it will be seen that many of the currents which now exist on the Mainland sports scene can trace their origin to pre-1949 Communist areas" (Kolatch, 1972, p. 82). In 1934 the Second National Chinese Soviet Congress reported: "A Red sports program has been developing rapidly. Even remote villages have held track and field athletics and sports fields have been made in many places" (Chinese Communists in Wartime, pp. 24–25). At Yenan College in 1941 the Communists established courses in dance, basketball, volleyball, track and field, gymnastics, anatomy, ice skating, swimming, and physical culture theory. In 1942 they organized a Yenan New Sports Institute for sport theory, including sport medicine and hygiene. In September of the same year a 6-day meet involving 1,300 athletes in basketball, volleyball, track and field, swimming, and military events was held. At this time Lenin Clubs in the province regularly had table tennis facilities.

Communist Organization of Sport

When Mao and his followers took over China in 1949, they set about to put Mao's 1917 principles into operation as part of their political program. Sport in China, as in Russia, is a function of the state, unlike in the United States, where sport is private enterprise and government commissions, such as that established by President Ford, are only advisory. *T'i yü*, in all its aspects, is carried on by mass organizations that do the actual contact work with schools and peasants and workers; government bureaus, which are responsible for organization and record keeping; and the party, which is responsible for making sure that athletes and administrators are not only technically competent but also politically "correct." All three function on national, provincial, municipal, and county levels. Below the county level, activities are carried on by the cultural, educational and health departments of communes, by schools, by trade unions, and by the Young Communist League.

What do the sport organizations do? They organize national, provincial, and local events; on a national level they are responsible for international competition; they provide technical and other assistance to specific sports; and they conduct public relations, which includes the publication of sport magazines. The sport bureaucracy takes very seriously the importance of *t'i yü* to the revolution. A former Chinese player and referee told Kolatch in 1969 that "if the Chinese claimed that there were 543,200 registered badminton players and they were called upon to do so, they would be able to produce all 543,200 in short order" (Kolatch, 1972, p. 109).

Sport and the Educational System

Sport is an integral part of the Chinese educational system. There, as here, mass education is primarily a public function. American educators, in general, would not disagree with the Chinese conception of its objectives: to promote intellectual, physical, and moral development and to teach comprehensive skills. The backbone of the Chinese sport system, says Kolatch, is in the primary and middle schools (most Chinese go no farther). The core sport program in primary- and middle-school education, as first set down by directives from Peking in 1958–59, consists of a daily early morning exercise program; 2 hours per week in a systematic physical culture class; and a 2-hour weekly program in competitive sport. Under the 1958–59 directives hours spent on sport surpassed those given to geography, biology, chemistry, music, and drawing and compared favorably with those devoted to history, socialist education, physics, foreign languages, and productive labor. The only subjects to get more attention than sport were Chinese language and math. The whole sport program is geared for four groups of students: those who are unskilled and uninterested; those who have basic skills and some proficiency in specific sports; the potential jocks who are very good at sports; and the physically unfit, who do light exercises.

For those who go on to the university level, the basic physical culture skills for labor and defense (gained in such activities as exercise, dance, the 100-meter dash, grenade throwing, and 10-kilometer marches) are required. Also mandatory under 1956 directives is competence in at least one competitive sport "so as to help develop a program of intercollegiate athletics which should involve 9 percent of the student body as players and 1 percent as referees and coaches" (Kolatch, 1972, p. 120). (One can consider how such a directive from the NCAA would revolutionize the American sport system: At the University of Miami at present this would mean about 1,300 student-athletes and 150 student coaches and referees.) Also different from American control of intercollegiate sports by alumni and professional administrators is typical control by youth groups—a Student Athletic Association and the Young Communist League.

A mass sport program for almost 1 billion people requires technically trained direction. This is provided by specialized schools of physical culture. It differs from American physical training in that graduates are not limited to school teaching. To enter a physical culture institute a man must show proficiency in the 100-meter dash, high jump, shot-put, and chin-ups; a woman must show proficiency in the dash, the high jump, and push-ups. Because the institutes emphasize the scientific study of sports, especially sport medicine, there are academic requirements for admission, but these are not as important as being tall, proficient in one sport, and politically sound. These requirements are stressed because "the institutes are major breeding grounds for top athletes and the Party wants assurance that athletes who might be called upon to represent China in international competition will behave as expected" (Kolatch, 1972, p. 129). In contrast to the poverty previously described, these institutes are generously supplied with facilities. In 1973 the Peking Physical Culture Institute covered 60,000 square meters, had indoor and outdoor swimming pools, an indoor track, three 75-by-20-meter gyms, two indoor basketball-volleyball courts, a weight room, five soccer fields, three track and field areas, and 20 outdoor basketball courts.

Those Chinese who don't go beyond middle school and want advanced sports training can get it at several thousand spare-time sport schools, which originated in 1955 and in the next 9 years produced over 3,200 athletes for municipal, provincial, and national teams. These schools hold 2-hour sessions, 2 to 4 days a week, some specializing in a specific sport, others training for several sports. Following the slogan "Cultivate from an early age, train for many years, establish a good foundation," the Chinese admit children into these schools for the sports of ice skating and swimming at ages 8 and 9; track and field, gymnastics, table tennis and diving at age 10 or 11; volleyball, soccer, basketball, tennis, badminton, ice hockey, and speed skating at age 12 or 13; and cycling and marksmanship at age 13 or 14 (Kolatch, 1972, p. 129). The spare-time schools face a problem similar to the conflict between mass participation and competitive sport that exists in the U.S.S.R. and the U.S.: "There must be enough students to maintain a pool of quality athletes. Yet if the school is to develop an elite, it can only defeat its own purposes by fully opening its doors to the masses" (Kolatch, 1972, p. 129).

Labor and Defense

Physical culture in the schools is part of the *laba-defense system* (an abbreviation for "labor and defense of the fatherland"—note the parallel with the Soviet Union). Early after the revolution, the Communist government set up a program of badges and certificates for completion of various levels of labor-defense skills: a youth class (under 15) and first and second classes for men and women 16 and over. A look at the events required in 1956 will show us what ordinary Chinese citizens (not elite athletes) were considered capable of doing at the very time that the famous Kraus-Hirschland study (1954) found many American children unable to perform even the simplest exercises. The required programs were these:

> *Youth stage (age 13 to 15)*
> • 60-meter dash,
> • 400-meter run,
> • long or high jump,
> • hand grenade or softball throw,
> • rope or pole climb, using both hands and feet.
> *Adult stage (age 16 and over)*
> • 60-, 100-, or 200-meter dash,
> • 800-, 1,500-, or 3,000-meter run,
> • long or high jump—plus weightlifting or pull-ups,
> • push-ups or rope climb,
> • shooting, hand grenade throw, or march with full pack 6 kilometers for men, 4 for women,
> • an event suited to local conditions, such as swimming in the south or ice skating in the north.

In the 1960s, partly under the influence of conflict with Taiwan and the presence of American troops in Vietnam, the labor-defense system took a military turn, eventually including paramilitary events that are nowhere else considered sports. The great emphasis on swimming was a preparation for events such as the 1935 Long March, in which Mao and his followers had retreated from the Nationalists to northern Shensi province, on the way swimming across rivers with full backpacks. In this connection, two events are interesting. In 1965 a film "Swimming for Beginners" was shown simultaneously in seven

Peking movie houses. On July 16, 1966, Mao himself, then 73 years old, is reported to have swum 10 miles down the Yangtse river in 65 minutes. (Kolatch notes that the winning time for 4 miles in the 1966 AAU Swimming Championships was about 1 1/2 hours.) The paramilitary activities that were practiced as sports after 1958 include marksmanship, mountaineering, gliding, model airplane building, parachuting, rowing, sailing, shooting from boats, driving motorboats, navigating warships, and telecommunications. All of these sports, says Kolatch, were intended to prepare the people, in the absence of sophisticated military technology, to wage essentially guerrilla warfare on their own terms. While this redefinition of sport was taking place, and school children were doing target practice on pictures of Chiang Kai-shek and Lyndon Johnson, the Chinese in their schools, in their factories, and even before their radios were carrying on the old-style *t'i yü*. An example is the official description of the exercises being broadcast to musical accompaniment in April 1963:

> *This set of physical exercises has nine parts. Namely, extension movement, chest expansion movement, leg kicking movement, abdominal and back movement, sideward and bodily movement, rotation movement, whole body movement, jumping, and readjustment. . . . These exercises give balanced training to all parts of the body, and are more profitable to people who do mental work or desk work. . . . There are two climaxes in these exercises, at the end of which the rhythm slows down gradually. The whole set of physical exercises requires a little more than four minutes to do. (Survey of the China Mainland Press, 1963, pp. 12–13)*

International Sport Relations

As in the U.S.S.R., an objective of physical culture in China is to develop athletes for international sport. That the People's Republic was interested in international sport from the beginning is shown by the fact that from 1949 to 1956 at least one Chinese athlete delegation went abroad every year. Over these first years the number of Chinese athletes going abroad increased from 9 in 1949 to 493 in 1956. Why did they go abroad? Primarily to learn, especially from the U.S.S.R., Poland, Czechoslovakia, Hungary, and Rumania. That in the early years they *needed* to learn is shown by the fact that they usually lost 90% or more of their engagements. That they *did* learn is attested to by the fact that in 1958 they had 221 wins, 171 losses, and 17 ties in 409 contests (Chi Yang, "Looking at China's Leap Forward in Sports from the Point of View of International Competition." Kolatch, 1972, p. 167.) These are of course China's records, but we should remember two things: I noted earlier that Chinese sport bureaucrats seem to be very adept at keeping records. Also, Kolatch says "Chinese accounts of international events in which they compete are unusually free of self-praise, and it is not at all unusual to find long accounts of a particular event without the slightest mention that China was the victor" (Kolatch, 1972, pp. 168–169).

The Olympics have been another story. Nationalist China was in the 1932 Games, but most of her Olympic Committee fled to Taiwan with Chiang in 1949. In spite of this, and in spite of the historic Maoist position that the International Olympic Committee is an agent of imperialist oppression, China informed the IOC in 1952 that she wished to participate in the Helsinki Games. A protest by Taiwan set off a long controversy as to which government was really China. Since then, until 1984, although the People's Republic almost made it to the 1952 and 1960 Games, Taiwan has been the only one to go. At the 1984 Winter Games at Sarajevo the People's Republic participated in five events. Two hundred athletes, with 100 coaches, doctors, and attendants, made the trip to the Los Angeles Summer Games, where the People's Republic won 32 medals—15 gold, 8 silver, and 9 bronze.

Kolatch tells us that the Chinese have always been interested in "holding international contests in China designed to counter what they consider the imperialist controlled meets of the West" (Kolatch, 1972, p. 109). In 1955 China hosted the International Friendly Shooting Competition and in 1958 hosted an international volleyball tournament. In 1961, Peking was host to the world table tennis championships. The Basketball Championships of Friendly Countries was held in Peking in 1963, and an invitational table tennis tournament was held in 1965. The friendly countries were mostly Communist nations from Asia or eastern Europe.

After breaking with the IOC, the Chinese set out to establish a competitive Olympics for friendly nations. The Games of the New Emerging Forces (abbreviated GANEFO) took place in Djakarta, Indonesia for 12 days in November, 1963 with 2,000 to 3,000 athletes present. The nations represented cover a wide geographic, cultural, and political spectrum and included:

- Bolivia
- Somali
- Dominican Republic
- Japan
- Philippines
- Algeria
- Mali
- Guinea
- Argentina

- Cambodia
- United Arab Republic
- Albania
- North Korea
- Iraq
- Lebanon
- North Vietnam
- Morocco
- Chile
- Finland
- Poland
- France
- Soviet Union
- Brazil
- Uruguay
- Saudi Arabia
- Bulgaria
- Czechoslovakia
- East Germany
- Yugoslavia (Kolatch, 1972, pp. 193–194)

China took 65 gold medals, 56 silver, and 47 bronze. The Soviet Union, which sent a small team, was second. Kolatch believes that the Chinese were anxious to compete in easier company than they would have found at the Olympics. He cites a Philippine commentator who says that his own country didn't send even second-rate athletes to Djakarta. As further evidence Kolatch presents his own calculation that only in weightlifting could the Chinese men's performances have won a gold medal in the 1960 Olympics; the women might have done better (Kolatch, 1972, p. 192). He feels that this, along with political ideology, may be the main reason why the People's Republic did not push for inclusion in the Olympics.

How successful has sport been in promoting friendship with China's major rival powers, the U.S.S.R. and the United States? To some extent, sport relations have blown hot and cold with the winds of international politics; but not completely. Like many things, the Chinese sport program was modeled after the Soviet program, and sport relations continued from 1955 to 1963. There were none between the 1963 GANEFO games and the December 1985 tennis competitions for girls and boys at Pompano Beach, Florida. This was a period of general unfriendliness between the two Communist powers. In table tennis, China's best competitive sport (and, as we saw, an American invention), China and the United States have met twice. The more publicized meeting was in China in 1971, at the time of the Nixon detente with the People's Republic. Less well known was a meeting in Tokyo at the world championships of 1956 while the Bamboo Curtain dividing the two nations diplomatically was still up and the Cold War was at its height. The 1984 Olympics could have afforded a fine opportunity for contact between athletes from all three powers. Unfortunately, pressure in California, hostile to both Communist teams, plus Russian retaliation for the 1980 U.S. boycott, prevented American, Chinese, and other athletes from living and competing together in the best Olympic tradition.

The Cultural Revolution

The conflict between mass physical culture and elite sport, common to all economically advanced nations, came to the fore dramatically in the People's Republic between 1966 and 1969 in an event that influenced sport as well as everything else in Communist China—the Cultural Revolution. Of this Johnson said, "The Cultural Revolution of the late '60s smashed across China like a violent sandstorm. Its targets were 'revisionist' officials who were accused of weakening the philosophies of Mao" (Johnson, 1973a, p. 93).

With regard to sport, the Cultural Revolution was marked by developments like these:

- Ho Lung, Chairman of the Physical Culture and Sports committee, was formally accused: "For the past ten years he has paid attention not to mass physical education, but to forming professional teams and highly developed activities. In 1962 he openly advocated that 'The National Physical Education Committee only pay attention to athletic teams and that the provincial and municipal levels take care of mass physical education, and national defense physical education.'" (The Crime of the Anti-Party, Anti-Military, Anti-Revolutionary, Revisionist Ho Lung, *Sports Battlefront*, No. 8–9, February 9, 1967).
- The second GANEFO games, scheduled for Cairo or Peking in 1967, were cancelled, without any formal explanation.
- Athletic schools for intensive sport training of children were discontinued in 1966.
- Swimming activity was essentially halted.
- Chinese teams stopped touring abroad.
- Specifically, the table tennis team that had made a 1965 sweep disappeared and missed the 1967 and 1969 World Championships. Chuang Tse-tung, three times world champion, was feared dead. In 1971, after defeat of the Cultural Revolution, Chuang reappeared, says Johnson, along with the rest of the

team, with a bourgeois potbelly and a post on the Central Committee of the Communist Party.

What was the meaning of all this? Let me venture my own interpretation and follow with a Chinese sport bureaucrat's analysis.

Mao, although a brilliant theoretician and a sort of Renaissance man, was a peasant, and the revolution was a peasant revolution, with the mentality of the American frontier—belief in spontaneous neighborly cooperation and distrust of impersonal bigness, bureaucracy, back-stabbing competition, and professional intellectuals. The struggle was a revolution *for* the kind of simple and locally controlled communal economy that E. F. Schumacher (1975) called the "intermediate economy," and *against* the mentality that would make China a big, impersonal, industrialized bureaucratic power like the U.S. and the U.S.S.R. In a sense it was a revolution against both advanced capitalism and Stalinism. Concerning sport, the revolution was suspicious of everything that looked like Soviet professionalism or American commercialism and favored a program of building healthy minds in sound bodies for the common people.

The Cultural Revolution lost in the short run—or did it? During his visit to China in 1973, shortly after the Cultural Revolution, Johnson raised the question with Tung Yi-wan of the department of mass sports of the All-China Sports Federation. Tung's opinion was that the Cultural Revolution had counteracted the tendency to put too much emphasis on winning. True, he said, this put a temporary stop to many sport activities (such as those I have detailed), but it brought about a new, healthy balance between training for the average citizen and development of international caliber athletes. "The idea of bringing up a super sportsman is one thing that the Cultural Revolution wiped out of our sports life" (Johnson, 1973a, p. 96).

Because Tung was a successful sport bureaucrat in 1973, after the defeat of the Cultural Revolution, he can hardly be considered an apologist. The worst that can be said is that, like many bureaucrats, he was talking out of both sides of his mouth. If he was, Tung was voicing the ambivalence of a China at a crossroads.

How will the People's Republic deal in the future with the *massovost-masterstvo* problem that plagues serious sport people everywhere? I think that China stands now about where the Soviet Union stood when Stalin took command after the death of Lenin and the assassination of Trotsky. Mao's peasant revolution died with its founder and is being succeeded by the top-heavy bureaucratic efficiency of what Galbraith called the "new industrial state," on the model of the United States and the U.S.S.R. (Galbraith, 1971).

Athletically, the 1984 Olympics suggest that the People's Republic is ready to try to move in with the big boys and girls. In the spring of 1986, women's soccer players were preparing intensively with their eyes on the first women's world soccer championship scheduled for 1987. They hoped to do as well as the women's volleyball team, which had won four world championships in a row, or the women's softball team, which in January had taken second place in its debut in world championship play. Although a sports writer had attributed their final defeat by the United States to technical inferiority, Don E. Porter, Secretary-General of the International Softball Federation, in an interview during the championships, had described the Chinese team as exceptionally competitive (*China Sports*, May 1986, pp. 4, 8). As Tung indicated, China will not go big time without conflict. Winning, we may guess, will not easily supersede the pursuit of friendship. Her *masterstvo* will be tempered by residues of the Oriental spirit of nonstriving and of the Maoist sense of community, as well as by her still-remaining poverty of resources. This tempering will be a healthy example for the rest of the world.

What it may mean is suggested by an exhibition in Peking in June 1985, sponsored jointly by the Chinese Olympic Committee and the Chinese Artists' Association, of 407 art pieces with sport themes. "All these works," said *China Sports* (October, 1985, p. 46), "reflect man's fight against nature, his efforts for self-fulfillment, and his aspirations to promote friendly relations among nations through sports." In a congratulatory message the chairman of the International Olympic Committee praised the exhibition as an important forward move from which the whole of mankind can benefit.

Chapter 9

*S*port in the Third World

Most of the world's population lives in the Third World, the area that is not directly affiliated with either the capitalist or the Communist bloc —primarily countries in Africa, Latin America, and southeast Asia. Economically, most of these countries are preindustrial and desperately poor. Politically, they are generally former colonies who have never known democratic self-rule. Since China and large parts of the Soviet Union are still basically economically developing areas, we have already encountered some of the issues involved in Third World sport. In this chapter we shall look at the Third World itself, comparing and contrasting sport there with sport in the First and Second Worlds.

We shall look first at how the development of sport is related to the history of these nations as colonies of major powers. Then we shall see what sport means in this context to Third World athletes. We shall then examine the kind of structures that developing nations have formed for physical culture and competitive sport. Finally, we shall look at some of the major problems of sport in the developing nations: the need for technical leadership, the problem of balancing elite sport with mass physical culture, differences in rural and urban involvement, the problem of spectator passivity, and the status of women athletes. Fortunately, there has been good sport research by Third World sociologists. Although this research only samples the enormous developing world, it suggests some major directions and problems.

Which Games to Play?

When the developing nations were colonies, the question arose that we saw in the less developed areas of the Soviet Union. Whose games shall be played—traditional local games or Western urban sports? The two solutions that we found in the U.S.S.R. have been paralleled in the Third World: A simultaneous practice of both forms and elimination of indigenous games in favor of Western sport. In India, native games have been maintained with the aim of preserving traditional culture and eventually transferring interest to Western sport competition. Both types of games are practiced side by side in Brazil. The same is the case in Ethiopia. Colonial Nigeria was a classic case of the other solution. Nigerian youth under the British had tribal youth games that trained them for adulthood and gave them a sense of identity: throwing spears, bearing swords, handling cross- and longbows, swimming, archery, wrestling, climbing ropes and trees, and acrobatic-tumbling gymnastics. They also had team games like *Ukepe ewan*, a lacrosse-like game (Adediji, 1979). The British, feeling a white man's mission to civilize and Christianize the natives, treated their indigenous games as savage and un-Christian as compared with Western sports like cricket, soccer, and netball. The result was to undermine the faith of young people in their culture and in themselves. After this debasement of the games that had traditionally trained youth for life, young Nigerians encountered another problem: When they tried to take up the white man's sports they were barred from his swimming pools and from his athletic clubs and teams.

Around 1960, Nigeria and other colonial nations achieved their independence. How would they assert this independence in sport? Not primarily by rejecting Western sport in favor of native games, but by striving to become adept enough to beat the Westerners at their own games. So native peoples, who had used Western education to develop techniques of rebellion and had used Judaeo-Christian concepts of justice and love to promote revolution, now used the colonizer's sport to win self-determination and dignity.

How this worked is suggested by the research of sport sociologists A. K. Maksimenko of the U.S.S.R. and Antoine Barushimana of Ruanda. They studied how top-class athletes in Central Africa had become interested in sport and the motives that kept them engaged. (Maksimenko & Barushimana, 1978). The investigation took place at the First Central African games, at Libreville in the country of Gabon, in 1976. Five hundred athletes from 12 nations participated. Of these, 300 returned a questionnaire submitted by the sociologists. Forty percent of the respondents played football (soccer), 14% volleyball, 15% basketball, and 30% were involved in track and field events. Ninety percent were men, 10% women. The average age was 22 years. Thirty-six percent came from families of poor peasants, 16% from working-class families, and only 2% from families of factory owners and private businessmen. Forty-five percent had a college education, 10% higher education, and a further 40% had finished elementary school. The authors comment on "the discrepancy between the level of edu-

The Brazilian football (soccer) star Pélé was once the highest paid athlete in history and may be the best known sports person in the world. Courtesy of Cosmos Soccer Club, Inc.

cation of athletes and the basic mass of the population of Central Africa where more than 60% of the population on the average are illiterates" (Maksimenko & Barushimana, 1978, p. 39).

The sociologists asked the athletes first about what had originally interested them in sport. School ranked first, friends second, family third, and leaders of sport fourth. Having established that school was the typical source of first interest, Maksimenko and Barushimana then asked the athletes for motives that (a) had initially interested them in sport as students and (b) kept them active at the present time.

The top-ranking *initial* motives for entering sport were

1. recreation (to get away from boredom, isolation, gaily to pass time),
2. the sport-achievement motive (achieve high results—to become a champion),
3. the prestige-personal motive (achieve moral recognition and popularity among surrounding people—to become a famous personality), and
4. the health motive (improve health, improve the body build and physical development).

To make a career in life, to build character, to have the pleasure of training, and to make money were not important motives for teenagers. The top *current* motives (for remaining in sport) were

1. to bring fame to one's country, heighten its prestige,
2. achieve high sport results (become a champion),
3. achieve moral recognition and popularity, and
4. get rid of boredom.

Making a career, earning money, becoming a professional sportsman, and feeding self and family were fairly unimportant for the mature athletes, for reasons stated by the authors:

> *The societies now under examination have not so far been able to build a show sport industry, while the population lacks money to spend on sport spectacles. . . . No country of Central Africa can afford to devote . . . attention to entertainments at a time when there exist more important tasks from the material point of view—the solution of economic problems, the elimination of illiteracy, the raising of the level of health and assuring nutrition to the population. (Maksimenko & Barushimana, 1978, pp. 45–46)*

Between the initial motivation (as pupils in school) and the current motivation (as top-level athletes) there has been a shift from personal to social motives. The researchers attribute this to a harder grip on the reality of life in a developing world and to a process of social maturation:

> *Ninety percent of sportsmen of various countries have noted the importance of their participation in sport with the aim of increasing national prestige. From our point of view this is explained by two causes: firstly, the social spirit of the population in the African countries which have freed themselves from the colonial yoke, connected with awareness of victory over the colonizers and the striving to achieve rapidly economic and cultural independence. Secondly, the polled individuals are top-class athletes, striving to defend in the best possible manner the honor of their nation. They are the strongest in the physical meaning of the word, and the people whose national honor they are defending, may be proud of them. (Maksimenko & Barushimana, 1978, p. 43)*

Organization of Sport

The Maksimenko and Barushimana study implies the existence of ongoing sport organizations to produce these top-class athletes as well as to conduct general physical education programs. It is generally assumed in the developing nations that physical education and sport will be coordinated by government, just as we in the United States assume a public school system. Now let's look at some of these structures as they have developed in Third World nations.

An interesting place to begin is Tunisia, in northern Africa, a French colony until 1956. Tunisia, as described by Mustafa Zouabi (1973) had some of the typical problems of colonial transition. Under the French, there were no independent Tunisian sport activities; all sportsmen belonged to French sport federations, and their activities were directed by Frenchmen. Very few sport facilities and little sport equipment existed in the country. Some large towns had no sport facilities at all. The country offered no center for training specialists in physical education. There had been little development of popular interest in sport, which was regarded as entertainment reserved for those with wealth and privilege.

Sport in independent Tunisia is now coordinated by the Ministry of Youth and Sport. Activities in the schools are under the guidance of the Director of Physical Education, School, and University Sport. Compulsory physical education in primary and secondary schools is coupled with efforts "to make the largest possible number of school-youth engage in sport activity, and . . . to enable them to obtain a higher technical level in the sport disciplines chosen by them" (Zouabi, 1973, p. 111). In 1973 there were in Tunisian schools 442 boys' and 135 girls' handball teams, 256 boys' and 115 girls' basketball teams, 240 boys' and 65 girls' volleyball teams, and 369 boys' soccer teams (no girls' teams). Also part of the school physical education program were gymnastics, swimming, fencing, and judo.

Outside of the schools, the principal activities of the Ministry of Youth and Sport are:

- to take care of the physical development of all citizens, irrespective of their social origins and to shape a sportive spirit.
- to popularize sport activity among citizens of the country.
- to train specialized personnel for various branches.
- to build proper sport facilities and to take care that these installations [will] be fully utilized, by giving access to them to a large number of participants.
- to give material and technical help to federations, clubs and all the organizations whose members are young people.
- to watch over the preparation of the national teams in various sport disciplines. (Zouabi, 1973, p. 112)

Syria, an Arab nation in the Near East, faced the old story: One of the major problems to be overcome in physical education, Zouheir

Chourbagi tells us in a report on *Physical Education and Sports in Syria*, is the inadequacy of facilities (that is lack of gymnasia and swimming pools) (1968, p. 197). Nevertheless, Syria has a healthy physical culture and sport program. In 1967 there were 127 sport clubs with about 15,000 members and federations in the specific sports of soccer, basketball, volleyball, wrestling, boxing, weightlifting, gymnastics, swimming, cycling, and horseback riding. A special directorate in the Ministry of Education supervised physical education, competitive sport, and scouting in primary to secondary schools. One to 3 hours a week of physical education were required in schools, and the Ministry supervised after-hours competitive games for both girls and boys. The two universities had competitive games but no compulsory physical education. Teachers for the program are now trained at the Institute for Physical Education, established in Damascus in 1968. Some of the deficiencies of economic and technical underdevelopment should have been relieved by a 5-year agreement with the Soviet Union in 1972 for competitions to be held in both countries, for sport seminars, and for the manufacture of sporting equipment.

The general direction of sport organization in Syria was first laid down in a legislative decree of August 4, 1952, which specified these activities:

- exclusion of political activities from clubs and federations.
- coordination of the work of the different sport organizations active in the country.
- banning all racial, religious, or confessional [but not sexual] prejudice from sporting and scouting activities.
- formation of national and Olympic committees.
- giving government allocations to sport clubs and federations. (Chourbagi, 1968, pp. 197–198)

Sport organization in the neighboring nation of Iraq involves a combination of state institutions and citizen bodies whose effectiveness has been the subject of a study by Abdul Mahmood (1981). In the most important case the state and citizen bodies are parallel: The establishment in 1968 of the Ministry for Youth Affairs (governmental) was followed in 1972 by the formation of the Iraqi Youth Union (citizen).

Each of the four ministries concerned with youth (Ministry of Education, Ministry of Higher Education, Ministry of Defense, and Ministry of Youth Affairs) has a directorate concerned with physical culture and sport. The General Directorate for Physical Culture in the Ministry of Education is responsible for required physical education in the primary and secondary schools. It encourages the development of talented youth in special sports by organizing sport competitions and sport festivals. It is in charge of standards for qualifying sport instructors and referees. "Activity in the sphere of school sports," says Mahmood, "is the principal foundation for physical culture and sport in Iraq" (1981, p. 118). The Ministry of Higher Education carries this further by doing the same thing for the universities and other institutions of higher learning. The Directorate for Sport of the Ministry of Defense similarly promotes mass physical culture among members of the armed forces and "focuses on raising the performance level of competitive army teams."

The Ministry for Youth Affairs has established 51 youth centers throughout Iraq, providing physical facilities and instruction for young people between 15 and 30. Youth hostels built by the ministry have recreational facilities for short visits by Iraqi youth and those from other countries. Youth holiday camps provide an opportunity for cultural and sporting events. The Ministry is responsible for maintaining, staffing, and supervising sport facilities and swimming pools. It has organized amateur gliding and parachuting activities since 1976 under a section called the Institute for Pre-Military Education. The Institute for Sports Medicine, which is also under this Ministry, provides free medical care for athletes injured in sponsored events.

Very important among the citizen organizations are 80 sport clubs throughout Iraq. The Ministry of Youth Affairs subsidizes club events and conducts nine training centers for top-class athletes who are candidates for national teams. Another important citizens' organization involved with sport is the General Council of Trade Unions, which organizes sport events in factories and other establishments. The General Union of Peasant Associations has set up 106 village social centers for youth between 10 and 18. One of the activities of these centers is sporting competitions. Unfortunately, the centers are pretty well isolated from the 51 urban centers established by the Ministry of Youth Affairs, which has set up no such centers outside urban areas. The General Union of Iraqi Students includes young people in secondary schools, vocational schools, and universities. The Union organizes student sport competitions and training programs for them and is also concerned with physical culture for the mass of students. The General Union of Iraqi Women has promoted team sport for women, especially in volleyball, basketball, and badminton.

All this would appear to be an impressively wide-ranging program of activities, especially for an underdeveloped country. How, then, does it look to a native sociologist? Mahmood did a study of Iraqi sport organization, contacting people on the top, middle, and grass-roots levels. He used interviews and questionnaires, studied organization documents, and participated in committee meetings and conferences. His conclusion, with which he felt that many people on all levels agreed, would probably apply to similar programs in other Third World countries. Mahmood found that although cooperation of government and citizen organizations has led to some positive trends in Iraqi physical culture and sport, the whole program seems to be lacking in coordination and communication except on narrow matters. He was critical of the failure of the government to bring rural areas into its urban-centered program. He found a shortage of long-range planning and the usual Third World story that "many institutions and organizations are lacking the necessary material and technical conditions, such as sports equipment, facilities, and other things" (Mahmood, 1981, p. 123). As a final result, he felt compelled to report "a scattering of many of the forces and possibilities [and] stagnation of the general level of physical culture and sport" (1981, p. 124).

The Third World nations whose sport structure we have looked at so far take sport for granted as a function of government, but only in the sense in which a United Nations ambassador from a pro-American and anti-Soviet Mediterranean ally said to me about 20 years ago: "We assume that there are important public functions that can be performed only by government; the trouble with you Americans is that you are so hung up on private enterprise." Cuba, the next nation whose sport structure we shall look at, is not hung up on private enterprise but, ironically, has a system of sport organization that was suggested as a model in 1975 when President Ford's Advisory Commission on Sport was trying to figure out how the United States can win more Olympic medals.

R. R. Aguilera of the Third World Communist power begins his article, "A Sociological Profile of Educational Sport in Cuba and its Development" (1973), with a humanistic emphasis on the individual that we did not hear in Soviet and Chinese discussions of how to make people more effective instruments for labor and defense: "Sport will reach its lofty objectives . . . as the development of sport corresponds with a social structure which recognizes that man represents the only wealth in the world and that his capacity for work and creation are implicitly the source of all values" (p. 119). By comparison with Cuba in the years before 1959—when sport was an activity of the privileged classes in private clubs and of poor athletes trying to escape poverty as professionals, especially in baseball and boxing—the sport program of Communist Cuba "has been adjusted to the characteristics and possibilities of our children, young people, workers, farmers, and military men in every corner of our country making [it] an actual fact that sport is a right of the people" (p. 119).

Aguilera states the premises on which Cuban physical education and sport are based. With one exception, there is nothing really different from the programs we have examined in other Third World countries:

- The program must give all citizens the opportunity and motivation to participate in physical culture and sport.
- The program must be geared to the needs of different socioeconomic groups in all parts of the country.
- There must be a wide diversification of available sports as preparation for international competition.
- The program must make use of available scientific, technical and teaching techniques so as to improve the quality as well as the extent of activities.
- Conscious involvement of the masses of people must be stimulated through the mass media.
- People must be made to feel that they have not only a right but a duty to support the sport aspect of Cuba's revolution.
- Ownership of sporting facilities must be in public rather than private hands. [This specifically socialist provision is where the Cuban program differs from the others we have reviewed.]
- An institute for the training of sport technicians and specialists is an absolute necessity.
- Factories must be established to produce sport equipment and other facilities. (1973, pp. 119–120)

How are these objectives implemented? A doctoral dissertation by Paula Pettavino (1982) explains it. The central government body concerned with sport is INDER, the National Institute of Sports, Physical Education and Recreation. With the Ministry of Education, INDER is responsible for sport and physical education in the regular schools. Technical sport personnel are trained at the national Higher School of Physical Education, which has a branch in each province. Promising athletes go to sport schools, which are both academic and athletic. There is a National Institute of Sports Medicine, where students learn to use computerization and other scientific techniques to produce the best athletic performance. The government operates a sport equipment industry near Havana that, among other things, produces homemade Cuban baseballs (very important in a country where baseball is the number one sport). As in Iraq, government bodies work with citizen organizations, or CVDs (*consejos voluntarios deportivos*—voluntary sport councils). The CVDs, which in 1982 numbered over 6,000, are described by Castro as "nuclei of citizens who, in every factory, on every farm, in every peasant association . . . in every cooperative, in every instruction center, in each military unit, in every municipality and every province . . . dedicate themselves to promoting sports activities" (Pettavino, 1982, p. 141). One sport official said, "When we look at our children, we are searching for diamonds." One way of doing this is through the LPV (*listos para vencer*—ready to run) physical proficiency tests, the equivalent of the Soviet GTOs. Another is through the

School Games, national competitions that produced 60% of the 1980 Olympic team.

Cuba seems to have done well in both the *massovost* and *masterstvo* aspects of sport. The right of all citizens to enjoy the same resorts, beaches, parks, social centers of culture, sports, recreation and rest is written into Article 42 of the Cuban constitution. Among other things, after 1959 the private sport clubs were opened to the people. By the mid-1970s more than a quarter of the population took part in INDER-sponsored competition. In a country whose whole population is less than that of New York, London, or Tokyo, over half a million Cubans play organized baseball.

The star athletes (such as world-known boxer Stevenson, middle-distance runner Guanterano, and 1980 Olympic javelin gold medalist Maria Colon) go to the advanced sport schools, where they participate on sports leave, earning the equivalent of the pay for the job for which they are training. The search for diamonds has been remarkably successful: A nation that ranked 57th in the world in population and 98th in land mass ranked 8th in medals at the 1976 Montreal Olympics. Jerry Kindall, the coach of the United States baseball team at the 1979 Pan-American games (a 10-year major league veteran) said that the Cuban team, which regularly sweeps the Games, could beat several teams in the U.S. major leagues (Pettavino, 1982, p. 240). First dominated by the United States, the Pan-American Games are now primarily a U.S.-Cuba showdown. Pettavino remarks that this performance by one of the neighborhood kids, plus the fact that Cuba gives technical sport assistance to the Soviet Union, must be very impressive to Third World nations. "Overall, Cuba provides the world with a clear example of how a communist system can help a developing country move from backwardness to excellence in a single area. The phenomenal success of this system of sport is inspirational" (Pettavino, 1982, p. 248).

The Cuban sport program, Pettavino suggests, is an interesting mix of American know-how, socialist planning, and Latin exuberance. Like the U.S.S.R., Cuba tries to promote both mass participation and competitive success. In general, their organization is modeled on the Russian model (centralization, special sport schools, national games, physical fitness tests, etc.) but is more like that of the young Soviet Union than the lumbering bureaucracy of today. It is, she says, less militaristic than the Russian program. It is still technically primitive—computerization in sports medicine is behind the U.S.S.R. as well as the United States. The Cuban athletes are less intense and humorless than the Russians. This, she says, is because they realize that their real livelihood won't depend on sport. The fans are more polite and less alcoholic. Cuban sport schools take seriously the future nonsport careers of their scholar-athletes. In general, Pettavino feels that the

Cuban sport system produces better people, closer to the ideal of communist man that both nations proclaim as their sport objective.

Transition and Sport

The problems of sport in the Third World grow out of the typical economic and political situation of developing ex-colonies. Economically, a Third World country has one foot in a traditional, rural, agrarian economy and one in a growing industrial economy. Some of its sport problems, which we saw foreshadowed in the outlying areas of the U.S.S.R. and China, grow out of underdevelopment—the shortage of stadiums, gymnasiums, swimming pools, and specific game equipment. Usually, this poverty is due to a combination of two factors: (a) colonial political domination in the past held back economic development, and (b) in the present, economic domination by major industrial powers and multinational corporations keeps the ex-colonies poor, except for an elite who go along.

Some sport problems, on the other hand, are an outcome of development. The conflict between elite and mass sport is an example. As underdeveloped nations move toward industrial takeoff, their populations are uprooted from their rural work and play activities and transplanted to jobs in the nonnatural setting of the city. Here their ordinary work activities do not keep them in shape as did rural farm work, and in city streets there is no longer opportunity for the rural games that relax country folk in their spare time. Because industrialization levels off the inequalities of income that usually exist in an agrarian society, people have more buying power than before. Also, for the first time in history, ordinary people have leisure time in which to spend their money.

Industrialism breeds specialization of all kinds, and one of the forms is that of athlete-entertainers who will give a vicarious sport experience to people who no longer have the opportunity to do their own physical playing. Specialization also produces technicians in mass physical education—teachers and coaches. Which of the two will it be? The situation of Tunisia, as described by Zouabi, is typical of the Third World; it is hard to do both. "In the present development of sport in Tunisia, the problem that has to be solved is whether to stress sport on a mass scale or competitive sport. . . . Activity on two fronts . . . gives rise to many obstacles, if one takes into account the modest material possibilities of Tunisia" (Zouabi, 1975, p. 113). Important factors swing the balance toward elite sport. In an underdeveloped country, because urban industrialism appears the key to economic advancement, country life and its ways tend to be downgraded, as we saw in Iraq, where the government established all its sport centers in the towns. Also, when the same country has been politically liberated recently, as Maksimenko and Barushiman's study of Central Africa showed, success in international sport becomes a way of establishing its identity. The outcome of these pressures is the same problem that was confronted by the Chinese Cultural Revolution—scarce human and technical resources are devoted to developing an elite of international sportspersons at the expense of the physical education of the masses.

Women in Third World Sport

A nation's stage of economic development affects women's participation in sport. I have said that the Third World nations have one foot in a traditional preindustrial society. This means, among other things, a patriarchial society. Pettavino points out that even in Cuba's highly developed sport program, Latin *machismo* has enough influence so that Cuban teams have fewer women than their Soviet and East German counterparts. Women are excluded from baseball, and sometimes are even discouraged from watching sports (Pettavino, 1982, p. 246). The other foot is in a society where woman's place is no longer exclusively in the home but also in the workplace and other social activities. Zouabi tells us that "a few years ago a young Tunisian girl had to cover her face when leaving home, even when going to school" (Zouabi, 1975, p. 113). This is a long way from playing on the runner-up women's basketball team on the African continent (the Tunisian team participated in the fifth African championships), or even more, taking part in swimming competitions. In Iraq, according to Akram Soubhi (1977), before the time of Mohammed, "birth of a daughter was . . . nothing to be proud of for the parents in Arabian territories . . . People were of the opinion that a woman is the property, one of the objects belonging to the master of the house, and her role was only to carry out the orders of the master, her husband" (Soubhi, 1977, p. 107). Although this view has been modified under Islam, says Soubhi, the religion still requires people "to treat women as weaker beings and to treat them in accordance with the role they perform, giving birth to sons and daughters" (p. 107).

Today in Baghdad and other towns, where rural tradition has given way, "the majority of women obtain higher education, conduct a lifestyle similar to that in Europe, take part in various kinds of cultural and sport entertainment" (p. 107). In 1958, following a revolution, about 4,000 young women from Baghdad took part in a sort of local Olympic Games, and in 1960 a women's sport club was founded in the capital city. Since the 1960s Iraqi women have participated in international competition. Since 1957 young women in the University of Baghdad have had available a wide range of subjects leading to specialization in physical education. Needless to say, whereas women formerly exercised in an attire that covered the whole body now they play in shorts and blouses. (If we look back 100 years in the United States, we will find a similar change.) These gains, says Soubhi, are still contested by conservatives, especially in rural areas. There are still parents who will not let their daughters go to coeducational schools and those who will present doctor's certificates to get them excused from physical education, not only in primary and secondary schools but also in the universities.

It is not only in the Arab nations that women's participation in sport has been restricted. In Nigeria women have had similar, although not so extreme, problems. These have been discussed by the Nigerian sport sociologist S. U. Anyanwu. "In the traditional Nigerian society," says Anyanwu, "women have been regarded as the weaker sex whose natural charm, beauty, and femininity may be destroyed by participating in vigourous physical activities" (1980, p. 85). In 1978 Adediji reported a small study of Nigerian women showing that 80% accepted the role of being "gentle, shy, fragile, conventional, and subordinate to the male sex" (1978, p. 39). Anyanwu points out that this prejudice is not Nigerian alone, but is part of our whole sport tradition that goes back to the Greeks and was continued when women were barred from the modern Olympics for some time after they began in 1896. Adediji says that female nonparticipation in sports stems from both the Nigerian culture and Victorian traditions of the Western world. Among the Nigerian natives, before the coming of the British, girls were trained to be nice wives and homemakers, whereas boys learned from their fathers to "develop dynamic qualities as leaders of their homes and defenders of the state" (Anyanwu, 1980, p. 87). The archery, wrestling, horseback riding, paddling, and canoeing that this training involved were taboo for women, who "were only allowed to dance and swim and take part in any traditional activity that entailed graceful movement." But they "were allowed to watch the men perform in local competitions in wrestling in order to cheer them up" (Anyanwu, 1980, p. 87). Note the American similarities. Nigerian sportswomen have to confront some of the same myths that plague American women's sport. A recent research project by Ugwuoke (1978) on participation in women's sport at the Nsukka campus of the University of Nigeria found 51% of the women reporting that they refrained from intramural sport because of fear of developing masculine features. Adediji speaks of a peer group taboo on sport participation by girls. "Boy friends reject girl friends on the basis of the girls' participation in sports. The premise of their action is based on the fear of alleged malfunctioning of some female organs in women who participate in sports. This attitude haunted the imagination of the girls" (Adediji, 1978, pp. 41–42). Anyanwu notes that in spite of Western research showing no harmful effects, Nigerian women, for whom marriage and motherhood are very important, often avoid sport because of these fears. Those who do participate typically hang up their gloves when they get married.

Adediji reports research on attitudes toward women's sport in and around a university community. When asked whether demonstrating equality was a valid reason for women's participation in sports, 90% of undergraduate women, 80% of university women workers, and 95% of women in the surrounding township said yes, as compared with 30% of undergraduate men, 32% of male university workers, and 25% of township men (Adediji, 1978, pp. 43–45, Tables 1–6). Adediji reports the following attitudes on male-female competition:

> When asked how they would feel competing against a member of the opposite sex, the women felt it would depend on the opponent and the situation. The majority believed there would be psychological pressures that would make them feel insecure. The men had mixed feelings about competing against a woman. Some felt that they would have a strong desire to beat her while others felt they [might] hold back. The majority of men expressed concern over the possibility of losing to the women. They felt that their worry would be not only for themselves but also for what their friends would say about them. (1978, p. 45)

A related problem is the coaching of female athletes by male coaches, along with male athletes, in light body-contact sports like basketball and field hockey. In terms of producing successful women's teams, practicing with and imitating males may be helpful. Anyanwu says it can lead to discouragement if the women find themselves unable to keep up with the men. On the other hand, joint practice may improve the women's performance toward the men's performance level. Male coaching of women, Anyanwu points out, also raises the question of role models. Speaking of the situation in southern Nigeria in the 1940s and early 1950s, Adediji says that "women began to imitate men in behavior and manners in an effort to be accepted into an all-male citadel. . . . These customs still affect the behavior pattern of the majority of Nigerian girls when participating in sports and games" (1978, p. 41). Anyanwu says that "the incentive, the challenge and motivation which the presence of female coaches offers to female athletes cannot be denied" (1980, p. 89). Part of the motivation may be the example of a woman who is athletically successful and still doesn't behave like a jock. The whole issue goes far beyond Nigeria. The

University of Miami has one major women's sport team coached by a male, and the same questions have been voiced.

In spite of these obstacles, women have been liberated in sport as in the rest of the Nigerian culture. Anyanwu speaks of a change in the attitude of the whole Nigerian community of a kind that now accepts sport heroines along with male heroes. Now women are involved in all sports except soccer, cricket, and boxing. Although Adediji says that "women are accepted in sports as long as they compete among themselves," and that to be challenged by a woman is to "debase one's masculinity," (1978, p. 42) secondary school girls do compete against boys in interscholastic matches in the noncontact sports of lawn tennis, table tennis, and badminton (Anyanwu, 1980, p. 91).

The first appearance of Nigerian women in international competition was in the Commonwealth Games at Cardiff, Wales, in 1958. In the 1966 Games at Kingston, Jamaica, a Nigerian woman won a bronze medal in the long jump. In the 1974 Games at Christchurch, New Zealand, Modupe Oshikoya won a gold medal in the long jump, a silver medal in the pentathlon, and a bronze in the 100-meter hurdles. Going beyond the Commonwealth, in the 1972 Olympics at Munich, Nigerian women competed in the 100-meter dash, the shot put, and the 400-meter relay.

Anyanwu concludes that "Nigerian women have moved from passive spectators to active participants. . . , thus breaking the barrier imposed upon them by the ancient cultural and value systems of their society" (p. 92). In so doing, they have moved in the direction in which women are moving throughout the Third World and throughout the whole world.

The chief factors shaping Third World sport are political and economic independence, modernization, and economic underdevelopment. Independence has produced a democratization of sport, as in Tunis, Nigeria, and Cuba, where ordinary people have begun to enjoy facilities and activities formerly monopolized by a French-, a British-, and a U.S.-linked elite. Modernization, by bringing industry, urbanization, a money economy, and the secular values that accompany them, has tended to produce a new specialized sport elite that becomes proficient at the games of the former masters. By undermining traditional sexism, modernization promotes the emergence of women athletes. How far Third World countries can promote both mass and elite sport is limited by the poverty of their economies. Economic underdevelopment makes more acute the choice between *massovost* and *masterstvo* that also exists in the more developed world.

The thorough and careful research on material for this chapter was done by Vasiliki Tolou of The University of Miami.

Part III

*S*port and *S*ocial Organization

Chapter 10

*T*he Sport Establishment

In this chapter we shall return to develop a theme that I introduced in chapter 3. There we saw that present-day sport, a development of the British and American Industrial Revolutions, involves (a) a continuity of organization, (b) highly specialized roles, (c) dynamic interaction with an audience, and (d) a sport order or establishment. Organized modern sport is not spontaneous play. It is not a pickup game. It is not even a single previously organized contest. The first American collegiate football game between Rutgers and Princeton in 1869 was what sport philosopher Paul Weiss called an *event*. The series of late 19th-century annual games in which Yale beat Harvard 19 out of 23 times, like the 20th-century series from Super Bowl I to XX, was an organized *pattern*. In the case of the Super Bowl, the pattern is part of a highly organized sport establishment, which the Yale-Harvard series was not.

Structure

What, then, is the sport establishment? In this chapter we shall examine the sport order from several angles: (a) as a system of interacting roles that sometimes mesh but often conflict, (b) as part of an athletic subculture, and (c) as a social institution that has its supporting system of beliefs. Our discussion will begin by outlining the *structure* of the sport order (the interacting components of which it is constituted) and move from there to its *dynamics* (the pattern of feeling and action through which the components are related).

William J. Baker in his *Sports in the Western World* (1982) gives us the barest skeleton of the role system that constitutes the sport order. Whenever we have had competitive sport, says Baker, we have had four groups of participants who like threads on a shuttle, weave in and out of the story of sports in the Western world:

- *players*—rough Roman gladiators or genteel golfers, medieval peasants or modern superstars, individual Greek competitors or modern teams.
- *patrons*—tribal priests and chieftains, village elders, kings, wealthy benefactors, modern club owners and league officials.
- *spectators*—at ancient Olympia and the Roman Colosseum, medieval tournaments, 18th-century boxing matches, and the latest Super Bowl.
- *commentators*—ancient sages, poets, philosophers, medieval theologians, preindustrial pamphleteers, 20th-century reporters and TV and radio announcers. (Adapted from Baker, 1982, pp. vii–viii)

To fill out the structure of the modern sport establishment (whether in the First, Second, or Third World, each in its own peculiar form), we will have to extend Baker's case of characters to read like this:

- *players*—genuine amateurs, formal amateurs, and frank professionals.
- a hierarchy of head and assistant *coaches* or *managers,* with their supporting personnel: physicians, trainers, equipment managers, physical therapists, masseurs, weight room coaches and attendants.
- a staff of referees, umpires, and other professional and semi-professional *game officials.*
- *training programs* for these sport personnel.
- *sponsoring bodies*—schools and colleges, religious service organizations (YMCA, YMHA), businesses, trade unions, military units, professional franchises, Olympic committees.
- *management*—collegiate athletic directors and their staffs, general managers of professional teams, recruiters, lawyers, money raisers, public relations personnel, ticket office personnel, stadium and field house personnel.
- *governing bodies*—leagues and Little Leagues, associations, conferences, government bureaus.
- stadium and media *fans.*
- *groupies* and "jock-sniffers" attached to athletes.
- bands, cheerleaders, organized opposite-sex friends of athletes (Hurricane Honeys, Gator Getters).
- alumni associations, booster clubs, and other *supporting organizations.*
- *the media*—press, television, radio.

- media *sponsors.*
- sport magazine and sport book *publishers.*
- *sporting goods* and equipment *industries.*

These elements of the sport establishment are related to it on different levels. Most of these roles are continuing, but some, like those of the Kazakh fans jetting to Moscow to follow their soccer heroes, are occasional. Most (including those of organized groups like the Hurricane Honeys) are formal roles; but some, like those of the groupies who trail a Namath, or Becker, or Tretiak, are informal. Some, like those of players, coaches, referees, and cheerleaders, are directly related to the production of games. Others, like those of the players', coaches', and officials' associations, and of investigators who monitor recruiting violations, importantly influence this production but are not part of the game activity itself. Stadium fans and media sponsors have the role of paying the bills; and the fans, who always give the home team an advantage, are also a direct part of the game. Producers of sporting goods and equipment are necessary for the physical operation of sports, and publishers of sport magazines and books keep fan interest alive and thus keep the supporting dollars, or rubles, or yens rolling in. But all mesh together to keep the sport order going.

As we know, their relationship is not one of total cooperation. In the words of the great sociologist William Graham Sumner, the sport establishment is a system of "antagonistic cooperation." It is this in the sense that a continuing system of sport competition (or, in fact, any single game) requires *an agreement to compete within mutually accepted rules* (see Figure 13.1, p. 261). But conflict and cooperation within the establishment are more than contact on the field. The coordination that keeps a system of sport going is shot through with conflicts of interest. At times these grow out of individual personality clashes, but what we shall examine is how they are related to the roles each party plays. Let us look at some of the more important areas of collision.

Conflicts of Interest

The first serious conflict involves *players and coaches* (or managers). This grows out of conflicts *within* the roles of both. The bottom-line fact about the role of the coach is that he or she has to win to survive. Thus team organization is usually semimilitary, with coaches running the gamut from near-psychotic George Patton types to benevolent father figures on the Eisenhower model. In my experience, most players accept this in general, with a preference for Eisenhower over Patton. But it creates conflicts. The player wants to win, but he also wants to survive physically, continue his career, and be a respected and self-respecting human being.

Players know that winning must sometimes involve rising above pain, but they are in a bind when coaches let it be known that their masculinity depends on endangering their welfare, and with it their careers. Sometimes, as when Jerry Kramer insisted on playing in a championship game with a detached retina (fortunately being overridden by the team physician), it is the players who are most at fault when they endanger life or limb; but a coach (and his players) are in a severe Catch-22 situation when the victory the coach needs to keep his job seems to depend on shooting up a severely injured athlete and sending him back into action. Furthermore, most players agree that on the field there has to be an expert in control, but some coaches like George Davis feel that players should participate in more decisions, including the choice of starting lineups; and some players, like quarterback John Reaves at the University of Florida, resent having all plays called from the bench. Players generally agree that the coach should be the ultimate boss on the field but sometimes question how restrictions on who can visit their rooms is related to field performance. Coaches may agree that the connection is remote, but insist that this kind of off-field control is necessary in order to establish their authority.

A second role conflict in American sport is between coaches (managers) and management (in formally amateur sport, collegiate athletic directors; in professional sport, general managers or owners). The most famous case in recent years was the perennial feud between Billy Martin and George Steinbrenner concerning who ran the Yankees. In both the formally amateur and the frankly professional situations the coach (manager) is the hired employee, management the employer. This *can* put the athletic director or owner in the position of saying: You work for me. I call the shots. This is exactly what the coach may in turn say to the scholarship athlete or the professional player. In professional sport, the owner is typically a well-heeled fan who keeps a team as a hobby (if profit were his main goal, he could make more outside of sport). As a fan, he is easily tempted to play grandstand quarterback to his coach (manager).

The coach's ace in the hole is his expertise; at running a team he is the professional, and the owner is the amateur. If the coach is successful, he has charisma; you don't arbitrarily fire an Earl Weaver or a Don Shula. Intercollegiate athletic directors also usually lack the charisma of successful coaches—have you ever heard of a college that had a 72–13 football record under athletic director X? They may use the leverage of being boss enough so that coaches who aren't top-flight may try to get rid of interference by becoming their own athletic directors.

A third serious area of conflict is between player recruiters and athletic governing bodies. In the Soviet Union, as early as 1925 a Disqualification Commission was established to control dirty play in soccer *and to prevent transfer of players from team to team.* More recently there have been problems with controlling the activities of sport brokers who sell the services of formally amateur soccer players to the highest bidder. In 1929 the Carnegie Foundation study of American intercollegiate sport reported the development of "a system of recruiting and subsidizing . . . demoralizing and corrupt, alike for the boy who takes the money and for the agent who arranges it" (Savage, 1929, p. xv). In recent years, the National Collegiate Athletic Association has placed on probation for recruiting violations such historic athletic powers as the University of Oklahoma, the University of Southern California, and Southern Methodist University.

I do not have any specific information on the interaction between recruiters and governing bodies in the U.S.S.R., but the situation in the United States is well known. No one claims any longer that American athletes in the major colleges are students who happen to go out for sports. It is accepted as customary and, indeed, proper that academic institutions should systematically recruit semiprofessional teams. To keep this system within bounds, the NCAA maintains an intricate system of recruiting rules and a staff of sport detectives who monitor the activities of its members. All this leads to discovery of activities that are sometimes near-criminal—for example, forging of high school transcripts and registration of athletes for nonexistent classes. Other violations are less blatant. Athletic recruiters, in their efforts to get the best talent, have to contend with regulations such as those requiring that visiting recruits be fed dormitory meals or the equivalent. In the mid-1970s this rule led to an internal hassle between the Miami *Hurricane* (student newspaper) and the Miami Hurricanes (football team) when the newspaper mistakenly received a bill sent to the athletic department after Hurricane Honeys entertained recruits at a restaurant whose fare was not that of the athletic dorm. Recruiters may risk, or actually receive, probation, as Miami did in 1981, for offenses such as the failure of a recruit to pay *interest* on a $10 bill he borrowed from a coach (he repaid the principal promptly). The Miami athletic directors' defense in the case of the misplaced restaurant bill was that everybody does it. In an intensely competitive struggle to be number one, where recruiting violations are regarded as business-as-usual and the regulating body is grossly understaffed it is not surprising that enforcement is inadequate and that enforcers are under tremendous pressure to apply the rules and recruiters under equal pressure to evade them.

A few years ago, Jerry Tarkanian, basketball coach at the University of Nevada at Las Vegas, brought the NCAA into court charging incompetence and favoritism in its investigative procedures. He raised the question of who gets investigated, and why. Clearly the answer is a mix of real rule violation and athletic politics. I think of at least three conditions that might result in investigation of and probation for an athletic program. One is flagrant and repeated violation of the recruiting code. A second is too rapid a rise to athletic prominence. This condition may tie in with the first in that recruiting violations may be a way of building a successful program. On the other hand, violations by a rapidly rising minor power may bring on investigation, whereas the same infraction by an established program might go unnoticed. A third condition also involves rapid rise to prominence, but in a very specific way—rival institutions in the same recruiting area may register complaints as a way of blocking out a competitor.

Another major conflict area is in collective bargaining between management and players' associations. On the undergraduate level the only serious attempt at collective bargaining was the 1970 University of Florida athletes' union. On the professional level, collective bargaining is established in the major sports and reached dramatic confrontation in the baseball strike of 1981 and the football strike of 1982.

This conflict is related to that between players and coaches, but it is different. The player-coach issue involves immediate personal survival and dignity. In the Gainesville players' union, which grew out of the counterculture of the 1960s, arbitrary control of athletes was an issue. In confrontations between management and professional players' unions, the first issue was, in Ed Garvey's words, whether athletes are persons or chattel. This has become a further question of who shall control sport. Collective bargaining has challenged the historic basis of professional sport—the reserve clause and the player draft—and advanced the concept of free agency. Unions have insisted on the capitalistic right of athletes to sell their labor to the highest bidder, whereas management has insisted on the capitalistic right to compensation for loss of its property through free agency. In the 1982 football strike, in the players' association proposal that athletes receive a specified share of management income, the confrontation came down to a question of control. Management, correctly, urged that the Garvey proposal was undermining the owner's capitalistic right to run his own business. Players insisted that there was no way for them to get a fair share without such participation in control.

Because no independent labor unions exist for anybody in the U.S.S.R. and the People's Republic (there is nothing comparable to Polish Solidarity in either country), we have as yet no similar account of athlete-management confrontation in the Communist countries. Perhaps, as Communist and capitalist athletes mix in the Olympics and other events, and if at the same time Polish athletes convey the spirit of Solidarity, we may begin to see jock liberation in the Soviet Union and China.

Another area of clash is between ticket offices and the media, between the stadium crowd and the media crowd. This is dramatized in the local TV blackout of professional football games. Two issues are present here—one of economics, the other of social psychology. Economically, blackouts assure that video viewing does not threaten stadium ticket sales. Because ticket sales, as a source of income, are less important than TV rights, this is not the real reason for TV blackouts—it is to assure a supporting crowd for the home team. An illustration is the recent remarkable success of both the professional Miami Dolphins and the formally amateur University of Miami Hurricanes in the Orange Bowl. In 1983, when the University of Miami won the national championship, the Hurricanes as well as the Dolphins blacked out TV coverage of their home games. This prevented the demoralizing audiences of 15,000 rattling around in a 70,000 seat stadium that had marked their losing years. The climax was the Orange Bowl Classic of January 2, 1984 (not blacked out), at which a more-than-full house (*and* a national TV audience) saw them clinch the number one position.

For media fans who cannot see a game because of a blackout, there may be resentment at being deprived, as they think, in order to serve the interest of management in ticket sales. This is only one instance in which fans have a sense of being ripped off by the establishment. Another is the sense of having to pay inflated ticket prices to support what they regard as the exorbitant salary demands of spoiled athletes. The more objective fans realize that player demands must be high (in terms of the fan's own income) in order for athletes to earn a lifetime's income in a brief playing span. They also realize that when salary demands do become excessive management has an alternative to meeting them by raising ticket prices—to absorb them out of profits. This is exactly what the Garvey percentage plan called for. Sometimes, in crises like the 1981 and 1982 strikes, fans may take the attitude of a plague on both your houses and threaten to boycott games when they are resumed. Predictions were made that fan interest and support would decline significantly after the strikes. They have not in any major way been fulfilled. 1982 baseball attendance and 1983 football attendance were not significantly down.

Another dramatic case of conflict with fans was Al Davis's action in ripping the Oakland Raiders out of their Bay Area community in 1983 and transplanting them to Los Angeles. This move also involved a clash within management in which Davis charged collusion by other NFL owners to deprive him of his rights of free enterprise. The other owners countered that ownership involves community responsibility beyond the sheer pursuit of profit. The three-sided clash raised fundamental questions about the dynamics of the sport establishment. Time will tell us who were the losers.

I said earlier that the whole sport order is a case of what Sumner called antagonistic cooperation. But the Raider case, the blackout, the player draft, opposition to free agency, insistence on keeping players in school until their class graduates, all indicate that American sport management itself is a special balance of competition and collusion. Well-heeled owners accused Garvey of socialism when he tried to cut the players' association into management, but they themselves act as a combination in restraint of trade, arguing that a free market for players would destroy competition on the field by allowing the richest owners to buy up the best athletes. What they say about Garvey and free agency may be true, but it all points to the fact that the sport establishment reflects the contradictions of a society split between the ideal of a free market and the reality of monopoly capitalism.

A final conflict is between the sport establishment and the educational system. Let us look carefully at the complicated relationship between organized education and the sport order. Michener points out that the attachment of semiprofessional athletic teams to universities has been found only in the contemporary United States. As contrasted with genuine student teams, which are an extracurricular expression of the educational community, formally amateur intercollegiate teams are an attachment that is usually related to the community only by name and location. In the American sport order, colleges and universities are a peripheral part not only of the formally amateur aspect of the sport establishment but also of the frankly professional aspect: College teams are a minor league where future pros are trained at the expense of educational institutions. True, some big-time university athletic departments make money, and athletic income has on occasion built academic buildings, but the usual relationship is academic subsidy of athletics—immediately of local sport entertainment and, more remotely, of professional sport. Educationally, one of the big areas of conflict is the *masservost-masterstvo* issue: A small minority of physically atypical athletes are given extreme attention, whereas the physical culture of the average student is neglected. Another conflict is between scholarships for academic performance and scholarships for athletic performance—when funds are limited, what goes to athletes must be withheld from serious scholars. Another problem is the educational fate of athletes themselves: The time, energy, and motivation consumed by sport deprives most of any real opportunity to benefit by the educational opportunity they have been given.

Most of these problems are peculiar to sport in the United States. We saw that Soviet and Cuban holders of athletic scholarships are required to give high priority to their studies along with their games.

The main reason seems to be that the institutions for which these semi-pros play are technical sport and physical culture institutes where their study has the recognized political function of preparing them as leaders in labor and defense—a situation with no clear American parallel.

The Athletic Subculture

So far in this chapter we have analyzed the structure of the sport order and of the antagonistic cooperation that makes it go. Behind the cooperation and the antagonism is a subculture—a system of attitudes, values, beliefs, and behavior patterns that all parties in the sport establishment share to some degree. To introduce us to the flavor of this subculture let us look at something that surfaced recently.

On December 27, 1983, the *Miami Herald* carried a story about the Orange Bowl committee that supervised the 1984 Miami-Nebraska championship football game (Fisher, 1983, p. 5A). What was reported was that membership on the committee has theoretically been open to all since 1972, when it was voted to admit women. But in 1983 active membership included three Hispanics, a handful of Jews, one black who saw himself as a token member and said, "I do not associate much with them," and no women. (Senator Paula Hawkins was an honorary member.) In that year four new members were admitted. All were white and male. Two were sons of committee members and two were Hispanics. A black, a woman, and two other Hispanics were rejected. The chairman justified all this by saying: "Our members come from all businesses. We have people who are very wealthy and of modest means. We had black members before it was common to do so. We had Jewish members when there was discrimination in this community. . . . It's only a matter of time until we have women members." He added that there really were already more than 100 female members since in most cases their wives were as active as they were. Patricia Ireland, regional director of the National Organization for Women, commented on this good old boy network, saying, "I don't know if the Orange Bowl committee is going to continue to ignore the 20th century." A further note came out after the game: The final game banquet was held at the exclusive Indian Creek Country Club, where the (black) majority of both teams ordinarily could not have gotten past the door.

The athletic subculture, at which this all hints, is a set of values, beliefs, and behavior patterns that is essentially authoritarian, sexist, racist, militarist, and nationalistic. In terms of chapter 2 of this book it represents the old culture as against the counterculture. Ex-football player Gary Shaw put it this way in 1972 for his particular sport: "Football is the strongest remaining unquestioned remnant of an old culture, and the struggle to change its current form is no less than a conflict between an old culture and a new culture" (p. 282). George Sauer, another Texas football alumnus, said a year earlier in explaining why he had quit at the peak of his career:

> *I think football has come to look a bit like our country does at certain times. I think the same powers that keep a football player locked in place are the same kind of powers that would tend to keep black and disadvantaged minorities, Mexican-Americans and Indians, locked in place. [A decade later Sauer probably would have added women.] The ideology of football's power structure is pretty much the same as that of the nation's power structure. (Scott, 1971, pp. 121-122)*

Authoritarianism

In chapter 2 we saw that for several thousand years before the Industrial Revolution and the American and French political revolutions social relations were typically based on unquestioned authority. The democratic counterculture that surfaced through these revolutions challenged this kind of authority. The decade of the 1960s further challenged it, and it has been questioned since. In general, the organization of sport supports the old authoritarian culture. This is what Sauer and Shaw were saying.

The struggle between the authoritarian and the postauthoritarian cultures focuses mainly on the coach-player relationship although, as we have seen, there are some owners and athletic directors who like to throw their authority around. The legendary authoritarian coach is Vince Lombardi. Today there are still coaches with the Lombardi approach; some others, like George Davis, avowedly believe in coaching democracy; and most coaches are a mix.

How authoritarian a coach will be depends on at least three variables: (a) the pressure to win, (b) the strength of authoritarian or democratic influences in his situation, and (c) the coach's personality. While coach at Arizona State, Frank Kush laid out the first variable concisely: "My job is to win football games. I've got to put people in the stadium, make money for the university, keep the alumni happy and give the school a winning reputation. If I don't win, I'm gone" (cited in Michener, 1977, p. 324). The most long-range example of the second variable is the influence of the counterculture over the past 2 decades. We saw earlier how Harry Edwards, from the left, and Woody Hayes from the right agreed that in the early 1970s athletes and coaches could not be isolated from antiauthoritarian influences on campuses. Another example: Other things being equal, a coach at a military service academy is likely to be more authoritarian than one at a liberal arts college with a humanistic tradition. As for the third variable, it could be that the coaching profession selects people who are unusually rigid and conservative. In the early days of the athletic revolution, under the influence of the famous post–World War II study of the authoritarian personality (Adorno, 1950) this aspect was emphasized.

A frequently quoted study by Bruce Ogilvie and Thomas Tutko (1971), based on a small sample of baseball, football, basketball, and track coaches, found them rigid, conservative, and insensitive to the needs of others. On the basis of such studies, Jack Scott (1969) described coaches as one of the most authoritarian groups in American society; they often outscore policemen and even military officers on measures of authoritarianism. All this was not supported by research conducted by George Sage in the early 1970s. In one study Sage (1974a) compared coaches with undergraduate students on a scale measuring Machiavellianism (the tendency to use and manipulate others) and found no significant differences between the two groups. Another study by Sage (1974b) compared coaches, students, and businessmen on a liberalism-conservatism scale. Coaches were somewhat more conservative than students and somewhat more liberal than businessmen.

About the role of the personalities of coaches, Jay Coakley's conclusion seems fair:

> *It is likely that the coaching profession attracts men and women who are highly achievement oriented, assertive, organized, and rather conservative in their beliefs. But it should be emphasized that an individual can be achievement oriented without being corrupt, assertive without being insensitive, organized without being manipulative, and conservative without being reactionary. (1982, p. 193)*

If many coaches are arrogant, overorganized, guarded and impersonal, inflexible, and unreceptive to the ideas of others, we shall find the main reason, I believe, more in their total social situation than in their inner psyches.

So far this discussion of the role expectations and behavior of coaches has dealt primarily with male coaches. A good reason for this is that traditionally most coaches have been male and thus most studies have dealt with males. However, the growth in competitive women's sport since Title IX has substantially increased the number of female coaches. How much will these women's behavior and attitudes be shaped by the fact that they are female *coaches*, and how much by the fact that they are *female* coaches?

In 1978 Linda Bain reported a study of 40 male and female coaches and physical education teachers (10 female coaches, 10 male coaches, 10 female PE teachers, and 10 PE teachers) from a random sample of 10 high schools taken from the Houston metropolitan area. Each person was observed on three occasions in interaction with students and scored, on a 1-to-9 scale, on seven aspects of the interaction. Bain made two comparisons: coaches versus teachers and females versus males.

By contrast with teachers, coaches were found to relate to others on the basis of their performance and to confine the relationship to the specific task at hand. They felt an obligation to provide learning experiences for all students. They were more accepting of the privacy of students, the right to seclusion of one's self, behavior, and property from public view, and of their autonomy, the right to regulate one's life by rules which one has accepted for oneself. Coaches talked more than teachers, and used more personal praise and criticism. They tended to treat the student as an individual, whereas to teachers the student was seen as a member of a group. Female and male coaches both exceeded their teaching counterparts on all of these variables.

However, there were gender differences in the whole sample of 40. These differences were all significant at the .01 level (differences this large would occur by chance alone less than 1% of the time). Women scored higher than men in promoting instructional achievement opportunities for all students. They were more protective of the privacy of students. They also engaged in more verbal communication of knowledge, and more praise and criticism.

In brief, coaches were more people-oriented than teachers. Women, in turn, were more people-oriented than men.

How do we explain Bain's findings? Although based on a small and local sample, they suggest that the attitudes and behavior of female coaches are shaped by both (a) the demand that they impersonally implant skills for individual competitive achievement (their coach role) and (b) the more nurturant and humanistic expectations that are learned as one grows up to womanhood in our culture (their female role). We may ask whether in the future women will be hardened by the competitive expectations of the coaching role or will, on the other hand, soften these expectations.

Sexism

As we noted in discussing sport in the Third World, the preindustrial age of authoritarianism was also patriarchal. Sport tends to continue, or restore, this patriarchy. Traditionally, the role of the male was to support his woman and children with his muscle, in work and in warfare; the role of the female was to be pretty, submissive, to attract a male, and then to bear and raise his children. The Industrial Revolution and the 20th-century automation and computer revolutions changed the nature of work and made muscle power obsolete. Technology applied to warfare made muscles nearly obsolete there too. What anthropologist William Arens says of football is true of all contact sport and perhaps of sport in general: "The game is a male preserve that manifests and symbolizes both the physical and cultural values of masculinity" (1975, p. 77). Masculinity here means preindustrial *machismo* based on the use of muscle. Contact sport is a preindustrial survival in a postindustrial age. (A more favorable way to put it might be to say that it is a survival of virility and bodily vigor in a time that has gone soft.)

What does male preserve mean? It means exclusion of women. Let's look at some dimensions of this exclusion. The most extreme dimension is banishment to the female preserve by exclusion from all sports. The bottom line of exclusion occurs when women are barred from entering the male preserve even to *watch* sport, as in the Greek Olympics; or when they are discouraged, as in present-day Cuban baseball. This ban may be modified for females who perform a feminine supporting role for male jocks as did women watching male wrestling in traditional Nigeria, or as do American cheerleaders. Less extreme is banishment from, or discouragement of, *participation* in all sports. We have seen this in traditional rural Poland and in the traditional Third World, especially the Islamic part. The reason given is that sportswomen lose their ability to perform their feminine role. Women in sport in the Western world still have to contend with the same feminine mystique.

The next form of exclusion from the male preserve is banishment from *contact sport*. The Soviet Union does not allow women to play soccer, and with some exceptions they are excluded from football in the United States. Many would say that these limitations are a reasonable protection of women's bodies. I am sure that few people would agree with Pettavino when she labels as Latin sexism the exclusion of Cuban women from boxing. On the other hand there are strong arguments that male genitalia are more vulnerable than female breasts, and that *nobody* should subject the human brain to boxing or the human knee to American football. Still, the central issue seems to be that violent collision isn't feminine.

Another type of exclusion is from intersex competition. We noted the mixed attitudes of Nigerian university athletes toward competing against the opposite sex. Michener makes a lengthy argument against intersex competition between adolescents (1977, pp. 161–168). Among young children and mature adults it may, he feels, be all right, but in the teenage period the young male ego must be protected against the trauma of losing to a girl. (He does not consider here the effect of exclusion on the young female ego.) In view of Michener's strong position, it is remarkable that Nigerian secondary school girls and boys, despite sexist traditions, do compete regularly in noncontact sports. We have no research on the effects.

Another dimension is exclusion of females from the male bond. Anthropologist Lionel Tiger (1970) contends that males have a genetic tendency to form strong cooperative bonds with their own sex and to exclude females. As examples we can consider the exclusion of women from most athletic dormitories and the segregation of male athletes from wives and girlfriends before games. Arens suggests that pregame celibacy resembles the practice of sexual abstinence by some primitive males before battle (1975, p. 79). Before games or battle three reasons may be advanced for female exclusion: (a) intercourse will drain male strength, (b) abstinence will stoke hostility before combat, and (c) the presence of women will weaken the team bond. Rather than attribute female exclusion to biological factors, it appears more a survival of the preindustrial male subculture, sometimes representing the desires of male athletes but normally emphasized by authoritarian coaches.

A bizarre example of athletic male bonding is the super-masculine behavior associated with British rugby clubs, described by the sociologists Sheard and Dunning (1973). Rugby is middle- and upper-class football, historically associated with the prestigious boys' public schools—Rugby, Eaton, Harrow, etc. Sheard and Dunning explain the violence of rugby as follows:

In Britain players of [Rugby Union football] have gained a reputation for regularly violating a number of taboos, especially those regarding violence, physical contact, nakedness, obscenity, drunkenness, and the treatment of property. Taboo-breaking of this kind tends to take a highly ritualized form. It has come to form an integral part of the subculture that has grown up and around the rugby game. One of its functions is that of providing an avenue of satisfaction for the players in addition to the game itself. (pp. 5–6)

Examples of the subculture: Roaring drunkenness is part of the tradition, accompanied by obscene songs that normally put down women and homosexuals. In a bar or in the bus after a match, a player may stage a ritual strip-tease, or he may be forcibly stripped and his body, especially his genitals, smeared with vaseline and shoe polish. In one case of a postmatch strip, the player was carried naked past women students at a university bar. Property may be stolen or deliberately destroyed. Unlike the lower-class violence that may occur on football specials after a soccer match, or unlike the supermacho behavior that used to be associated with the culture of the American pool hall, this violation of recognized standards is not considered hooliganism but is accepted with the attitude that the old boys will be boys.

Now why does this stereotyped wild behavior on the part of young British gentlemen occur? Sheard and Dunning see it as an assertion of masculinity in the face of doubt about one's male sex role. With the development of industry in the 19th century, these sociologists say, the British gentleman or would-be gentleman lost the outlet for physical expression that he had previously and substituted the physical inertia of an office existence. His grandfather, who had been able to ride to hounds for example, could thus assert his role as a male. Now the middle- or upper-class youth could assert it, not so much in the rugby contest itself but in the ritualized extracurricular masculine subculture. Also, the sex role of these young males was questioned from another quarter. Females of their class were becoming emancipated. Sheard and Dunning note the following:

The balance of power between the sexes is now beginning to veer toward a more egalitarian form of relationship. . . . One of the principal initial responses of many men as the attack from women first began to be mounted was to withdraw into the all-male culture and celebrate its values. In them the singing of obscene songs which symbolically expressed their masculinity in a virulent form, men's fear of women, and their simultaneous dependence on them, became one of the central elements in the club subculture. (1973, pp. 13-14)

Furthermore, in this male preserve where the strongest ties are to other males, homosexuality is to be feared. In the segregated male public schools from which rugby sprang it was quite common. "And even the game situation, where the players grasp each other in a hot sticky mass, their heads between each other's thighs, has become the butt for frequent jokes" (p. 15). Thus "queers" are reviled and mocked, along with women.

Sheard and Dunning tell us that the excesses of the rugby clubs have declined in recent years. This, they say, is in part because rugby has become more competitive and the men want to be in shape. But it is also because the new woman wants a man's life to be centered on her, not on the old boys. Rugby clubs are breaking down and admitting wives and other women friends. It appears likely that the old-style rugby player will become just an historical curiosity. So, perhaps, on this side of the Atlantic, may the macho American athlete.

Another bizarre aspect of the male athletic subculture is the tendency to dehumanize women. In traditional patriarchy two things typically happened simultaneously to women: They were degraded into impersonal sex objects and elevated onto pedestals. Usually this involved separation of women into two classes—idealized women whom one might marry and degraded women whom one might use for sex. Dave Meggyesy says that to many football players he knew ''wives are virginal creatures keeping the home and the kids; other women are meat on the rack'' (1970, pp. 182–183). How this kind of attitude degrades both sexes is shown by Jim Bouton's description of the ballplayer's pastime of beaver shooting (beaver being female pubic hair): crawling under the seating of stadiums so that to the tune of the Star-Spangled Banner an entire baseball club of clean-cut American boys would be looking up the skirt of some female (1971, p. 36). Meggyesy, reports that to football players he knew, a female was typically a cunt or a piece of ass. One sad case he related is that of a married player, returning from a road trip, who said, ''I'm really going to punish the old lady tonight'' (1970, p. 183). In terms of power, a male who reduces a female to a ''cunt'' at the same time psychologically reduces himself to a *schmuck* (the translation of the Yiddish is prick—a creature totally identified with his penis). He does this when, as Meggyesy's own case shows, the most important thing in maintaining one's own identity in the face of the athletic and nonathletic establishment is the love of a woman whom a man regards as a person. As Sheard and Dunning said of the rugby subculture, countercultural tendencies have no doubt softened the kind of attitudes Bouton and Meggyesy reported around 1970. Yet it was in 1981 that a female physical education major wrote on an exam for me of her resentment at being regarded by some of her male fellow-majors as just a piece of meat.

This was the year that male domination spread in another dimension: Men took control of women's sport. For a decade the male National Collegiate Athletic Association had insisted on what one woman administrator caustically described as its divine right to govern all collegiate athletics. Finally it succeeded in moving the female Association for Intercollegiate Athletics for Women out of the picture and taking over governance of the women athletes generated by Title IX. The process was exhaustively analyzed by Donna Lopiano in a 300-page affadavit presented at AIAW's antitrust suits against NCAA (Lopiano, 1981).

The change from female to male control offers an interesting study in the loss of democracy under patriarchy, for in several respects the AIAW had been less authoritarian than the NCAA, and sometimes even countercultural.

- A significant difference was rooted in the systems of classification used by the two associations. Both employed the terms Divison I, Division II, and Division III. With NCAA this is a three-layered hierarchy of *institutions* that compete across the board with their peers, meet and establish policy with their peers through their peer organizations, and exercise different power in the whole association according to their level in the hierarchy. This applies to income too, of which the most important part is television rights. Lopiano says that "in an economic sense, the NCAA is its Division I program" (1981, p. 14).

AIAW's classification applied to performance level in specific *sports*. Thus, a school could play Division I basketball, Division II volleyball, and Division III field hockey. This was a more flexible and egalitarian system than NCAA's hierarchy of *schools*.

- The lower commercial value of women's sport made it unnecessary for AIAW to develop a machinery of regulation and enforcement as complex (and, as we have seen, sometimes bizarre) as that of NCAA.
- Member institutions in AIAW were generally represented by working sport personnel (athletic directors and athletes) rather than, as in NCAA, by faculty representatives without such direct sport involvement and primarily concerned with the promotion and regulation of sport as a commercial venture.
- Student representatives, chosen by their peers, played a recognized and active role in all aspects of the organization of AIAW.
- AIAW was actively concerned with minority representation in the organization as a whole and in its committee structure.

The absorption of women's sport into the male preserve is further documented by Milton Holmen and Bonnie Parkhouse's study of the selection of coaches for women's sport between 1974 and 1979, as reported by 335 randomly selected directors of women's athletics at AIAW member institutions. They revealed (a) a 37% increase in the number of coaches for female athletes, (b) a greater increase at the assistant (229%) than at the head (8%) coach level, (c) a substantial increase in male coaches (724) in comparison to their female counterparts (44), (d) a significant decline (294) in the number of female head coaches, and (e) a large increase in the number of male head coaches (437) (1981, p. 9). Statistically, an increase as large as that of men in women's programs would have occurred by chance less than one time in a thousand ($p < .001$). The same was true of the decline in female head coaches (Holman & Parkhouse, 1981, pp. 12, 13).

In short, it is male coaches who have cashed in on women's lib in sport; relatively, women coaches have lost out.

Racism

In beginning this section, I named five patterns that are associated with the athletic subculture. Because they are all aspects of the preindustrial male preserve I think that authoritarianism, sexism, militarism, and nationalism will be found wherever we find organized contact sport. Because it is so pecularily American, racism is, I think, special to sport in the United States.

Blacks have experienced in American sport the same sequence of exclusion from the white preserve followed by admission with discrimination, that women have experienced almost everywhere from the male preserve. (Black women athletes have experienced both.) From the vantage point of the 1980s, when most major sports are dominated by black males, it is hard to grasp such facts as that, with rare exceptions, big-time football was entirely white until 1946, baseball until 1947, and that there were no blacks in national professional basketball before 1950. Florida students born in the early 1960s find it hard to believe that in the year of their birth there were no blacks on any major college team in the state, and that the idea of their inclusion was at that time almost unthinkable.

In a sense, sport was ahead of the rest of the country in racial desegregation. Professional baseball, football, and basketball introduced blacks before the 1954 Supreme Court school desegregation decision. Athletic desegregation on the professional and formally amateur levels has occurred, however, primarily because it is good business. One sports writer said of Jackie Robinson, ''Jackie's nimble, Jackie's quick, Jackie makes the turnstiles click'' (Coakley, 1982, p. 244). As soon as the deep-South Universities of Alabama and Mississippi became convinced that blacks could win ball games, these institutions—where George Wallace has personally barred the door to a black woman and federal troops were necessary to admit a black man to graduate school—began to recruit black athletes. But this does not mean that they were accepted as equals.

What do I mean by not as equals? I refer to several things: (a) segregation by sport, (b) social segregation, (c) segregation by position, and (d) segregation from professional opportunity.

First of all, blacks are not usually found in those sports (such as swimming, bowling, tennis, and golf) in which there is ordinarily off-the-field personal contact, including contact between the sexes. They are segregated in team sports in which relationships are usually confined to the field, and even there are so impersonal that a team can be successful without its members liking one another, or even when some actually hate others. (It is true that the sports that remain in the white preserve are also, except possibly for bowling, sports that are too expensive for young blacks to enter or that require facilities from which they are ordinarily excluded.)

Second, blacks are not recruited to become an integral part of a college or university body. At training tables, in recreation after practice and games, in casual campus and classroom contacts, and in dating, blacks are likely to be found with blacks and whites with whites. Michener described plainly the situation of the young black athlete, especially the man recruited to a predominantly white university, in an unfamiliar and distant place like Lincoln, Nebraska, Laramie, Wyoming, or Manhattan, Kansas:

> *The black athlete, cut off from black society of any kind, is supposed to spend four of his most virile years playing games for his university, and sitting alone in a room, forbidden to speak to any female. If he dares to do so, the whole weight of the athletic establishment falls on him; he is castigated verbally, threatened with the loss of his scholarship, demoted by his professors in class. (1977, p. 161)*

Michener cites a black University of Wyoming player who tried to date a white girl whose cowboy brothers thereupon organized a posse "to gun down the nigger if he makes another move."

Third, blacks are ordinarily subjected to positional segregation on the field (stacking) in noncontrol positions whereas the control posts go to whites. In baseball, blacks are usually excluded from the positions of pitcher, catcher, shortstop and second base and are segregated in the outfield. In football centers, quarterbacks, offensive guards, and linebackers are generally white; running backs and defensive backs are usually black. In basketball, control positions are guard and center, with forwards primarily black. In the pros this pattern was generally true in 1970 but not in 1980; in 1980 positional segregation was still found on both women's and men's college basketball teams. In the 1970s there was some tendency for positional segregation to decline, but Coakley points out that sometimes the decline wasn't real—for example, when blacks assume new control positions it is in situations like the football wishbone offense in which the quarterback is really a running back and the coach calls the plays from the bench. Another reason for the decline may be that with pro basketball and defensive football becoming predominantly black racial differences have to be erased.

Why are blacks positionally segregated? One reason may be that segregation by position perpetuates itself through role modeling—young blacks who aspire to greatness will want to be like older successful blacks who are positionally segregated—slugging outfielders and running backs, for example. Another reason is the attitudes of coaches. Williams and Youssef in 1975 asked football coaches to identify the qualities necessary for the control positions of center, offensive guard, and quarterback. The answers were reliability, quick comprehension, and thinking ability. They were then asked to name the qualities for noncontrol positions—running back, defensive back, and wide receiver.

For these they named physical speed, physical quickness, and motivation to achieve. Finally, the coaches were asked to name the qualities typical of white and black athletes. The "white" qualities were (a) thinking ability, (b) quick comprehension, and (c) reliability. The "black" qualities were (a) speed, (b) quickness, and (c) high motivation (Williams & Youssef, 1975). "With such attitudes," says Coakley, "it is easy to see how coaches would tend to systematically assign blacks and whites to different positions" (1982, p. 252).

Finally, positional and social segregation lead to segregation from professional opportunities in sport. As players, whites, whether in central positions or not, are more likely to be asked to endorse products. (Mean Joe Greenes with their Cokes, Bubba Smiths with beer, and O. J. Simpsons flying through airports, are rare.) A black player is likely to make less in an off-season job. Whereas white players are picking up $1,000 to $2,000 for appearances, a black player may have to settle for $100 high school talks. A clue to professional futures was given by Oscar Grusky, who found in 1963 that a disproportionate number of major league managers were ex-catchers (the catcher is the baseball quarterback, and usually white) (Grusky, 1963). In the light of all this, Gene Upshaw's and Ed Garvey's findings in the NFL in late 1978 were not surprising:

> *Of approximately 280 assistant coaches, there were only ten to twelve blacks; there had never been a black head coach in the history of the NFL; no black offensive or defensive coordinators were currently employed; there have never been any black general managers; no blacks in the collective bargaining arm of the National Football League, the Management Council, and no blacks in policy-making positions in the NFL office. (Upshaw & Garvey, 1980, p. i)*

Richard Lapchick (1984) reported that in 1983 only 6.9% of coaches, executives, and administrative staff of the NFL were black. In the previous year the NBA, where 75% of the players are black, had only 5.3% of blacks in coaching, management, and administrative positions. We shall explore sport racism further in chapter 11.

Militarism

The connection between sport and war has often been noted. There is the famous cliché that Britain's wars are won on the playing fields of Eton. In chapter 7 we heard an anti-Bolshevik Britisher lament that the opposition to the Russian revolution of 1917 had not prepared adequately on the soccer fields of Moscow. After World War I Walter

Camp, father of modern American football and brother-in-law of the great social Darwinist sociologist Sumner, wrote that the "grand old do-or-die spirit that holds the opponent on the one-yard line was what won the critical battle of Chateau Thierry" (Powel, 1926). At a later time General Douglas MacArthur phrased this ode to sport:

Upon the fields of friendly strife
are sown the seeds
that upon other fields, on other days
will bear the fruits of victory. (Goodhart & Chataway, 1968, p. 63)

In 1969, Max Rafferty, formerly a successful high-school coach and then California Superintendent of Public Instruction, drew a standing ovation from California athletic directors by linking sport, war, and authoritarianism: "There are two great national institutions which simply cannot tolerate either internal dissention or external interference: our armed forces and our interscholastic sports program. Both are of necessity benevolent dictatorships" (Scott, 1971, p. 14). In a 1971 *Philadelphia Inquirer* article Sandy Padwe pointed to the linkage of the sport and military establishments: jets flying over stadiums in halftime shows; ABC refusing to televise a halftime program by the University of Buffalo band with an antiwar, antiracist, and antipollution theme, but broadcasting an Army-Navy show honoring the Green Berets; the Rose Bowl committee refusing to allow the University of Michigan band to present a 4-minute peace segment in its halftime show, but authorizing the usual military floats and red-white-blue pageantry; a neon American flag over the Orange Bowl end zone and 50,000 spectators at the Memphis Liberty Bowl simultaneously waving little American flags provided by the management (Padwe, 1971).

Let's look at what underlies the athletic-military connection. War is a territorial intimidation-strategy game in which the most complicated and sophisticated weaponry is justified by the fear of invasion—for Americans, "the Russians are coming," and for the Russians, "the Nazis came." For this terminal contest similar games (a) are a preparation and (b) create a taste. The connection between war and sport is twofold. Games, especially physical contact territorial games, are seen as war. And war is seen as a game. As early as Old Testament days, war was a spectator sport. In the Second Book of Samuel, two contending military leaders say of their warriors, "Let the young men arise and play before us" (2:14). On the most sophisticated intellectual level of game theory military establishments practice deterrence through pseudomathematical calculation of how their opponents will react in a number of situations: If we do this, they will think this, and do this, whereupon we will counter thus and they will think this and do this, etc. The similarity to the strategic calculations of athletic coach-

ing staffs is obvious. On the gut level, all this sophisticated technological preparation is experienced as a preindustrial contest between the
good guys and the bad guys: a pitched battle when knighthood was
in flower, or more recently, Cowboys and Indians and cops and
robbers. In the mid-1980s the good guy is Rambo. When I say that the
athletic subculture, as well as being authoritarian, sexist, and racist,
is militaristic, I mean that both war and contact sport are a throwback
to the preindustrial macho culture and reinforce each other.

Nationalism

For obvious reasons, the militaristic aspect of the subculture merges
into the nationalistic. Nationalism in sport wears several different faces,
depending on the situation. We have seen that in the Communist and
Third Worlds it is assumed that sport is a function of government and
an instrument of national power. Although most sporting events are
directly sponsored by such private bodies as sport clubs, schools, industrial plants, unions, and cooperatives, both mass physical culture
and competitive sport are coordinated by government, which actively
organizes the pyramidal process by which superior athletes are chan-
neled upward from the mass base to the peak of international competition for the honor of country. In this kind of situation it is highly
unlikely that a hockey star like Vladislav Tretiak will become an international free agent and sell his services to the Montreal Canadiens.
Tretiak's freedom was as limited by his role as a national symbol as
the freedom of his American counterparts is limited by the reserve
clause in their contracts. The capitalist world has generally rejected this
kind of sport nationalism, except when a president like Ford assem-
bles a Commission on Olympic Sports that asserts that "winning is
a reflection of our national spirit and purpose," or when one like Carter
imposes an Olympic boycott on the assumption that the United States
Olympic Committee is subordinate to the national government.

Nevertheless, every 4 years capitalist, Communist, and Third
World countries join in a process whereby, as Alex Natan (1958) has
put it, athletes become soldiers of sport with the international prestige
of their nations at stake. The origin of the modern Olympics, promoted
by Pierre de Coubertin, was a mixture of idealism and nationalism that
has persisted ever since. According to the Olympic ideal the games
were to be an international sport forum in which amateur athletes
would compete as individuals over the heads of their governments.
The ideal was tainted from the start, however, by the fact that
Coubertin was an intense French nationalist who saw the games in
part as a way in which France could regain the prestige she had lost
when defeated by Germany in the Franco-Prussian War. Today,

although the ideal is still promoted by the International Olympic Committee and partially realized in the community of athletes in the Olympic Village, all three worlds accept and are motivated by the unofficial national scoring. The Communist nations deride capitalist commercialism and claim that their athletes are amateurs while they give them *government* subsidy; the capitalist world accuses the Communists of professionalism and hypocrisy and itself generates medal winners by *corporate* subsidy. Both systems join in regarding the Olympics as an arena of national power. This conception may destroy them. In a 1981 sociological perspective on the Olympics the Finnish sociologist Paavo Seppänen finds one significant recent example of the Olympic spirit as an independent force in the world: the action of the British Olympic Committee in sending a team to the 1980 Moscow Olympics in the face of a government-ordered boycott.

One phenomenon is worth consideration by anyone who doubts that the American athletic subculture is nationalistic—the unique association of patriotic and military symbolism and ritual with sporting events. We do not routinely open a scientific conference, a convention of physicians, lawyers, or teachers, a school or university commencement, or an art exhibition with a rock, pop, western, operatic, or religious soloist singing "The Star-Spangled Banner" against a magnified flag in the background with all participants standing with heads bared or hands over hearts. However, we take it for granted that a major team sporting event cannot begin until such homage has been given to national identity and power.

The Sport Creed

All social institutions, of which the sport order is one, are supported by a system of beliefs (ideology). Some of these beliefs have a basis in fact, some are false, and some are unproved. True, false, or unproved, they are generally believed by participants in the institution. Harry Edwards has systematically outlined the "dominant sports creed," the ideology of the sport establishment (1973, pp. 103–130, 318–330). Although teaching experience has shown me that athletes and other students may differ sharply on particulars, as a whole these 12 beliefs are generally accepted by players, coaches, officials, management, fans, and media personnel:

- Sports participation develops good character.
- It develops a value on loyalty.
- It generates altruism.
- It generates a value on social and/or self-control.

- It develops fortitude.
- It prepares the athlete for life.
- It provides opportunities for individual advancement.
- It generates physical fitness.
- It generates mental alertness.
- It is supportive of educational achievement.
- It develops religiosity.
- It develops patriotism.

Let's look more closely at the items in the sport creed, with some of Edwards's comments and my own.

- *Sport promotes good character.* If we ask why young men and women go into the coaching profession, one of the big reasons is the influence they hope to have on the personality and emotional development of young people. Is their hope justified? Ogilvie and Tutko's comprehensive study of the personalities of athletes, published in 1971, is titled, *If You Want to Build Character, Try Something Else.* Studies by Harry Webb (1969b) and others indicate that as one grows into organized sport the ethic of sportsmanship typically diminishes in favor of the desire to win. Francis Ryan (1958) found admirable qualities of character in his study of the personalities of successful competitors—openness, sociability, humor, and self-discipline. However, he also found less admirable traits—hatred of opponents, a need for grudge matches, inability to accept defeat, and unquestioning acceptance of the coach's authority.
- *Sport promotes loyalty.* There is little doubt, I think, that sport promotes strong group loyalties. What this means is best understood by applying Sumner's (1940) treatment in *Folkways* of the characteristics of in-groups (which always have an enemy out-group). Strong feelings of hostility toward the opponent create strong feelings of loyalty within the team. The individual identifies so strongly with the team as to risk health or life for it. He or she has a double standard for judging the acts of the team and those of the adversary. What is good clean aggressiveness by his or her team is a cheap shot when the opponents do it. In-group loyalty may be less true of individual sport than of team sports. Even in team sports it has been weakened in the affluent society by the rise of the well-paid individual star whose team victory may be less important than personal record making.
- *Sport generates altruism.* Altruism is, by definition, concern for the other (Latin, *alter*). Whether sport develops altruism depends on whether the other is a member of one's loyalty group (team). Sumner reported that primitive (and not so primitive) cultures

tend to define only members of their own group as people. One does not feel toward members of the out-group, who are really nonpersons, the obligation that one has to real people. There is much of this kind of thinking in sport, along with some humanism. The Webb studies found altruism in sport declining with adolescence. Ogilvie and Tutko reported a low need in athletes for giving support to others and receiving it from them.

• *Sport promotes social and self-control.* In the old days before the counterculture, teachers and other adults would point to athletes as models of the clean-cut boy or girl. Research by Walter Schafer (1969) showed midwestern high-school athletes with a lower delinquency rate than nonathletes. Soviet sport sociologists consider sport an important tool against delinquency. In fact, there are special sport sections in Moscow for delinquents (Riordan, 1977, pp. 197–198). An interesting case of self-control is the outcome of three psychological tests reported by Edwards that showed black athletes to be more reserved, more orderly, more controlled, and more self-examining than whites (1973, p. 225). Apparently the hope of using sport as a way out of the ghetto was a strong motivation to keep their noses clean.

• *Sport develops fortitude.* There can be no doubt that sport, especially contact sport, requires fortitude, but Edwards believes that it *selects* athletes who have fortitude more than it develops it in those who do not. There is also the question: Could other activities provide fortitude as well or better? If they are more like the situation one will meet in later life, they well may. Undergraduate in-service experience in an emergency ward or a minimum security prison might well be more relevant for a premedical or prelaw student than playing on an athletic team.

• *Sport prepares the athlete for life.* This idea of sport had more reality when school and college sport were amateur. But now, as Edwards points out, for amateurs as well as pros, sport *is* life, and so the aspiring athlete has no youth. Another problem is that in his nonyouth the athlete leads a very artificial existence that may actually handicap him or her. What Harvard President Eliot (1905) wrote close to a century ago is still true. He said that there is no poorer way to prepare for life than to learn to believe that one can perform well only in the presence of applauding friends. Therefore, the athlete often faces an identity crisis when he or she must confront life after sport. Moreover, there is the problem, often encountered in Little League, of the young person who is shattered by failure to make the team.

• *Sport promotes individual advancement.* The truth is that for some it does, but for most it does not. We shall see later how sport has been an upward ladder for minorities—Irish, German, Polish,

Jewish, Italian, Latin, black, and French Canadian. About 1% of athletes in sport make it big, and 99% either wind up where they started or are actually held back by sport. Sport tracks some minority members up to more money, prestige, and achievement. It may track others down out of higher goals they might have reached if they had not been athletes.

* *Sport promotes physical fitness.* This is true for participants in the minor sports—tennis, golf, jogging, swimming—who develop lifelong habits of exercise. As for the major contact sports, Edwards points out that both college and professional athletes are rated as high insurance risks. Few participants in the major sports finish their careers without some lifetime disability. But even the battered and overstressed major athlete will probably live longer and better than the person whose participation is limited to watching from the stands.

* *Sport participation promotes mental alertness.* On this claim Edwards concludes that there is no evidence pro or con. Clearly organized sport *requires* mental alertness, at least enough to remember the plays. Some of it is selected, some developed. The big question is, How much is transferred to nonsport situations? Strangely, this claim is similar to the one traditionally made for the mentally sharpening effect of math as a school subject. In sport as in math, transfer of training is likely to be greatest in areas similar to the original one, and less in dissimilar ones.

* *Sport promotes educational advancement.* There are two basic facts here: (a) some youths use their athletic ability to get much further in school than they otherwise might; and (b) when they are there, they usually have to choose between their sport and their academic work—there are rarely time, energy, and attention for both. Some use an athletic scholarship to prepare themselves for a nonathletic vocation; but many others become so absorbed in sport that they are tracked out of other educational opportunities for advancement.

* *Sport participation develops religiosity.* Sport in the United States has traditionally been associated with the authoritarian syndrome, which promotes conventional religiosity along with militarism, sexism, racism, and free enterprise capitalism. The ritual prayer before players go out to knock each other's heads off is as much a part of the pattern as is The Star-Spangled Banner. The Fellowship of Christian Athletes (FCA) sees sport as properly expressing and promoting an orientation to winning for Christ. Billy Graham enthusiastically claimed that "there are probably more really committed Christians in sports, both college and professional, than in any other occupation in America" (*Newsweek*, January 11, 1971, p. 51). The NFL sanctioned a spe-

cial Weekend of Champions at the 1971 Miami Super Bowl, featuring Christian athletes from almost all major sports. However, the FCA and other religiously committed athletes are only a minority, and the ritual prayers, like the national anthem, are generally rather routine. Edwards is probably right in concluding that there is no hard evidence that sport either significantly promotes or detracts from formal religiosity.

* *Sport participation develops patriotism.* We have observed that the athletic subculture has nationalistic as well as authoritarian, racist, sexist, and militaristic overtones. As we noted earlier, sport is more clearly and frankly an instrument of national policy in the Communist and Third World nations, but for all three worlds the myth that sport is good clean amateur self-actualization is long dead. The athlete who entered international competition and made his way on his own is also long in the past. Today he is a formal amateur paid by government or private agencies to compete for his country. There are ecstatic patriotic episodes like the United States Olympic-hockey victory in 1980 and some World Cup soccer championships, but what kind of long-run national loyalty they create is still open to investigation.

In this chapter we looked first at the structural components of the sport order. Then we viewed the whole establishment as a system of antagonistic cooperation and highlighted some of the most prominent areas of conflict. After that we looked at the different aspects of the authoritarian-sexist-racist-militaristic-nationalistic pattern of action, feeling, and belief that undergirds the sport order. We have concluded with the myth system by which the sport establishment, like all social institutions, is supported. In chapter 11 we shall examine further what this whole complex system does for socially powerful people and for the socially powerless.

Chapter 11

Sport and Social Power

In chapter 10 we saw that an important item in the myth system of the athletic subculture is the belief that sport is an important way for powerless people, especially minorities, to move up in the world.

Let us examine this belief, looking first at the situation in other countries and then comparing the situation in the United States.

Sport and Social Stratification Abroad

In a 1979 study Zbigniev Szot and Bogdan Jurkiewicz compared the social backgrounds of Polish gymnasts of the beginning level (first class), participants in the Polish national championships (national champion class), and participants in international competition (international champion class) (Szot & Jurkiewicz, 1979, p. 78). First, it was found that first-class and national-class gymnasts from intellectual families did better than those of working-class origin. But, "this thesis found no confirmation in the highest (international) class, where competitors of working class origin obtained results better . . . than their counterparts coming from the families of intellectuals" (Szot & Jurkiewicz, 1979, p. 78). The reason? At the beginning, on the lower levels of competition, the white-collar athletes have the advantage of not having to work to help support their families and can go to school, where they have required physical education. But on the higher levels, the working class have started earlier, are helped by their experience in physical work, and are more strongly motivated. "Men who started to train gymnastics at the age of 10–12 years achieved the biggest success and they come from workers' families" (p. 79). Furthermore, for gymnasts of blue-collar origin there is "a possibility of promotion through practising of gymnastics which is greater than in the case of competitors from the families of intellectuals" (p. 79). Therefore, "they

are more strongly committed to sport activity and show more perseverance in the difficult training for gymnastic exercises" (p. 79). I think
that the factors of early beginning, physical work, and motivation outlined by the Polish sociologists would also help us understand why
working-class Polish-American athletes and athletes from other ethnic minorities succeed in the American sport system.

In another Communist country, Yugoslavia, in a 1976 article
Kresimir Petrovic summarized efforts to study how sport was related
to social stratification in his country. A 1965 study of 283 top athletes,
male and female, showed only 5% to be the children of farmers (pp.
97–98). A 1972 study found sport achievement positively related to
socioeconomic status and residence. A 1973 sample of 24,000
Yugoslavian athletes showed "children of parents with a higher social position are more active in more expensive sports, or rather in
sports having the nature of a status symbol, both in Yugoslavia and
outside of it" (p. 97). A 1974 study of skiers spelled out the status rankings in that sport: downhill slalom first, ski jumping second, and cross-
country racing third (pp. 98–99). Petrovic found that such ranking in
sports contributed to the increasing separation of social status groups.
He concluded that "sport is predominantly the privilege of those who
have more than average social status" (p. 97) and that "those individuals who need sports activity very much, are practically without any"
(p. 99). He concluded that sports organizations should be aware of this
stratifying effect of sport and try to become less exclusive.

A 1981 report by the Nigerian sociologist A. H. Sohi studies how
sport is related to social stratification in India. Indian sportsmen, says
Sohi, are predominantly from the lower middle class. After becoming
sportsmen they are higher in social class and educational level than
their fathers (15% of the fathers of sportsmen are just literate, 17% having no more than a primary-school education). One reason for upward
mobility is that "a trend is emerging in India now which provides a
weightage to be given to sport performance at the time of employing.
The private industrial concerns show a keen interest in sport" (Sohi,
1951, p. 73). Another reason is that as education has become available
to all classes sportsmen are likely to have places reserved for them in
institutions of higher education and to receive athletic scholarships.
But this does not mean total democracy exists in sports. A rank order
of sports follows the hierarchy of social classes. Sohi's study showed
these social prestige scores for persons playing the different sports:
badminton 7.0, field hockey 5.3, gymnastics 4.7, basketball 4.0, track
and field 2.7, soccer 2.7, weightlifting 1.7 (1981, Table 9, p. 72). The
facilities for the higher prestige sports are more available to youths of
higher social status. Also, as they grow up, children of each class learn
the sports typical of that class. (We can see the similarity in the absence of American ghetto youths in such sports as tennis, golf, and
swimming.)

How social background, individual achievement drive, and choice of sport activity can work together is indicated by Belgian research conducted by Famaey-Lamon, Hebbelinck, and Cadron (1979) involving 5,500 children aged 6–12, and their parents. The children, who were from 107 primary schools representing all parts of Belgium, should have been a pretty good sample from that country. The problem studied was choice of team sports as compared with individual sports. How, the researchers asked, is this choice related to social position and educational attainment? They tabulated the choices of team versus individual sports for the parents of the 5,500 children and for the children themselves. The answer: For parents, "team-sports are more practiced by manual workers. In the other professional groups, mainly individual sports are chosen, in a most pronounced way in the category of the self-employed and the intellectuals, that means the professions in which the sense of responsibility is most strongly developed" (p. 43). The term *responsibility* seems here to refer to individualistic motivation and choice in a person's life. The children follow their parents: Team sport is practiced more by children whose parents left school after the primary grades, and individual sport by those whose parents went further in their schooling. It appears that those who "succeed" individualistically in the world outside sport also choose those sports in which they are most likely to star as individuals.

In the Cuba before Castro there existed a situation somewhat similar to that in India: high-status people playing gentlemen's games in exclusive sport clubs and low-status young men seeking fame and fortune through boxing and baseball. From Luque to Tiant, this group produced some outstanding stars for the United States major leagues. Under Castro, the gentlemen's clubs have been opened to the masses. Baseball is still the number one sport. Pettavino says that Cubans still avidly follow the U.S. majors. Although professonalism is downgraded by the Communist regime, young baseball players who are successful in Cuba fantasize about making it to real success in the United States. In the early 1984 season Barbero Garbey, a Marielito, was leading the American League in hitting. In time, perhaps, the restoration of U.S.-Cuban relations will bring another flood of Cuban stars to prominence and affluence in the United States.

Sport mobility in Brazil is very much like some things we shall see in the United States, and is also very different. Brazil has an extreme case of what Janet Lever (1969) calls soccer mania. When Brazil lost in the 1966 World Cup finals, after thousands of fans followed the team all the way to London, black streamers and clouds of black carbon paper came down from office buildings, flags flew at half mast, and people wept in the streets. Lever cites a recent Brazilian study by Antonio Teixeira that shows production in São Paulo increased 12.3% in the weeks that their top team won and that industrial accidents increased by 15.3%

Barbaro Garbey, 1984. World Wide Sports.

in losing weeks. Fans ritually burn candles in their team's colors to enlist divine support.

When Lever studied Brazilian soccer in 1969 this mania was kept going by 5,000 professional athletes playing for about 100 teams. Eighty percent were from the lowest social class, many of them black. "Scouts for various teams scour the beaches of coastal towns and the lots and playing fields of the inland cities" (Lever, 1969, p. 49). Hoping eventually to attract these scouts, boys from the age of four or five up, "too poor to afford soccer balls, . . . will practice the whole day through on beaches or empty lots with only a tightly rolled stocking for a ball" (p. 49). Many poor, uneducated boys rise fast to the big city teams, but a number fall back down as fast as they rose. "Around the age of 30 they find themselves with no work skills, no money and only memories of their brief career. . . . Because he neither studied nor worked during his brief playing career, a lower-class retiring player has no choice but to accept a menial, unskilled job" (Lever, 1969, pp. 41–42). For reasons that Lever discusses interestingly, soccer players on the less professionalized, smaller city teams very often come out better than the top-flight big city stars.

"It is certain," says Lever, "that any ladder of mobility such as professional sport takes on a much greater significance in a traditional, rigidly stratified society than in a relatively open social system such as in the United States" (p. 43).

Now let's look at the site of the most widely and highly organized sport activity—the United States. The basic fact with which to begin is that the culture of the United States has historically been dominated by male WASPs (White Anglo-Saxon Protestants). The specific question here will be: How has sport increased, or decreased, the power of male WASPs in American society?

Historically, sport in the United States has spread from the English-Scottish group that has historically been dominant to include members of one after another non-WASP minority—Germans, Irish, Poles, Italians, Jews, and most recently, blacks and Latins. Before the Civil War, as we saw in chapters 3 and 6, sport was primarily an upper-class game in the British tradition, centering around such activities as fox hunting and horse racing. The latter part of the 19th century was the period of industrial takeoff, with rapid growth of cities and immigration of eastern and southern Europeans who made up a large part of the labor force. Around the turn of the 20th century, along with other industries, they began to move into sport, which had become a mass spectator business.

What happened, in terms of ethnic mobility, is illustrated by Kirson Weinberg and Henry Arond's (1952) study of the ethnic origins of boxers in the first half of this century. Table 11.1, showing how ethnic groups ranked first, second, and third in number of top fighters for a number of years, is as clear a picture of the ethnic athletic succession as we are likely to get.

Table 11.1 Rank Order of Number of Prominent Boxers of Various Ethnic Groups for Certain Years

Year	Rank 1	Rank 2	Rank 3
1909	Irish	German	English
1916	Irish	German	Italian
1928	Jewish	Italian	Irish
1936	Italian	Irish	Jewish
1948	Negro	Italian	Mexican

Note. From "The Occupational Culture of the Boxer" by S.K. Weinberg and H. Arond, 1952, *American Journal of Sociology,* **57,** p. 460, Table 1. Copyright 1952 by the University of Chicago Press. Reprinted by permission.

Football and Ethnic Mobility

Another illustrative case is football. Allen Sack (1973) has written interestingly of the rise of Yale to football prominence over Harvard in the late 19th century. Harvard football, played mainly by Anglo-Saxons from around Boston, was until then a gentlemen's sport in which excessive concern with winning was not quite proper. Yale, under the leadership of Walter Camp with non-WASP players recruited from a much wider section of the country, played to win in a manner that in the British tradition was unsporting and beat Harvard 29 times in 33 years. In one year in the late 1890s almost all the Harvard team came from near Boston, whereas Yale represented Connecticut, New York, Ohio, Illinois, Kansas, Virginia, and Arkansas. One of Yale's heroes, Pudge Heffelfinger, was in 1889 the first non-Anglo-Saxon to be named to the All-America team. Until then the top gridiron jocks had names like Adams, Ames, and Channing.

The history of All-America teams from then to the present shows the ethnic shift, which was also a shift away from the Ivy League schools and a shift away from players of New England origin (Powel, 1926, Appendix A). In 1889 and 1890, the team came entirely from Harvard, Yale, and Princeton. As the years went by, the team spread geographically to include these schools:

> 1891–95 Pennsylvania
> 1898 Chicago
> 1900 Columbia
> 1907 West Point, Cornell, Brown
> 1909 Michigan
> 1912 Wisconsin
> 1915 Pittsburgh
> 1916 Minnesota, Ohio State
> 1918 Nebraska

Ethnically, after Heffelfinger broke the WASP monopoly, there came, from 1895 to 1924, Murphy (the first Irishman), Hershberger, Daly, Hagarty, Rafferty, Sheahin, Pierkarski (the first Pole), Bowditch, Eckersall, Hogan, McCormick, Ziegler, Schultz, Fish, Goebel, Tobin, Schillmiller, Hollenback, Fisher, Bomeister, Mulbetsch, Schlachter, Oliphant, Callahan, Allendinger, Stein, Schwab, Garbisch, Bedenk, Bjorkman, Stuhldreher, and Koppisch. In the 1920s, there were Friedman and Luckman, in the 1930s Goldberg. The first black All-America player was William H. Lewis of Harvard, in 1892 and 1893; the next was Paul Robeson, in 1918. Although there were black professional baseball players in the late 1800s, and a black man finished fifth in the 1896 United States Open Golf tournament, it was not until Jackie Robinson broke the baseball barrier in 1947 that more than a few isolated blacks (like the early pro Fritz Pollard, Buddy Young at Illinois, Willis Ward at Michigan, and Marion Motley of the Cleveland Browns) appeared on the major football scene. Today blacks have superseded the previous minorities—Germans, Irish, Poles, Italians, Jews—and dominate football, basketball, and baseball, as well as boxing. The only significant non-black minority remaining are Latins in baseball.

In 1948, when the minorities in sport were still predominantly white, George Saxon, a refugee intellectual working as a coal loader, wrote of the significance of sports for young men of eastern and southern European extraction in America's industrial areas. He saw athletics as a way out for those on the bottom of the heap:

The impossibility of attaining human goals in real life, in production and in social relations led to sublimation in the fanciful reflex world of sports. . . . To the chosen few, athletics became a road to success. Individual ability could find expression in sporting events . . . to an extent not discoverable elsewhere in society. The worker no longer dreamed of being a capitalist; he wanted to be a football hero. . . . Multi-syllabic Eastern European names became the means by which great universities were identified. For every ten thousand who became aware of a shadowy Bertrand Russell [British philosopher] there could be ten million acutely aware of the diet and vital statistics of a Goldberg who could run back punts. But to become a Goldberg required only ability, to become a Russell required membership in another class. (Saxon, 1953, p. 314)

Such was the way out, and up, for longtime football star George Blanda, who said of his childhood, "Hell, first thing you wanted to do was to escape the mines and that image of being a drunken, stupid, dirty Polish coal miner" (Novak, 1976, p. 14). It was the way for the bus driver's son who got his best football offer from the University of Miami: "I've broken a leg, my nose, and my ass for this place, but at least I've gotten a degree. I won't have to drive a bus now." It was also the way for the other Miami football player who said:

Being from Pennsylvania, I have seen guys leave those steel mill and coal mining towns by athletics. Most of them understand life at a very early age. The reason is perfectly clear. They see their parents work themselves into the ground and don't want to end up that way. So, the only solution is to do well in college.

In the summer of 1985, James C. Penny, a student of mine and a football player, researched the Saxon hypothesis in his home town of Youngstown, Ohio, through in-depth interviews with 12 college football players (seven blacks, four Caucasians, and one black-Hispanic), and reached a different conclusion. He felt that although "there are probably still some athletes who see football as a way out from their troubled times and financial distress," his interviews showed him that "just as a parent loves and protects a child, so a football player loves the game of football and protects his dream of becoming a professional athlete and being able to show the world new moves, long passes, and excruciating tackles" (unpublished class essay).

The most dramatic example I know of successful mobility after football comes from the coal-steel belt. It is the case of the 1963 University of Pittsburgh football team, which had a 9–1 record against top opposition and was ranked third nationally in the final polls. Ten years later this football squad had produced 3 physicians, 15 dentists, 5 attorneys, 7 educators, 2 ministers, and 28 in high positions in industry. Of this team, which significantly was all white, Randy Jesick, who studied them said, "They were winners in the game of football, and now they're winners in the game of life" (Michener, 1977, p. 297).

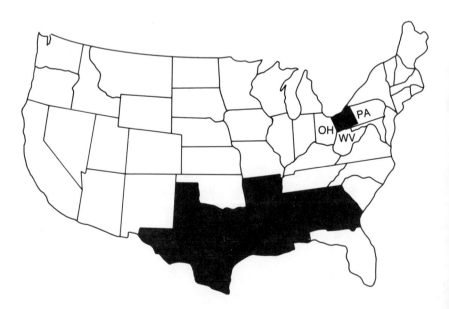

Figure 11.1 Football players come from the northern coal-steel belt and the rural south. Adapted from Rooney (1974).

I spoke earlier of a shift in the area from which athletes originate. John F. Rooney's *A Geography of American Sports* shows two major areas from which football players come at present (see Figure 11.1). One is a belt running from Johnstown, Pennsylvania, through the Pittsburgh area, across West Virginia, then to Cleveland. This area Saxon, the intellectual coal miner, described in 1948 as a coal mining area where the degradation of modern society is epitomized by an enervating industrial complex. The other area is the South from Georgia to Texas. James Michener explains this geography of athletic origins: "We don't find young people of promise from the advantaged states like Wisconsin, Iowa, Connecticut, and Oregon bothering with professional sports. They don't have to" (1977, p. 243).

Fathers and Sons

Research by sport sociologists John Loy and Harry Webb throws further light on the upward mobility of athletes on the social ladder. Loy (1969) studied the social origins of 1,021 Life Pass holders at the University of California at Los Angeles. To be a Life Pass holder, one must have competed in college sport for 4 years and earned at least three varsity letters. Each Life Pass holder filled out a long questionnaire and was scored in terms of a social status scale devised by Otis Dudley Duncan. Wrestlers, boxers, and baseball and football players (three of these in contact sports) typically had lower-class fathers (Duncan scores of 43 to 49) and had themselves moved to the status of college graduates. Fencers, crewmen, ice hockey, cricket, tennis, and golf players typically had upper-class fathers to begin with (status scores of 60 to 74) so had nowhere to rise. Another measure was the percentage of athletes in different sports who had moved up from blue-collar backgrounds. The figures ran this way (Loy, 1969, Table 2, p. 114):

Wrestling	48.1
Baseball	36.5
Football	34.6
Track	30.5
Soccer	26.3
Gymnastics	26.3
Basketball	16.4
Swimming	14.3
Tennis	13.3
Crew	10.4

Again, the wrestlers and baseball and football players had the greatest mobility. If the figures for basketball players with blue-collar figures seem low, this is probably because these figures cover all UCLA athletic history, most of which was before basketball became a sport mainly for ghetto graduates.

The percentages of those whose fathers had not finished high school again show football, wrestling, and baseball at the top (Loy, 1969, Table 3, p. 114):

Football	51.59
Wrestling	49.99
Baseball	49.98
Track	43.30
Gymnastics	38.21
Basketball	37.38
Swimming	27.15
Tennis	25.19
Crew	23.87
Soccer	22.85

A longitudinal picture of mobility over an athlete's lifetime was given by comparing the status of the father's regular job with that of the son's first job after graduating and then with this present job (Loy, 1969, Table 4, p. 115):

Status Scores

	Father's Main Job	Son's First Job	Son's Present Job
Wrestling	43	70	77
Football	48	63	74
Baseball	49	64	75
Soccer	51	74	79
Track	53	67	77
Basketball	57	69	77
Gymnastics	58	67	80
Crew	62	67	78
Swimming	63	67	78
Tennis	64	70	75

Again, the sports are in essentially the same order, but we have a more detailed view. Loy comments that "perhaps the most striking aspect . . . is the great degree of social mobility achieved by athletes whose parents had the lowest socio-economic status" (p. 115).

Athletes had a surprising degree of academic success. About 44% had earned degrees beyond the bachelor's (Loy, 1969, Table 5, p. 116):

Gymnastics	61.75%
Soccer	54.28
Wrestling	50.00
Track	45.79
Swimming	45.67
Basketball	43.91
Tennis	40.72
Baseball	37.11
Crew	29.85
Football	29.21

Another indicator of mobility was political preference. Since party preference is associated with social status (as one moves up in the world, he is more likely to be Republican), it is interesting that two groups with lower-class fathers had strong Republican preference (wrestlers 60.71%, football players 55.70%). In this connection, it is again relevant that Michener reports that of 60 athletes he has known well, only 1 was a Democrat, and that he knows no football coach who is a Democrat (Michener, 1977).

The overall picture we get from the Life Pass study is that sport at UCLA, particularly the bodily contact sports, has offered a way up in the world to sons of lower-status parents. Another study, by Harry Webb, of 253 Michigan State athletes between 1958 and 1962 indicates that sport is not a significant way up for those at the very bottom of the ladder. He found Michigan State jocks drawn mainly from the middle three fifths of the population. The United States Census classifies families in terms of five income groups from the top fifth (in 1960, over $9,000) to the bottom fifth (in 1960, under $2,800). Webb ranked his 253 athletes in terms of the fifth in which their family fell. The result: Very few of the athletes come from [the] bottom fifth and not many of them come from the top fifth either. Athletes come . . . not from the poorest or the richest fifth, but from the middle income level (Webb, 1969a, p. 124). The chance that the result could have occurred by chance alone was less than 1 in 1,000 ($p < .001$).

It was possible that individual sports (such as fencing, tennis, and golf) had loaded the results. To check this, Webb compared the income for families of 166 team sport athletes with the national distribution and found them, too, coming from the middle three fifths. Again, the probability of chance was less than 1 in 1,000. Finally, calculating for 111 football players alone, he found them coming from the same middle three fifths (again, $p < .001$).

Webb's results are reconciled somewhat with Loy's when we look at his classification of athletes in the major team sports (baseball, football, hockey, and basketball) in terms of their fathers' occupations. Close to three times as many major team sport athletes (65.6%) had fathers listed in trades or labor, as had fathers who were listed as professonal, technical, clerical, or sales (23.2%). From Webb's census data, we could judge that they were predominantly skilled or semiskilled rather than unskilled. His listing of sports in order of father's occupational status does not look very different from Loy's (Webb, 1969a, p. 127).

1. Golf
2. Fencing
3. Tennis
4. Swimming
5. Baseball
6. Wrestling
7. Gymnastics
8. Track
9. Hockey
10. Football
11. Basketball

Webb's sample, active as athletes much later than most of Loy's, reflect the recent drop in the social origins of basketball players.

The False Lure of Upward Mobility

We have looked at what is true in the American dream of making it through athletics. Now what is false about it? I shall start with three sociological researches, the first two with uneducated athletes, the third with a group of educated ones.

In their study of the occupational culture of the boxer, Weinberg and Arond (1952) found that boxers are typically uneducated. They refer, for example, to an article in *Ring Magazine* (July 1950, p. 45): "A fighter with an education is a fighter who does not have to fight to live and he knows it. . . . Only for a hungry fighter is it a decent gamble" (cited in Weinberg & Arond, 1952, p. 462). Boxers also come from ethnic minorities in areas of social disorganization, near the center of the city. There has been the ethnic succession typical of the bodily contact sports: "First Irish, then Jewish, then Italian were most numerous among prominent boxers; now, Negroes" (Weinberg & Arond, 1952, p. 460). What happens in terms of social mobility? If a boxer is good, he may rise rapidly and early. But his decline is as spectacular as his rise. The tremendous physical beating boxers take, plus their tendency to squander their sudden earnings, plus their lack of non-boxing skills, is likely to make for an unhappy future.

Of ninety-five leading former boxers (i.e., champions and lead-ing contenders), each of whom earned more than $100,000 dur-ing his ring career, eighteen were found to have remained in the sport as trainees or trainer-managers; two became wrestlers; twenty-six worked in, fronted for, or owned taverns; two were liquor salesmen; eighteen had unskilled jobs, most commonly in the steel mills; six worked in gas stations; three were cab drivers; three had newsstands; two were janitors; three were bookies; three were associated with the race tracks. . . ; and two were in busi-ness, one as a custom tailor. (Weinberg and Arond, 1952, p. 460)

The Weinberg-Arond research was done 30 years ago, but Norman Hare's 1971 study of 48 retired black boxers found no one who had been able to save much of his earnings and told much the same story as Weinberg and Arond:

In the gyms, I watched the active fighters working and waiting for the lucky break which, they believed, would take them to the wealth and glory of a championship. I listened to the former fight-ers reliving their own fighting careers, boasting to sustain their pride, dissatisfied now with their present lot and trying to call back in conversation the youth and skills that had once been theirs. (Hare, 1971, p. 8)

Now the formally educated athletes. In 1974 Paul Dubois compared 160 athletes and 450 nonathletes who had been graduated 2 years be-fore from San Francisco, San Jose, and Hayward state universities. On a social prestige scale developed by the National Opinion Research Center he found no significant difference between the two groups. He also found no significant difference in annual income. He did find that team athletes had significantly higher job status ratings than individual sport athletes, perhaps because they were more sociable. In general Dubois said that his results "raise questions, especially for minority students, about whether they should put more time into academics and less into athletics. It's a myth that athletics is a steppingstone to success for most college athletes and students should know this" (Johnston, 1976, p. 6F).

Athletes are likely to forget the tremendous odds against their in-dividual success in sports. There are, of course, Joe Louis, Rocky Marciano, Muhammad Ali, Bronko Nagurski, O. J. Simpson, Henry Aaron, Carl Yastrzemski, Bill Russell, Bill Bradley, Kareem Abdul-Jabbar, Pancho Gonzales, Lee Trevino, Nancy Lopez. But 99% of ath-letes do not reach this kind of stardom.

In basketball, the current hope of black kids for exit from the ghetto, in 1974 there were 200,000 high-school seniors and 5,700 college seniors of whom 211 were drafted and 55 signed (Tutko & Bruns, 1976, p. 126). Thus the men signed were 1% of the number of college seniors and 3/100 of 1% of the number of high-school senior players. Of such chances Bob Cousy, a nonblack who did make stardom says,

> *Looking back, I'm amazed at how few individuals or teams ever make it in pro sports. Competition decrees that every year the losers outnumber the winners by twenty to one in the standings, by hundreds to one in the draft. Hating to lose as much as I do, I'm coming to realize that losing is the fate of almost everyone in one way or another, even those with talent, brains, and desire. (1975, p. 173)*

In football, in the fall of 1968 there were 900,000 boys playing high school ball and fewer than 30,000 college players (*Sports Illustrated*, September 29, 1969, p. 11). In baseball, the other major sport, Department of Labor figures show millions of boys in Little League, 400,000 in high-school ball, and 25,000 college players, about 100 of whom will make it to the majors. "And just a handful of these will have a career that lasts as long as seven years" (Tutko & Bruns, 1976, p. 126).

Thomas Tutko and William Bruns tell us, in summary, that as an avenue of upward mobility the whole sports industry, which is only about half as big as the canned soup business, in 1975 fielded in six major team sports (football, basketball, hockey, baseball, tennis, and soccer) about 135 teams, with no more than 3,500 active players, of whom no more than 1,740 were starters (1976, p. 126).

Calculating specifically for the currently most important ethnic minority, Coakley says that in 1980–81 there were approximately 1,000 blacks on major professional sport teams and perhaps another 1,000 on minor league teams or the equivalent—meaning that with 26 million blacks in the United States, one in 30,000 is a top athlete. (Virtually no professional career opportunities exist for black female athletes.) Coakley observes that if any corporation encouraged all black males to train for jobs open to only 2,000 men, it would be denounced as irresponsible. "Yet professional sport has been able to do this for years and receive praise for its 'contributions' to the black population" (Coakley, 1982, p. 261). Arthur Ashe (1977) has noted that there are actually more openings for blacks in medical, law, business, and other graduate schools than in professional sports. Coakley says that a young black would do better to set his sights on being president than on being a top athlete, because in so doing he might learn something that would prepare him for a realistic career. Edwards has said of all this that "the persistence and calculated perpetuation of the belief that sport offers blacks unique opportunities for advancement amounts not to mere naiveté but to inhuman mockery" (1979, p. 117).

Most athletes fall by the way. Some do so at the beginning. All the way, most athletes are substitutes. Many parents of Little League youngsters have become acutely aware of what this fact implies. The sport experience does not really prepare the substitute for anything because he doesn't really share the experience. "Another prevailing myth in sports," says Tutko, "is that a hard-working substitute will come out of the experience with a stronger character. On the contrary, unless a child is extremely mature or unless he has a great deal of support from his parents, being a substitute will affect him adversely" (Tutko & Bruns, 1976, p. 84). His being home on the bench labels him as inferior in the eyes of his peers. With no game experience, he generally gets worse instead of better. He may do poorly in school or shun friends to avoid ridicule. Jonathan Brower, after studying boys of 8 to 14 in a California baseball program for nearly a year, said of poor players: "Like most young competitors, their athletic involvement constitutes a major part of their lives; they have fewer alternative activities than adults and thus if they are poor players, they define themselves as inferior human beings" (cited in Tutko & Bruns, p. 85).

A University of Miami football player whose rank was somewhat less than that a substitute wrote bitterly of his experience:

Scout team players do not play or even travel. They just practice every day and watch with the rest of the spectators come game time. Playing, or rather not playing, is really not the major cause of my dissatisfaction and disenchantment with the game. Most of my grief is a result of the loss of respect . . . that is shown towards me. I, personally, feel I am treated very unfairly as a human being. Because I do not exhibit the talent that other players do, I am looked down upon by coaches and fellow players on and off the field.

In high school I was one of the best players on the team. Because of this I was looked up to and respected by almost everyone in the school. Now all of sudden I am a fourth team member and have lost all that respect. . . . You are judged as a person on how well you perform on the field. Athletes should be treated as humans, not as machines. Why should someone be loved as a person because he plays good football, and someone else disliked because he does not play so well? (unpublished essay)

Harold Charnovsky, in his study of how baseball players see themselves, has stated very concisely the plight of the athletic failure:

Those who fall by the wayside represent a poignant study in disappointment and frustration, a failure to fulfill the American dream. The real tragedy lies not in their failure alone, for all men may fail, but in their failure after total commitment. They are unprepared to do anything else, despite baseball's claim that unsuccessful players are young enough to enter other fields. (Charnovsky, 1968, p. 41n)

Discrimination in Recruitment

How do the youngsters who don't start their athletic life as bench-warmers find their dreams withering, in Lorraine Hansberry's words, like a raisin in the sun? As one moves up the ladder from Little League to junior high to senior high to college he confronts discrimination in recruitment: If one is nonwhite, one must be outstanding. There is room on the bench for mediocre white athletes, but not for mediocre minority athletes. Brower says, "Mediocrity is a white luxury" (1973, p. 3). A 1977 triethnic study by Leonard showed blacks in baseball to be superior to whites. From 1947 to 1973 (the period since Jackie Robinson broke in) "blacks and Latins have had significantly higher batting averages, doubles (with one exception) and stolen bases than whites. Moreover, blacks have had consistently higher home run rates and slugging averages than both whites and Latins. . . . Black and Latin pitchers have had a significantly higher percentage of victories, strikeouts per inning and lower earned run averages than whites" (Leonard, 1977, p. 92). In 1973 black hitters averaged 17 points above whites, and, in 1974, 14 points. In 1975, according to Yetman and Eitzen (1982), black batting superiority was 21 points. What this means is that on the average the black baseball player who isn't a 15 to 20 point better hitter won't make it to the majors, whereas an inferior white player may. Scully put it this way in 1974: "Not only do blacks have to out perform whites to get into baseball, but they must consistently out perform them over their careers to stay in baseball" (p. 263). A recruiting model for baseball would go like this: Given six athletes of different race and ability (with the letter indicating race and the number indicating ability on a 1 to 10 scale), on a major league team B10, W10, and B7 will start, W7 and W5 will ride the bench, and B5 will be shipped to the minors.

The same general model holds for football: Brower (1973) concluded in 1973 that "if they are going to make it in professional football, black athletes must be better than their white counterparts." And also for basketball: In 1979, 92% of leaders on National Basketball Association teams in scoring, field goal percentage, rebounding, shots blocked, and assists were black (Simons, 1980). In basketball, as the sport has become predominantly black, the discrimination is weakening: less-than-outstanding blacks are recruited and ride the bench along with the whites. The same thing may happen in baseball and football as whites become rarer.

What happens when an athlete beats the tremendous odds and makes it to the top? First of all, he can anticipate only a few years of earning power before he is over the hill (in major league sports, about 5). In those years he must earn his lifetime income, unless he is well enough known to cash in on his reputation in a big way while he is active or after he retires. When we consider that this is his lifetime income, the $150,000 per year earned by the average major league baseball player may not be so outlandish as it can seem to a college assistant professor who compares it with his own mere $25,000. In addition to the brevity of the athlete's earning span, there is the risk. Apart from the fact that he is unlikely to retire from a bodily contact sport without some degree of permanent disability, the athlete's whole lifetime income is wagered on his chance of maintaining through his active career a high degree of health and efficiency in a body that was not constructed for the kinds of stresses that are routine in major sports. There is no lifetime income insurance to protect against what may happen when a running back's trick knee or a pitcher's arthritic elbow gives out (especially if he is a minor player).

Stacking Revisited

Even at the top the upward-bound athlete encounters positional segregation (stacking), which I introduced in chapter 10 and which we shall explore in more depth now.

The most-quoted work on stacking is a 1970 study by Loy and Joseph McElvogue. These researchers started with the hypothesis that nonwhites would be segregated in the noncentral positions—the central positions being so located physically and also involving a high degree of interaction with other team members and frequent exercise of independent judgment. Loy and McElvogue studied the makeup of the teams in the National and American baseball and football leagues in 1968 to find out how positions were distributed racially. The central baseball positions were catcher, shortstop, and first, second, and third base. It was, of course, necessary to distinguish offensive and defensive units in football. Central offensive positions were quarterback, center, and guards; central defensive positions were (in the 4-3 system of linemen and linebackers then prevalent) the three linebackers. Loy and McElvogue's results are summarized in Table 11.2, adapted and abbreviated from tables in their report. The results demonstrate statistically significant racial segregation by position in baseball and football; none of them could have occurred by chance as many as five times in 10,000. Yetman and Eitzen found essentially the same positional segregation in baseball in 1975. In 1980 Coakley in football (Coakley, 1982) and Simons in baseball (Simons, 1980) found basically the same stacking pattern described by Loy and McElvogue.

Table 11.2 Whites and Blacks in Central and Noncentral Positions in the National and American Baseball League and the National and American Football Leagues, 1968

Baseball Position	White	Black	Total
Central (Infield, including Catcher)	94	19	113
Noncentral (Outfield)	38	36	74
Total	132	55	187

$(p < .0005)$

Football Offense Position	White	Black	Total
Central (Quarterback, Center, Guards)	100	4	104
Noncentral (Others)	120	62	182
Total	220	66	286

$(p < .0005)$

Football Defense Position	White	Black	Total
Central (Linebackers)	72	6	78
Noncentral (Others)	120	88	208
Total	192	94	286

$(p < .0005)$

Note. Based on "Racial Segregation in American Sport" by J.W. Loy, Jr. and J.F. McElvogue, 1970, *International Review of Sport Sociology,* **5,** pp. 10, 12, 13, Tables 1, 2, 3. Original data from *1968 Baseball Register* and *Autographed Yearbooks* of NFL and AFL and from *Pro Football 1968* by J. Zanger, 1968, New York: Pocket. Reprinted by permission.

The data all show blacks competing for positions that require Supermasculine Menials (Eldridge Cleaver's term) with speed, quickness, good hands, and aggressiveness, whereas the positions that require judgment and leadership have gone to whites. The bottom line is that positions that involve dramatic control of game outcome are white; how else explain the fact that in 1975 all but one of the NFL punters and placekickers were white, and that there was no black place-kick *holder?* Apparently strong legs and good hands were not enough to justify putting a black player in that kind of game control position. That the central positions tend to be control positions is further shown by Grusky's finding, cited earlier, that a disproportionate number of catchers become baseball managers, and by Scully's discovery that 68% of all baseball managers from 1871 to 1968 were former infielders (Scully, 1974, p. 246). Both studies fit in with Gill and Perry's (1979) report on the 1973 University of Illinois women's intercollegiate softball team, in which the players ranked catchers and infielders highest in team leadership.

So pervasive is the stacking pattern that on their way up blacks tend to shift from control to noncontrol positions—for example, the black college quarterback who becomes a pro running back to leave the signal-calling post to a white. Eitzen and Sanford found in 1975 that of 387 professional football players a statistically significant number of blacks had changed from control to noncontrol positions as they moved up from high school and college to pro ball.

More than game control is at stake for blacks who play a noncentral position. Dubois showed in 1974 that the central positions are the highest paid (pp. 55–56). The 1975 *Football Register* revealed that only 4.1% of the players in predominantly "black" positions (running back, defensive back, wide receiver) had been in professional football for 10 or more years, whereas 14.8% of players in the "white" positions (quarterbacks, center, offensive guard) had (Yetman & Eitzen, 1982). Shortening of career means that the black player when he quits has a smaller lifetime nest egg and a smaller pension because this depends on years of service. It also means that he is more likely to leave football with a permanent disability.

When stacking was first studied, some sport sociologists felt that because basketball lacks the kind of fixed zone positions found in baseball and football positional segregation could not occur there. But in 1974 Eitzen and Tessendorf, by studying basketball instruction books, established that coaches generally agree on position differences in control: the guard as the floor general and "quarterback," the center as having outcome control because of his pivotal position under the basket, and the forward as the "animal" with speed, strength, and rebounding ability (Eitzen & Tessendorf, 1978). They concluded that blacks would be stacked in the forward positions. In the 1970–71 NBA season this turned out to be the case, but stacking was not found in 1979. In college basketball one 1980 research found that stacking persisted in some athletic conferences; another found that it had disappeared. Apparently the black takeover of the game during the 1970s had about the same effect on positional segregation as on discrimination in recruitment.

Life After Sport

When the cheers of the crowd have died down (after high school, after college, or after a pro career), what comes next? Jack Scott, who was himself a coal country jock on college football scholarship, answers the question realistically for the high-school level: "Schoolboys who spend four years of high school dreaming of collegiate gridiron glory are suddenly confronted by reality on graduation day. For every Broadway Joe Namath there are hundreds of sad, disillusioned men standing on street corners and sitting in the beer halls of Pennsylvania towns such as Scranton, Beaver Falls, and Altoona" (1971, p. 179). With regard to preparation, tracking has disqualified most athletes (especially black athletes) for nonsport careers. Time is an element here. Most professional athletes retire before they are 30. Michener notes of several outstanding athletes he knew:

> It suddenly occurred to me that these superlative men . . . had been forced to retire from their athletic careers at an age when I, in my profession, had yet to write word one. Their public lives had ended before mine began. In their middle thirties these gifted men had reached the climax of their fame; they had scintillated for a decade, then been required to find other occupation; I had stumbled into a career at which I could work till eighty, if I lived that long. (1977, p. 282)

Also, minority group athletes, if they try to use their careers to move up within the sport world, find the same discrimination that has beset them on the field. I will expand here some facts introduced in chapter 10. In coaching, in 1979 that were no black head coaches or managers in the NFL and major baseball leagues and only two in the predominantly black NBA. There was one black baseball manager in the Class A Western Carolina League. Assistant coaches, who are hired as tokens or to deal with the special quirks of black players, are usually stacked in noncontrol positions—excluded from jobs such as third base or pitching coaches, or offensive or defensive coordinators (no blacks at these positions in the NFL in 1979).

Although they have not addressed today's main problem of a postsport career—racial discrimination—various students of the subject have suggested that an athletic career may unfit the athlete for a full life after sport. Speaking to the 1968 International Congress of Sport Psychology, José Cagigal, Director of the Spanish Institute for Physical and Sport Education (Madrid), saw sport as disqualifying the athletic prima donna for the realities of life:

*Generally speaking, to excel at any human activity calls for many
years of sustained effort, making the individual spiritually mature
enough to take his final triumph in stride. In sport, it is different;
although effort and will-power are necessary to become an outstanding performer, public triumphs are obtained with relative
ease in comparison with other walks of life. . . . The caste of champions is in danger of becoming an outrageously spoiled social
group, dragging its members down through successive stages of
regressive immaturity to leave them finally with a wholly distorted
sense of values incapable of taking their place in normal society.
The champion who has belonged to the caste, when he leaves his
hot-house world either on account of age or failure has the typical reactions of the unadapted psychopath. (1970, p. 347)*

Although his language was somewhat less strong, sociologist
Walter Schafer also told a symposium on the sociology of sport that
sport in our culture tends to create a severe conflict when the athlete
confronts real life:

*Athletes whose sense of identity and self-worth is entirely linked
to athletic achivement often experience an identity crisis when the
athletic career has ended, and it becomes necessary to move on
to something else . . . and as a result, linger on as marginal men
in the world of athletics, have family or personal problems, or fail
to adjust to a new work role. (1969, p. 35)*

Wiley Lee Umphlett reviewed the ex-athlete as presented in
American fiction and found him unprepared for life. Typical was Yale
All-America football player Tom Buchanan in Scott Fitzgerald's *The
Great Gatsby* (Fitzgerald, 1925, cited in Michener, 1977, p. 283): "One of
those men who reach such an acute limited excellence at twenty-one
that everything afterward savors of anticlimax." Then there is Rabbit
Angstrom of John Updike's *Rabbit Run,* an ex-basketball hero from a
coal town. "He cannot unravel his relationships with his wife, or with
the bar girl he has made pregnant; he cannot resolve his interior conflict between his longing for a free open space . . . and his actual life
in the northern urban sprawl in which he is trapped. . . . He can only
do one thing: run furiously as he had once run during the closing
minutes of basketball games" (cited in Michener, 1977, pp. 284–285).
Umphlett (1974) concluded that fictional athletes (a) distrust urban life
and live in dreams of a simpler life close to nature, (b) are antifeminine
and unable to deal with women, and (c) like Fitzgerald's all-American
hero are unable to put past glory behind and cope with today's realities.

It can be said that fiction is not life, but it may be truer and certainly is more interesting than some statistics. Michener concludes that the 60 athletes he has known well don't resemble the cultural myth of the ex-athlete, but it must be said that athletes who are close to Michener are not likely to be typical jocks. (In sociological language, they are not a random sample of the athletic population.)

Back from fiction to the nitty-gritty world of the retiring athlete.

In 1980 one major college had a black head football coach and six had head basketball or track coaches. On the high-school level desegregation has worked in reverse for coaches as well as for principals. Between 1954 and 1971 more than 2,000 coaches at all-black schools lost their jobs (Edwards, 1979, p. 126). The hiring of a black head coach at a predominantly white Southern school in 1970 was so remarkable as to receive feature stories in *Sports Illustrated* and the *New York Times*. The situation is little different outside the South.

There have been three black umpires in major league baseball history; one was working in 1979. In the same year 8% of pro football officials were black, and in basketball 20% of the officials were black.

In the sport-related media, the 1968 Equal Opportunity Commission Report stated that in the fall of 1966 blacks appeared in only 5% of 351 sport-related commercials in the New York area. Yetman and Eitzen (1982) studied one pro football team in 1971 and found that, of the starting players, 8 of 11 whites and only 2 of 13 blacks were able to do TV spots.

Sport and Power—The Balance

What does sport do for the powerless in our society? In terms of our discussion in this and the previous chapter, it is doubtful whether, on balance, organized sport in any way significantly changes the distribution of social power. It does enable a few gifted people to attain wealth and fame. It does enable a somewhat larger number to move a notch or two up the socioeconomic ladder. It does give formal education to some who might not otherwise have it, but it makes demands that make it next to impossible for the average athlete to make use of his opportunity. It gives large or small rewards to the winners at the price of raising and smashing false hopes in the vast majority of losers, meanwhile exploiting these dreams for corporate profit. Even the winners may be tracked out of significant contributions they could have made to the mainstream of human achievement. Organized sport, as we saw in chapter 10, teaches underprivileged people to submit to unquestioned authority while setting them at each other's throats in a minor form of warfare. It widens the polarization into dominant male and passive female. By calling its activities masculine, it enhances some males' sense of virility at the expense of females, and therefore at their own expense.

Chapter 12

Social Character of the Different Sports

In chapter 11 we examined how sport is related to the whole pattern of social power. Organized sport, although it is an establishment with a certain common ideology and organization, is not a monolithic unity. It is, so to speak, a federation of different sport activities, each of which has its own special relationship to the whole social structure. In this chapter we shall look at the different social functions of the specific sports.

As a beginning, let's examine four basic characteristics in terms of which we can distinguish the separate sports. There are territorial and nonterritorial sports, time-bound and non-time-bound sports, bodily contact and noncontact sports, and striking and nonstriking sports.

The territorial sports are variations of the Papremis spring fertility rites, involving movement in territory, against opposition, toward a goal: soccer, American football, basketball, hockey, lacrosse, polo. All have a fundamentally warlike relationship to space. Other sports also occur physically in space but do not have the same warlike relationship to territorial goals: baseball, tennis, golf, swimming, track and field competitions. George Grella describes dramatically the difference between the territoriality of football and the nonterritoriality of baseball: "The winning team in baseball, because of the shape of its field, cannot acquire territory, operating instead in a realm beyond spatial measurement. . . . No other game opens rather than encloses space. If the stands were removed from the football field, the game would still be conducted within its dreary box; if baseball's outfield bleachers were removed, the game could continue its space across the land" (1975, pp. 562–563).

Some games are timed by the clock: all the territorial sports, also track and swimming events. If Lewis Mumford is right (and I think he is) in describing the clock as the basic machine of industrial civilization, then these time-bound sports are part of the industrial complex: Those who watch the clock in their working hours also watch it in their recreation. Baseball, tennis, and golf are non-time-bound as they are non-space-bound. Their duration is determined by factors other than the running of a clock. In baseball, three outs add up to an inning, nine innings to a game. There is no such thing as a tie, so a game could go on forever. In tennis, points add to game, games to set, sets to match. Before the tie breaker (an invention of, or for, the clock-conscious television industry) a tennis match could also theoretically continue to eternity. Of both games, as contrasted with the time-bound sports, what Grella says of baseball is probably true: "The game succeeds in creating a temporary timelessness" (p. 563).

The chief sports in which bodily contact plays a fundamental and legal role are boxing, football, and hockey. Between these and the clearly noncontact sports are those, like basketball, soccer, and lacrosse, that formally outlaw contact but actually allow much of it by officials' interpretation. Whether or not bodily contact sport is a throwback to our prehuman ancestry, it is clearly a throwback to the preindustrial days before brain (human or electronic) took the place of sheer brawn.

Finally, some games (baseball, tennis, golf, hockey, polo) feature the striking of a ball with some kind of stick. The other territorial games, track and field, and swimming, do not. Some see the hand-eye coordination involved in the striking games as a preparation for industrial activity.

Now, further into the particular sports. Leonard Koppett (1973), in an excellent book on the social context of basketball, has described the essence of the game as deception. I shall use Koppett's terminology in analyzing first our three major American spectator sports.

The Essence of the Game Is Individuality: Baseball

Baseball, the grand old American game, is best seen, I think, as an expression of 19th-century rural Yankee individualism. Michael Novak contrasts the key player in football with the star in baseball:

When Bart Starr completed a pass for the Green Bay Packers, all the Packers could be said to share the deed; one man alone is quite helpless. When Joe Di Maggio stepped to the plate in Yankee Stadium, with his unforgettable stance and fluid swing, Di Maggio

*stood in spotlighted solitude and none of his teammates could act
in his behalf. Football is corporate, baseball is an association of
individuals . . . often taciturn, plying each his special craft, col-
laborating, but at each crucial point facing events alone, solving
the mathematical possibilities of each task in the reflective quiet
of his own hunches, instincts, and lightning moves. (1976, p. 58)*

Describing the drama of Ted Williams' final game at Fenway Park
in Boston, novelist John Updike also speaks of baseball's individualism: "Of all team sports, baseball, with its graceful intermittencies of
action, its immense and tranquil field sparsely settled with poised men
in white, seems to me best suited to accommodate, and be ornamented
by, a loner. It is essentially a lonely game" (Updike, 1960, p. 112).

Grella points out that where each individual stands alone, each
is also individually accountable: "Every player is potentially responsible for victory or defeat; just as his triumphs are visible to all, so are
his mistakes. He cannot hide an error in a mass of struggling bodies
or commit it in some obscure corner of the field, for it is there in the
open for everyone to see" (1975, p. 557).

David Voigt (1974), in an historian's reflection on baseball's relationship to American culture, suggests the peculiarly American type
of hero that this game of personal accountability has produced. The
hero is a man of the people: Babe Ruth, a refugee from an orphan
asylum; Shoeless Joe Jackson, an illiterate Carolina country boy playing the outfield in his bare feet; Lou Gehrig, home-loving son of an
immigrant German steelworker; Bob Feller, an Iowa farm kid; Joe Di
Maggo, an Italian-American batting genius who also married the
nation's sex symbol; Mickey Mantle, another country boy from
Oklahoma; and in the post-Vietnam era, socially conscious Tom Seaver
with his lovely wife—as David Halberstam (1970) suggests, a Mr. and
Mrs. America for the 1970s. The hero has a nickname to give him the
common touch. He is unselfish, strong but not a bully, manly, salty,
earthy, a lover of his country.

He is also imperfect, like his fans, confronted with their own lonely
tasks. Grella remarks that in baseball's legends it is the mistakes or
bonehead plays that have been remembered the longest—Fred Merkle's
failure to touch a base, Fred Snodgrass's muff of a crucial outfield fly,
Mickey Owen's passed ball on a third strike. The flaw is sometimes
of behavior or character: Ty Cobb's almost psychopathically vicious
disposition; Babe Ruth's gargantuan appetite for hot dogs, booze, and
women; Hack Wilson rising above an almost constant hangover to hit
56 home runs and drive in 190 runs (still a record) in a season. The
baseball hero also suffers: Iron Man Gehrig played over 2,000 consecutive games and practically died in harness before he reached 40. Di
Maggio patrolled the outfield with bone spurs and Mantle with osteo-

myelitis. Peter Reiser beat his brains against outfield fences. Jackie Robinson played brilliant and dedicated baseball when every day was an encounter with the stress of racial hatred and finally succumbed prematurely to diseases of stress—diabetes and hypertension. Sandy Koufax set strikeout records over the excruciating pain of an arthritic elbow.

Baseball is fundamentally a rural sport. The first recorded case of a baseball game played under essentially modern rules took place in June 1846 in a part of Hoboken, New Jersey, called the Elysian Fields. Grella thinks it is not accidental that baseball is mythically associated with Cooperstown (where it did *not* originate)—the town named after the novelist of the frontier who created such heroes as Hawkeye, Deerslayer, Pathfinder, and Leatherstocking, and where Natty Bumppo (a great baseball name, Grella thinks) roamed the hills. Novak says that although baseball's commercial centers are urban, its players are typically small-town boys, a large percentage from the South. Although blacks and Latins today play a large part, I think Novak is right in describing baseball as symbolically white and Protestant. "In baseball, the form of Anglo-American culture, especially rural culture, is perfectly reflected" (1976, p. 96). This gives sense to the widely expressed feeling that the 1985 Missouri World Series brought baseball's classic back to the heart of America, where it belongs. Novak points out that whereas a black basketball coach is easily accepted, to most people a black baseball manager just seems out of place. Voigt remarks that although baseball is played well in Latin America and Japan, it is not really the same game. Using David Riesman's terms, I think we can describe baseball as the game of inner-directed 19th-century American values, oriented to individual achievement and personal responsibility.

Voigt points out another connection with 19th-century individualism: The whole concept of ownership of a player, which underpins the reserve clause, reflects the right of a 19th-century entrepreneur to do as he pleased with his property. Novak sees baseball as playing an important role in the civilization of the nation: "It is a triumph of law over the lawless spirit . . . that so civilized, orderly, and lawful a game could have arisen from the plains, the Southlands, and the eastern cities of the nineteenth century, when the frontier and badlands still loomed upon the horizon" (1976, p. 64).

In the late 20th century, baseball is not too well adapted to the television age. "Timing and waiting are of the essence," says William O. Johnson, "with the entire field in suspense waiting on the performance of a single player. By contrast, football, basketball, and hockey are games in which many events occur simultaneously, with the entire team involved at the same time. With the advent of TV, such isolation of the individual performance as occurs in baseball became unaccept-

Baseball was played on Boston Common in 1834, years before it was supposedly invented by Abner Doubleday at Cooperstown. Reproduced courtesy of the Racquet & Tennis Club.

able. . . . Baseball is a game that was designed to be played on a sunny afternoon at Wrigley Field in the 1920s, not on a 21-inch screen" (1971, p. 103).

However, before we write its epitaph, we should note some points baseball has for our time. Novak says, "Baseball is an antidote to the national passion for bigness. It is a slow, careful, judicious game" (1976, p. 64). It is also an antidote to the excessive passion for rationality. Baseball is, or was until it came to terms with the 20th century, a zany game. None of what Grella calls the improbabilities of baseball history could occur in the world of organized football, or organized basketball, or especially in the world of corporate business: three Dodgers occupying third base on the same play; a World Series being decided by *two* ground balls hitting a pebble and bouncing over the head of 18-year-old Freddie Lindstrom; the holder of the all-time highest batting average starting his career playing for the Bloomer Girls; Bill Veeck sending a midget to bat; Wilbert Robertson, Dodger manager, trying to catch a grapefruit tossed from an airplane by one of his players; Giant manager John McGraw warming up the nonplaying Charles Victory

Faust before every game of three pennant-winning seasons because a fortune teller had said the Giants couldn't win without him.

In a world of territorial push, the symbolism of baseball's spatial arrangement is also important. As Grella points out, baseball is "the one arena of American life where you can go home again. The diamond . . . is merely an arrangement of bases, small islands of security in the perilous avenues leading from and toward home; most of the diamond is dangerous territory, with only three small spots where a man can be safe" (1975, p. 562). Novak sees the same symbolism against the background of frontier America:

> One dusts off the sacred "home," starting place, Keystone, source and touchstone of triumph: those who cross it most often . . . carry off the victory. "Around the world" is the myth: batter after batter trying to nudge forward his predecessors in this most American of games until the whole universe is circled, base by base, and runners can come "home." One imagines Yankee Clipper ships blown silently across the sparkling sea, sails creaking in the wind, the sound of wood, the silence and isolation of each sailor at his post, encircling the world for trade. (1976, pp. 57-58)

Finally baseball is, as Grella says, the American rite of spring, of life and hope, as no other game is, especially not football, the game of autumn and dying life: "It is . . . the Summer Game, played by the Boys of Summer, an ongoing celebratory dance in the golden season. Its limits in time are April and October, including our happiest months. Even in cold climates we know that if Opening Day has come, spring cannot be far behind" (1975, p. 551).

The Name of the Game is Intimidation: Football

Football *is* for the late 20th century. "The intensity that characterizes football," says Stanley Eitzen, "resembles the tensions and pressures of modern society, contrasted with the more relaxed pace of agrarian life and baseball" (1984, p. 53).

J. H. Duthie points up the significance of American football for our century by contrasting its appeal with that of Olympic sports:

> The individual events of the early Olympics Games . . . spotlight, in face of the inevitability of individual defeat and death, the importance of human force, speed, strength, cunning, and individual skill. The strong-man-alone was exalted. . . . Olympic contest

events, like running, jumping, wrestling down an opponent or throwing outdated weight objects are forms which retain their enormous emotional appeal because they demonstrably have no technological significance for today. They clearly educe nothing but the consciousness of what it means to be human, to strive, to wrestle, to impose our will for a short period on obdurate nature. . . . Individual contest has an appeal deeper and more real than much of our everyday work life. Modern men, dwarfed by the technology they have created, still thrill to athletic events glorifying the energy and achievements of the single individual. (1980, pp. 94–95)

On the contrary, American football does not transcend technological society; it *is* technological society:

Players disappeared to be replaced . . . by specialists with narrowly defined duties and clear-cut responsibilities. Carefully calculated tactics planned by squads of non-playing experts and educated officials who are measurement specialists provided quantifiable achievements denoted in exact intervals of space and time. Above all the submission of the individual as a shift worker to be called on and dismissed as required is mandated. American football, in which specialists in defense oppose an equally specialized offensive unit at all times, provides the most highly evolved athletic metaphor of a technological society. (Duthie, 1980, p. 97)

Clearly, American football has 19th-century roots. My student Mark Melzer has written very imaginatively about these. He likens the game to the 19th-century American passion for land. "Football is a game of land, ownership, and possession." In neither hockey nor basketball does one capture or lose land. In them penalties are imposed against individuals, but football teams are penalized by taking away territory. Although computerization may have changed techniques and strategies, the basic 19th-century motif is still there:

Nothing illustrates more the "Manifest Destiny" of Americans than the game of football. Americans have always felt we must push our borders further and further west. We need more land. Our early settlers let no barrier stop their inexhaustible push forward. We conquered mountains, valleys, rivers, Indians, and you name it, all for that precious earth. And Americans stopped at no cost to gain this land, whether it meant breaking treaties with the Indians, deceiving Mexicans, or just out and out war. In football we also see this factor. Football is a game of deception; you try to fake or fool the opponent. Yet if that doesn't work you can al-

ways use brute force. The need for more land, the deception, the spirit, and the technological advancement, all factors evident in the game, provide us with an interesting insight into our own culture and heritage. (Melzer, class essay)

Like baseball, football does have a place in the cycle of seasons. Historically, it has been intimately associated with the fall harvest rite—Thanksgiving. If however, it has any of the spiritual quality of humble gratitude that characterized that Pilgrim holiday, it is the thankfulness of Anglo invaders for having been allowed to capture and survive in Indian territory. Novak believes that football, teaching that violence is the ultimate human reality, has a more pessimistic view of human possibilities than baseball's springtime view (I agree). He holds that the football view is the more realistic view (I disagree).

Anthropologist William Arens begins his analysis of the great American football ritual thus: "Violence is one of our society's most obvious traits, and its expression in football, where bodily contact and territorial intrusion are essential, clearly accounts for part of the game's appeal" (1975, p. 77). But only part of it. "Football's violence is expressed within the framework of teamwork, specialization, mechanization, and variation, and this combination accounts for its appeal." Conrad Dobler, a college political science major, described in 1977 (whether rightly or not) as "pro football's dirtiest player," on his NFL personnel form put this essence of 20th-century football in one sentence, "It is still the only sport where there is controlled violence mixed with careful technical planning" (Hurford, 1977, p. 30). Another of my students, Patricia Edelman, sees this product of two centuries as "cut along the lines of the American grain, savage, violent, militaristic in its meticulous organization, moralistic in its celebration of performance and high purpose, remorseless in the contempt for failure and its adulation of success." "The game," she says, "is ideally suited for television; the barrage of cameras, the zoom shots and the instant replays reveal subtleties the fan in the stadium could not see, and penetrate the hand-offs, traps, pile-ons, wedges, and other concentrations that obscure the action" (class essay).

In terms of social appeal, Novak describes football as the immigrant myth and the corporate myth. As we saw in chapter 11, football in this century is typically played by escapees from one or another lower-middle-class urban ghetto. Whereas baseball has typically been played by rural WASPs, football is promoted and watched mainly by urban middle-class spiritual WASPS, already arrived or on their way up the corporate ladder. "Baseball and bowling . . . appeal to the less educated and the older segments of the population while both college and pro football appeal to the better educated and middle aged" (Robinson, 1967, p. 79n).

The Football Fan - 1903

Writing on the psychology of football in the early days of the modern game (1903), a professional psychologist, G. T. W. Patrick, described his observation of football in this way:
   In this game more than in any other there is a reversion to aboriginal manners. The game is more brutal, that is, more primitive than others. The lively chase for goal, the rude physical shock of the heavy opposing teams, and the scrimmage-like melée character of the collisions awaken our deep-seated slumbering instincts. By inner imitation the spectators themselves participate in the game and at the same time give unrestrained expression to their emotions. If at a great football game one will watch the spectators instead of the players, he will see at once that the people before him are not his associates of the school, the library, the office, the shop, the street, or the factory. The inhibition of emotional expression is the characteristic of modern civilized man. The spectators at an exciting football game no longer attempt to restrain emotional expression. They shout and yell, blow horns and dance, swing their arms about and stamp, throw their hats in air and snatch off their neighbors' hats, howl and gesticulate, little realizing how foreign this is to their wonted behavior or how odd it would look at their places of work.
   Note: From "The Psychology of Football" by G. T. W. Patrick, 1903, *American Journal of Psychology*, **14**, p. 116.

   Novak puts it together this way:

Football is preeminently the sport of the new white collar and professional class, of the statesmen, bureau chiefs, managers, executives, ad men, consultants, professors, journalists, engineers, technicians, pilots, air traffic controllers, secret service men, insurance agents, managers of retail chains, bank officers, and investment analysts. . . . But football is also the liturgy of the working class, the immigrants, the rednecks. (1976, p. 76)

The preference of middle-class people for football poses a problem in explanation. Common sense tells us that working-class people are generally more violent and less restrained than the middle class. Scientific research shows that middle-class children, in growing up, typically learn to suppress and repress emotional expression more than do working-class children. On this basis we should expect the working class to prefer the violence of football and the middle class to prefer the greater restraint of baseball. The opposite is in fact the case. Why? Harry Edwards says that people prefer aggressive sports in proportion to their "degree of active involvement in the mainstream of American life" (1973, p. 270). Yuppies who are pushing aggressively, and somewhat successfully, to get ahead of their fellow humans easily identify with the aggression of football. They are likely to claim that "baseball is too slow." We will note that the middle class, upward bound in the mainstream of American life, are not *playing* football, they are just enthusiastically watching those not in the mainstream (the working class, the immigrants, the rednecks) beat *their* brains out.

As a strategy game, football's peculiar kind of territoriality places it in the same category as chess, which we have seen is a board model of war. "Basketball," says Novak, "is continuous action, but football is played as a set piece like chess. In chess, opponents alternate single moves" (1976, p. 82). There is, however, a difference. Carrying out the moves in their playbooks, football players are sometimes called pawns, and in a sense are. But they are also alive. The chess player (the coach) can plan his moves, but he cannot execute them. Execution depends basically on the ability of his players to intimidate the opposing pawns. Here is the essence of football.

The Essence of the Game Is Deception: Basketball

Comparing games to musical forms, Novak tells us that baseball is like chamber music. Vivaldi, he says, though not a right fielder for the Mets, should be: The name is right, and his style, "slow, pastoral, each instrument distinct, intensely grasped," penetrates the whole spirit of the game. He would agree with Pete Axthelm, who said that "baseball is basically a slow, pastoral experience, offering a tableau of athletes against a green background, providing moments of action amid longer periods allowed for contemplation of the spectacle" (1970, p. ix). Football, says Novak, is like Ravel's Bolero or Beethoven's Fifth Symphony: Football games build like symphonies to climactic resolution. And "basketball is jazz: improvisatory, free, individualistic, corporate, sweaty, exulting, screeching, torrid, explosive, exquisitely designed for letting first the trumpet, then the sax, then the drummer, then the trombone soar away in virtuoso excellence" (Novak, 1976, pp. 98–100).

Basketball shares with jazz the quality of improvisation. It is improvisatory by contrast with baseball and football, both of which involve set plays. For this reason basketball is much easier for the television or radio broadcaster than for the newspaper sportswriter—for who can report a jam session in print? For the same reason, fans rarely remember specific plays, or even specific games, as they do with baseball or football. Basketball is also improvisatory by comparison with nonset play games like soccer and hockey, the field sports that it much resembles. The difference is that the world of basketball is three-dimensional (the goal is off the ground), whereas the goal in soccer and hockey is bound to the earth (or ice). The symbol of the difference is the jump shot (which made contemporary basketball), during which one can improvise in many ways while airborne. The dunk, which doesn't require that one be 6–10, or even 6–2, further verticalized basketball. When basketball was limited to the earthbound set shot, with feet on the ground, the scores, although not like those in soccer and hockey, were abysmally low by today's standards (as on November 22, 1950, when the Fort Wayne Pistons of the NBA beat George Mikan and the Minneapolis Lakers by the score of 19 to 18). Of course, the introduction in 1954 of the 24-second rule, requiring a team to shoot or surrender the ball, also played a part in skyrocketing scores.

The two men who first advanced improvisation in basketball were white sons of immigrants—Angelo Luisetti and Bob Cousy. Luisetti's one-handed shot changed the world of the two-handed set. Cousy, who became ambidextrous by constant practice carrying books, opening doors, turning keys, and eventually dribbling, passing, and shooting left-handed, in turn rescued basketball from a rigidity imposed by Luisetti's one-handed shot. "Cousy saved pro basketball," said a veteran. "Until he came along, the game followed a rigid pattern. It was the practice of every team to work the ball into the giant pivot man and he turned around and hooked a basket. Cousy changed all that. The fans ate up his razzle-dazzle" (Novak, 1976, p. 104). Koppett (1973) says it was Cousy who brought *style* to basketball—*how* one does it is as important as the result.

Jazz, improvisation, and style embody the essence of basketball—deception. Basketball, says Koppett, is the game of the poker face. A large part of the game consists of a feint with a hip here, a feint with a shoulder there, a look or a head movement in the wrong direction, fake passes, false dribbles, fake breaks toward the basket, fake shots. "Three or four times under the basket a man may pump before he actually lets go" (Novak, 1976, p. 107). Deliberately invented in the late 19th century by a Christian clergyman to promote the physical well-being of young men in winter months, basketball was intended to provide sport without the bodily contact of football and, in the process, to develop moral values. A hundred years later, the game maintains its legal barriers against physical contact, although the interpretation of them would probably shock the Rev. James Naismith. He would also probably be shocked to learn that in the eyes of an astute observer like Koppett the basketball player is the supreme con artist in sport, and basketball tends to recruit players and spectators who have (or would like to have) a talent for deceiving their fellow humans.

Basketball is an art form and is increasingly becoming a black art form. Teams are becoming more black, and audiences are becoming more black. In Chicago and Philadelphia basketball crowds tend to be black, whereas the whites watch hockey. Basketball is also played well by whites in the rural Midwest, Novak reminds us, but it is a different game, "a game of the head, solid, deliberate, strategic, grinding" (1976, p. 107)—no jazz. Axthelm puts it this way: "Kids in small towns—particularly in the Midwest—often become superb basketball players. But they do so by developing accurate shots and precise skills; in the cities, kids simply develop moves" (1970, p. x).

Black basketball is put-on. Although the first great put-on artist was Cousy, the term is a black term, central to the black experience. "Like the stories and legends of black literature, the hero does not let his antagonist guess his intentions; he strings him along, he keeps his inner life to himself until the decisive moment" (Novak, 1976, p. 107). In brief, he puts on the Man, Uncle Charlie. Thus, the game symbolizes the centuries-old struggle for black identity. "Available records of life among black slaves," says Edwards, "indicate that a slave's wits were more important to insuring his longevity than physical prowess" (1973, p. 198). Surviving black work songs embody the same put-on of the Man. As much as the physical grace that stacks blacks in the forward positions, this is the quality that basketball celebrates. What does this celebration, by athlete and audience, do for black social power? Novak sees it as a positive affirmation of black identity. Others believe that it siphons black energies off into symbolic gratification and away from fulfillment in the mainstream of social and economic life.

Edgar Friedenberg sees another dimension of deception in basketball. This is violation as an accepted part of game tactics. To Friedenberg, basketball is a caricature of "our legalism and the intricate web of regulations among which we live and on which we climb" (1967, p. ix). In most other games, actions that are illegal are generally dangerous or disrupt the game and so are usually avoided. But in basketball, one does not observe the rules, but rationally balances the penalties of violation against the advantages to be gained. The deliberate and open tactical foul is found only in basketball and soccer. The coach, says Friedenberg, manipulates rule violations much as a businessman manipulates the Internal Revenue Code. Thus, while the player is putting on his opponents on the floor (a typically black move), the coach is calculating how profitably to break the law (a typically middle-class move). Moral lessons are being learned that Naismith never dreamed of. We can see what Friedenberg meant by calling basketball "an abstract parody of American middle-class life" (p. ix).

A final comparison of our three major spectator sports:

Several factors make basketball more democratic and communal than either baseball or football. The smaller size of teams and the fluidity and unpredictability of play make impossible the benevolent despotism of the playbook football coach or baseball manager. The physical arrangement of the basketball arena brings the crowd much closer to the actions of players and officials. What Grella says of baseball is even truer of basketball—it is impossible to hide or avoid accountability for one's actions. Another democratizing and humanizing factor is that, in basketball, players engage almost naked, not in violent collision, but in intimate physical contact. Compare baseball, where Grella speaks of "the odd uniform, with its high stockings and knickers, the collarless shirts and boys' caps, all of it not very far removed from the uniforms of the Currier and Ives illustrations, a vestigial survival of what must have been gentlemen's leisure wear a century ago" (1975, p. 555). Or compare the Superman appearance of the football player, for whom "the donning of the required items results in an enlarged head and shoulders and a narrowed waist, with the lower torso poured into skintight pants accented only by a metal codpiece" (Arens, 1975, pp. 78–79). By contrast, the basketball player is about as close as one can be, in a public team spectacle in our culture, to the nudity required of the Greek Olympic athlete.

Putting everything together, if one were to ask for a model for baseball it would be 19th-century capitalist individualism. A model for football would be 20th-century totalitarianism. A model for basketball might be the communes of the 1960s or earlier, the kind of combination of individualism with team spirit that led Cousy to make this criticism of the 1970 New York Knicks: "If anything, they pass when they could shoot, and that's a fault every coach would love to worry about" (Axthelm, 1970, p. 18). It is not mere coincidence that an excellent example of a basketball player who has combined individual brilliance with team dedication is Bill Walton, whose political convictions are democratic socialist.

Soccer: The Game Is Football

When the dribbler wants to elude a defender and change direction, he must do so by faking with his legs and feet without losing control of the ball. Three things are really happening at once—the dribbler is controlling the ball, faking, and changing direction, all with the same part of the body. There is no move in baseball, football, or basketball which demands as much from one part of the body at the same time, because control of the ball in these sports comes primarily from the hands. (Cascio, 1975, p. 198)

Thus Chuck Cascio describes the essence of soccer. In the United States, baseball, football, and basketball (which, as Cascio says, are all forms of *hand* ball) are the overwhelmingly most popular spectator sports. But not so in the world as a whole. Kyle Rote, Jr., a former student of theology and the law, and probably the best known soccer player born in the United States, estimates that there are about 250 million soccer players in the world. This would mean that about 1 human being out of 20 plays soccer. Even in the United States, Pelé, with his 3-year contract with the New York Cosmos, was the highest paid athlete in history. Cascio says that he is better known throughout the world than Larry Csonka, Johnny Bench, Wilt Chamberlain, Gerald Ford, Carol Burnett, and Frank Sinatra. Among Americans, only Ali might compare. The World Cup, unlike the so-called World Series in baseball, is a global event. "The contests," says Cascio, "become part of a national movement, a country rallying behind a team involved in a war fought with feet and a ball" (1975, p. 21).

Soccer, although popular in Britain, Germany, Holland, Italy, Hungary, and the Soviet Union, is primarily a game of the southern hemisphere. It is played on big green fields, which can be as large as 130 yards long and 100 wide, on which a player can run 7 to 12 miles in the course of a game. Novak describes it as "an almost total commitment to fluid form, to kinesis, to the patterns in motion of a unit of runners" (1976, p. 96). Periodically, the fluidity is interrupted, or intensified, by bursts of action. Soccer, says Novak, lacks the physical aggression and the tactical control of small, detailed activities that mark the major sports in the United States. As our opening quote emphasized, soccer is a game of the feet as contrasted with the hand games of the northern hemisphere. *Homo Faber* (man the maker) has built the northern hemisphere, says Novak, with manual dexterity and manufacture (from the Latin *manus*, hand). So we might say that soccer is basically a Third World game. (This is demonstrated by the fact that in all four of the World Cup finals, including 1986, that have matched a European team against a Third World team, the Third World team has won.) It makes sense that, in the days when manufacture was transforming England, the event occurred that is recorded on a commemorative stone at Rugby: "William Webb Ellis, with a fine disregard for the rules of the game, first took the ball in his arms and ran with it, thus originating the distinctive feature of the Rugby game." This manipulation (again, *manus*) began the series of events that finally ended with the transformation of soccer into American football. In soccer, in the upper body, the head takes the place of the hand as an instrument of propulsion: "Good headers use the neck and head like a baseball player uses the wrist and hand. The wrist snaps the hand to provide force. In soccer, the neck snaps the head with much the same effect" (Cascio, 1975, p. 201).

Despite the trend to American football, soccer has also been here in the United States, but not as an American game. Baseball was fitted to the space of rural pastures, and basketball could be played wherever there was a barn to which to attach a peach basket. Soccer was played mainly by urban immigrants—German, Irish, Italian, and Polish immigrants in New England, New York City, and Pennsylvania, who attached themselves to clubs or teams sponsored by businesses like Bethlehem Steel, J. P. Coats Thread Company, American Woolen, and Interborough Rapid Transit. It was also played in the Ivy League colleges, but not in the heartland. In 1913 there was formed an amateur United States Football Association, but it was not until after the 1966 World Cup Games in England brought films of 32 matches that had drawn 1 1/2 million people and grossed $7 million that United States promoters became seriously interested in soccer. The outcome was the formation of two pro leagues that merged to form the North American Soccer League. At first the member cities imported whole foreign teams, who had in fact a soccer vacation with pay in their home off-season.

A 10-year contract with CBS did bring the game into middle America, and Pelé boosted attendance wherever he played, although it tended to drop back to normal afterward. Individual imported players still make up the largest and the best part of the teams. However, the United States has developed a few native stars like Kyle Rote, Jr., and Bob Rigby. In 1975 the United States Soccer Federation estimated that there were 600,000 boys *and girls* playing soccer in the United States. (Compare the U.S.S.R., where women are barred from soccer.) There were probably about 50,000 young players around Dallas (Rote's home town), 35,000 around St. Louis, and 40,000 in the Washington, DC–Maryland–Virginia area. St. Louis University, Howard, Penn State, Clemson, and several smaller schools have excellent soccer teams. The St. Louis Stars professional team, rooted in an area of soccer enthusiasm, was predominantly United States–born, many locally recruited. However, in an age of manipulative technocracy, world-style football may be expected to have a hard time rooting itself in the American heartland and attaining the appeal of its somewhat illegitimate, but hand-oriented, violent, tightly coordinated, and authoritarian American grandchild.

Hockey: Game of the North

Hockey is a game of the north. It can technically be played in Miami, but it is native to the subarctic, where people live a profound confrontation with nature, where the ground is frozen solid 6 feet deep half of the year, where in winter blizzards are routine and a temperature of 0°F is warm, where there is ice on lakes in June and the possibility of frost in August. (Having grown up in the relative warmth of southern New York state, and having later taught 4 years in Minnesota, I can say that no one who has not experienced a subarctic winter can understand how different in quality it is.) Living in the subarctic breeds expectation of extremes, develops the habit of physical endurance, and raises the threshold to pain.

On this continent hockey players come typically from subarctic farms and small towns, where the only way out of this routine confrontation with nature is to go to the city, and the only way to the city for some may be hockey. I think this is the background against which we must understand the fact that hockey is the most violent of team games, the only team game where fighting is taken for granted, a game where collisions are so violent that part of a trainer's standard equipment are forceps to loosen swallowed tongues, where a team may carry a player with no real talent other than the capacity for mayhem.

Its native climate shapes the medium of the game and, therefore, the game experience. On skates on ice, players can reach velocities of up to 30 miles an hour, which no other sport approaches. By contrast with soccer, which he calls graceful, flowing, evasive, and quietly impassioned, Novak describes hockey as swift, physical, brutal, and violent. The swiftness given by its icy medium lends to hockey a crowd appeal unique among games. It may also detract from its appeal by making it the least strategic of the territorial games. Ross Atkin says that the major drawback of hockey may be its disjointed nature:

Even the polished Montreal Canadiens have a hard time controlling the puck for any length of time. With bodies zooming all over the ice, the puck is constantly being intercepted and deflected, leading to a great amount of offensive futility. In basketball, by contrast, a team can more easily control the ball and set up shots. The attacking team in hockey often resorts to dumping the puck over the blue [line], then chasing after it. This sort of catch-as-catch-can play results in a fast-paced yet chaotic game that is not always interesting to strategy-minded fans. (Atkin, 1977, p. 11)

Another element making strategic control difficult may be the unique fact that, in hockey, substitutions are made while play is in progress.

The speed imparted by the ice increases the possibility of violence in hockey. The bodies zooming all over the ice bear lethal weapons in their hands and on their feet. The puck is also lethal because, being flat to slide on ice, it can gash as well as bruise. Violence ultimately converges on the goal. "A lone oncoming shooter against a goal tender is the true one-to-one relationship," says Gerald Eshkenazi, ". . . a pure confrontation" (Eshkenazi, 1972, pp. 21–22). A hockey slap shot does not travel much faster than a fast pitch in baseball, but the ball is round and *the batter is not standing on the plate.* The goalie is heavily padded, true. Until fairly recently, however, his face was not protected by a mask. He was wide open to the kind of thing that happened in 1928 when New York Ranger goalie Lorne Chabot stopped a Montreal shot just above his left eye. If his 44-year-old coach has not skated out to take Chabot's place, the Stanley Cup finals would have been terminated by doctor's orders then and there.

Hockey players are tough. "They dress for a game without fanfare," says Eshkenazi. "First they take out their false teeth and drop them into paper cups. Then they put on the gear that protects their kidneys, shoulders, groin, kneecaps, and toes. They know they will be hurt, that sometime during the evening they will be bruised" (1972, p. 13). Dr. James Nicholas, the orthopedic surgeon who took care of Joe Namath's knees and has done research on the demands imposed by different sports, has said, "Their tolerance to pain is remarkable. Hockey players are the most uncomplaining athletes I've met" (Eshkenazi, 1972, p. 13). Some young players are said to collect the stitches from their healed wounds, and to boast after a bloody game about the new trophies they have won. There is a hockey cliché, "If you can walk to the bench, you can play."

This toughness and willingness to play when injured are tied to an intense emphasis on winning, which is in turn tied to the fact that for many players hockey is the only way out of the life in which they grew up. All these factors explain why hockey, although it does not have the tactically controlled violence of football, at all times skirts much closer to the brink of uncontrolled violence. The temper tantrum is close to being an accepted part of the game. The practical question for officials is not whether players should fight, but how soon, and how the fights will be stopped. For example, although fighting is technically illegal *per se,* officials are not too concerned about two men fighting but must intervene before a third man joins because that is likely to bring benchsitters on the ice (which is illegal) or trigger crowd involvement.

Hockey, like basketball, is played in a confined area in which the spectators are very close to the action. Although sport statistics generally show a higher percentage of games won by all teams at home, in hockey, as in basketball, the advantage is very great. For example, in

1971 the New York Rangers had a 19-16 record on the road, whereas at home they won 30 games and lost only 2 (Eshkenazi, 1972, p. 14). Knowing the ricochets off one's home boards is an advantage, but probably the main reason why home teams win is that, although the officials are honest and the players physically tough, in a basketball-hockey type of crowd situation both are psychologically intimidated by the home crowd.

A final point—hockey is still the only major sport to remain almost totally white (in the 1976–77 season there were two blacks in the National Hockey League, and in 1984 the name of Edmonton's black goalie Grant Fuhr was inscribed on the Stanley Cup). I have referred to the tendency of hockey to become the white hope for white spectators as basketball teams and crowds become more black. Why have blacks not moved into hockey as they have into baseball, football, and basketball? There is no reason to think that the same physical abilities that have brought success in these sports could not be transferred to ice. The answer probably takes us back to where we started this section—hockey is a game of subarctic Canada. As long as there is a pool of young rural Canadians culturally attuned to the game and ready to use a stick and a puck to get up in the world, blacks from the ghetto, as well as whites from the mines and the mills, will probably seek their upward mobility in other sport channels.

The Democratization of Tennis

Billie Jean King once captured tennis' combination of tradition and modernity when she described it as violent action against a background of complete tranquility.

In November 1970, according to a Nielson survey, there were 10.6 million tennis players in the United States; in the same month of 1974, there were 33.9 million (Winder, 1976, p. 9). This is not the first time tennis has been a popular mass sport. In the early days of the modern era, two travel guides told their readers about tennis abroad. In his *Description of England and Scotland,* in 1558, the Frenchman Estienne Perlin reported, "Here you may commonly see artisans, such as hatters and joiners, playing tennis for a crown, which is not commonly seen elsewhere, particularly on a working day" (Henderson, 1947, p. 59). In 1598 Sir R. A. Dallington, in his *Method for Travell,* gave Englishmen this information about the French: "Ye cannot find that little . . . town in France that hath not one or more courts. . . . Ye would thinke they were born with Rackets in their hands. . . . There is more tennis players in France than ale drinkers with us" (cited in Henderson, 1947, p. 64).

Tennis has not always been for the masses. In fact, it seems to have begun in monasteries. The French game *jeu de paume,* so called because it was played with the palm of the hand instead of a racket, was *court* tennis (lawn tennis was invented in the late 19th century). ''Court tennis is played on a court shaped like a stylized cloister. The ball must travel over the net, as in lawn tennis, but may also be bounced against the walls, or from the roof of a low gallery which extends along three sides of the court, much the same as the cloister in a cathedral'' (Henderson, 1947, pp. 47–48). Jeu de paume was played first at Easter. It seems to have been an adaptation to Christian architecture and tradition of the pagan spring fertility rites. ''By the year 1287, at least within church walls, the rough and tumble ball games had become more refined, and . . . in certain churches . . . the game of tennis is officially recognized'' (Henderson, 1947, p. 50).

The game was fun enough so that it ceased to be only an Easter ceremony and became the favorite sport of young monks. An illustrated calendar of the early 16th century shows a game in which a priest has taken off his religious garb, and his undershirt is showing. The church took action against such scandalous performances, as it did also against priests who played with laymen on public courts (Cochard, 1889, cited in Henderson, 1957, p. 54). By the 16th century the game had become a sport for the kings and nobility and then for the common people. The racket had been introduced; by the year 1400 the manufacture of rackets and balls in France was controlled by a Guild of Tennis Masters.

By the 16th century tennis was established in England as the game of the courtier and gentlemen. Charles II was an avid player, who once lost 4 1/2 pounds of weight in a single match. Tennis was also the badge of an educated man. J. Earle, a Fellow of Oxford, in 1628 described a ''mere Young Gentleman of the University,'' saying that ''the two marks of his Senioritie, is the Bare Velvet of his Gowne, and his proficiencie at Tennis, where, when he can once play a set, he is a Freshman no more'' (Earle, 1628, cited in Henderson, 1947, p. 66). Henderson points out that ''by the time of Shakespeare tennis was the popular sport of the common people.'' However, because of its association with gambling and other vices, it had practically disappeared by the beginning of the 19th century. Lawn tennis was developed in 1873, but at the time Henderson wrote, in 1947, what he said was essentially true: ''Today tennis is played in the private courts of a few wealthy men in England and America, and a few select sporting clubs in the United States, England, and France. It is a splendid game, ideal for exercise in the young and old, but unfortunately restricted in its use because of its excessive cost'' (p. 58).

The only exception is that it had developed also as a minor spectator sport, played by young men and women variously known as ten-

Lawn Tennis as invented by Major Wingfield, 1873. Courtesy of Racquet & Tennis Club.

nis bums, kept amateurs, shamateurs, who received travel and expense money, and sometimes a little more under the table. The game was still on the face of it a gentleman's (or lady's) sport, played for fun by people who had no monetary interest. The decorum was upper class; applause or booing was not permitted. Until a Mexican man named Gonzales and a black woman named Gibson shot to the top, the personnel was essentially WASP, the kind of people admissable to a place like the West Side Tennis Club.

The realities of tennis a quarter of a century ago are graphically demonstrated in an exchange between the English press and American tennis player Gardnar Mulloy over a 1953 incident in which Mulloy lost his temper at Wimbledon. Suggesting that Mulloy had violated the tennis code of the gentleman, columnist Jack Peart wrote in the Sunday Pictorial: "Don't run away with the idea that the pick of the world's semiprofessional sun-chasers are out for the honor and glory that goes with a coveted Wimbledon title. Not on your life. Kudos mean cash to amateur tennis players—especially the men. No wonder they call it the tennis racquet" (Mulloy, 1960, p. 160).

Mulloy's reply places the tennis amateur in social context. He describes a hypothetical young man who has been groomed for international tennis since the age of 13:

After seven years of training, practice, striving, playing, he goes on to the center court at Wimbledon. For a game of tennis? Baloney! There's only one thing in the whole wide world that kid wants—to win. What the hell else is he there for? What do the folks back home think he is doing there? Playing a game of tennis? Under these circumstances a player who loses his temper deserves to get his ear slapped back. But our boy is involved in an international contest. National honor and prestige are at stake. A chance of becoming a world Champion is within reach. He's got to win. (1960, p. 163)

During the period of the kept amateur there were tennis pros, but their activity was essentially limited to exhibitions. The major tournaments and Davis Cup play were still open only to amateurs. In this game of gentlemen there were no open tournaments. In the 25 years since the incident related by Mulloy, tennis has become frankly professional. A top player in his or her 20s, today can make as much money in a year as the best and most experienced amateur players were able to pick up in a lifetime of expense and under-the-table money. Tennis is broadcast to the nation as TV entertainment and tailored to the needs of television.

In the 1970s Michael Mewshaw, a novelist and tennis buff, joined the tour for 6 months as an observer. The report he gave told how far tennis has come from jeu de paume in a cloister:

Mewshaw found . . . that the tour was accompanied by a numbing sideshow of girls and drugs and dominated by financial arrangements never before revealed. He found fixed matches; he found gambling. He learned about the illegal, under-the-table money that is regularly paid by tournament directors to superstars. He discovered conflicts of interest involving umpires that would be a scandal in any other sport. He unearthed a pattern of activity—much of it involving the most famous, talented, and wealthy athletes on the tour—that led one important tennis figure to tell him, "Tennis was born in dishonesty and has never grown out of it." (Mewshaw, 1983, jacket)

Of his discoveries Mewshaw said sweepingly that "much about professional tennis is unfair—unfair to more than ninety percent of the players on the circuit, unfair to the honorable men and women who have devoted their lives to the game, and finally unfair to the sponsors and fans who have a right to expect more than a shabby burlesque" (1983, pp. 305–306).

As our beginning statistics indicated, the decline of shamateur tennis has had another outcome than money for TV networks and careers for rising young stars. It has changed tennis from a game played in stuffy hushed decorum by a minority for a minority to a game for the expanding middle classes in an affluent society. It is, as the young monks found, an optimistic springtime and summertime game. Like baseball, tennis is noncontact, nonterritorial, and non-time-bound. Thus, it offers a respite from the clock and the rat race. Being a striking game, it provides movement against an object rather than against people. It is active enough to engage the cardiovascular and respiratory systems. For these reasons, played as singles into middle age and as doubles thereafter, tennis remains perhaps the best participatory sport for lifetime health and pleasure.

Ultimate Self-Confrontation: Golf

Golf, which like tennis has traditionally been an elite sport, likewise exemplifies clearly the transition from play to commercialism. Like tennis, golf involves no territorial imperative, is non-time-bound, noncontact, and involves the striking of an object with a stick. For these reasons—with the shortcoming that it does not as actively engage heart and lungs—it also is an excellent lifetime participant sport. Golf is the ultimate solo sport. There is really nothing in golf to compare to doubles in the other individual sport of tennis. In his history of the pro golf tour, Al Barkow describes what he sees to be the essence of golf:

> It can be said that there are only two things in life we do alone: die and play golf. . . . Where a home run or a sixty-yard forward pass may have the captivating properties of a well-hit golf shot, . . . they depend on the machinations of others—a mispitch at the waist, a fleet, sure-handed receiver, or a lax defender. The golfer, though, stands alone. He starts and finishes the deed; every shot he plays is a one-on-one confrontation with his own nervous system, power of concentration, ego. He can blame no one for failure, can take full credit for success. It is just he and the golf course. . . . The golfer is Don Quixote attacking a windmill, a windmill that is literally . . . himself. Golf teases the existential soul with the loneliness of the long distance runner. (1974, pp. viii, 25–26)

What about this solo act draws spectators? In 1900, the fine English golfer Harry Vardon toured the United States and had this to report: "The Americans were not sufficiently advanced to appreciate some of the finer points of the game. They did, however, appear to thoroughly appreciate the type of ball I drove" (cited in Barkow, 1976, p. 42). Barkow describes the same thing in Space Age terms: "A golf spectator is satisfied when he gets to see . . . a ball struck with consummate power and amazing control; a ball sent soaring from a standing start, then floating to earth and stopping within a prescribed swatch of lawn. It is an awesome sensation, not unlike watching a rocket launch" (1974, p. 25).

The golfer has not always been alone. So far as we can trace its history, golf originated in a team game. In the French *jeu de mail*, as early as the 14th century, two teams would drive wooden balls about the size of tennis balls cross-country with a mallet to a marker—a stone, a tree, or other vertical objects. The game was played along country roads with high ditches that furnished natural obstacles. In the 17th century jeu de mail became popular with the wealthy, and the course was reduced to a single set ground. The Dutch played a similar game, *kolven*, in the 16th century, both teams using the same ball, the distant goal still upright. It was in Scotland, out of a form of a shinty, that a game emerged that involved driving a ball into a series of holes, and thus the distinctive character of golf as a ball game developed. Henderson believes that golf can be traced back through shinty to the Egyptian fertility rites. "But," he says, "the development of the game itself is Scottish" (1947, p. 12).

Mary Stuart, Queen of Scots, was fond of golf. Here she is playing at St. Andrews. Courtesy of The Bettmann Archive.

Golf remained a predominantly British game until well into the 20th century, with St. Andrews, in Scotland, its Mecca. The first United States Open was held in 1895, with 10 players and a purse of $335. In the *Atlantic Monthly*, in June 1902, William Garrot Brown sized up the situation: "Empires, trusts, and golf were three topics of conversation in the land. The future historian . . . will not rate golf as the least of the three new things which came with the end of the century" (Barkow, 1974, p. 51). In 1914 a Harvard philosophy professor remarked that the British, in golf as elsewhere, muddled through, but that the scientific approach would lead Americans to success. They did suceed. In 1921 Jock Hutchinson (an American, not a Scotsman) won the British Open. In 1922 Walter Hagen won it. In 1930 Bobby Jones completed a grand slam of British Open, British Amateur, American Open, and American Amateur tournaments.

Jones was the last great amateur golfer in the best traditional sense of the word—a lover of the game and a Southern gentleman of culture and means. At the time of his grand slam, there were essentially three kinds of golfers in the United States, with status in this order: (a) amateurs, (b) club pros, and (c) touring pros. The amateur could afford to play without being seriously concerned about tournament purses. The club pro was primarily a golf teacher who occasionally played a tournament. The touring pro played the circuit for a living, traveling the country in Depression days in a beaten up car over beaten up roads for a hopeful cut in a meager purse. The man most responsible for giving respectability to the touring pros was Hagen, the son of a German-born blacksmith and a tremendous competitor; the most spectacular event was a severe trouncing of Jones in a special match-play engagement. Gene Sarazen, son of an Italian carpenter, was also influential in taking the game away from the elite. An important part in professionalizing golf was played by George May, an ex-Bible salesman who, in the 1940s, promoted the Tam O'Shanter tournament in Chicago with bleachers around greens, name tags on players, and the first $100,000 purse. A pivotal point in the rise to recognition of pro golf took place in 1953 when Lew Worsham, before a national TV audience of 2 million, won the Tam O'Shanter by one stroke by holing out a wedge shot on the last hole for an eagle.

We have come a long way from jeu de mail, kolven, and St. Andrews. Post-war affluence and TV coverage have made the pro tour a major commercial event, organized of course more for the national television audience than for the spectators on the spot. As Robert Lipsyte points out in his history of sport in the 1970s, "Corporate America's television sponsorship made golf an enormously rich spectator sport—our latest livingroom heroes were men in picnic clothes who charted their comparative standings not by victories or even great performances but by the amounts of money they earned" (Lipsyte, 1975, excerpted in *Miami News*, July 3, 1976, p. 18). Lipsyte cites the case of Arnold Palmer who, even with fading skills, remained a culture hero jetting "from engagement to appearance to board meeting to match to the opening of a trade show."

The "old school" in golf is still represented by the Masters tournament, held since 1934 at the Augusta National golf club. By contrast with the Chicago gangsters who sometimes hung around Tam O'Shanter, at Augusta National "the membership list is composed of the quiet powers that are part of the industrial-military complex" (Barkow, 1974, p. 173).

Jones was prominent in initiating the Masters, and President Eisenhower was also president of Augusta National. At Augusta, says Barkow, golf is played in the Victorian manner, "and not without the attendant hypocrisy" (1974, p. 173). It is said that at the Masters dogs do not bark and babies do not cry. To avoid a commercial image, attendance and the size of the purse are not publicized, but golf course architects and equipment and clothing manufacturers are on the scene making deals and taking orders. On one occasion a very pregnant young women was refused use of the clubhouse restroom because she did not have proper credentials. The younger generation of pros is sometimes put off by the elitist atmosphere. Former National Open champion Lee Trevino has complained that at the Masters Mexican-Americans have less status than caddies. However, Barkow does believe that the Masters is one of the best run tournaments.

Those who think golf is a pastoral escape from the rat race should consider the harassment of Jane Blalock, an ex-tomboy and college history major, who in her 20s became one of the most effective players on the women's tour. Blalock is, in the words of her coach and by her own agreement, a very intense competitor. I have not seen a more concrete and insightful account than she gives of the physical and psychological stresses of athletic competition (Blalock, 1977, chap. 7). In 1972 the Ladies' Professional Golf Association suspended Blalock on the basis of unsubstantiated charges that she had repeatedly cheated in placing her ball in play. Under a temporary court injunction she was able to continue tournament play with success despite ostracism by many of her fellow players. In 1974 federal judge Charles A. Moye finally sustained his earlier ruling that the suspension was in violation of the Sherman Anti-Trust Act because it was imposed by competitors of plaintiff who stood to gain financially from plaintiff's exclusion from the market (cited in Blalock, 1977). The court did not rule on the facts in the case, but only on the conspiratorial nature of the procedure.

I have tried in this chapter to place the most important sports in the context of social history and social change. Where do we go from here? Let us close with one suggestive attempt at an answer.

Marshall McLuhan, the very influential student of media, advanced some ideas about how audience preference for sports is related to historical periods (McLuhan, 1967). McLuhan began with three historical epochs: the preliterate, up to the invention of printing; the literate, based on printed media; and the postliterate, which would begin with the visual medium of television. What he meant by postliterate is indicated by the frequent complaint of adults that children don't read any more, just watch TV. For adults, the difference would be between the morning newspaper (literate) and the morning network news (postliterate). Susan Birrell and John Loy (1979) have developed some of McLuhan's ideas about sport in the literate and postliterate periods.

McLuhan distinguished between hot sports and cool sports. In hot sports action is focused; in cool sports it is diffused, both as to location and as to action. Wrestling, diving, gymnastics, and fencing are examples of locationally focused sports; baseball, golf, and the territorial sports are spatially diffused. Diffusion of action measures the pace of the game and the degree to which action is unexpected and unpredictable. From this standpoint a professional wrestling match is less action-diffused than a tennis match, a baseball game less diffused than an American football game or a soccer match. Table 12.1 shows how Birrell and Loy, following McLuhan, classify sports in terms of diffusion (coolness). Class I sports are the coolest, Class III the hottest.

Table 12.1   Diffusion Rankings of Selected Sports

Sports	Locational Diffusion	Action Diffusion
Class I auto racing, basketball, football, hockey, lacrosse, soccer, rugby, roller derby	high	high
Class II baseball, golf, most races, tennis	high	low
Class III bowling, boxing, diving, fencing, field events, gymnastics, pool, wrestling	low	low

Note. From "Modern Sport: Hot and Cool" by S. Birrell and J.W. Loy, Jr., 1979, *International Review of Sport Sociology*, **14**, (1), p. 8, Table 1. Copyright 1979 by International Society of Sport Sociology. Reprinted by permission.

Cool sports, the sports of the postliterate television era, diffused in location and action, make more demands on the spectator and leave more room for spectator involvement in experiencing them. Hot sports, the sports of the literate era, are more limited in action and/or area and present a ready-made experience to a receptive spectator. Baseball, with its slow pace and constant focus on the pitcher-batter confrontation, is a typical action-focused hot game. Football's more constant action makes it a diffused-action cool game that permits and requires the spectator to fill in the action. McLuhan would agree with Grella's description of baseball as a typical 19th-century sport and with Novak and Duthie in calling football the game of the late 20th century. Like Johnson, he sees baseball as giving way to football in the era of TV, because the more wide-ranging action of football is better suited to television than is "isolation of the individual performance" (Johnson, 1971, p. 103).

Birrell and Loy are not completely satisfied with the predictive ability of McLuhan's hypothesis. For one thing, after a period of slump, baseball is still very much with us. According to McLuhan, a Class II sport like tennis, and especially a Class III sport like gymnastics, should be on their way out, but both have experienced strong popularity in recent years. Personally, I have a problem with McLuhan's terminology, as do some of my students. The classifications in Table 12.1 seem valid, but the hot-cool designations feel backward to me. Football feels hotter to me than baseball, auto racing hotter than gymnastics. However, McLuhan's hypothesis clearly has something to say about the relationship of sport preference to social trends and could well be explored further.

Part IV

The Social Psychology of Sport

Chapter 13

*S*ocialization:
The Rules of the Game

There is a widespread belief that play, games, and sport teach the rules of life. In this chapter we will examine this belief in the light of what we know about *socialization*, the process through which one becomes a participating member of society. Let us look first at several representative statements of this belief.

H. G. Wells, the British author who wrote a comprehensive world history and was a forerunner of science fiction also wrote in 1911 a little book on simple floor games for young children, in which he said, "Upon such a floor may be made an infinitude of imaginative games, not only keeping boys and girls happy for days together, but building a framework of spacious and inspiring ideas in them for later life. The British Empire will gain new strength from nursery floors" (Wells, 1911, pp. 9–10).

At about the same time the prominent American psychologist G. Stanley Hall wrote of the role of adolescent games in developing social qualities. In adolescence, Hall said,

> *A new spirit of organization arises which makes teams possible or more permanent. Football, baseball, cricket, etc., and even boating can become schools of mental and moral training. The rules of the game are intricate, and to master and observe them effectively is no mean training for the mind in controlling the body. . . . The reason for every detail of inner construction and conduct of the game requires experience and insight into human conduct. Then the subordination of each member to the whole and to a leader cultivates the social and cooperative instincts. . . . Group loyalty can be so utilized as to develop a spirit of service and devotion not only to town, country, and race, but to God and the Church. (1937, Vol. 1, pp. 221–222)*

Otto Mallery, a contemporary of Wells and Hall, told political and social scientists about the socializing functions of organized play:

In the games of the street every boy is for himself. Victory belongs to the shrewd, the crafty, and the strong. Team games of the playground require the submission of the individual will to the welfare of the team. Rigid rules inculcate fair play. A boy has the option of obeying the rules or not playing at all. New standards are set up; standards of self-control, of helping the other fellow, of fighting shoulder to shoulder for the honor of the team, of defeat preferable to unfair victory. These standards when translated into the language of political life we call Self-government, Respect for the law, Social Service and Good Citizenship. (1910, p. 156)

In 1925 W. O. McGeehan paid tribute to such a good citizen in an obituary to the magnificent baseball pitcher Christy Mathewson:

He was the incarnation of all the virtues with which we endow the ideal American. If baseball will hold to the ideals and example of Christy Mathewson—gentleman, sportsman, and soldier—our national game will keep the younger generation clean and courageous, and the future of the nation secure. (cited in Literary Digest, October 24, 1925, p. 42)

At about the same time Stuart Sherman used tennis to illustrate dramatically the socializing effects of sport. In a game of tennis, he says, the server is *physically* free to do all kinds of things. He can walk up to the net and drop the ball over instead of serving, shoot it over the net with a gun, or hire a boy to carry it around the net. But he is not *mentally* or *morally* free to do any of these things. He realizes that the rules make the game, and he believes in the game. "The ethical implications of athletic games are immense. Democracy itself is a complex athletic game. Its existence depends, more than upon anything else, upon our hearty willingness, for the sake of the game, to refrain from doing what we are physically perfectly free and able to do" (Sherman, 1924, p. 21).

George Davis, the soft-nosed football coach best known because in the 1960s he compiled an unbeaten record while having his high school players vote on their starting lineups, explains that team democracy in football is the best way he knows to help young men find themselves. A person's task in life, says Davis, is to find what he can do best and mesh it with what others can do best, so as to enrich the lives of all. "How do I know this is true?" he asks. "Football taught me. The better I blocked, the better my halfback ran. The better he ran, the better I blocked. Life is finding what is best in *you* and presenting it to society in performance. I don't mean giving society what it wants necessarily, but giving it what *you* have to give" (Amdur, 1971, p. 304).

The Process of Socialization

Now let us move from these preliminary impressions to analyze systematically the part played by play, games, and sport in the process of socialization. By way of definition, socialization is *the process by which we acquire personalities as functioning members of society.* The fact that we acquire them in a process of experience means that our social qualities are not as such inborn. Our basic physiological, psychological, and social drives—for food, sex, recognition, response, emotional support—are. Our capacity for adapting to new situations (intelligence) has an inborn neurological basis as well as a basis in experience. The same may be true of special mechanical, musical, and mathematical aptitudes. But we clearly develop social potentialities only through social interaction. In a sentence suggested by Lenin, socialization is the process of learning "the elementary rules of social life that have been known for centuries and repeated for thousands of years in all school books" (Lenin, 1932, pp. 73–74). It was described by the sociologist Charles Horton Cooley when he said that "always and everywhere men seek honor and dread ridicule, defer to public opinion, cherish their goods and their children, and admire courage, generosity, and success" (1962, p. 28).

Where, now, do play, games, and sport fit into the process? Writing of play among the children of the Australian aborigines, R. M. Berndt says, "For the student of primitive life the chief interest in . . . imitative play lies in its educational value. The primitive child's school is its playground, and his playground is everywhere" (1940, p. 293). The best general statement I know as to how play is related to socialization also comes from down under. In *The Games of New Zealand Children* Brian Sutton-Smith says:

> *Group life is very precarious among young children six to nine years of age; in their game organization these youngsters can rise above the limitations of their own relatively unorganized personalities; the structure of their games makes group activity possible amongst them when there might otherwise be none; their games provide the first behavior patterns that (as a group of children reaching toward social organization) they can readily comprehend, enjoy, and maintain. (1959, pp. 44–45)*

Earlier, Cooley had written of how our highest principles of social judgment grow out of concrete experience in the simplest group relationships like play:

Where do we get our notions of love, freedom, justice and the like which we are ever applying to social institutions? Not from abstract philosophy, surely, but from the actual life of simple and widespread forms of society, like the family or the play group [my emphasis]. In these relations mankind realizes itself, gratifies its primary needs, . . . and from the experience derives standards of what it is to expect from more elaborate associations. Since groups of this kind are never obliterated from human experience, but flourish more or less under all kinds of institutions, they remain an enduring criterion by which the latter are ultimately judged. (1962, p. 32)

Before we go into the socializing effects of sport as such, let me illustrate how socialization works concretely through a simple central person game that I played as a child in New York state in the 1920s and which a 1980 publication tells me is still played in southern California up to the age of 9. Sutton-Smith does not list it among the games of the New Zealand children, but I imagine it is played there too, perhaps under a different name.

The game is "redlight." For those not familiar, it is played this way: Players (except one) line up at a starting line. The object is to reach a finish line. An It person, chosen by some chance procedure, turns his back to the starters, facing in the same direction, and shouts greenlight! Everyone tries to move toward the finish line. Periodically the It person shouts redlight! and turns and faces the other contestants. Everybody must stop. Anyone who doesn't will be sent back to the starting line. The game is won by the person who first reaches the finish line by advancing during the "greenlight" periods. The winner becomes It, and the previous It returns to the ranks. The process is repeated over and over.

We can call redlight a metaphor of social authority—of leadership and followership, of superordination and subordination. The game is the authority system of home, school, work, and public life, and it is also *not* that system (see chapter 3). Redlight raises and answers such questions as: How do leaders get where they are? (Possibilities in the game and in real life are chance, performance, deception, and cheating.) How much power should a leader have to judge and punish the actions of his followers, and what right do followers have to disagree and control him? (Suppose the It person says, "You moved," and I say, "I didn't" or "I didn't intend to" or "I didn't move enough to

count" or "I moved but you didn't really see me." Or suppose the
It person plays favorites. How are these situations to be resolved?)
    The theme of redlight, says Christine Van Glascoe, is "the relation-
ship between access to power and its exercise, and the social control
of power in its abuse. . . . In the game, one matures, as it were, from
player to director in a period of about 10 minutes, and, furthermore,
is allowed to practice the transition from player to director over and
over again" (1980, pp. 230–231).
    We will be able to examine just what sport does for our socializa-
tion by looking at it as *internalization of roles in a system of antagonistic
cooperation*. Figure 13.1 portrays this visually.

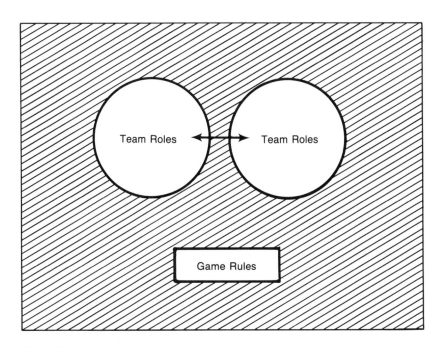

Figure 13.1   The Game as a Social System

    The term antagonistic cooperation comes from the book that also
gave the words folkways and mores to our language (Sumner, 1940,
p. 18). William Graham Sumner used the term to describe a situation
in which two groups are in conflict within a wider system of cooperation. As an example he cited the kind of relationship by which preda-
tors refrain from killing their prey in order to avoid exterminating their
source of food, thus benefiting both parties. He also saw industrial organization as an advanced form of antagonistic cooperation among

groups struggling to wrest a living, and more, from nature and one another. Huizinga reminds us that the basis for preliterate tribal organization has typically been opposition of two phratries into which the tribe is divided. "The mutual relationship of the two tribal halves is one of contest and rivalry, but at the same time one of reciprocal help and the rendering of friendly service" (Huizinga, 1964, p. 55).

A game is such a system of antagonistic cooperation. George Sauer, telling why he loved football even though he had to quit it, said, "At its highest level athletic competition is a cooperative venture much more than it is an antagonistic one" (Scott & Sauer, 1971, p. 55). Huizinga describes the potlatch in terms of "two groups standing in competition but bound by a spirit of hostility and friendship combined" (1964, p. 59). Sutton-Smith observes that "it is clear that games can take place only between people who have confidence in each other, at least to some extent. Games and sports imply a higher level of agreement among the antagonists than exists between those who do not have games" (1972, p. xv). Writing of modern sport (especially football—soccer and rugby) Norbert Elias and Eric Dunning state clearly the nature of antagonistic cooperation:

> *In present-day industrial societies, a game is a group configuration of a very specific type. At its heart is the controlled tension between two sub-groups holding each other in balance . . . a tension-balance. . . . Just as the mobility of a human limb is dependent on the contained tension between two antagonistic muscle-groups in balance, so the game depends on a tension between two and at the same time antagonistic and interdependent players keeping each other in fluctuating equilibrium. (1966, p. 397)*

Internalization of Roles

Within this equilibrium of antagonistic cooperation, each person plays his role, as one does in life as a whole. The most famous statement about role is by Shakespeare: "All the world's a stage, and all the men and women merely players; they have their exits and their entrances, and one man in his time plays many parts" (*As You Like It*, Act 2, Scene 7, lines 139–142). The classic scientific definition is by the anthropologist Ralph Linton:

> *A role represents the dynamic aspect of a status. The individual is socially assigned to a status and occupies it with relation to other statuses. When he puts the rights and duties which constitute the status into effect, he is performing a role. . . . Each person has a series of roles deriving from the various patterns in which he*

*participates and at the same time a role in general, which
represents the sum total of these roles and determines what he
does for the society and what he can expect from it. (1936, pp.
114–115)*

Roles, to be effective, have to be internalized, so that not only are
they expected of us by others, but they are expected of us by ourselves.
Freud once compared the upbringing of a child to the siege of a city.
Having established its superiority, the attacking army (society), to avoid
having to keep up the siege indefinitely, establishes a garrison within
the city. We do not have to believe, as Freud seemed to, that the relationship between society and unsocialized child is inevitably war. But
his image of the internal garrison is valid to the extent that social controls over behavior are not effective until they are internalized.

The social psychologist George Mead's description of how internalization takes place is especially relevant for us because he specifically stresses the function played by games (Mead, 1967, especially
"Play, the Game, and the Generalized Other," pp. 152–164). Role taking begins in the young child when he takes the role of *specific* others—
plays Mommy, Daddy, cowboy, Indian, teacher, postman, policeman,
and so on—and in these capacities carries on conversations with himself. In so doing he internalizes the character he plays. (Freud stressed
the importance of internalizing the specific other of—identifying with—
one's parent.) But in a game, says Mead, the process is carried farther.
The child internalizes not an individual, but a group; not a specific
other, but a *generalized other.* "If [a child] gets in a ball nine, he must
have the responses of each position involved in his own position"
(Mead, 1967, p. 151). To perform his role, he must be able to take in
fantasy the role of everyone else on his team (and, we may add, the
roles of the players on the other team). Mead being a philosopher, not
a jock, is not as specific as he might be. We can take a specific illustration from baseball.[1] Suppose there are runners on first and second.
The batter drives a low liner to right field for a hit. Immediately we
have 10 players (the batter and the two runners on the team at bat,
and the right fielder, the four infielders, and the pitcher and catcher
on the fielding team) who are potentially involved in the play. Each,
to play his role at this moment, must have inside him the roles of the
other nine. The simplest outcome is a throw that goes directly to the
plate, with the pitcher backing up the catcher. Another possibility is
a cut-off throw and a play at third base. All the players have to have
in them a range of possible actions by all 10 men. With this illustration
we can see what Mead means when he says: The fundamental differ-

[1]I am indebted to my former "A" students, catcher Tom Holliday and pitcher Stan
Jakubowski for this illustration.

ence between the game and play is that . . . the child must have the attitude of all the others involved in the game. The attitudes of the other players, which the participant assumes, organize into a sort of unit, and it is that organization that controls the response of the individual (1967, pp. 123–124). The unit is the generalized other.

In the game, the generalized other is the team, the little society that each player internalizes. Looking at Figure 13.1, we could also say that the player internalizes the roles of *both* teams, who are involved together in the antagonistic cooperation of the game.

In the child's socialization, internalizing the generalized other in the game is a preparation for life in society. This internalization, says Mead, is a constant part of the child's playing the game of life. Cooley found the basic sources of personality in the three main primary groups—family, neighborhood, and play group. Mead says that games are such a powerful preparation for life because they may grip the child more intensely than either his family or the community to which he belongs. It is through internalization as generalized others that one's family, school, religious organization, clubs, country become a part of one's life—as also may the whole human race. "Ask not for whom the bell tolls," said John Donne. "It tolls for thee" (1929, p. 538).

Another perspective: The German sociologist Georg Simmel observed of the game that it is "not only that the game is played in a society (as its external medium) but that with its help people actually play society" (1950, p. 50). In his study of Little League baseball, Geoffrey Watson spells this out:

From the first step of the player's passage through the game— warming-up to bat—to the next step of the outcome of "MAKING IT on base" or disconsolately returning to the dugout, to the final and ultimate stage of witnessing or making the third "out," parents are exposed to a symbolic "departure" of their sons to the depths of game interaction where unpredictable and totally uncontrollable events flow with dramatic speed. The game adopts a position of central importance due to the public display of a son's ability: on center stage at bat, when base running, or when his skills are tested in decision-making fielding performances. Throughout the immediate concerns of the wider community are temporarily "ruled out" as the late evening's action engrosses both parent and son in a family game which is as much a sport for mother and father as it is for an aspiring son. Families actually "play" "society" in what appears to be in every way an intensely competitive and achievement-oriented socialization laboratory. (1977, p. 20)

Sport and Gender Roles

A very central part of socialization is learning a role as female or male. Let us look at the part that play, games, and sport can have in acquiring a gender identity.

During the 1970s sociologist Janet Lever studied the play behavior of 181 10- to 11-year-old fifth graders in three Connecticut schools, looking for differences between the play of girls and the play of boys (Lever, 1978). Girls' play was more informal, less formally structured, more cooperative, more spontaneous, and more personal. The play of boys was more formally organized and more complex, with more rules, more impersonal competition, more specialized positions, and more teamwork. The boys played more outdoors. Male groups were larger, with more of a mix of different ages. Boys were less likely to play in a predominantly female game than girls were to participate in a predominantly male group. Boys were more likely to prefer team games, girls individual games.

Reviewing studies of gender roles in children between 5 and 12, Sutton-Smith and Savasta (1976) found the play of boys stressing group competitive games, in large spaces, with the body used as a whole as an instrument of power, more emphasis on winning and losing, much individual initiative, and a continuous flow of action. In a much-debated experiment the psychologist Erik Erikson asked girls and boys to use toys to construct a movie scene. The boys preferred to erect structures, buildings and towers, or to build streets, whereas the girls preferred to arrange the furniture and place people within a house. Erikson concluded that the play of girls, as females, was oriented to inner space and that of the boys, as males, to outer space. The girls' play, Erikson said, showed that the female has "a finer discrimination for things seen, touched, and heard. To these she reacts vividly, more personally, and with greater compassion." In addition, "in the employment of larger muscles she shows less vigor, speed, and coordination" (Erikson, 1964, p. 598).

Some interesting studies by Roberts and Sutton-Smith (1962) link preferences of boys and girls for physical skill, chance, or strategy games with similar choices by adult men and women. They analyzed game choices of 1,900 third to sixth graders in 12 midwestern schools and found the results that are abbreviated in Table 13.1. These differences were all significant at the .05 level; that is, they would have occurred by chance alone fewer than 5 times in 100 samples from such a population. It is interesting that the pure strategy games and chance games were predominantly female, and the physical skill-strategy games (sports) predominantly male. They compared these results with

Table 13.1   Game Choices of 1,900 Boys and Girls, Grades 3 to 6

Game type	Girls	Boys
Strategy	5	0
Chance	7	1
Pure Physical Skill	4	9
Physical Skill and Strategy	1	11

Note. From "Child Training and Game Involvement" by J.M. Roberts and B. Sutton-Smith, 1962, *Ethnology, 1,* p. 177, Table 7. Reprinted by permission.

those of an earlier Minnesota poll that had asked adults: Which of the following games have you played in the last year? The researchers selected golf and tennis as examples of physical skill games; bridge and checkers as strategy games; and dice, craps, and bingo as examples of chance games. For tennis and golf a higher percentage of men than women played; bridge and checkers were played significantly more by women. Dice, craps, and bingo were also played significantly more by women (Sutton-Smith, Roberts & Kozelka, 1963).

Webb's (1969) study of children's attitudes toward fairness, skill, and victory in games, reported in chapter 6, includes differences that tell us about the relationship of sport to gender roles in our culture. From 6th to 10th grade *both* sexes emphasize skillful play and victory. In the last two high-school years, however, the girls move away from the emphasis on winning. Webb thinks the reason for this is that the adolescent girl's ambitions—traditionally, to get a boyfriend—depend on qualities other than competitive skills (this I question), whereas the boy's career ambitions do require skill and winning.

What this all adds up to is that play, game, and sport in our culture still play a role in preparing boys for teamwork in the traditional male preserve of work and war (which stresses the competitive, physical, outer orientation) and in preparing girls for the traditional female preserve of childbearing and homemaking (which emphasizes the nurturing, sensitive, inner orientation). The kind of problem that such sport socialization raises in a world of changing gender roles is suggested by Margaret Hennig, one of the first women admitted to the Harvard Business School, in 1963. Hennig spoke of the difficulty posed by the fact that girls do not usually have the long and intense team sport experience that boys have in working with others, taking risks, plotting strategy, and experiencing victory and defeat. She reminisces: "My business policy professor began talking about goals, strategy, and objectives. I suddenly realized that I had no idea what 'strategy' meant. All the men just nodded their heads and the professor went on" (Hennig, 1976, p. 2). We may wonder how many women have been disqualified from managerial careers by the kind of loss of interest in winning that Webb reported.

Game Rules and Life History

The socializing function of play, games, and sport is a process that takes place within a person's life history. What is the chronology— what follows what? Ivor Kraft tells us what comes first:

Typically, the child first grasps the meaning of the abstraction, rule, in simple life situations which have nothing to do with games. He is punished, rewarded, deprived, or offered some pleasure in connection with what seem to be arbitrary aspects of life: He gets his bottle if he cries lustily; the cat scratches him if he pulls its tail. The child later applies this concept to games. (1967, pp. 71–72)

Mead sees a succession of play, with internalization of specific others, and games, in which a generalized other composed of one's peers is incorporated into one's personality. Several other students of play and games have stressed the transition that takes place as parents lose significance as the center of the child's life and are replaced by his peer group.

In a study published in the last years of the 19th century, Luther Gulick (1898) outlined five stages in psychological development in play, from babyhood to late adolescence. His conclusions were based on reminiscences of his own five children and of children in Springfield, Massachusetts, and in English schools; on boys' books; and other studies. Gulick found children before the age of 7 doing things like building with blocks, climbing, and investigating (even to the point of dissection of animals that he felt expressed not cruelty, but inquisitiveness). But "children before the age of seven rarely play *games* spontaneously" (Gulick, 1898, p. 800). If they play them, it is generally on the initiative of adults or older children. Unless influenced by adults, play at this age is also almost exclusively noncompetitive. There is typically little finely coordinated manual dexterity—hand-wrist movements.

Gulick found children between 7 and 12 playing games individualistically and competitively—making little streams and dams, paddlewheels and boats, and simple machinery of all kinds. Typical games were blindman's bluff, prisoner's base, tiddly winks, marbles, somer-saulting, and rolling over backwards. Boys were more competitive than girls.

Early adolescence (12 to 17) Gulick found marked by the beginning of team games. Young adolescents played baseball, football, hockey, and basketball and formed gangs to play cowboys and Indians or cops and robbers. The key here was co-operation among a number for a given end, with the individual subordinated to the group and to a peer leader.

In late adolescence, "the plays [games] are pushed to the limits of endurance and strength: They correspond more to organized savage warfare—for instance, college football. There is a depth and intensity about it that older people can hardly realize, unless they have themselves been through it. It seems to be a real thing and not merely a game" (Gulick, 1898, pp. 801–802). We will remember that this was 1898.

Gulick writes the following summary:

The plays of early childhood are individualistic, noncompetitive, and for the accomplishment and observation of objective results. The plays of later childhood are individualistic, competitive, involve active muscular coordination and some judgments. The plays of adolescence are socialistic, demanding the heathen virtues of courage, endurance, self-control, bravery, loyalty, enthusiasm. (1898, p. 802)

The succession Gulick describes is from parent-centered (early childhood) to individualistic-competitive (later childhood) to team-competitive (adolescence). We well remember that, when Gulick wrote, there was no adult organization of Little League baseball or Pop Warner football for children.

Gulick's sequence is in general supported by recent studies by Brian Sutton-Smith in New Zealand and Maximilian Stejskal in Finland. Sutton-Smith's study of the developmental psychology of children's games in New Zealand revealed that the earliest games are central person games that are play representations of the relationships which children normally experience in their family life. The central figure is a parent substitute. She or he may play a limelight role, of which Sutton-Smith gave as examples the game in which the group dances singing around Sally, "Who is a-weeping," or Punchinello, the "funny fellow." In the "it" games of tag or hide-and-seek the group tried to avoid or outwit an aggressive central person. In scapegoat games the central figure is made a villain by the group. In games like King of the Mountain the group members attack and try to displace the central person. These central person games, says Sutton-Smith, "are a symbolic bridge between the child's primary tie to his parents and his secondary ties to his peers.'' In these games the child learns to act out his conflicting attitudes of submission and rebellion toward parents in such a way as at the same time to become prepared for his cultural role.

At the age of 10 or later, central person games typically give way to competitive team skill games. Two kinds of games serve as transitions from the central person games to competitive team sports. One is individual games of physical skill—hopping, jumping, running, catching, marbles, tops. Another transitional type is the "pack against pack" contest without specialized individual roles. In our culture, cops and robbers and cowboys and Indians are examples. When individual skill contest and desultory pack contest give way to confrontation or organized teams before audiences, we have come all the distance from parentally modeled play to modern sport (Sutton-Smith, 1972, p. 213).

Stejskal's description of the traditional folk-athletic games of rural Finland (as contrasted with modern athletics) emphasizes the socializing role of games as *rites de passage* celebrating and legitimizing the transition from childhood to manhood (Stejskal, 1970). Stejskal's conclusion that children under 8 rarely compete in their play consciously with one another sounds like Gulick. From 12 to 15, Stejskal found, rural boys fight a lot to test and demonstrate their strength and agility. But about 15, the age at which the church customarily confirms them adults, the matter gets serious. When boys can lift confirmation stones up to knee level "tradition occasionally defines that maturity or marriage ability is proven," although sometimes it may be necessary only to lift one end of the stone, not to raise it off the ground. But this weight lifting may go so far as to resemble the severe puberty tests of some preliterate societies or the competitive bench pressing practiced by American athletes. With the help of a rope, these Finnish adolescents may lift up to 250 kilos (550 pounds). Although Gulick had found them characteristic of the then-urbanized culture as early as the 1890s, team games, or collective sport in which the individual subordinates himself to the team are in Finland a part of the development of modern athletic games, which are much more structured and take place at sport grounds rather than fields, backyards and country roads, the traditional scene of the rural folk-athletic games.

Authoritarian and Self-Generated Roles

Linton's definition of role, cited earlier, is a little too rigid (as may be Shakespeare's also): It sounds as though the roles we play in life (and also games) are the reading of a predetermined script. In real life, and real games, this is not the case. In life and games we have two kinds of roles: (a) those in which we follow to the letter patterns assigned to us and (b) those in which we exert initiative in meshing our behavior with that of other people whose precise response we can predict roughly but not exactly. An illustration from modern sport is the difference between the quarterback whose plays are called from the bench and the quarterback who has a great deal of freedom to call the play as he reads the defensive alignment. The other players may also run the gamut, from carrying out assignments memorized from their playbooks to improvising their own tactics to conform to the quarterback's audibles.

In Finland, the rural folk-athletic games of adolescence lead to organized sport. Statue of the great Finnish distance runner, Paavo Nurmi, in front of the Helsinki Olympic Stadium, site of the 1952 Games. Courtesy of Finnish National Travel Bureau.

Writing in 1938 about the play of the Tallensi children of Ghana, anthropologist Meyer Fortes said that play "is the paramount educational exercise of Tale children," and went on to make the distinction I have made:

In his play the child rehearses his interests, skills, and obligations, and makes experiments in social living without having to pay the penalty for mistakes. . . . But the Tale child's play is never simple and mechanical reproduction: it is always imaginative construction based on the themes of adult life, and the life of older children. He or she adopts natural objects and other materials . . . which never occur in the adult activities copied, and rearranges adult functions to fit the specific . . . configuration of play. (Fortes, 1938, cited in Harris & Park, 1983, p. 392)

The Rumanian sociologist George Ciuciu distinguishes two aspects of socialization—adaptation and innovation—and says that they correspond to two kinds of games—organized and extemporized. "With the help of the two kinds of games the child and the teenager get trained for two fundamental elements of the social life: the observation or integration into the social norms on the one hand, the change or modification of the social environment on the other" (Ciuciu, 1979, p. 9).

The most famous research on the two kinds of rules and roles was done in the early 20th century when Jean Piaget (1948) studied children of both sexes in Geneva and Neuchatel, Switzerland, to learn about the rules by which they played marbles. Piaget found the same general progression from parent-governed to peer-governed games that Gulick did, and that Sutton-Smith found in New Zealand. Children under 10, if asked who had invented the game of marbles, would almost inevitably attribute it to their fathers or to the elders of the community. Asked whether one child or a group of children could change the rules if they wished, they typically answered no, explaining that what has been handed down by the elders is right and should not be questioned. Strangely enough, although verbally the young children said the rules were unchangeable, in practice they did not observe them very well. To the question about who invented the game, the children over 10 were likely to answer something like "a bunch of kids". To the question whether the rules can be changed, their response was typically "Why not?" Unlike the younger children, who said the rules are sacred and unchangeable but broke them, the older children, while saying they are open to improvement, were more likely to observe them.

Piaget, like Mead, was studying games not for their own sake but for what they could teach about socialization—the development of social morality. He found a progression in marbles from a *morality of constraint*, which is *heteronomous* (other-directed) to a *morality of reciprocity*, which is *autonomous* (self-directed):

We have recognized the existence of two moralities in the child, that of constraint and that of cooperation. The morality of con-

*straint is that of duty pure and simple. . . . The child accepts from
the adult a certain number of commands to which it must submit
whatever the circumstances may be. Right is what conforms to
these commands; wrong is what fails to do so. . . . But first, parallel
with this morality, and then in contrast to it, there is gradually
developing a morality of cooperation, whose guiding principle is
solidarity and which puts the primary emphasis upon autonomy
of conscience. (Piaget, 1948, pp. 334, 335)*

In chapter 2 we saw that Piaget's distinction is central to the counterculture, in sport and elsewhere.

A Harvard study by Michael Maccoby, also dealing with the game
of marbles, supports the trend toward reciprocity found by Piaget.
Maccoby asked boys, "When you are playing marbles with your father
and you have each got ten marbles, how many are you prepared to
lose to your father and how many are you prepared to win off him,
and when you are playing with your best friend how many marbles
will you lose and how many will you win?" The 5-year-olds, when
playing with their fathers, wanted to lose a lot; playing with their peers,
to win a lot. The 11-year-olds wanted to win a lot from their fathers
but to break even with their best friend. Here we see a sharp change
in attitude toward the authoritarian figure (from let him have all to
clean him out) and toward the peer (from clean him out to share and
share alike) (Reported in Sutton-Smith, 1969, pp. 185–186).

Piaget's findings were stated as though they were true of all children, everywhere, at any time. But he did note that the children he
studied were from the economically poorer areas. An Englishman,
M. R. Harrower (1934), compared responses to game rules and situations in two groups of British children: a group of lower income children comparable to those studied by Piaget and a group from a
progressive middle class school (Harrower, 1934). Of the middle-class
school children, Harrower said, "There is certainly no evidence of
Piaget's 100 percent in terms of appeal to authority at the age of 6-7
years in this group" (p. 88). It would seem (and this corresponds with
other things we know) that respect for authority is much stronger in
children of lower income families. Thus, Harrower found that "there
is a much greater shift away from an arbitrary ethics of authority in
the [lower-class children]" (p. 88). Perhaps Piaget's results were biased
by the socioeconomic group he studied.

Piaget's distinction was further amplified when Jay Coakley and
his University of Colorado sport sociology students observed and questioned children of 6 to 13 in formally organized, adult-controlled league
sports events (constraint) and informally organized, player-controlled
backyard, park, or playground games (reciprocity) (Coakley, 1982, pp.
83–90). The children were predominantly middle class and Anglo

white, with about 10% Chicano or black. They were two thirds male and the majority were between ages 10 and 12. The main questions the students asked both groups were: What about playing gives you the most fun? and What are your biggest problems in playing?

The children playing 84 pickup games emphasized having a lot of action, having a close contest, and strengthening friendships. There was so much action that most of the games were very high scoring. Ordinary game rules were modified so as to give everybody a chance to participate regardless of skill. With regard to friendship, they were modified so that teams were chosen partly on the basis of personal preference rather than on skill. Rule enforcement was informal, maintained by such sanctions as joking. Over half the games didn't have an argument serious enough to stop play.

The children playing in 121 formal league games also liked action and personal involvement, but playing efficiency and game outcome were their biggest concern. Control was by adults, with much emphasis on game rules and specialized positional roles. Eventually, everybody got to play a little, but most of the children sat on the sidelines bored or interested in things outside the game. Highly skilled players, when taken out of the game, would typically stay close to the coach, hoping thus to be sent back in. There was typically more concern with team victory than with personal performance. Arguments were characteristically not with opponents but with teammates who were felt not to be doing their part. There were visible expressions of friendship during breaks in action, but not during the game.

Coakley concluded that, in terms of socialization, children in formal sports learned much about technical sport skills and observance of adult-enforced rules, but the children in pickup games learned more about interpersonal skills, participation in decision making, and how to live with the outcomes of personal decisions. Coakley (1982) comments:

My feeling is that most young people in our society have numerous opportunities to engage in highly structured activities and that caution should be exercised when their "free time" activities are organized by adults. Developing technical athletic skills and learning formalized game rules are not nearly as important as developing interpersonal skills and learning to live with the consequences of personal decisions. (p. 90)

Also, he commented critically on how children's enjoyment often suddenly ends when an informal prepractice scrimmage is terminated by the coach's whistle: "The spirit of play suddenly disappears, and sport becomes joblike" (p. 93).

The two kinds of rules and roles (authoritarian-organized-heteronomous and self-generated-extemporized-autonomous) are likely to be promoted by two types of athletic leaders. Football coaches like Vince Lombardi and Paul Brown, or leaders in baseball like Little League manager Mike Maietta, are likely to demand rigid performance of predetermined roles or to call all plays from the bench. Ex–Green Bay Packer Bill Curry said of the Lombardi method: "What he seemed to do was to select a role for each player. He wrote the play, and he did the choreography, and if you didn't fit the role he would change your personality so you could play the part" (Plimpton & Curry, 1977, p. 32). Martin Ralbovsky's *Destiny's Darlings* gives a similar profile of Maietta's authoritarian leadership as seen by his individual players and by himself in interviews 20 years later (Ralbovsky, 1974). More humanistically oriented coaches like George Davis or Weeb Eubank of the spectacular 1969 New York Jets Super Bowl champions, or baseball managers like Red Schoendienst of the 1967 St. Louis Cardinals, are likely to encourage more flexible role performance. By contrast with the Lombardi image, Curt Flood describes Schoendienst as "a friendly, unobtrusive, considerate man who did not distract us from our jobs" (Flood, 1970, p. 87). Flood's picture of the Cardinals is one of genuine socialization:

> Nobody on that team had occasion to utter the usual petty platitude, "I don't care if he's white, black, purple, or green, just so he does his job on the field." On that team we cared about each other and shared with each other and . . . inspired each other. As friends, we had become solicitous of each other's ailments and eccentricities, proud of each other's strengths. We had achieved a closeness impossible by other means. . . .
>
> There we were, Latins, blacks, liberal whites and redeemed peckerwoods, the best in the game and the most exultant. Victorious on the field and victorious off it, by God. A beautiful little foretaste of what life will be like when Americans finally unshackle themselves. (1970, pp. 88, 90)

The authoritarian and self-generated role behavior found by researchers can both produce effective teams. Here is a dramatic example of authoritarian role assignment, geographically and culturally very far from Vince Lombardi and Mike Maietta, taken from the textbook for civics used in native schools in the Fiji Islands in 1949:

Section 1 What does Government mean?

1. Here is a story:

Some boys wished to play [rugby] football. Sam had a ball, and Tom had one, too. But Sam hid his ball, so that they would use Tom's. Tom was angry.

When they played, they all wanted to play "forward." There were no "backs." Then they began to quarrel about it. Their game was stopped. They could not agree, so they could not play.

Inosa was the biggest boy. He said, "This is very foolish. We cannot play like this: I will be captain, and you must all do what I say. If you do not, then you shall not play."

They all said, "Yes." So he said, "We shall play with Sam's ball today. Tomorrow we shall play with Tom's ball." He then told each boy where to play. Now the game was good. They won the game.

When Inosa became captain, and made laws, that was GOVERNMENT. You cannot play games without laws, and you cannot play without a leader. (Cited in Frederickson & Cozens, 1947, p. 13)

A different answer to the question, What does government mean? and also to the question, What does sport mean? would be given by George Davis:

The biggest problem is motivating your athletes to perform. You know what he's going to have to do. Well, who will he do it better for? Will he do it better for an authority, or will he do it better for his peer group?

People associated with sociology know the answer. It's the peer group. Most of us all our lives have been cast in roles so tight that we don't dare escape them. I think many coaches feel if they take away the threat of not playing an athlete, the athlete won't obey them. That's not true. They'll be more closely disciplined by their peer group and what they think of them than they would possibly be by what their coaches think of them. Joe Namath is a good example. He's independent, a free soul, but his commitment to his teammates is complete. He would rather hurt himself than his teammates. I believe that. . . .

College and pro teams should vote on starting lineups. The coaches need not accept the players' view, but at least they will know what the athletes are thinking. Who knows? The vote might surprise them. It certainly will make for more cohesion and confi-

dence between players and coaches. . . .

I . . . feel I know as much about democracy and its relationship to human beings as anybody. I know how it works—not by studying statistics or researching out somebody's opinions. . . . It's a great way to go. It's the only way. (Cited in Amdur, 1971, pp. 197, 307)

As I said, both constraint and autonomy can produce successful teams in many ways. Sutton-Smith points out the interesting fact that authoritarian role assignment can generate peer group solidarity. In the very young children in New Zealand playing games with a central figure (It, for example, in tag), he shows how in play children can form a cohesive group through symbolically acting out their resentment against authority.

Although these players do not as yet have much experience in getting along with one another, they do have in common their experience of the relationship between inferior and superior beings. Such common experiences, when represented in the form and fantasy content of these games, can bind the children into a group where other things might fail. . . . In the . . . games there is . . . identification with parent figures seen as arbitrary and fearsome. All children have had the experience of contending, in fact or fantasy, against such figures. In these games they can explore these feelings, but can do so without the dangers that would be involved in exploring such feelings in real life. The games invite exploration (screaming with fear, roaring with rage) but with their rules and the agreement that it is only "play" they safeguard the children from the anxiety which might otherwise result from unguarded exploration and expression of impulse. (Sutton-Smith, 1972, pp. 213-214)

On the adult level, this kind of solidarity can be manipulated by intelligent authoritarians. Bill Curry relates how mutiny against Vince Lombardi erupted in the Green Bay locker room one day. One player, who had to be restrained from hitting the coach, told Lombardi off. Then Lombardi said, "All right. Now *that's* the kind of attitude I want to see. Who else feels that way?" One player said, "Yeah, me too!" Then all through the room rose cries, "Yeah, hell, me too!" "And suddenly," says Curry, "you had 40 guys that could kick the world." Then Lombardi went through the room and asked each man, nose to nose, "Do you want to win football games for me?" "And the answer was, 'Yes, sir,' 40 times, and we did not lose another game that year" (Plimpton & Curry, 1977, pp. 37-38).

Cheating, Winning, and Socialization

There are still further questions to be asked about socialization. In discussing how the child applies the concept of rules to games, Ivor Kraft comments: The child . . . also quickly grasps the concept that sometimes one can get away with breaking the rules (cheating) in such a way as to enable the game to go on functioning. Cheating happens to be a widespread phenomenon wherever games are played (Kraft, 1967, p. 72). Of the lessons taught by games, Sutton-Smith says: "In games children learn all those necessary arts of trickery, deception, harassment . . . and foul play that their teachers won't teach them, but that are most important in successful human relationships in marriage, business, and war" (Sutton-Smith, 1972, p. 339). (I always invite my students to analyze this statement item by item, and see how much they agree with.)

In *The Ultimate Athlete* George Leonard elaborates on this point. He says that we have come to take cheating for granted in the sports we watch on TV. In football, for example, along with the game between the two teams there is a game between players and officials. Offensive holding is forbidden by the rules. But players, coaches, and officials all know that a certain amount takes place and is permitted, *and taught by coaches.* The point, then, is not *whether* to hold, but *when* to do it and *how* to do it sneakily. Leonard reminds us that fouling is accepted basketball strategy and an expected source of spectator enjoyment in hockey. He also notes the following:

> We who cheat for a team are by no means individualistic tricksters. We are good corporation men. By playing sneaky games with officials, we prepare ourselves for success in the world outside of games. We learn to press for advantages in making out expense accounts and tax returns; we depend upon corporate and government officials to show us just how far we may go. We push to the limit traffic laws and antitrust laws and laws concerning political contributions. (Leonard, 1974, pp. 17–18)

All this is *not* socialization in the sense of learning the basic rules necessary to get along with others.

Let us look again at Figure 13.1, which depicts the game as a system of antagonistic striving within rules, and ask two questions: (a) Is learning to win by violating the rules a desocializing experience, even if it increases the solidarity of the team and prepares one, as Leonard and Sutton-Smith suggest, for later life? and (b) Is learning to win by observing the rules always a socializing process? Or can fair winning desocialize a person?

Many social scientists confuse people by using the word socialization loosely to signify learning the accepted culture pattern. I think we should limit the term, as I have tried to in this chapter, to learning the elementary rules and attitudes necessary for human social life anywhere, anytime. (Margaret Mead made this same distinction in 1935 when she defined *socialization* as "the set of species-wide requirements and exactions made on human beings by human societies," and *enculturation* as "the process of learning a culture in all its uniqueness and particularity" (Mead, 1963, p. 198). It is quite possible for a culture to survive, temporarily, while violating the elementary rules of social life. We don't know how long temporary is. Nazi Germany, which hoped to last 1,000 years, is one example.

Light is thrown on this whole question by Francis J. Ryan's (1958) comparison of two kinds of people produced in our culture—college athletes who are good competitors and those who are poor competitors. Ryan, a coach of field events and research assistant at the Yale Department of University Health, contributed his study in a symposium by members of the Yale Division of Mental Hygiene on problems of college men. His definition of good competitor is clear: A good competitor is one whose performance in competition exceeds his practice performance; a poor competitor is one who performs better in practice than in competition. In other words, Ryan was studying the difference between the man who rises to the occasion and the one who chokes under competitive stress. This is a commonly observed distinction in track and field events.

He sent 65 coaches questionnaires on which each was asked to rate on 13 items the best competitor, past or present, he had ever coached, and the poorest. Although coaches were not asked to name the athletes they described, many did so, and Ryan says that "our good competitors include most American world record holders and Olympic champions" (Ryan, 1958, p. 116).

The questionnaires showed a substantial difference between good and poor competitors in general social qualities, practice habits, and attitudes toward performance. Socially, the good competitor was considered to be very friendly, the poor one a lone wolf. The good competitor was usually in good spirits, with plenty of belly laughs, the poor competitor smiled easily but seldom laughed heartily. The good competitor's communication was good; the poor competitor was about average or difficult to talk to. One coach worked 4 years with a man and never had a conversation with him. The good competitor was well liked by his teammates; the poor competitor was about average or unpopular.

Ryan felt that the sport behavior he studied reflected more general attitudes. "The poor competitor would appear to be unhappier, more constricted, and in general, more poorly adjusted . . . seems to have difficulty in expressing his aggression generally, and his inability to compete in athletics may be a specific instance of . . . an over-all difficulty" (p. 119). His problem is *fear of success*. This, says Ryan, is likely to affect his behavior in some other areas of life, though not all. Poor athletic competitors are sometimes, he points out, very successful in academic competition. This fact may indicate that the poor competitor is specifically afraid of performance that is culturally defined as masculine. "He may be relatively free to express himself in a more neutral or possibly even traditionally feminine activity" (p. 138). As for his future life as a whole, the more masculine his job, the more likely he is to be disabled.

Some aspects of Ryan's study raise questions about the whole masculine competitive syndrome as it appears in sport and in our culture as a whole. The good competitor, as defined by Ryan, is friendly and affable except in competition. Then he follows the model of the boxers who routinely touch gloves, then perform 45 minutes of mayhem upon one another, and at the end may fall into each other's arms like long-lost brothers. The good competitor, as discovered by Ryan, apparently lives in two worlds—the world of ordinary life, where people are fellow human beings, and the field of sport competition, where one's adversary is an enemy. By contrast, "the poor competitor prefers an atmosphere of friendliness" (1958, p. 127). He may even go so far as to offer encouragement or even coaching hints to an opponent. If the good competitor does anything like this, it is probably a con, gamesmanship.

The good competitor may expect to have a number of grudge matches, in some of which he doesn't even make a show of being friendly. Ryan says that some personality clashes are of course inevitable if one encounters many opponents, but that some good competitors seem psychologically to need these grudge matches. Contrariwise, the poor competitor does not have grudge matches, nor is he angry or bitter toward opponents. The good competitor Ryan finds hard to live with after a defeat: He may be bitter, morose, and even vicious. The poor competitor may on the other hand be relaxed, talkative, and in good spirits. One other contrast is that the good competitor accepts the coach's instructions without question, whereas the poor competitor is likely to make alternative suggestions.

At the time that he wrote, in 1958, it is clear that in Ryan's mind the poor competitor has a psychological problem, about which a conscientious coach may justifiably be concerned in terms of what it may mean for the athlete's whole future life. Twenty years later, after an athletic revolution, many would be inclined to feel that it is the good competitor, as described, who has a problem. This, I believe, would be the view of George Sauer, reflecting on football and the American ethos:

I think the values of football as it is now played reflect a segment of thought . . . that is prevalent in our society. The way to do anything in the world, the way to get ahead, is to compete against somebody, work your way up, and in so doing you have to judge yourself or be judged in relation to somebody else. . . . As it is played now, football reinforces the social ethic that aggression and competition is a healthy thing—that that's the way to become a success. This kind of thought has a potential for tragedy and to the degree that it is exercised and carried out in football, it is tragic. (Scott & Sauer, 1971, p. 53)

Fred Mahler, a Rumanian sport sociologist, made the point eloquently in telling the Fourth International Symposium on Sport Sociology at Bucharest in 1973 that play transmits the moral contradictions of a society and in calling for a counterplay to protect the players from the negative effects:

We certainly are in favor of competitive games but . . . one should awaken the consciousness of the participant . . . that affirmation of his personality integrated with the collective is the most precious result of play, success being nothing but a means and not an end in itself; that what is precious in a competition is the effort to surpass oneself, achieved not at the expense of the others, but together with them; that the true conquerer is the one who, thanks to a dignified behavior and observation of the rules, has unanimously been accepted, has obtained the affirmation of his human qualities, even if he is not the one who has personally conquered the laurels. (Mahler, 1975, pp. 112–113)

One can learn the rules of one's *cultural* game without learning the rules of the *human* game. This will become clearer as we examine the relationship of sport violence to social violence in chapter 14.

Chapter 14

Sport Violence and Social Violence

In this chapter we will explore one of the most important questions about sport, culture, and personality—the relationship between violence in sport and nonsport violence in society and in life in general. Violence we may define as the use of destructive personal force against objects (including people) that are believed to stand in the way of one's goals. Violence is related to hostility. Hostility embodies the wish to hurt another human being. It may or may not be acted out in the form of actual damage. There may be a hostile intent without a hostile act, or there may be a violent act without hostile intent. Dean Ryan suggests an important distinction between violence that is hostile and violence that is instrumental. Hostile violence is destructive behavior in which damage is intended. Instrumental violence may damage people in the course of achieving a goal (for example, incinerating a civilian population to win a war or disabling a key opponent to win a ball game), but the intention need not be hostile (Ryan, 1974, p. 24).

Violence is also related to aggression. The term *aggression,* as used by some authors, is synonymous with *hostility*. Others use it to describe all outgoing manipulation of one's environment (by contrast with passivity, defense, and escaping behavior). A great deal of confusion is often created by loose use of the term aggression. In this chapter violence will mean destructive aggression, whether or not hostile in intent.

Levels of Sport Violence

Violence in sport has many levels. The most extreme is the kind of violence that is outside the rules of even the bodily contact sports. (Although the sport establishment tries to keep such things in the family, such violence has recently been taken into the courts as also a violation of criminal law.) Among the violent operations that are almost standard operating procedure in the National Football League are sticking (ramming one's helmet into the base of an opponent's spine), stripping (pinching, biting, slugging, twisting arms and fingers to pry the ball loose from a ballcarrier), ringing the bell (slamming a fist into the earhold of a lineman's helmet), leg whipping (kicking hard in the shins), and clotheslining (extending a forearm in front of a charging opponent's throat) (Surface, 1974, pp. 151–154).

Extreme violence is also possible, indeed approved, *within* the rules of bodily contact sport. A University of Miami football player, describing a situation in which he whooped with glee over putting an opponent in the hospital, wrote, "There is a certain something that a football player has, and that is why he loves the game. He can go absolutely berserk and even hurt an individual without getting into any trouble" (unpublished class essay). Frank Champi, before he quit as Harvard quarterback in 1969, described the legitimate violence of football: "You see people hit, getting hurt, it goes on and on . . . If somebody tries to break your leg, what can you expect? To play as hard as you can is to hit as hard as you can" (Amdur, 1971, p. 61). Boxing is the other major body contact sport. In it assault and battery are legitimized.

All of the territorial games modeled on the spring festival contests described in chapter 5 (basketball, hockey, soccer, and lacrosse, as well as American football) easily cross the line into violence. Although Robert Ardrey has oversimplified and sensationalized the idea, possession and protection of a home and homeland have deep human roots. They can easily be associated with the defense of Good against Evil. The territorial games, like the original Osiris ritual at Papremis, involve a goal located in space that is attacked and defended. Intense emotions are easily mobilized. Although the rules of most territorial games theoretically minimize or outlaw bodily contact, in actual practice they are usually interpreted so as to maximize it.

In the nonterritorial and noncontact sports, power exerted against objects and people can play a large part. Most baseball fans prefer heavy hitting and scoring to close, low-scoring games featuring skill and finesse but little raw power. Force exerted on the inanimate baseball is not all that attracts fans. Baseball owner Branch Rickey, a devout Christian churchman, once said that his ideal ballplayer would break both legs of anyone who got between him and a base. Although the net makes bodily contact almost impossible in tennis, George Leonard gets the feel of contemporary amateur tennis when he says of doubles that "net play more and more resembles World War II, with red-faced, tense-muscled middle-aged men crouching at the front lines every Sunday, itching to fire their nylon howitzers down their opponent's throats" (Leonard, 1974, p. 111). In his history of pro golf, Al Barkow says the women's pro tour may never catch on as has the men's. Although golf essentially lacks the violence spectators seem to crave, men do provide some. But females, no matter how skillful, "just do not propel a golf ball with the same crack and rocketlike force as do the men" (Barkow, 1974, p. 119). Leonard, describing golf as a game of contemplative strolls and shimmering distances, attributes much of the charisma of Arnold Palmer to the fact that even when past his prime he could turn the game into a cavalry charge. (With respect to Barkow's comment, it is unlikely that a woman golfer could do that.)

As Ryan suggests, "It is possible that competition, by its very nature, leads to aggression" (1974, p. 25). Muzafer Sherif and Carolyn Sherif describe how, in their famous Robber's Cave experiment with group behavior in adolescent boys, competitive athletic contests led to hostility so intense that the experiment had to be terminated. They state the principle that was illustrated: "When members of two groups come into contact with one another in a series of activities that embody goals which each urgently desires, but which can be attained by one group only at the expense of the other, competitive activity toward the goal changes, over time, into hostility between the groups and their members" (Sherif & Sherif, 1969, p. 239). In short, a zero sum game (see chapter 3), in which winning is everything, is bound to become hostile. Therefore, from this viewpoint, the way we define competition in our athletic subculture makes it inevitable that it will teach us to be cutthroats. Dreams of clean competition are just that—dreams.

Hughes and Coakley (1978) think that team organization itself, especially in contact sports like football and hockey, may be so oppressive and threatening as to incite violence. Noting that some athletes have compared an athletic team to a prison, Hughes and Coakley started with Gresham Sykes' (1958) study of prison organization:

> According to Sykes, inmates become aggressive because prison life confronts them with threats to their (1) moral worth, (2) adult status, (3) physical well-being, (4) masculinity, and (5) personal feelings of adequacy. Our investigation of the organization of heavy contact sport teams leads us to conclude that athletes are often confronted with the same kinds of threats. (Coakley, 1982, p. 63)

Four Theories

Let's rephrase the problem with which we began this chapter: How is violence in competitive sport related to violence in everyday life, for the participant and for the spectator? For the rest of this chapter, we will explore four basic answers that, in turn, tell us that sport violence

(a) decreases, (b) increases, (c) parallels, or (d) symbolizes social violence.

Sport violence may be held to *reduce* social violence by drive discharge (hostile impulses in player or spectator are worked off through sport), social learning (by playing violent sports athletes may learn to keep their hostility under control), or by negative modeling (spectators observing the pain of a hurt athlete may be reluctant to inflict similar pain). (Drive discharge catharsis for player and spectator is the most commonly held theory of sport violence; in fact, we might call it Plank 13 in the myth system of the athletic subculture.)

Violence in sport may be held to *increase* social violence because, physiologically, the activity that is supposed to discharge excitation may serve instead to arouse it; because, having come to take violence in sport for granted, the athlete may do the same in everyday life; or because the spectator, having seen admired models rewarded for violence, may imitate his or her heroes.

Sport violence may be held to *parallel* social violence in the sense that every culture is a pattern whose parts hang together, so that in a violent society play will be violent, whereas in a peaceful society play will be more peaceful. In both societies sport will be a particular way of expressing the dominant cultural theme.

Some students of sport stress that sport violence may *symbolize* the violence by which frustrated members of a society would like to express their frustration; the desire of just people to overthrow the unjust; or the perpetual struggle of frail humans to master a hard world. Here, it is held, unconscious and denied impulses are acted out dramatically on the field of sport.

Evidence for Reduction

The drive discharge version of the hostility reduction theory sees the violent tensions that are worked off as originating in innate hostile impulses (the view of Freud and more recently of Robert Ardrey and Konrad Lorenz) or in the frustrations imposed by social life (the hypothesis of John Dollard and Neal Miller that frustration inevitably breeds aggression). The most impressive single piece of research evidence for the drive discharge view is, I think, a psychological experiment conducted by Seymour Feshbach (1961).

Feshbach's research studied the effect of seeing a film of a violent athletic event. It involved the relationship among three factors: (1) treatment of a person by experimenters, (b) exposure to a violent film, and (c) testing of the level of aggressiveness after exposure.

One hundred and one male University of Pennsylvania students volunteered for the stated purpose of their judging the main character in two 10-minute films. One group was given fairly routine instructions. In the other group, instructions were given by Feshbach's assistant Abraham Wolf in such a way as to arouse anger by questioning the students' intellectual and emotional maturity. These two groups were labeled Noninsult Group and Insult Group. (In a footnote Feshbach expresses his gratitude to Wolf for his competence and courage in doing the insulting.) Following this preliminary treatment, the students were then shown either a prize fight sequence from the movie *Body and Soul* or a neutral film depicting the spread of rumors in a factory.

After this viewing, all were given two measures of aggressiveness. In a word association test they were asked to give 10 written associations to each of five words (*choke, massacre, murder, stab,* and *torture*) shown them on 5 × 8 cards, mixed into a series of 11 cards, along with six neutral words (*wash, travel, walk, relax, sleep,* and *listen*). Each student was scored on the number of aggressive responses in his first 10 associations to each of the five violent words (total possible score 50). In the second test of aggressiveness the original experimenter left the room and an associate entered and asked the students to fill out a multiple choice questionnaire evaluating the experimenter and the whole experiment. The questionnaire included six items, each with six possible responses, which were scored from 1 to 6 for aggressiveness (total possible score 36).

On aggressiveness toward the experimenter, among those who had previously been insulted, those who had seen the fight film were significantly *less* aggressive than those who had watched the neutral film. Table 14.1 shows the number of each group who fell above and below the average (in this case, median) aggressiveness score. A difference so large would have occurred by chance less than one time in a thousand ($p < .001$). The word association test also produced a significant difference in the same direction (students who had seen the fight film were less aggressive) but the level of significance was lower ($p < .05$).

Table 14.1 Distribution of Aggression Questionnaire Scores Falling above and below the Median as a Function of Insult Fight Film and Insult Neutral Film Treatments.

Treatment	Below Median	Above Median
Insult Fight Film	20	6
Insult Neutral Film	7	22

Note. From "The Stimulating versus Cathartic Effects of a Vicarious Aggressive Activity" by S. Feshbach, 1961, *Journal of Abnormal and Social Psychology, 53,* p. 383, Table 4. Copyright 1961 by the American Psychological Association. Reprinted by permission of the author. $p < .001$.

Feshbach's conclusion was that vicarious exposure to violence has a cathartic effect when a person has been specifically angered, but not otherwise. He also hypothesized that under other conditions vicarious aggressive experience would have a stimulating effect, but the results for his Noninsult groups do not show this.

A real-life example of the drive discharge hypothesis is the role of soccer among the urban Zulu of South Africa, as analyzed by the anthropologist N. A. Scotch (1961). Within a short time, these Zulu have moved from a preliterate tribal culture to an urban environment in Durban and other South African cities. The shift from rural to urban life is usually stressful for people anywhere. For the tribal Zulu, it meant moving to crowded housing and competition for scarce jobs. (Scotch does not mention that, as blacks, in the city the Zulu were brought into sharpest confrontation with apartheid—the South African separation of the races.) The whole result has been that in the city "interpersonal and intergroup hostility and aggression are much greater . . . than in the traditional rural Zulu community" (Scotch, 1961, p. 71).

Soccer football plays an important part in this rural-urban transition. Much of the limited leisure of male Zulu is spent playing, watching, and discussing soccer. Organized football leagues, resembling in their hierarchies of skill our major and minor leagues in baseball, engage in complex rivalries no less extreme, bitter, and unremitting than in Chicago or Cleveland. Players, although amateurs, are recruited, paid, and enticed away from one team to another. Star players have been known to pass from team to team looking for the best deal.

The soccer syndrome transfers to football the emotions and rituals that in tribal life accompanied war. Players practice ritual sexual abstinence before a match as previously before battle. They smear on their jerseys and shoes the medicines traditionally put on weapons to give strength in battle. They purify themselves by an emetic the morning of the match as previously before combat. The teams approach the playing field in military formation. An educated Zulu describes the intensity of ritual preparation the night before a match, typically presided over by an *inyanga* (a tribal doctor):

All the football teams have their own inyanga *who doctors them all for each match. The night before a match they must camp together around a fire. They all sleep there together, they must stay naked and are given . . . medicines by the* inyanga. *Incisions are made on their knees, elbows, and joints. . . . Almost every team I know has an* inyanga *and does this—it is necessary to win. Even though players are Christians and have lived in towns for a long time they do it, and believe in it. (Scotch, 1961, p. 71)*

Scotch believes that this substitute warfare (whose tribal survivals clearly resemble some of our athletic rituals) play an important part in Zulu adjustment to the pressures of urban living:

Football . . . is one of the few opportunities open to the Zulu for release from the anxiety and tensions of . . . urban life; and more specifically, it allows the expression of the increased aggression and hostility that arises in the city between Africans, within the framework of a modern, acceptable form. (p. 71)

Scotch was mainly interested in the broad pattern through which tribal customs were translated to an urban setting. To give clear evidence on the cathartic effect of soccer, we would need to make two comparisons. We would need to know whether urban Zulu in highly frustrating situations were more involved in football than were people in less difficult situations. We would also have to compare the amount of intergroup and interpersonal hostility among Zulu involved in sport with the amount of Zulu not so involved.

It is argued by some that since competitive sport is a form of *controlled* violence, one learns how to be aggressive without letting one's hostility get out of hand. This training, it is held, carries over into everyday life. Dean Ryan suggests that "Bubba Smith could wipe out one entire end of town in an evening, if he chose. He doesn't, however. It may be that experience at controlling aggressive behavior gained through athletics keeps him from acting aggressively except in situations that he considers justifiable" (Ryan, 1974, p. 29). A piece of research evidence that supports this idea is perhaps A. A. Stone's (1950) Harvard honors thesis in which he found that football players at the end of a season were less aggressive generally and less personal in their aggression as measured by a Thematic Apperception Test (TAT) than were a control group of nonathletes.

As for the spectator, in laboratory situations it seems that seeing the painful results of violence may alert people to the possible outcome of their own violence and thus lead them to control it. In a series of experiments Richard Goranson showed two groups a fight film. One had a positive outcome showing the winner leaving the ring undamaged and going on to success. The other had a negative outcome, stressing the loser's injuries, a cerebral hemorrhage, and agonizing death. The subjects who had seen the negative outcome film afterward gave fewer shocks to a learner. Goranson had the subjects rate their mood before and after the film. Those who saw the negative outcome film felt significantly less happy after the film than before. If it had drained off tension cathartically, they should have felt better. So

Goranson prefers the interpretation that "the horrible effects of the violence served to *sensitize* the subjects to the potential harm that they themselves might inflict" (1970, pp. 21–22).

Evidence for Increase

Now for the evidence that sport violence increases violence in other activities. A 1972 experiment by Zillman, Katcher, and Milavsky contradicted the bottom-line form of the drive discharge theory—the belief that vigorous muscular activity reduces emotional tension. On the contrary, in this experiment it raised it, thus throwing in doubt the simple common-sense view that one works off aggression by chopping wood or hitting a bag.

Twenty-eight University of Pennsylvania students were recruited for research that was supposed to (a) test their ability to perceive while distracted and (b) test the effect of electric shocks on learning. The procedure was this: The experimental group were first angered by giving them shocks for wrong answers to 12 questions. They were then put to work pedaling for 2 1/2 minutes on a cycle machine (bicycle ergometer) and while pedaling shown a series of slides on which they were to report. (Control groups had no arousal of anger and performed a fairly simple manual task instead of pedaling.) Finally, all groups were invited to give shocks, from 10 switches labeled quite mild to rather painful, to help in a learning task. Throughout the experiment, the metabolic state of all groups was tested several times by taking a combination of pulse rate, systolic blood pressure, and skin temperature (the last as a measure of contraction or dilation of periphal blood vessels).

The arousal of anger through electric shock raised the level of metabolic excitation. The bicycle riding raised it very significantly ($p < .001$). Those who had been angered and had pedaled the bike (and thus were doubly aroused) gave significantly stronger shocks to the learner than the control groups ($p < .05$). Zillman, Katcher, and Milavsky said of their results: "The findings are clearly counter to the expectation that strenuous physical exercise, at least as long as elevated excitation lasts, and as long as the individual does not reach a state of acute exhaustion, can serve to drain aggressive tensions and thus induce catharsis" (pp. 258–259).

In another classic film-viewing experiment Donald Hartmann (1969) found that vicarious aggressive experience stimulates violent activity, rather than reducing it as in Feshbach's experiment. Hartmann used as his subjects 72 male adolescent offenders under court commitment to the California Youth Authority for crimes ranging from minor offenses to strong-armed robbery. The young men were asked to take part in an investigation of teaching machines and audiovisual displays. As in Feshbach's experiment, the first step was arousal of anger by the experimenter's assistant in half of the subjects, through critical and unjustified statements about their intelligence and competence. The other half received neutral comments.

After the arousing or nonarousing instructions, the young men were each assigned at random to one of three 2-minute films. The first minute of all three films was identical, showing two boys on a basketball court shooting baskets. The second minute of the first film showed the two boys in an active and cooperative basketball game. In the other two films the boys got into an argument that ended in a fist fight. These two films differed in that one showed one of the boys being hurt, while the other focused on his opponent's hostile behavior and attitudes. There were thus a neutral film, a pain-cues film, and an instrumental aggression film. "The pain-cues film focused almost entirely on the victim's verbal and gestural pain as he was ferociously pummeled and kicked by his opponent. The instrumental aggression film . . . focused on the aggressor's responses including foot thrusts, flying fists, aggressive verbalizations, and angry facial expressions" (Hartmann, 1969, p. 282).

After he had seen one of the films, each young man was then told that he would eventually be questioned about its content. He was then invited to participate in an experiment on the effect of pain in learning. He was set in a room equipped with lights that were supposed to signal when a partner in another room had got a learning task right or had made an error. These lights were under the control of the experimenter; there was no actual learner. The young man also had at hand a panel of switches through which he was supposed to shock the learner when the light flashed that the learner had made a mistake. He was first invited to use each of the switches to shock himself, so as to know how strong a shock it delivered. Then the learner was supposedly put through a series of 25 tasks, for 10 of which the young man's light flashed an "error." Each time he was to pull a switch to shock the learner and thus help him learn. The duration and intensity of the shock were registered in an adjoining room and thus gave a measure of each young man's aggressiveness after seeing his film.

The results of the Hartmann experiment appear in Figure 14.1. Contrary to Feshbach's results, both violent films were followed by a *higher* level of aggression, as compared with the neutral film, regardless of whether the young man had been insulted or not. The difference shown would occur by chance less frequently than 1 time in 100: $p < .01$. The young men who had been insulted were more aggressive after seeing the film than those who had not been insulted. The opposite would have been expected from Feshbach's theory of catharsis. In addition, viewing a victim's pain stimulated more aggressive responses than

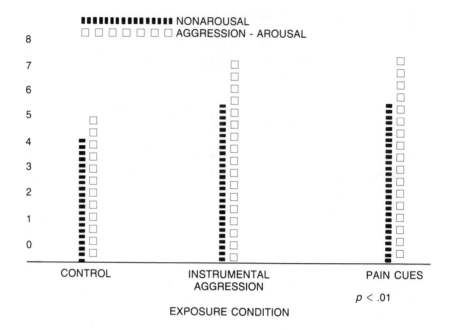

Figure 14.1   Mean shock intensity for subjects viewing the control film, the instrumental aggression film, and the pain-cues film. *Note.*   From "Influence of Symbolically Modeled Instrumental Aggression and Pain Cues on Aggressive Behavior" by D. P. Hartmann, 1969, *Journal of Personality and Social Psychology,* **11,** p. 283, Figure 1. Copyright 1969 by the American Psychological Association. Reprinted by permission of the author.

did viewing of an aggressor's hostility. Also (not shown in Figure 14.1), young men with longer records of antisocial behavior, particularly when they were angered and saw pain, delivered more intense shocks than those with shorter records. Overall, Hartmann said, these results contradict the theory of catharsis as developed by Feshbach and others.

Hartmann's conclusions are supported by several earlier experimental studies by Leonard Berkowitz, also using an aggressive sport film and a neutral or less aggressive film. One violent film was the boxing picture *Champion,* starring Kirk Douglas. Less aggressive control films showed a sailing race and the mile race between Roger Bannister and John Landy in which Bannister ran the first 4-minute mile. Consistently, Berkowitz has found that his subjects behave more aggressively after seeing a violent film than after seeing a less aggressive one.

For example, in his experiment using the Douglas fight film, reported in 1965, Berkowitz used the same sequence of angering → exposure to film → opportunity to give shocks later employed by

Hartmann, with the added twist that in some cases he identified his assistant, who was to receive the shocks, as a boxer, and in others as a speech major. Angered subjects who saw the fight film gave the boxer an average of 5.35 shocks as compared with 4.95 for those who saw the neutral film. In average duration of shock, the figures were: fight film, 16.56, neutral film, 11.47. (Here, $p < .05$.) (Berkowitz, 1965, p. 315).

Research dealing directly with the results of sport violence (of which there is not very much) is supplemented by a large body of experimentation on the general results of participating in or viewing violence. Richard Walters and E. L. Thomas compared a group that watched a fight scene from the James Dean-Sal Mineo movie *Rebel Without a Cause* with a group that watched a film showing adolescents doing art work. Afterwards, the fight scene group behaved more aggressively (Walters & Thomas, 1963). Albert Bandura (1973) has repeatedly found that children will repeat adult aggression seen live, on film, or on television.

In 1969 Jeffrey H. Goldstein and Robert L. Arms (1971) took the sport violence problem out into the real world, comparing spectator attitudes before and after the Army–Navy football game in Philadelphia and also before and after an Army-Temple gymnastics meet. Student assistants from Temple University interviewed 97 fans coming into the stadium, asking them which team they favored. From a hostility scale constructed by Buss and Durkee (1957) they asked the spectators 28 questions (9 scoring indirect hostility, 8 scoring resentment, and 11 scoring irritability), mixed with 8 filler questions about football. Having thus measured pregame hostility of a sample of fans by use of an accepted measure, the interviewers asked the same questions to another sample of 53 fans leaving the stadium after the game. The spectators leaving the stadium were significantly more hostile than those entering. This was true for both supporters of the losing team (Navy) and supporters of the winning team (Army). Table 14.2 shows the average before and after hostility scores. The range of possible scores was from 0 to 28 (the number of questions). A difference of this size would be expected by chance fewer than 25 times in 1,000 ($p < .025$). "No support for a catharsis effect is obtained in the present study," said Goldstein and Arms, "contrary to the many popular notions that it would occur" (1971, p. 89). (The results would be more convincing if *the same* spectators had been interviewed before and after.)

At the Army-Temple gym meet, where the same interviewing techniques were used, there was no significant change in the level of hostility. Why? Although the gym meet was not a neutral noncompetitive control situation, in terms of the scale presented earlier in this chapter the level of violence was much lower. "One major difference between the nature of the two events is that a football game involves multiple players in direct physical contact, while a gym meet involves individual performance in which no contact can occur. It seems likely . . . that watching an aggressive sport leads to an increase in hostility among spectators'' (Goldstein & Arms, 1971, p. 88).

Table 14.2   Mean Spectator Hostility Scores, 1969 Army-Navy Football Game

| | Preferred | | | |
	Army (winning team)	Navy (losing team)	No preference	Total
Pregame	$n = 38$ 10.42	$n = 47$ 11.72	$n = 12$ 11.67	11.20
Postgame	$n = 18$ 13.33	$n = 30$ 13.17	$n = 5$ 15.00	13.40

Note.   The higher the score, the greater the hostility; $p < .025$. From ''Effects of Observing Athletic Contests on Hostility'' by J.H. Goldstein and R.L. Arms, 1971, *Sociometry,* **34**, p. 88, Table 1. Copyright 1971 by the American Sociological Association. Reprinted by permission.

In 1979 Arms, Russell, and Sandilands replicated the Goldstein-Arms research with a hockey game and a wrestling match as the contact sports and a swimming meet as the noncontact event. By using students on class assignment, rather than randomly selected fans, these researchers were able to score the same persons on aggression tests before and after the sport events. They also felt they were able to avoid another criticism of the Goldstein-Arms study—that the results may have been due to alcohol intake. The effect of contact sport on fan hostility was essentially the same as in the football study.

In another venture into the real world, Edward Turner (1974) gave sentence-completion and thematic apperception tests to males at the University of Maryland and after they had watched football and basketball games and wrestling matches involving tension and a doubtful outcome. There was a significant increase in the number of aggressive words produced after these experiences as spectators.

These studies of spectator behavior in laboratory and stadium are supported by research like that of Michael Smith, a former Canadian hockey and football player and hockey coach, now a sociologist, who examined 68 newspaper accounts of crowd violence during or after sporting events and found 75% of the episodes triggered by game violence. Similarly, another former football player and track coach, John Cheffers, and sociologist Jay Meehan found spectator fights ignited by player fights 57% of the time in soccer, 49% in football, 34% in baseball, but, interestingly, only 8.5% in hockey (Gilbert & Twyman, 1983). ''Yet,'' says Smith of the drive-discharge theory, ''for decades and decades eminent scholars wrote without a shred of evidence that acts of violence in sport are cathartic or therapeutic for spectators'' (cited in Gilbert & Twyman, 1983, p. 66). (I must note that already in this chapter we have looked at some shreds of evidence.) If crowds typically responded like Feshbach's laboratory subjects, we would not find precautions like those related by Robert Yeager, in a description of Rio de Janeiro's 200,000-seat soccer stadium:

> *A twenty-five-foot-wide, fifteen-foot deep moat, rimmed with jagged glass, isolates the playing field from the stands. Police armed with tear-gas guns stand guard around the moat; players and officials reach the field through underground tunnels that run from locker rooms to a trap door in the turf (Yeager, 1979, p. 83)*

One-third of baseball spectator fights are ignited by player fights. Courtesy of *The Miami Herald.*

Evidence for Parallelism

The view that sport violence parallels social violence was supported by Richard Sipes' (1973) study of the relationship between war and combative sport in 20 societies (all preliterate except for the Hutterites, a communal pacifist group in the United States and Canada). Data on these societies were taken from J. P. Murdock's *Ethnographic Index,* to which we were introduced in chapter 4. Sipes selected what he thought were the 10 best examples of warlike societies and the 10 best examples of peaceful peoples. There are two main models, says Sipes, of the relationship between war and combative sport. According to the drive-discharge model, the members of every society have a certain amount of hostility that must be discharged somehow. War and violent sports are alternative ways. "Warlike sports serve to discharge accumulated aggressive tensions and therefore act as alternative channels to war, making it less likely" (Sipes, 1973, p. 64). According to the cultural patterning theory, on the other hand, war and sport are both expressions of a common underlying pattern of cultural *mores.* "Behavior patterns and value systems relative to war and to warlike sports tend to overlap and support each other's presence" (Sipes, 1973, p. 65). If the drive-discharge hypothesis is correct, in warlike societies we should expect to find few combative sports, and in peaceful societies we should find many. If the cultural patterning hypothesis is correct, we should find that the more warlike societies have more violent games, and the peaceful societies have fewer. In a sentence, the discharge theory would predict an inverse (negative) correlation between frequency of warfare and number of combative games; the cultural patterning hypotheses would predict a direct (positive) correlation. Which hypothesis was supported by the data in the 20 societies? "The cross-cultural study shows that where we find warlike behavior we typically find warlike sports and where war is relatively rare combative sports tend to be absent" (Sipes, 1973, p. 71). (See Table 14.3.)

Table 14.3   Relationships between Warfare and Combative Sports in 20 Preliterate Societies

| | | Combative Sports | | |
		Yes	No	
Warlike	Yes	9	1	10
	No	2	8	10
		11	9	20

Note.   From "War, Sports and Aggression: An Empirical Test of Two Rival Theories" by R.G. Sipes, 1973, *American Anthropologist,* **75,** Table 2. Reprinted by permission of the American Anthropological Association. $p < .003$.

Sipes' study contradicts the opinion of the British psychiatrist Anthony Storr (1968) that the encouragement of all kinds of competition in a society will reduce the kind of hostility that leads to war and the observation of the historian Jacob Burckhardt that "a people knowing war has no need of tournaments" (cited in Huizinga, 1964, p. 72).

A somewhat similar study by Keefer, Goldstein, and Kasiarz (1983) examined modernized nations rather than preliterate societies. These psychologists investigated the relationship in 60 countries between participation in war and Olympic participation (especially in contact sports) between 1896 and 1965. The relationship between months at war and entry into contact Olympic sports is shown in Table 14.4, whose form resembles Sipes' fourfold table. As explanation, the authors suggested that "international athletic competition fosters conflict or that the two stem from a common set of factors, such as basic values" (pp. 185–186).

Table 14.4 Relationship between Warfare and Olympic Contact Sports

		Number of contact sports entered	
		Below median	Above median
Frequency of	Below median	24	12
War	Above median	6	18

Note. Adapted from "Olympic Games Participation and Warfare" by R. Keefer, J.H. Goldstein, and D. Kasiarz, 1983, in J.H. Goldstein (Ed.), *Sports Violence* (p. 189), Table 11.3. New York: Springer-Verlag. Copyright 1983 by Springer-Verlag. Reprinted by permission. $p < .01$.

Another example of sport violence paralleling social violence is the civilization of violence with the move from a preindustrial to a modern society, as analyzed by Eric Dunning (1983). The preindustrial society, on which we touched in chapter 10, was described by Huizinga in his classic work on the late Middle Ages (1924/1984), whose first chapter is "The Violent Tenor of Life." Social organization was what sociologists call primary, based on face-to-face communal relationships. For our purpose, the most important form of the tie was the bond between the members of the local male gang, which emphasized masculinity, *machismo*, bravery, skill in fighting other enemy gangs. There was no central force to control the activities of these male vigilante groups—as political scientists say, the national state didn't yet have a monopoly on violence. The form of violence was affective; that is, fighting and hunting were sources of pleasure. Typical participant sports were ones like Dane's Head and Kneppen (Welsh football), which were symbolic gang wars. Spectators typically enjoyed activities like bearbaiting, cockfighting, prizefighting, burning cats in baskets, and watching public executions. Enjoyed is the key word for this affective violence.

With the coming of industrialism, social organization became secondary, based on the impersonal sale of services in the market. Violence was civilized: Its cruder forms came to evoke repugnance rather than pleasure. It became instrumental rather than affective, a means to an end rather than an end in itself. (People were killed in factories to make a profit, and in war to serve national interest, but not out of an enjoyment of pain.) Along with everything else, sport became competitive and highly organized around the goal of winning, and its violence became more controlled. It is true, says Dunning, that in recent years the instrumental goal of victory has evoked waves of player and spectator violence, but on the whole sport, like social life in general, has been civilized.

Sport anthropologist Kendall Blanchard (1976) agrees with Sipes's culture patterning view. He believes that *both* those who make general claims that combative sport reduces social aggression and those who claim that it generally increases it are wrong. Rather, "team sport behavior provides a specialized, artificial context for the expression of learned aggression needs through competitive forms of conflict" (Blanchard, 1976, p. 97). It is a part of the culture, shaped by the culture. How combative sport in turn shapes the culture depends on the particular social situation. Sometimes sport competition may prevent unnecessary social violence. An example is the stickball games arranged by the traditional Mississippi Choctaw Indians when two communities appeared headed for open hostility. "On the other hand, team sport contests can become the scene of violence. This is not to say that these competitive sports *cause* that violence" (p. 97).

We may better understand what Blanchard means by considering three unrelated events that occurred in 1969. In Central America, Honduras and El Salvador went to war after a soccer game led to rioting. In Milwaukee, Wisconsin, after losing a basketball game, black high-school students threw a white college professor off a bus. In eastern Europe, a crisis between Czechoslovakia and the Soviet Union followed a Czech hockey victory that elated fans celebrated by tearing up the furniture in the Russian airlines depot. Did combative sport *cause* the war, the international crisis, the interracial violence? Could they have occurred without the sporting events? Were the clashes in the sport arena like the fuse that ignites the explosion of sticks of dynamite?

Evidence for Symbolization

Sport violence may symbolize social violence that, for one reason or another, is suppressed or repressed. Let us begin with the dramatic example of cockfighting in Bali, reported by Clifford Geertz (1972).

In the Balinese cockfight, owners arm their prize cocks with spurs, "razor sharp, pointed steel swords 4 or 5 inches long." They are placed facing one another in the center of a ring about 50 feet square, and then:

Most of the time . . . the cocks fly almost immediately at one another in a wing-beating, head-thrusting, leg-kicking explosion of animal fury so pure, so absolute, as to be almost abstract, a Platonic concept of hate. Within moments one or the other drives homes a solid blow with his spur. . . . The cock who landed the first blow usually proceeds to finish off his weakened opponent. But this is far from an inevitable outcome, for if a cock can walk he can fight, and if he can fight, he can kill, and what counts is which cock expires first. If the wounded one can get a stab in and stagger until the other drops, he is the official winner, even if he himself topples over an instant later. (Geertz, 1972, p. 8–9)

Meanwhile, "the crowd packed tightly around the ring follow in near silence, moving their bodies in kinesthetic sympathy with the movements of the animals" (p. 9).

The Balinese, like many Polynesian people, are openly gentle and restrained, legendary for their graceful dancing. According to Geertz, in their everyday life they obsessively avoid any kind of open conflict. But "as much of American surfaces in a ball park, or a race track, or around a poker table, much of Bali surfaces in a cock ring. For it is only apparently cocks that are fighting there. Actually, it is men. . . . The deep psychological identification of Balinese men with their cocks is unmistakeable" (p. 5). The pun, says Geertz, is Balinese as well as English, for the Balinese word for cock, *Sabung*, also means penis, hero, warrior, champion, lady-killer, tough guy.

Now from the South Seas to postindustrial society, where men identify with their jocks instead of their cocks. Analyzing the wave of sport violence that arose in the mid-1970s, sociologist Irving Goldaber, director of the Miami-based Center for the Study of Crowd and Spectator Behavior, speaks of violence for vicarious power:

*More and more people aren't making it. You work hard, you ex-
ist, but you haven't got much to show for it. There are increasing
numbers of people who are deeply frustrated because they feel
they have very little power over their lives. They come to sporting events to exercise, vicariously a sense of power. . . . Because
winning, being No. 1, is everything, they are likely to be very
ferocious if they—their team—are thwarted and they vent their
frustrations physically against players, officials, or other spectators. That's the nub of the problem. (cited in Gilbert & Twyman,
1983, p. 71)*

A related example of symbolism in sport violence is British soccer
hooliganism, analyzed by Pearton and Gaskell (1981). In chapter 10
we noted that, unlike rugby, British soccer is a game traditionally
played by working-class youth, with a working-class following. From
here came the 75% increase between 1960 and 1970 in serious offenses
on the soccer field, and with them the hooliganism of the "apparently
mindless, rowdy, destructive and sometimes violent young football
supporters" (p. 58). To understand this, according to Pearton and
Gaskell, we must know what has happened to British working-class
youth, for whom "the economic and social problems of the 1970s . . .
created a 'backs to the wall' mentality in contrast to the 'you've never
had it so good' mentality of the previous decade" (p. 57). We must
understand what football has symbolized to working-class youth:

*Football . . . represented the possibility of success to large parts
of the population who had not only never experienced success but
had been led to believe they had no right to it, and came to believe
they could only win it through collective action. . . . Supporting
a team was never merely watching a match, it meant being a part
of something bigger—a major expression of the reality and the
hopes of the industrial working class. (pp. 62–63)*

Frustrated working-class youth have none of the ways of coping
with frustration open to other members of society—overdrinking, il-
licit drugtaking, rugby tours, office parties, continental holidays, and
wife swapping. "For the working class youth living at home there are
few such opportunities. The football match is one" (p. 63). Pearton
and Gaskell throw much light on how the same Liverpool slums that
produced the protest music of the Beatles in the 1960s, in the 1980s
produced the traveling drunken hooligans who ignited the Brussels
soccer massacre.

In the cases of Bali, 1970s spectator aggression, and British soccer
hooliganism, sport violence compensates symbolically for social sup-
pression or repression. Michael Novak sees its significance as cultur-

ally patterned and also existential in the sense that it makes us more aware of our place in the universe (Novak, 1976, especially chapter 5). To Novak the life of our culture and life in general are vicious and brutal. Violence in sport is a symbolic expression that enables us to experience directly or vicariously a dimension of existence that we often deny. Novak considers it healthy that males, unlike females, don't repress their anger but can feel it and act it out. He feels that sport, especially football, contributes to the richness of our life by providing a culturally approved area where those who are less repressed can help others to experience this aspect of existence. They are dramatic heroes who challenge others to be heroic. "Football externalizes the warfare in our hearts and offers us a means of knowing ourselves and wresting some grace from our true nature" (p. 91). Thus, violent sport, particularly football, is essentially a religious drama. "If you think football is a violent liturgy reflect upon the Eucharist [the symbolic eating of the body and blood of Christ in the Mass]" (p. 91).

Perceived Intent

Through all these interpretations must run the basic sociological principle that how people act depends as much on what they see a situation to be as on what the situation objectively is. In his study of Choctaw Indian youths and Anglo young people in Murfreesboro, Tennessee, Blanchard shows how the two groups, because of their cultural training, perceive the same sport activity in different ways (1976, p. 102). Blanchard asked 13 Choctaw and 12 Anglo basketball players to pick out of a list of feelings the ones most important to doing well in the sport. Both groups named aggressive, tough, and mean as qualities of a good basketball player. But the Choctaws, unlike the Anglos, also picked feelings like cheerful, friendly, and loving. When shown sketches depicting violent conflict in football games, the Choctaw high-school students typically disapproved strongly, and the Anglos approved.

The Choctaws tended to see a game as a friendly contest, the Anglos to see it as a violent conflict. In the terms we used earlier (not Blanchard's) a basketball or football encounter seemed to be to the Anglos a zero-sum game and to the Choctaws a positive-sum game (see again chapter 3).

The Choctaw fan may yell the violent words he has learned from the Anglo as part of the game—tear off his head, bust his ass, kill him—but since he also sees games as cheerful, friendly, and loving, the expressions are routine and don't convey the violence they do for the zero-sum Anglo for whom winning is the only thing. The same event in a game (for example, a legal football tackle) a Choctaw spectator is likely to see as less violent. This is because he does not see the person making the tackle as hostile, as the Anglo fan is likely to. In a basketball game, if a Choctaw is roughly guarded, he is less likely to see this as a hostile act and to react violently. "Violence is thus a more likely possibility in the Anglo situation" (p. 106).

Perceived intent thus varies from situation to situation, person to person, culture to culture. When Berkowitz manipulated his scene from the movie *Champion* so as to make Kirk Douglas a good guy, even subjects who had been angered didn't react aggressively, but when he was shown as a bad guy, they did. Ryan summarizes the point: In sports if the opponent is perceived as a good guy, little aggression will result, but if the opponent is perceived as likely to act unfairly or aggressively, more aggression should be expected, both from the spectator and the participant (Ryan, 1973, p. 26). Berkowitz says, "The scene really isn't an aggressive stimulus, unless the observer thinks of it as aggression, as the deliberate injury of others (Berkowitz, 1972, cited in Ryan, 1973, p. 27).

In an experiment reported in 1967, Seymour Epstein and Stuart Taylor studied how willingness to inflict punishment in an aggressive competitive situation was affected by (a) whether one won or lost the competition and (b) whether one saw the opponent as intending to inflict harm. On these two points, hostile response was significantly related to perceived hostile intent ($p < .001$) but not to winning or losing. "Instigation to aggression in a competitive aggressive interaction is determined largely by perception of the aggressive intent of the opponent, whether or not the attempt finds its mark" (Epstein & Taylor, 1968, p. 288).

A. H. Hastorf and Hadley Cantril (1954) did an on-the-scene study of perceived intent in a real-life situation at the 1953 Princeton-Dartmouth football game. Before the game, it was clear that Dartmouth needed to stop Princeton's All-America back, Dick Kazmeier. He was stopped early, leaving the game before the half with a concussion and a broken nose. How this was seen depended on who was seeing it. The Princeton student newspaper editorialized about this intentional unsportsmanlike crippling of a star. The Dartmouth paper pointed out that, as football injuries go, Kazmeier's were not really major and reminded Princetonians of previous games that season when *they* had won by ganging up on an outstanding opponent. On a questionnaire given to students of both schools, 39% of Dartmouth students saw the game as rough and fair. Only 3% from Princeton saw it that way. Asked to check rule infractions by both teams while watching a game film, Dartmouth students checked an average of 4.3 by Dartmouth and Princeton students checked a mean of 9.8 infractions by Dartmouth ($p < .01$).

Perceived Injustice

This last Hastorf-Cantril finding was a measure of perceived injustice—to Princeton students the Dartmouth team had been getting away with murder and presumably the officials were perceived as having let them do it. In Smith's analysis of 68 cases of crowd violence that, as we saw, found player violence to be the main instigator, the *second* most important triggering factor was unpopular officials' decisions. In turn, Smith (1975) noted, assaultive player behavior may have been triggered by perceived injustice at the hands of officials. Mark, Bryant, and Lehman (1983), in analyzing the causes of crowd violence, point out that perceived injustice is a particular kind of frustration: Whereas Dollard defined frustration as deprivation of what one *expects*, perceived injustice is deprivation of what one feels one *deserves*, and is a much more powerful inciter to violence. Thus, bitterly intense cold or intense heat at a football game will generally be less violence-provoking than the callback of a winning touchdown. Also, of 1,947 fans polled at college and professional hockey games, most judged referees to be the most important cause of crowd misbehavior (Cavanaugh & Silva, 1980). Again, it is not what objectively happens, but what is seen to happen, that incites: Injustice is very much 'in the eyes of the beholder.' Aggression is aroused by injustices *as they are perceived* (Mark, Bryant, & Lehman, 1983, p. 87). Here, I must add, it is very important what intent is perceived behind the perceived injustice—riotous behavior is more likely to occur if the officials are seen as biased than if they are seen as merely incompetent. In crowd or mass behavior there is great danger that those who perceive favoritism will carry the day over those who perceive error. That perceived injustice and perceived intent can have far-reaching results will be obvious if we remember such facts as that, in 1955, a perceived unfair suspension of Montreal Canadien star Maurice Richard led to the smashing and looting of 15 blocks of stores in Montreal, and that in 1964 nearly 300 people were killed in the riot and panic that followed when fans tried to attack a referee who had nullified a potentially tying goal in a soccer match between Argentina and Peru.

Earlier in this chapter I referred to the argument by Hughes and Coakley that sport violence may grow in part out of the organization of the sport team, which in some respects resembles a prison. The late psychologist Philip Brickman (1977) believed that there is an aspect of sport organization that makes perceived injustice (and the violence that grows out of it) *less* likely to occur than in everyday life. This is the way sport organization handles violation of the rules. If there were as many illegal acts in everyday life as are usually detected in a basketball game, or as usually go undetected in a football game, says

Brickman, society would break down. The sport establishment does not break down because the sport system, unlike the criminal justice system, uses penalties based on equity rather than penalties based on deterrence.

The strength of the sport system, according to Brickman, is that it realistically assumes that violations are going to occur and seeks to restore a fair situation whenever they do, rather than to punish the violator in the hope of eliminating violations. Sport penalties are based on what objectively happens rather than on the reading of intentions. They are proportionate to the offense. They are enforced immediately on the spot so that interaction is not disrupted. Sometimes the injured party is given the option of refusing the penalty. Very importantly, penalties are generally imposed on offenders regardless of their status (top-flight star or lowest benchwarmer), and the offender is not labeled or branded after the penalty has been imposed (for example, the hockey player just out of the penalty box has the same status as everybody else).

The sport system does use some deterrence-based penalties: disqualification of a golfer for moving his ball or not signing his scorecard, or of a boxer for repeatedly hitting below the belt, or forfeit of a game for using an ineligible player. But, in general, sport penalties are equity-based, aiming to restore fairness. Brickman and his interpreters believe that this is why, although sport events usually occur under conditions conducive to violence (anonymity, crowding, heat, noise, alcohol, big money at stake), they are rather rarely disrupted (see also Mark, Bryant, & Lehman, 1983). (It is noteworthy that the spectacular Montreal hockey riot, in which over 100 people were arrested, followed a pair of deterrent penalties: Hockey commissioner Clarence Campbell suspended Maurice Richard for the season and playoffs for hitting a referee; fans greeted Campbell with fruit, galoshes, and other missiles when he appeared at a game; the Montreal fire chief evacuated the Forum; the game was forfeited to Montreal's opponent; and hell broke loose in the streets.)

It is interesting to close a chapter on sport violence and social violence with Brickman's idea (which is clearly arguable) that if society's system of justice were modeled on that of the sport establishment we might substantially reduce perceived injustice and the violence that can follow it.

Chapter 15

Self-Actualization: Play as Freedom

Reflecting on a lifetime's experience as a physical educator in a 1968 Temple University lecture, Eleanor Metheny said of why people play sports,

During the past ten years I have talked with countless people about the dimensions of their interest in the rule-governed competitions of sport. In those conversations I have heard the word "freedom." Freedom to go all out, holding nothing back—freedom to experience myself at my own utmost as a wholehearted, fully motivated, fully integrated, fully functioning human being. (1975, p. 140)

Fleeting Moments

Let us make concrete what Metheny was talking about.

Pete Reiser, one of the all-time great outfielders in baseball history, looks back on his years in the game:

No, I don't have any regrets. Not about one damned thing. I've had a lot of good experiences in my life and they far outnumber the bad. Good memories are the greatest thing in the world, and I've got a lot of them. And one of the sweetest is of the kid standing out on the green grass in center field, with the winning runs on base, thinking, hit it to me. Hit it to me. (Honig, 1975, p. 315)

A 15-year-old high-school football player tells social psychologist Edgar Friedenberg:

> *I was in a [football] game last year that we lost by a very bad score but in the midst of it I was, seemed to be, having a fairly good day. And I just felt light-headed . . . —I played for the heck of it, for the fun of it, just because I wanted to. And . . . I'd be schmeared a couple of times—I'd get up and laugh my head off and I wouldn't know why I was laughing, and I certainly shouldn't have been laughing because I really got schmeared. And I'd go back to the middle and I'd be dying laughing and they'd think I was crazy, but I enjoyed it. . . . After the game was over I felt terrible because we lost so bad. But during the game it was just this feeling of exuberance. (Slusher, 1967, pp. xi–xii)*

John Brodie, San Francisco 49er quarterback, explains why he rejects both of the popular images of the football player as beast or computer:

> *Often, in the heat and excitement of a game, a player's perception and coordination will improve dramatically. At times . . . I experience a kind of clarity that I've never seen adequately described in a football story. Sometimes, for example, time seems to slow way down, in an uncanny way, as if everyone were moving in slow motion. It seems as if I have all the time in the world to watch the receivers run their patterns, and yet I know the defensive line is coming at me just as fast as ever. I know perfectly well how hard and fast those guys are coming and yet the whole thing seems like a movie or a dance in slow motion. It's beautiful. (Brodie, 1973, pp. 19–20)*

Chicago Bear Mike Singletary describes a jarring stop of Eric Dickerson for a 1-yard loss on a third and one play; "I don't feel pain from a hit like that. What I feel, is joy. Joy for the tackle. Joy for myself. Joy for the other man. . . . It's football, it's middle-linebacking. It's good for everybody" (Telander, 1986, p. 39).

A professional basketball player, Houston NBA guard Calvin Murphy, tells how it feels to sink a free throw before a hostile crowd: "The most beautiful sight in the world is that ball falling through the net, and then the sudden silence. It's like taking on 15,000 people at once and beating them all" (Pileggi, 1977, p. 10).

Charlie Hodgson, who coached two University of Miami women's swimming teams to national championships, describes what keeps him going:

I don't have any super long-term goals, except that I like to be 100 percent successful in anything I do. I drive a '67 Volkswagen with the front end bashed in, I live at home and I can't afford much of anything. . . . I figure I get paid about 15 cents an hour. But anything worthwhile is not easy. For something to be meaning-ful, you have to struggle and I'm willing to struggle—for a little while longer. (University of Miami Hurricane, *April 23, 1976)*

A rock-climber speaks of the self-actualization that draws him to this harzardous sport:

You see who the hell you really are. It's important to learn about yourself, to open doors into the self. The mountains are the greatest place in the twentieth century to get this knowledge. . . . Nobody hassles you to put your mind and body under tremen-dous stress to get to the top, there's nobody to . . . force you, judge you. . . . Your comrades are there, but you all feel the same way anyway, you're all in it together. Who can you trust more in the twentieth century than these people? People after the same self-discipline as yourself, following the deeper commitment. The facades come rolling off. A bond like that with other people is in itself an ecstasy. (Csikszentmihalyi, 1975, pp. 94–95)

Jesse Owens relives his gold medal 9.4 100 meters in the 1936 Berlin Olympics:

Your mouth goes as dry as cotton. Your palms are wet with perspi-ration. Your stomach is jumping. You feel as if your legs can't sup-port your body. You feel all those things in a flash, an instant. . . .

Nine years of work and it's all over in 10 seconds. Your arms, your legs, your knee action . . . that's what you think of in those 10 seconds. You must keep them working together.

You can't worry about the guy at your side or the guy behind you. You've got to get in front and they've got to catch you if they can. You've been trained for this. You can't let them catch you. They must not catch you.

Then you hit the tape and all the joy flows. It comes through all at once. On that day, the dream is complete. A dream you've had for nine years. And when you step on the victory platform and watch your flag raised above the others and you hear the crescendo of your national anthem being played, you say to your-self, "Today, I was the best." (Rubin, 1980b, p. 4A)

Dimensions of Sport Freedom

Now, having illustrated it, let us analyze in what ways play (or sport, so far as it *is* play) contributes to people's self-actualization and freedom. First, the play situation is an island in which the ordinary conditions and pressures of life are suspended and a new set of play rules set up. Sutton-Smith says, "For me play is what a person does when he can choose the constraints within which we will act or imagine. . . . The player substitutes his own conventions and his own urgencies for those of society and nature" (1972, p. xiii). It is not a lone player, however, who ordinarily sets up the rules of play. In analyzing this, Metheny takes us back 3,000 years, to the 12th century B.C., to the legend of Patroclus as recorded in Homer's *Iliad*. The Greek nobleman Patroclus died a bloody hero in the Trojan war. To honor his brave life, his comrades at his funeral "threw javelins, hurled stones, drove horse drawn chariots at full speed, ran as fast as a man can run, and wrestled with each other in hand-to-hand combat." But they did not do these things just as Patroclus did them, for under the conditions of real life Patroclus could not perform his best. "On the battleground he had to throw on the run, and he had to throw at other men who were running toward him with their own spears at the ready; so he had to adjust his aim and force to the requirements of the movement, always keeping his own guard up to ward off the enemy spears and arrows. As he threw, other warriors often jostled him, or his feet slipped in the muck" (Metheny, 1975, p. 136).

So, at Patroclus' funeral, his companions tried to rule out all these hindrances and give everyone a free and equal chance to do his very best. They did this by establishing what Metheny calls "the paradoxical rules of sport competition," which imposed equal conditions on all competitors:

> *Thus, each warrior . . . freed of all the hampering circumstances of war, . . . was free to go all out, holding nothing back; he was able to focus all the energies of his mortal being on one supreme attempt to hurl his own javelin at the nothingness of empty space . . . or he was free to run as fast as he could run, to hit as hard as he could hit, to leap, to jump as high, as far as he could leap or jump. He was free to bring all the forces of his own being to bear on the performance of one self-chosen human action. (Metheny, 1975, p. 136)*

The *Iliad* is legend, based on fact, reconstructed later by a blind poet and not by the all-seeing eye of Wide World of Sports. But as a description of the paradox (seeming contradiction) by which rules bring freedom, the funeral of Patroclus, as analyzed by Metheny, comes very close to the core of what sport can be.

Aside from the mud and blood and other distractions of war, from what does play give relief? There are kinds of social freedom. In the play situation people can overcome the group antagonisms that ordinarily separate them from one another. Stumpf and Cozens, who pioneered in introducing anthropological insights to physical educators, say, "It is above all in the leisure and play aspects of human culture that the hard crust of conservatism that divides one people from another is at its weakest" (Frederickson & Cozens, 1947, p. 215). A case in point is a 1983 study by South African sociologists showing that *all* ethnic groups (white, black, colored, and Indian) sampled in urban South Africa favored interracial soccer-rugby, tennis, and swimming on both a club and national level (Scholtz & Olivier, 1984).

Also, sport is freedom from work. Stumpf and Cozens quote the historian Arnold Toynbee as saying that sport "is a conscious attempt to counter-balance the soul-destroying specialization which the division of labor under industrialism entails" (Toynbee, cited in Frederickson & Cozens, 1947, p. 617). This is no doubt true of many people's play, despite the fact that modern sport has in some cases embodied and raised to a peak this soul-destroying specialization. Here is the truth in the image of football player as computer to which Brodie referred. However, I believe George Leonard in his book *The Ultimate Athlete* has best expressed what Toynbee was referring to. Leonard speaks of the running of O. J. Simpson "tuned into the rhythmic, pulsing, dancing nature of existence":

> *Out of a lifetime of sports spectating, the moments that live with us . . . are pure dance. We may forget league standings and final scores and even who won, but we can never forget certain dance-like moments: that supernatural Brodie to Washington pass in the 1971 playoff game with the Redskins; that classic, utterly pure blow with which Sugar Ray Robinson ended his 1957 bout with Gene Fullmer; that transcendent running catch by Willie Mays in the first game of the 1954 World Series in the Polo Grounds. Perhaps it is this desire for the transcendent rather than mere victory that keeps us locked to our television sets on those sunny afternoons when we ourselves might be out playing. . . . Indeed, we can say that the whole complex structure of pro football was created so that O. J. (and others like him) can dance. (Leonard, 1974, p. 230)*

Another kind of self-actualization that sport gives is dramatic knowledge of self. Metheny describes the moment of truth in which the Greek Olympic athlete must stand, naked of all pretense and stripped of all justifying excuses by the rules of sport:

In that self-revealing moment, no man can delude himself, for every competitor must experience himself as he is—in all the complexity and ambivalence of his own feelings about himself, his gods, and other men who claim the right to share the universe of his existence. If he is a proud man, he will experience his own pride. If he is a domineering man, he will experience his own need to dominate the lives of other men. So, too, a fearful man will know his own fears; a resentful man his resentments; and an anxious man his anxieties. An idealistic man must realize the reality of his own ideals—and the conflict he experiences as he tries to live up to them. A chauvinistic man must come to terms with his own chauvinism; a loving man must reveal the limits of his love; and a hating man will experience his own fearful hate. (1975, pp. 137–138)

Transcendence through dance and through self-insight are aspects of the existential experience of one's ultimate condition, a face-to-face encounter with how things really are that seems, for many people, to intensify their sense of aliveness. This encounter involves an intensified sense of being (life) and also a sharpened awareness of the possibility of non-being (death). Some find an ecstasy in their sport through this possibility of death. Let us begin with Janet Guthrie, in 1977 the first woman ever to drive in the Indianapolis 500:

Everything tastes better, smells better, looks better, feels better after a race. That's why I do it, I guess. It's the exhilaration, the worry of thinking you might not make it, the coming down afterward. I know of nothing else that is so life enhancing. . . . Every driver is immortal behind the wheel. The possibility of bodily injury does not occur out there. The cocktail party instinct, of course, is to say that race track drivers are suicidal. Well, I have a highly developed sense of self-preservation. Yet, the idea of putting yourself in a position where life is . . . forfeitable . . . I mean you tell all your friends and relatives that it's not really dangerous. But still. . . .'' (Miami News, *May 29, 1977, p. 5B*)

George Leonard is so impressed by the value of confronting death that he advocates protecting people's right to risk their lives through Right-to-Drown laws for those who do it in water and comparable legislation for those who find their confrontation on land or in the air. Leonard explains why:

We need no roundabout theories to explain the fascination of death and the salutary effects of calculated risk. We simply must remember that, from the vantage point of embodied consciousness, death provides us our clearest connection with the eternal. It can be said that in our present condition of flesh and blood, we are playing a game—I have called it the Game of Games—and somehow, at some level, are always aware of a boundary, a line we cannot cross and still return to this game. To cross that boundary we surrender the particular arrangement of molecules that we call the body. We surrender the particular arrangement of awareness that we call our ego. In surrendering, even in preparing to surrender, we begin to learn something about our present state. We learn something about the ever-shifting balance, the trade-off between the particular and the cosmic, about the necessary and unnecessary limitations imposed upon ourselves on this field of play. We gain hints of possibilities we had not dreamed of. (Leonard, 1974, pp. 224-225)

The Fascination of Risk

I am personally inclined to feel that one best intensifies life by focusing on life, but Bruce Ogilvie (1974), a sport psychologist, has done some impressive empirical research that gives some support to Leonard's argument. Ogilvie used questionnaires, standardized psychological tests, and depth interviews to study over 250 high-risk performers—professional and amateur football players, race drivers, sky divers, scuba divers, acrobatic airplane pilots. Why, Ogilvie asks, will a person fall free for 8,000 feet while aiming at an 8-inch target on the ground; dangle at the end of a rope on a mountain 10,000 feet above the earth; strap himself into a high-powered midget plane for acrobatic competition; take the wheel of a racing car when Ogilvie's research showed that 67% of race drivers he studied were dead or disabled from competition within 5 years?

Ogilvie found some people explaining the risk takers in terms of psychopathology—in brief, they are sick. His research shows us, Ogilvie believes, that the risk takers are as psychologically healthy as the average person, perhaps healthier.

To get perspective, we may look at some of the negative interpretations of risk taking by psychologists and others.

- To some, skydiving, mountain climbing, and so forth are a form of what the psychoanalyst Alfred Adler called a masculine protest—an effort to overcome feelings of inferiority through being recognized as superior; to prove oneself omnipotent (we will remember Guthrie's statement that race drivers feel themselves immortal), to prove oneself sexually adequate and reassure oneself of one's masculinity.

- Some see the risk taker as a psychopathic personality who has an immature, shallow contact with reality.
- Risk taking has been described by some as a counter phobic reaction, through which one reduces anxiety by constantly and compulsively exposing oneself to the things of which one is physically and psychologically most afraid.
- Another view is that the risk taker displaces fear from another situation in which the risk is greater. Thus, a woman who is afraid to stand up to her husband or a man afraid to confront his boss might overcome the sense of cowardice by conquering fear of falling off a mountain or jumping from a plane (my illustration, not Ogilvie's).
- Ogilvie says that the most frequent psychological explanation of habitual risk-taking behavior is an unconscious death wish. One flirts with death because one really wants to die. (Why one would want to die would need explanation, but there is plenty of clinical evidence of people who court death because somehow dying seems more attractive than living.)

There is, says Ogilvie, plenty of evidence that people take risks for all of these reasons. "Each has received support based upon clinical experience at every level from Pop Warner football through Olympic and professional sports over the past two decades" (Ogilvie, 1974, p. 45). But this is not the whole story. If it were, we should find two things: Risk takers should score low on standard measures of mental and emotional health. Also, the different sports should vary in mental health according to the degree of risk, with the most emotionally stable athletes in the nonrisk sports and the most emotionally unstable in the risky sports. The tests and interviews do not show all this to be the case. Let us see what they do show.

Whatever risk takers may be, they are generally not stupid. Delk's study of sky divers found an average IQ in the superior range (122) (1971, pp. 12–15). Another study of mountaineers gave a similar result. Ogilvie estimates that high risk takers will score in the top 15% of the population in abstract reasoning ability. The Minnesota Multiphasic Personality Inventory and other personality tests show that risk takers have a high energy level; are not anxious, depressive, or excessively dependent; and do not worry about their health. In ability to set goals, ambition, desire for success, and drive to be regarded as exceptional, Ogilvie says risk takers will typically score in the top fifth or top quarter of the population. Some of the people he studied have been very successful in business and the professions.

Risk takers are typically aggressive and take it for granted that they will dominate situations. They are independent. Unlike the traditional establishment athlete, they are socially rebellious, reject traditional standards, and are impatient with routine.

It is in interpersonal warmth that the risk takers come closest to being emotionally deprived. In keeping with their aggressiveness, they are forthright and have a strong interest in the opposite sex, but they have slight respect for the advice of others. Though their tough mindedness and unsentimentality may seem qualities of strength, and they appear extroverted, the risk takers are nonaffiliative, that is, aren't joiners. Their typical emotional relationships, says Ogilvie, are flat—they are typically cool, reserved loners. In his study, the professional football players were an exception—warmhearted and outgoing. (This may be partly because football is a team sport, whereas the other risk activities studied are individual.)

Ogilvie says that he found no significant differences between the female and male risk takers, that they have an almost identical personality structure. He thinks that for this reason we can dismiss the idea that risk taking can be attributed to some form of masculinity device. (This does not necessarily follow: In a male chauvinist culture, which the sport world generally is, the risk-taking women might well be trying to prove that *they* are men.)

The problem is to explain the paradoxical (seemingly contradictory) behavior of people who seem to relish life but habitually and deliberately risk ending it. These risk takers, says Ogilvie, "are humans with a much greater need for stimulation and excitement who find that flirting with fate and living on the brink of their existence produce a special form of ecstasy that cannot be provided by any other form of behavior" (Ogilvie, 1973, p. 50). For them, risk taking satisfies "a tremendous need to escape from the drabness of predictability," from the "bland tensionless states associated with everyday living." This, Ogilvie says, can be true of even a 747 pilot who controls his plane via an electronic master panel, or of the surgeon or the attorney for whom the youthful challenge of putting his skill on the line has waned. "I have found from my interviews with men and women who are the best in the world in their particular field of endeavor," says Ogilvie, "that they experience little joy in life when their true ability remains uncontested. They much prefer to place their considerable talent on the line and face the ultimate truth as to their ability" (1973, p. 50).

Ogilvie's explanation receives some support from Bratton, Kinnear, and Koroluk's (1979) study of 266 members of the Calgary Section of the Alpine Club of Canada. There were two classes of members: hill walkers and rock climbers (the difference should be obvious). Both groups were asked to score on a 1 to 5 scale each of 22 reasons for climbing. The most prevalent reasons were enjoyment of fresh air, recreation and relaxation, enjoyment of scenery, exercise and physical fitness, and escape from routine. Except possibly for the last we have nothing very relevant to Ogilvie's explanation of high-risk athletes. But when the hill walkers and rock climbers were compared, the rock climbers scored much higher on reasons such as exhilaration, excitement, accomplishment and pride, challenge, self-expression, desire to test oneself, to conquer peaks, to do something that few others have done. Possibly contradicting Ogilvie's finding of no significant sex difference in the personalities of high-risk athletes, on most of these reasons the male rock climbers scored higher than the women. "This," say the authors, "is in line with the culturally defined role of the male in Western society" (Bratton, Kinnear, & Koroluk, 1979, p. 31).

Even with the rock climbers, to flirt with danger scored only 0.93 out of a possible 5.00. "To flirt with danger was important for only three young male rock climbers, thus supporting the view that most climbers play down the danger aspect of climbing" (Bratton, Kinnear, & Koroluk, 1979, p. 30). Before we accept the verbal response here as the complete gut reaction, let us remember how Guthrie minimized the risk in the Indy but also stressed the thrill of mastering danger.

Deep Play on the Mountain

An important study of a specific high-risk sport is the research conducted by John MacAloon and Mihaly Csikszentmihalyi (1983). Rock climbing is a special, technical form of mountain climbing that stresses *diretissima* (the most direct, i.e., vertical, ascent) as against a traditional roundabout climb. Rock climbing is what the philosopher Jeremy Bentham (1931) called *deep play:* "play in which the stakes are so high that it is . . . irrational for men to engage in it at all" (p. 106). It ordinarily has no audience. "No one but the climber (and other skilled climbers) knows what he has accomplished and how well. . . . Rock-climbing is thus the exact antithesis of the American preoccupation with spectator sport" (MacAloon & Csikszentmihalyi, 1983, p. 362).

MacAloon and Czikszentmihalyi studied 30 rock climbers who had an age range from 19 to 53 with a mean age of 28. Five were female and 25 male. Educationally, they ranged from high-school students to PhDs; the typical climber had a college BA. From them the researchers learned the sense of the deep activity that the philosopher would have called irrational.

What attracted the climbers to this hard and dangerous sport? In terms I used earlier in the chapter, it is a sort of existential venture, embracing the climber's whole experience of nature, self, fellow-climbers, and society. These experiences, MacAloon and Csikszent-mihalyi report, are central to rock climbing: centering of action on a limited stimulus-field, a feeling of competence and control, unambiguous feedback (an immediate sense of well-being reports that one is climbing well, an immediate sense of fear says that one is not). Awareness and action merge; there is a sense of transcending ego boundaries in what the psychologist Maslow called a peak experience (no pun intended).

In 1985, 1,591 rock climbers successfully scaled the 865 foot perpendicular face of Devil's Tower in Wyoming. Data and photo courtesy of Richard A. Guilmette.

On the mountain the climber experiences obvious danger that he or she can evaluate and control, rather than the hidden, unpredictable dangers and unrecognizable fears of life in the real world. In place of anxiety, worry, and confusion there is happiness, health, and vision. For slavery to the clock the climber exchanges a timeless sense of time out of time. Concern for the immediate, intrinsic reward of the climb itself replaces the daily carrot-and-stick concern with extrinsic social rewards. Instead of a separation of mind and body, the climber experiences a body-mind unity. Whereas in everyday life one does not understand oneself and may be at war with oneself, on the mountain there is a sense of self-integration and self-understanding. In place of isolation from nature the climber experiences oneness with nature. Direct, immediate communication with one's fellowclimbers replaces the masks, statuses, and rules of daily life. A society of intense inequality is replaced by a community of equals. In place of the superficiality of most daily concerns, up there there is a dimension of depth.

Autotelic Experience and Flow

The rock-climbing study was part of a broad program of research by Csikszentmihalyi (1975) on autotelic behavior in work and play. As contrasted with extrinsic motivation, in which the reasons for action lie outside the activity, autotelic behavior (Greek: *autos*, self; *telos*, goal) is valuable in itself. Examples of extrinsic motivation are playing for money, for fame, or to improve one's health. Autotelic motivations are pleasure in companionship, emotional release, enjoyment of the activity itself, the sense of fun.

Csikszentmihalyi's study, which was not limited to sport in the sense of audience games, included 30 rock climbers, 30 male chess players, 23 female chess players, 22 composers of modern music, 28 female modern dancers, and 40 city high-school championship basketball players.

Csikszentmihalyi asked the respondents to rank in order of importance eight motivations for their activity. For each motivation the range of possible averages for the whole group would run from 8 (ranked highest by all respondents) to 1 (ranked last by all). Table 15.1 shows three highly autotelic motivations (enjoyment of the experience, the activity itself, and development of personal skills) ranked highest and the most extrinsic motivation (prestige, regard, glamor) ranked lowest.

Table 15.1   Rankings Given to Reasons for Enjoying Activity (rock climbers, composers, modern dancers, chess players, basketball players; N = 173)

Rank	Reason	Mean
1	Enjoyment of the experience and use of skills	5.99
2	The activity itself: the pattern, the action, the world it provides	5.78
3	Development of personal skills	5.37
4	Friendship, companionship	4.77
5	Competition, measuring self against others	4.22
6	Measuring self against own ideals	3.81
7	Emotional release	3.75
8	Prestige, regard, glamor	2.49

Note: From *Beyond Boredom and Anxiety: The Experience of Play in Work and Games* (p. 15, Table 1) by M. Czikszentmihalyi, 1975, San Francisco: Jossey-Bass. Copyright 1975 by M. Czikszentmihalyi. Reprinted by permission.

At this point Csikszentmihalyi studied the differences among his different groups. In total autotelic rank, from most autotelic to most extrinsic, they ranked: 1. composers, 2. dancers, 3. rock climbers, 4. male chess players, 5. female chess players, 6. basketball players (Csikszentmihalyi, 1975, Table 2, p. 29). The most autotelic item, enjoyment of the experience and use of skills, was ranked very high by all the other groups but lower by basketball players. (The lower autotelic ranking of the basketball players may be due to the fact that basketball was the only competitive team game among the activities studied, or it may have to do with the fact that the basketball players were high-school students and thus less mature.)

In another test, the 173 subjects were asked to rank a list of 18 experiences from 1 to 18 in terms of how much they resembled their own activity. Unlike in Table 15.1, here a *low* number is autotelic. On one of these items, designing or discovering something new, the basketball players stood apart. Composers, dancers, and female chess players scored designing or discovering something new as the item most like their experience; basketball players scored it sixth, and gave playing a competitive sport first place. On another item, running a race, basketball players ranked the item second in similarity to their activity; composers scored it 16.5, extremely dissimilar. On the item making love, the answers were interesting and in line with the other results. Dancers ranked this 4.5 on a scale of 18 in similarity, rock climbers ranked it 6, and composers ranked it 6.5. Neither male nor female chess players nor basketball players could see a similarity between their activity and the experience of making love (ideally, perhaps, the most autotelic activity). The basketball players ranked lovemaking 14 on the 1 to 18 scale of similarity, male chess players ranked it 16.5, and for the female chess players making love, at 17.5 on a scale of 18, seemed to be the activity least resembling chess (Csikszentmihalyi, 1975, Table 3, p. 29). Here again, both basketball and chess are intensely competitive, win-oriented games, as contrasted with the other activities.

On the basis of his studies, Csikszentmihalyi has developed the model of the flow situation to describe activity in which extrinsic motivation is at a minimum and autotelic factors at a maximum. In the flow experience, action and awareness are merged—one does not stand apart at all and watch oneself playing, working, or whatever. Attention is intensely concentrated on a very limited field. There is a loss of self-consciousness (not of consciousness as such). One's goals are very clear and one gets an intense and immediate feedback on how well one's action is approaching them. Abstractly, flow is described by Csikszentmihalyi in this way:

In the flow state, action follows upon action according to an internal logic that seems to need no conscious intervention by the actor. He experiences it as a uniform flowing from one moment to the next in which he is in control of his actions, and in which there is little distinction between self and environment, between stimulus and response, or between past, present, and future. (1975, p. 36)

Elsewhere, he speaks of the "paradoxical feeling of simultaneously being in control and being merged within the environment." More specifically, the experience is expressed this way by a rock climber who is also a poet:

Climbing is recognizing that you are a flow. The purpose of the flow is to keep on flowing, not looking for a peak or utopia but staying in the flow. It is not a moving up but a continuous flowing; you move up only in order to keep the flow going. There is no possible reason for climbing except the climbing itself; it is a self-communication. (p. 47)

Another rock climber speaks of "one of those rare moments of almost orgiastic unity as I forget myself and become lost in action."

Csikszentmihalyi cites George Steiner's description of what it is like to fall out of flow in a chess game and then get back in flow again as demonstrated in the Fischer-Spassky world championship match:

The bright arcs of relation that weld the pieces into a phalanx, that make one's defense a poison-typed porcupine shiver into vague filaments. The cords dissolve. The pawn in one's sweating hand withers to mere wood or plastic. A tunnel of inanity yawns, boring and bottomless. As from another world comes the appalling suggestion . . . That this is, after all, "only a game." If one entertains that annihilating proposition even for an instant, one is done for. (It seemed to flash across Boris Spassky's drawn features for a fraction of a second before the sixty-ninth move of the thirteenth game.) Normally, the opponent makes his move and in that murderous movement addiction comes again. New lines of force light up in the clearing haze, the hunched intellect straightens up and takes in the sweep of the board, cacophony subsides, and the instruments mesh into union (Steiner, 1974, p. 94).

In case rock climbing and chess may seem a long way from the major spectator sports that are the main concern of this book, it may be helpful to relate the idea of flow to the novel and widely read treatment of sport as self-actualization by Timothy Gallwey (1974), a tennis pro who applied eastern philosophy to the teaching of the game. To Gallwey, a correct understanding of tennis (and of life) depends on distinguishing two selves: Self 1, which is the teller, and Self 2, which is the doer. The difference between the two selves Gallwey illustrates by the dance. With formal instruction as to which foot to put where, when, as a young man he took weeks to master the fox trot. Sometimes he would be so preoccupied with the next step that he would almost forget that he had a woman in his arms. At a disco today, a kid who may be failing both math and English can, by picking up the body language of his peers, learn the Monkey, Jerk, and Swim (all more difficult dances) in one night. The secret for tennis: The most important word in the language is let. "You trust the competence of your body and its brain, and you *let* it swing the racket. Self 1 stays out of it." Gallwey cites a personal case in which, just before a tennis match, an attractive girl phoned to break a dinner date for the third time. Neither he nor his opponent could understand the fantastic tennis Gallwey then played. It was not anger, mainly; he just played out of his mind, letting go with a "what the hell" attitude that swept his opponent off the court.

What can Self 1 do, positively, in the game of tennis and the game of life? It can help program Self 2, whose actions are based on information it has stored in its memory of past actions of itself and the observed actions of others. Self 1 can also establish goals for Self 2—for example, to break a service game by upsetting the opponent's net-rushing. Beyond this, Self 1 must trust Self 2 to react. Between points and games, Self 1 can plan. But in action Self 2 must execute. The reason, I would say: Self 1 can *talk* about flow; Self 2 *is* flow.

At this point I would like to add two illustrations of a self-realizing flow situation in a football game.

The first is John Brodie's description to Michael Murphy of his relationship to his receiver Gene Washington:

> Brodie: *We room together, and we are good friends. We've worked out a series of signals that can change even after I've begun my snap count. But most of all, I guess, is that we read each other so well. He knows where I want him to be on a given pass play. Sometimes he will run a set pattern, but at other times he has to get to a place on the field any way he can.*
>
> Murphy: *Could that place be marked by a set of coordinates, say at a particular yard line? Or is it better to say that you meet somewhere in the field of existence, in the field of your relationship, amidst all the flux on the playing field?*
>
> Brodie: *I think the more poetic way says it better—it's a highly intuitive thing. Sometimes we call a pass for a particular spot on the field, maybe to get a first down. But at other times it's less defined than that and depends upon the communication we have.*

Sometimes I let the ball fly before Gene has made his final move, without a pass route being set exactly. That's where the intuition and the communication come in. But then we don't know what the other team, what those cornerbacks and safety men, might do next. That's part of the fun of the game, not knowing what they are doing to do. The game never stops. . . . (Brodie, 1973, pp. 21-22)

Then another pass play, described by Jerry Izenberg:

. . . a man named Harlon Hill came sprinting down toward the dugout end of the [Yankee Stadium] in the final seconds of a Chicago-New York football game, which the Giants were leading, seventeen to ten. A back named Jimmy Patton matched him stride for stride, and then Hill and Patton were leaping for the ball. I saw Hill go up twice on that single play, and I saw Patton go up twice with him: I saw Hill touch the ball three times before he pulled it in, held it, and stumbled across the goal to tie the game. I remember in that brief instant, Harlon Hill was the perfect receiver and Jimmy Patton was the perfect defensive back, and never have I seen anything that more personified the artistry and competitiveness and the poetry of what two professionals can achieve in a mano a mano *confrontation. (Izenberg, 1972, pp. 221-222)*

Brodie and Washington, and Hill and Patton, illustrate what Csikszentmihalyi feels to be the main condition for the existence of flow: a proper ratio between the abilities of the performer and the demands of the situation. Here we come to the title of Csikszentmihalyi's book, *Beyond Boredom and Anxiety*. If the demands on one exceed one's aptitude and training, the result is likely to be anxiety. If aptitude and training are greater than situational demands, the performer is likely to be bored. Flow may occur when the balance is just right. Csikszentmihalyi illustrates this principle with rock climbing, in which both demand and aptitude are quantified (see Figure 15.1). Slopes are rated from F^1 (a scramble) to F^{11} (the limits of human potential). Climbers are also rated from F^1 to F^{11} in terms of the most difficult climb they have made. Faced with an F^7 slope, an F^4 climber (A) will feel worried, an F^{10} climber (C) will feel bored, and an F^6 climber (B) will experience flow. On a very hard F^{10} slope, A (F^4 skill) will feel anxious, B (F^6 skill) will be worried, and C (F^{10} skill) will be in flow.

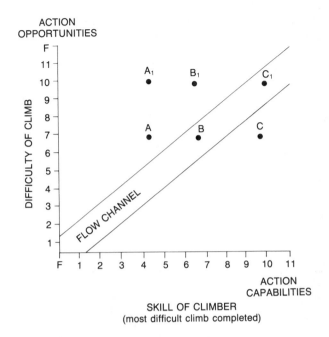

Figure 15.1 Example of Flow and Nonflow Situations in Rock Climbing. *Note.* From *Beyond Boredom and Anxiety: The Experience of Play in Work and Games* (p. 51, Figure 2) by M. Csikszentmihalyi, 1975. San Francisco: Jossey-Bass. Copyright 1975 by M. Csikszentmihalyi. Reprinted by permission.

However, Sutton-Smith thinks that the flow situation, in which competence equals challenge, is more characteristic of work than it is of play. And the situation in which abilities exceed challenge is not necessarily boredom. It can also be play:

> *In play our competence does exceed the challenge. Because of that it is a harbor to which we can retreat and envisage our possibilities rather than our real accommodations. When we rise out of play or in play tackle external objects in such a way as to be challenged excitingly (rather than to be overwhelmed or underwhelmed) then flow occurs. Flow is a state of integration with reality, play is not. (Sutton-Smith, 1979, p. 12)*

Csikszentmihalyi studied flow in other activities, beyond his original 173 cases. In rock dancing, the dimming of lights and the overpowering loudness of the music so reduce distraction as to lead many dancers to report a loss of self and a merging with the music. Because there are also other factors that impede one-mindedness, Csikszentmihalyi rates rock dancing as a shallow flow activity as compared with the deep flow of chess and rock climbing. An example he cites of the distracting factors is the uncertainty that sometimes arises as to whether a partner's moves are part of the dance or a sexual advance.

Rock dancers were subjects for a further study of flow. On the basis of interviews, Csikszentmihalyi selected dancers whom he felt would be really in flow and others whom he felt would not be. He asked the two groups to score themselves on a 4-point scale (from never to always) on their experience in rock dancing: sense of harmony with the environment, greater awareness of one's body, less awareness of distracting problems, less awareness of the passage of time, knowing what to do at all times, and getting immediate feedback from one's partner. The results showed that the in flow dancers were significantly closer to a 1–1 ratio between skill and challenge in terms of the movements, the music, the partner, and the overall activity (Csikszentmihalyi, 1975, Table 6, p. 313).

Another group of subjects was 21 surgeons. Surgery is not usually considered a form of athletics, although one of the respondents did say, "Surgery is a body contact sport, not a spectator sport." Answering the question Why do you do surgery? only a third named a cure as the main reason. Another third spoke of the challenge. A final third described their work in such terms as fun, exciting, feels great, feels real good, aesthetically pleasing, dramatic and very satisfying, like taking narcotics. They compared surgery to skiing, water skiing, mountain climbing, driving a fast car, competitive sailing, competitive softball, tennis. None of the 21 would exchange his specialty for another branch of medicine. Csikszentmihalyi sees surgery as possessing the main characteristics of flow activities: opportunities for action and enjoyment, limitation of stimulus field, clarity of goals and feedback, competence and control, transcendence of ego boundaries. All of these add up to the kind of fascination described by one surgeon: "It's incredible to put in a kidney [transplant] and have it start putting urine out even before you're closed."

Flow Experience and Social Structure

Csikszentmihalyi's subtitle is "The Experience of Play in Work and Games." He believes that the autotelic satisfaction, flow, that he has studied is possible in both. Surgery is a dramatic example, but flow can be part of the work life of the ordinary person. He cites the supermarket checker interviewed by Terkel (1975) who keeps in rhythm with

the cash register (It's like playing a piano), learns to know each cus-
tomer, and so is as absorbed as the surgeon.

The surgeon and the checker are two examples of how work in
our society can have the autotelic quality of play. Three years after the
publication of his book, Csikszentmihalyi reported interviewing a cross-
section of working people in Chicago, reading them from the book
descriptions of the flow experience, and asking them whether they had
had work experiences of this sort. Twenty-six percent said yes
(Csikszentmihalyi, 1980).

In chapter 6 we saw how the Puritan ethic rejected play as taking
time from work. Perhaps it did this, Csikszentmihalyi suggests, because work was the Puritan's game. Max Weber (1958) said of the
Protestant's money making:

> He [got] nothing out of the work for himself except the irrational
> sense of having done his job well. . . . In the field of its highest
> development, in the United States, the pursuit of work, stripped
> of its religious and ethical meanings, tends to be associated with
> . . . passions which often actually give it the character of sport.
> (pp. 71, 82)

Some work is flow, but we know that most work, as yet, is not.
What, then, is the role in society of the kind of activities that
Csikszentmihalyi has studied? Using the language of the anthropologist Victor Turner, he suggests that flow activities are antistructural
and also protostructural (Turner, 1969).

In everyday language, they *challenge* the accepted patterns of social life, and they also furnish a *model* of what it might become. He
cites the study by Clifford Geertz of the addiction to cockfighting in
Bali. The Balinese spend a great amount of time and resources training and wagering on roosters. Those who are successful gain temporary
social status. "It is," says Geertz, "a Balinese reading of Balinese experience, a story they tell about themselves" (1973, p. 418). But, says
Csikszentmihalyi, "The Balinese find true but unsettling what they
see of themselves in the cockfight. The cockfight displays the social
order in a new light" (1975, p. 97). A parallel example would be athletes like George Sauer, Dave Meggyesy, Chip Oliver, Bill Walton, and
others who in the last 15 years have come to see the structure of organized sport as an expression of a violent and competitive culture and
have rejected both.

The protostructural function of flow goes beyond criticism and rejection. The autotelic experience provides a model for change in the
normative order—the system of cultural norms and institutions. "Deep
play and other complex flow activities are like laboratories in which
new patterns of experience are tested" (Csikszentmihalyi, 1975, p. 93).

*In chess the structure involves the actor through intellectual com-
petition, in climbing, danger draws the actor into physical and
mental concentration. In each case, the person discovers a state
of being which is rare in normative life. The comparison affords
a relativizing perspective on the culture in which one is usually
immersed. (Csikszentmihalyi, 1975, pp. 99–100)*

This confrontation is stated very strongly by a mountain climber:

*Too many stimuli in the world, it's a smog, a quagmire. In civili-
zation man doesn't really live reality. One never thinks about the
universe and man's place in it . . . you think about cars, schools,
parties. . . .*
  *The mountains and nature bombard the mind with the ques-
tion of what man is meant to be doing. The fact that man's mind
freaks out in civilizations shows how abnormal and unhealthy they
can be. We are the animals that have been the most fucked up
in the last thousand years. Up there you know you're right, down
here you think you're right. (Csikszentmihalyi, 1975, p. 95)*

What do you know up there? Play or work for extrinsic motivations of status, money, and power are self-defeating. "Status differen-
tials tend to follow a zero-sum pattern: The psychic benefits for those
who get recognized are paid for by the decreased self-respect of those
who do not" (Csikszentmihalyi, 1975, p. 4). Play, says Csikszentmihalyi, should be the model for a positive-sum society, where in work
and play everybody wins, because all experience flows together.
  What this might mean concretely is expressed by George Leonard
in interpreting the views of a tennis instructor, Dyveke Spino:

*She suggested the possibility of considering the person on the
other side of the net not as your opponent but as your partner.
In this context, a well-hit ball becomes a gift of energy, freely delivered. The gift may be returned, then exchanged again and again,
linking the two players in a single energy field. The breathing of
the two can be synchronized, with each player exhaling as the ball
leaves [his] racket and inhaling upon its return.*
  *Does this mean that you always hit the ball to the other player's
strong side so that it is more likely to be returned? Far from it.
In actual play you hit the ball to your partner's weakness, to the
underdeveloped area of the energy field, and you expect the same.
Thus both of you have the opportunity to achieve more of your
potential and the total field between you is strengthened.*

You might also be a "winner," which could be all to the good. But I can't help thinking that there are ways of keeping score that don't appear on the sports page. (Leonard, 1974, p. 107)

Speaking of the antistructural aspects of our experience, Turner describes them as

the liberation of human capacities . . . from the normative require-ments incumbent upon occupying a sequence of social statuses, enacting a multiplicity of social roles, and being acutely conscious of membership in some corporate group such as a family, lineage, clan, tribe, or nation. . . , or of affiliation with some pervasive so-cial category such as a class, caste, sex- or age-division. (Turner, 1983, p. 147)

I like especially the sport simile through which he describes the protostructural peak experience: "There is an instant of pure poten-tiality when everything trembles in the balance like the moment when the trembling quarterback with all the 'options' sees a very solid future moving menacingly toward him." (p. 147)

Chapter 16

*A*thlete and Spectator

Many Americans worship at the church of sports. Services are held for each personal belief, whether it be football, racing, golf, or diving. One is thrilled by the splendor of the occasion and the beauty of the surroundings. On the walls hang the trappings and accounts praising past heroes. The offering freely asked is cheerfully given. The renditions of the colorfully clothed musicians stir one to action. Dramatically delivered is the powerful image of overcoming the adversary. Here each is brought to his own style of fulfillment. As one turns to leave, one muses, It is good to have been here, for I have felt the power. (Cheska, 1979)

Agon and Athlete

The sense of self-realization in sport, as elsewhere, always involves a relationship to other people, to spectators present or absent. A sporting event is a dramatic ritual, an *agon*, of which the actions of the watchers are as much a part as are those of the performers. In a 1977 article on the corruption of sport Christopher Lasch critizes the view, seemingly held by some critics of modern sport, that spectators are irrelevant to the success of the game. "The attainment of certain skills," says Lasch, "unavoidably gives rise to an urge to show them off . . . the performer wishes . . . to ratify a supremely difficult accomplishment, to give pleasure, to forge a bond between himself and his audience, a shared appreciation of a ritual executed not only flawlessly, but with much feeling and with a sense of style and proportion" (Lasch, 1977, pp. 24, 25).

Social psychologists generally hold that our self-feeling depends on others who mirror us to ourselves. To William James, the self-sense was always social; we have as many selves as we have groups significant to us. In the absence of supporting social groups, a fantasied observer—God—may support our sense of fitness in our selves. Charles

Horton Cooley used the simile of the "looking glass self"—what we feel ourselves to be is what we perceive others see us to be. George Herbert Mead said that to have a satisfying self is to receive a sense of satisfaction from significant other people who observe our activity. Later research in social psychology has verified and supported these early insights.

The critics of whom Lasch speaks sometimes talk as though large sport audiences were something peculiar to the 20th century. However, audiences much outnumbering the performers were part of the game scene at Papremus, at Olympia, at the Roman Coliseum, and at the medieval tournament. In these rituals, past and present, spectators have never been purely passive onlookers. As well as furnishing a mirror by which performers judge their own performance, crowd response stimulates and intimidates. If this were not true, it would not be a general principle in sport that home teams usually win. The agony and ecstasy of spectators shapes the outcome of the *agon* on the field, so that bad guys (visiting teams) generally lose.

What *is* different about contemporary sport we can visualize by thinking of a continuum of spectator participation. At one end is the informal gathering of people who may casually observe a pickup game. The modern critics of sport, with whom Lasch disagrees, appear to idealize this kind of game situation, except that to some it would seem to be best if nobody were watching at all. In the middle of the continuum is the stadium crowd—Olympia, Coliseum, Yankee Stadium, Superdome. At the far end is something peculiar to the 20th century— the radio or television audience of scattered observers. The difference between being part of a crowd of even 100,000, which is still an interacting group, and being part of an absent audience of 100 million separated viewers, is one of the most critical changes this century has brought to sport. Modern media of communication (telegraph in the late 19th century, radio and TV in the 20th) have created audiences that are not only much vaster but are also absent and incapable of interacting immediately with the athlete on the field, or with one another.

In addition to the agonizing crowd, the athlete of today has a *public*. What difference does this make for his experience of self-actualization? The athlete does not hear the fan at home in front of the TV set when he blasts one out of the park, smashes a service ace, or makes an acrobatic catch of a forward pass. But he hears from him eventually, and Lasch believes that what he hears is reliable. Lasch argues that the modern sport audience, mainly composed of men who took part in sport as boys "and thus acquired a sense of the game and the capacity to make discriminating judgments," are a more trustworthy judge of quality than are the viewers of drama, dance, and painting, for which skilled amateurs make up only a small part of the audience.

Hans Lenk, in his *Philosophy of Sport* (1973) says that the presence of spectators emphasizes the seriousness of sport. He attaches great importance to the spectator's emphatic sharing of the athlete's movements. Francis Keenan combines this idea with Lasch's and observes that "the competent observer can follow a performer sympathetically, if not overtly, in his body. He has prior movement experience of a similar nature" (Keenan, 1975, p. 41). Lasch says that the true sport fan can distinguish between the committed performer and the grandstander. Thus judgments by sport fans, unlike those of followers of the arts, are little influenced by fad and fashion, novelty and shock appeal. (Lasch's impressions are, incidentally, not supported by Harold Charnovsky's study of about 15% of all active major league baseball players, whom he found believing that "adult fans are 'squares,' people who lack understanding of baseball or the men who play it. They are seen as uninformed, naive, and volatile, as fickle as the weather, and to be trusted even less" (Charnovsky, 1968, p. 52).

Sport as Tragic Drama

A sport event can be a tragic ritual *agon*, a dramatization of the struggle of human beings with nature or of the struggle of good people against antisocial people. In both the American Indian games analyzed in chapter 4 and the original territorial games discussed in chapter 5, both elements were present: the good guys on the side of nature or the gods against the bad guys. By saying that sport can be a tragic drama I mean that it is a symbolic experience of the ultimate human condition. We touched on this theme in chapter 14. Cheska calls the sport spectacular a "ritual model of power," "a tenseness of victory and defeat communicated within the compressed arena of time and space" (1978, pp. 51, 54, 66). In "The Athletic Contest as a Tragic Form of Art," Keenan says, "The tragedy teaches us that for many men the ultimate achievement is defeat and that the highest level of performance, the most noble effort, may end in defeat" (1975, p. 51). The competitors are antagonistic collaborators in the existential drama. "The 'other' athlete is not 'another,' but . . . is a participant in the same order of consciousness as are the victors. Both 'achieve' and fail to 'achieve.' . . . The athlete who is second best symbolizes both excellence and failure" (Keenan, 1975, pp. 48, 51). A football game like the 1984 Nebraska-Miami confrontation in the Orange Bowl illustrates exactly such a community in tragic drama. Such a tragic agon has a number of elements:

- The certainty that one performer, no matter how excellent, will lose

- The tragic flaw that may undo even the most excellent player
- The spectacular reversal of game momentum by which defeat may be snatched from the jaws of victory
- The player's recognition, in action, of his identity, the revelation of his ultimate strengths and limitations as an athlete—and as a person
- The ability of the tragic loser to turn a natural defeat into a spiritual victory by contending to the end
- The pity, fear, and empathic sharing in the transcendence of Fate through which the *agon* may cleanse the spectator

Because the *agon* is a microcosm of the spectator's life (all spectators' lives), it appeals to and enriches that life. It does this better than the stage play because the state must rely on imitation; athletics present life first hand and thereby increase the drama.

Keenan points out that "athletic contests, like dramatic tragedy, are divided into time periods of varying length. Periods, quarters, halves, innings are the counterpart of the 'acts' of drama" (1975, p. 46). Cheska (1979) spells out further the elements in the "sport spectacular":

- *Like the regularly repeated national celebrations (Memorial Day, Independence Day, Thanksgiving) and religious holidays (Sundays, Easter, Christmas) sport drama is likely to be part of a regularly repeated athletic pattern (Super Bowl, Wimbledon, World Cup, World Series).*
- *As Huizinga said, the sport drama takes place within a set of rules that are considered absolutely binding, and determine who is the legitimate victor in the agon. Brickman (see chapter 14) would very likely agree with Cheska that "a sport event represents one of the remarkable displays of fair play known today" (p. 59).*
- *The whole situation is ritualized so as to charge everyone up emotionally into communal participation or group unity transcending individual existence. Two collectivities (players, band, cheerleaders, spectators) have a sense of belongingness within their own group and separateness from the other collectively. Thus, in modern life, the sport spectacular produces in an impersonal society the kind of communal sense that existed before the growth of industry and cities.*
- *A dramatic make-believe transforms the actors (athletes) into superhuman creatures who must perform on a more-than-human level lest the drama be brought down to earth and shattered.*

• *The importance of the drama is that it symbolizes the power struggles of everyday life (see chapter 14). Because the game is like the real world but isn't actually the real world, spectators can, through the supermen on the field, exercise power without the problems and dangers that accompany power in real life. Also, "the simplicity of a game stands in orderly contrast to the complicated, confused, chaotic real world of power transactions. In the real world of social transactions it is difficult to know if one has won or lost." (Cheska, 1979, p. 57)*

The sport spectacular is so attractive because it is a metaphor, as it was described in chapter 3: A (the agon) is like B (real-life conflicts), but it is also not like B.

The Athlete as Hero

As Cheska says, a part of the tragic drama is heroic acts performed by athletes. What is a sport hero? A Polish sport sociologist (Swierczewski, 1978) and an American physical educator (Smith, 1973) have both addressed the question of how the athletic hero is related to his sport and to his audience.

Swierczewski begins an article on the international athlete by telling what the sport hero is *not*. He is not an entertainer. Swierczewski argues strongly that the typically American conception of the athlete as entertainer will not fit such facts as the letters that he read in a study of Polish soccer players, written by fans about a dramatic soccer victory over England. An entertainer is "somebody representing the prowess of athletes in a given country, their physical strength, agility, nimbleness, sometimes even gracefulness and charm" (1978, p. 90). He is admired as a culture hero like members of a rock group, film actors, heroes of cartoons, people jumping a motorcycle over a number of cars or trying to master Niagara Falls. Swierczewski contrasts this kind of adulation with that of the Polish fans who compared their feelings after the Wembley stadium victory with their feelings at the end of World War II. Anyone who can produce that kind of reaction, says Swierczewski, is no mere entertainer.

Neither is the true sport hero what Zygulski (1973) called the "hero of the day." As an example of such a hero, Swierczewski suggests a brave airline stewardess who is the only survivor of a disastrous plane crash. He says an athlete can be this kind of hero but does not illustrate how. I would suggest Bobby Thomson, whose dramatic clutch home run won the 1951 pennant for the New York Giants. That single event did not make Thomson the kind of hero that another giant, Willie Mays, subsequently became over a long stretch of years.

The true athletic hero, Swierczewski believes, is best described by Stefan Czarnowski's definition: A hero is a man who within certain rites, due to services rendered during his life or by his death, possesses powers influencing a certain group or cause, of which he is a represen- tative and the personification of its basic social value (1954, Vol. 4, p. 30). This true hero is a *moral* hero. "The perfection of a hero," says Czarnowski, "consists in the fact that he fully represents some strict- ly defined value" central to his culture (1954, p. 15). The particular moral quality that makes a hero varies with his society. Of the ancient world, Czarnowski says,

> *The characters in Homer win the title of heroes thanks to physi- cal strength, cleverness, and cunning. In a later period of this same Greek civilization heroes turn into the personification of the moral ideal. Finally, in the Greek-Roman world the heroes are above all philosophers, mystics, and moralists and simultaneously the Chris- tians begin to glorify their martyrs and ascetics. (1954, p. 15)*

The hero need not die to be heroic, but a choice of values involv- ing self-sacrifice helps. Swierczewski cites the case of the Polish cyclist Szozda, seriously injured in a race crash, who got out-patient medical treatment, including a leg bandage and anaesthetic, and then rode on. The applause in favor of Szozda gained momentum with each lap, celebrating his solution to "the conflict between the health value and success in sport." (Playing over pain for Alma Mater is also, of course, a hero-producing factor in the United States.)

Another important element in heroism is the underdog factor— athletes in the role of David versus Goliath are easily worshiped, as were the Poles who upset the British at Wembley (or, we could add, the 1980 U.S. hockey team upsetting the Russians at Lake Placid). Another interesting thing about the hero that Swierczewski empha- sizes is his dual image in the media: exposé of his all-too-human qual- ities along with his glorification as superhuman:

> *In both cases we deal with the same human being, in the physical sense, nevertheless in the second case . . . the athlete is being en- nobled. He is being raised to the dignity of a hero. Obviously the transformation from an "entertainer" into a hero is no guarantee of eternal glory for the given athlete. (p. 98)*

Garry Smith's (1973) treatment of sport heroes builds on O. E. Klapp's general study of heroes (1962, 1969) and relates hero types to the collision between old culture and counterculture introduced in chapter 2. Smith outlines some of the qualities that can make a hero. One is exceptional talent. He agress with Swierczewski that the hero is much more than a highly skilled entertainer. In speaking of a number of extremely talented athletes, he uses the word awesome, which makes the ability possessed by an individual or team more than merely mortal. If, he suggests, this quality persists year after year, as in Gordie Howe, Bart Starr, Stan Musial, and Billy Casper, sheer ability may eventually lead to hero status. Like Swierczewski, Smith refers to the man of the hour—again, Thomson, and "Ken Dryden almost singlehandedly winning a Stanley Cup for Montreal in 1971" (Smith, 1973, p. 66). Playing superlatively despite a handicap is also hero-making: Ben Hogan transcending a near-fatal auto accident and Jackie Robinson a black skin. Flair or charisma is another factor—Arnold Palmer's cavalry charges, Willie Mays' basket catches, and Bobby Orr's unique defensive style.

From Klapp, Smith takes three relationships of heroes to their followers: reinforcement, seduction, and transcendence.

Reinforcement keeps the individual within the social structure and directs him toward socially approved goals. Seduction keeps the individual within societal bounds, but tempts him to break rules. Transcendence takes the individual outside of the societal structure, and provides him with a new identity, new experiences, and new norms. (Smith, 1973, p. 61)

Before the counterculture, Smith points out, sport heroes were usually reinforcers and role models for the dominant cultural values: "decent, honorable, unassuming individuals . . . usually quiet, respectable family men who personify middle class values" (1973, p. 66). From my own youth, I would take as examples two men who embodied the basic values of the 19th-century America out of which baseball grew: Christy Mathewson, whose obituary I noted in chapter 13—a superbly talented, clean-cut, Christian young man; and Lou Gehrig, a gifted German-American lad, son of a steel worker, who adored his mother, rarely missed a school day from grade school through Columbia University, established a consecutive game record that will probably never be broken, and eventually almost died in uniform.

Smith points out that in the 1950s and 1960s football, for reasons I discussed in chapter 12, became the sport of the highly bureaucratized times. In all sports, highly efficient and rationalized teams like the Green Bay Packers, New York Yankees, and Boston Celtics were heroic because of their efficient dominating over competitors in the same marketplace. Sport heroes emerged who were the equivalent of business executives (remember the description of Arnold Palmer in chapter 12).

The counterculture of the late 1960s rejected all this. The years since the rise of the counterculture have tended toward seductive heroes, Smith feels. "Some modern sports heroes are brash and arrogant, they are people who have supreme confidence in their ability and often can back it up" (Smith, 1973, p. 66). He considers Joe Namath and Muhammad Ali to be examples. Swinging antiheroes like Namath and Dwight Sanderson were antiheroes in the sense of rejecting both the Mathewson-Gehrig and corporate lifestyles; and they were heroes in the sense of being talented, famous, and rich countercultural role models. "Both have penchants for the limelight and the more they irk the older generation, the more they are lionized by the young." As role models, they "may induce young men to bend the rules and flaunt the established order" (Smith, 1973, p. 67).

Smith believes that transcendent heroes are very rare among athletes. "An athlete hero normally does not have the power to take his followers outside the bounds of the social structure to produce a person with a new identity" (1973, p. 67).

Using Turner's terms from the previous chapter, the years since the countercultural push of the late 1960s have produced a number of antistructural heroes but no outstanding protostructural hero to envision and model a new sport order. Although Csikszentimihalyi says that "no one would suggest that the course of American culture has been seriously affected by the small band of visionaries [rock] climbing has produced," (Mac Aloon & Csikszentmihalyi, 1983, p. 381) possibly from flow experiences on a mountain or elsewhere a protostructural hero may appear.

Agon and Spectator

We have seen so far that an audience of some sort is indispensable for the athlete's self-realization as a player. What, in turn, does the athlete contribute to the self-actualization of the spectator? This can be boiled down to several basic questions: (a) Does sport make the spectator more passive or more active?, (b) How does sport affect his health?, (c) Does it make him more or less violent?, and (d) How does it affect his social power?

The answer in each case will be different according to the kind of spectator we are talking about. The biggest difference is between the participating spectator-at-the-event and the nonparticipating watcher-at-home (or elsewhere). Even at the event itself there are several kinds of spectators, as suggested by Leonard Koppett (1973). Koppett distinguishes the rooter, the bettor, the analyst, and the thrill-seeker.

The rooter is blindly loyal to ''his'' team. He attaches to the team the same emotions that the patriot attaches to country. For the rooter, we may add, the game is significant because, as Sutton-Smith puts it, the game may invert the social experience of everyday life—those who are daily losers can be winners by identification with their heroes. A good example is the meaning for New Yorkers of the 1969 Jets and Mets. Another is Hans Hermann's study of East German soccer fans, whom he found participating as compensation for feelings of dissatisfaction and deprivation in their work or school life. He explains that this is why there is such an excessive representation among the fans of those who have had bad experience at school (Hermann, 1978). Other examples are in chapter 14: Goldaber's observation about the relationship between empty lives and sport identification in the 1970s and Pearton and Gaskell's discussion of the meaning of soccer team identification for British working-class youth.

The bettor can be either a professional or a personal wagerer. Like the rooter, says Koppett, the bettor is interested primarily in who wins, rather than in how the game is played. He may love good playing, but is primarily a businessman. Sometimes, like three fascinating gamblers whom Michener accompanied to the Liberty Bell racetrack in eastern Pennsylvania, he may rarely watch a race but quietly pocket his winnings, with no communication beyond a standard, ''I'm making expenses'' (Michener, 1977). His difference from the rooter is that his loyalty is determined by the team he bets for, which may change from game to game.

The analyst is the spectator whose ego trip involves knowledge of strategies, statistics, and esoteric information, all of which make him a more or less disinterested expert observer.

The armchair quarterback plays a game of wits. He anticipates action and attempts strategic decision as if he were coaching or actually playing. He parades his expertise by announcing proper actions in advance of actual occurrence; when his pronouncements find concurrence with actual events, the spectator is fulfilled and delighted with the drama. The action becomes in a sense, imitative of his forecasts and representative of his will. (Keenan, 1975, p. 46)

The thrill-seeker is awaiting the circus catch (in baseball or football), the homer with the sacks loaded, the backboard-shattering slam dunk, the 60-foot three-point basket at the closing buzzer, the spectacular accident on the speedway, the 70-yard punt that bounces out of bounds on the 1-yard line.

In terms of activity and passivity, we have seen that the spectator-at-the-event tends to be emotionally and vocally involved in the agon. This will probably be truer for the rooter, the bettor, and the thrill-seeker than for the analyst. But the analyst too is a mirror for the participant's self-sense. He is adept at comparing today's performances with the great (or lousy) performances of the past. Particularly if he is a media writer or broadcaster, he is actively engaged. (No one is going to accuse Howard Cosell of being a passive bystander). The spectator-at-home, of whatever type, is not active in the sense of giving immediate feedback to the players or giving and receiving it in interaction with other fans. Being a viewer of TV may lead a person to become actively engaged in attending sports. But it may not. In 1954 the National Opinion Research Center found that over half the public (who had much less TV exposure then than now) had never attended an intercollegiate football game, that in any given season only one in seven attended, and that only one in five was an active fan (rooter). We must remember that in chapter 6 we saw that throughout this century the rise of commercial spectator sport has at times been paralleled by increase in mass sport participation (as the intensive commercialization of tennis on TV in the 1970s was matched by a boom in sales of tennis equipment and a spread of tennis participation beyond the old leisure classes). So in many ways the late-20th-century spectator is not the passive dolt he has been caricatured as being.

The fact that the spectator is much less physically and emotionally inert than the stereotype says something about the effect of spectatoritis on health. Although some of the evidence cited in chapter 14 may raise doubts, the athlete on the field is likely to work off the stress of agon physically and directly, whereas the equally stressed fan in the stands does not. Players rarely drop dead in a game; fans on occasion do. In chapter 1, I suggested that although much has been made of the danger of athlete's heart, it appears that over the long run the development of supplementary blood supply to the heart muscle is likely to make the athlete a lesser coronary risk than the fan. The same would be likely to be true for other diseases of stress.

In chapter 14 we explored at length the experimental evidence on whether sport makes players and/or spectators more or less violent. The evidence did not seem to support the theory of catharsis, particularly for spectators. One of my football players commented that the average American's reason for coming to see football played "is really no different than the Romans watching the lions eat the Christians or the gladiators killing each other." Is this self-realization? Michael Novak would say, in a way, yes: Football brings everybody face to face with his own usually hidden inner violence. It may be, however, that it obscures one's more loving potentialities.

In chapter 11 we examined how sport is related to social power. Our emphasis was more on the athlete than on the spectator. We found that sport serves as a ladder of upward escalation for a few members of socially powerless groups, and that the upward mobility, as well as often increasing income and status, identifies the athlete with an athletic subculture that is exploitative, authoritarian, militarist, racist, and sexist.

Spectators share this upward mobility with athletes vicariously, that is, by identifying with their success. Do they thereby realize themselves more adequately? Some, like Novak, would say yes. He believes that it is healthy and positive for blacks, who are shut out of ordinary professional and business opportunities, to be able to identify with black basketball players who are running rings around their white opponents. Others would say that success by identification with successful black athletes, as with other successful black entertainers, makes it easier for blacks to accept their exclusion from other high-status careers. This, particularly, is the case for young blacks who could be successful physicians, lawyers, or architects but who are sidetracked into futile efforts to become Kareem Abdul-Jabbars, Reggie Jacksons, or Mean Joe Greenes.

Koppett compares the fan's loyalty to his local team to the patriot's unquestioning devotion to country. Through his team's success, the fan achieves a triumph that could never be his in real life, outside sport. Consider the Detroit fan, as seen by Denny McLain, the major leagues' most recent 30-game winner:

> *Detroit's not a sophisticated city. It's a factory town. It's a blue collar place. The fans seem to have a closer identification with the player.*
>
> *They don't go away for weekends, they go to the ballyard. Their release is their favorite sports team, not a yacht or a trip to Acapulco. They live and die with their guys on the field, and they're a hardy group of sometimes rowdy, sometimes hard-drinking and leather-lunged people. (McLain, 1975, pp. 199–200)*

As McLain says, Detroit is a blue-collar factory city. Specifically, it is an automobile city. A writer, Harvey Swados, worked on the assembly line in an auto plant to get background for his novel, *On the Line* (1957). If some day you buy a new car, says Swados, and along with the familiar new car smell there is a strange rotting odor, there may be no dark mystery. An assembly line worker, fed up with his job, may have had no better way to strike back than to leave his unfinished lunch in the body of a car as it went by him down the line. The same worker, on a weekend when his team was a contender, might be rowdy and leather-lunged at the ball park, and live and die with the team on the field. These factors, coupled with unemployment in the auto industry, may throw light on the rioting after the 1984 World Series.

Or take another worker with another job in another city, in a steel mill in Pittsburgh. As has been found of American workers in general, this steeler probably hates his job and certainly finds in everyday life no triumph that can approach the four Super Bowl victories of the Steelers football team.

Or, a touching little story, told by Woody Hayes, about a Filipino girl, married to a graduate student at Ohio State, who turns down her husband's suggestion that she sell their football tickets for $100:

> *Here's a little girl who wouldn't earn a hundred dollars in a week, and yet she's gonna work a week to see Ohio State play football because that was her only connection with Ohio State University. She was off campus all week. Her husband was on campus. But here was her connection—Ohio State football on Saturday, in there with 88,000 people. She's a little girl a half a world away, who comes to America, and the thing she likes best is football. (Seiden, 1977, p. C1)*

As good a profile of a fan as I have ever seen is James Michener's description of Herman Fly, a German-American locomotive plant worker. Herman's odyssey, recounted in typical Michenerian style, embraces the fall of two great Connie Mack baseball teams in 1914 and 1931; the departure of the As to Kansas City and thence to Oakland (where Herman's allegiance still followed them); Fly's final switch to the basketball 76ers and at age 70 to the hockey Flyers.

> *Herman Fly never knew the joy of positive participation, but that he derived spiritual pleasure from being a mere spectator, there can be no doubt. In an age when big-league franchises were being callously shifted in order to pick up a few more dollars, he was unique in continuing to pay his devotion to a team which had abandoned him. . . . For the small amount of money he spent each year on his admissions, Fly received a maximum return. For him, sports were a bargain. (Michener, 1977, pp. 42–43)*

To what degree are all these experiences of spectators self-actualization? In the early days of European football, when local pick-up teams contested from one village green to another, a local citizen might have cheered them on with some meaningful sense that his neighbors' victory was his own. When my small college team won the state baseball championship over the state university in 1936, in the days I described in the opening pages of chapter 1, all of the victors were walk-ons who shared my classes and dormitory and my identification with them was easy, reasonable, and gratifying. But when Detroit factory workers identify with baseball professionals who are Detroiters only temporarily, by contract, or Pittsburgh steel workers rise and fall with the fortunes of similarly hired diamond and gridiron aficiandos, or a Filipino girl finds the meaning of Ohio State University in a group of semiprofessionals, most of whose only real tie to the institution is an athletic scholarship, there is none of the same kind of organic connection, and it is hard to see how these people realize *themselves*.

Are Sport Spectacles Corrupt?

At the beginning of this chapter I referred to the idea that games would be better off without spectators. I said that this view runs counter to the basic principles of social psychology. However, it seems to be held by a number of concerned and competent people. What truth can we find, then, in the notion that in becoming spectacles games have been corrupted?

Lasch agrees that there is some basic corruption in modern sport. Games are corrupted, he believes, when in order to appeal to a mass that doesn't really understand or care for the game promoters introduce *irrelevancies*. Exploding baseball scoreboards are an example. The midget whom Bill Veeck sent up to bat for the White Sox would be another. So would cheerleaders without bras and bat girls in short shorts, who have nothing to do with the skillful playing of football or baseball. Encouragement of deliberate rough play and fighting draws to the hockey arena people who have no real appreciation of a well-played game. Lasch believes the game is corrupted whenever it is shaped to attract mass audiences rather than to promote the best play. Artificial tennis courts make possible profitable all-weather tournaments in unnatural surroundings, like Caesar's Palace, rather than promoting the fastest and most skillful play, as does grass. World Series night games geared to TV prime time and played in freezing weather change the whole nature of the summer game for both players and fans. The American League's designated hitter rule is aimed to promote high scoring that is supposed to be crowd-pleasing rather than demanding that a hurling ace be a completely rounded performer.

Sport is corrupted, says Lasch, when the *unpredictability* that is central to a good game is lost. This may happen, as in the fixed wrestling match, when the contest becomes pure show biz, a ritualized good guy-bad guy drama devoid of surprise. Sport may become routine

when the dread of losing becomes so uppermost, as it understandably does with some coaches, that management "makes every effort
to eliminate the risk and the uncertainty that contribute so centrally
to the ritual and dramatic success of any contest." "When sports,"
says Lasch, "can no longer be played with appropriate abandon, they
lose the capacity to raise the spirits of players and spectators, to transport them into a higher realm. Prudence and calculation, so prominent in everyday life but so inimical to the spirit of games, come to
shape sports as they shape everything else" (Lasch, 1977, p. 30). Several dull "Stupor Bowls" of the past are an example.

Some observers also feel that sport is corrupted when the medium
event displaces the stadium event (Brien R. Williams's terms). To
understand this, let us first go back to the times when 19th-century
industrialism in the United States created an urban mass with no opportunity for the healthy play of town and country, who flocked to
the stadium to get their exercise and experience their agon vicariously
through the professionals on the fields. Although the same industrialism found that profit could also be made by selling baseball bats, foot-
balls and basketballs, tennis rackets and golf clubs, bikinis and
tanksuits, snow and water skis, and jogging shoes, the fan who uses
none of these himself, but only sits and roots, is still with us. To the
extent that hired hands do people's playing and take their exercise for
them, professionalism in sport is itself a corruption. Columnist Sydney
Harris agrees with Huizinga that play is a central and vital human activity but feels that for grown men to play games for money before
passive onlookers is a perversion.

> "Professional sports" don't interest me, because I think that the
> phrase is a contradiction in terms. . . . It is good and necessary
> that men should work for a living. It is a monstrous perversion
> that men should play for a living. . . . In true sports, the contes-
> tants are ranged against each other. In professional sports, they
> are ranged against the public. The ultimate object is to attract as
> many customers as possible. They are merchandisers and
> promoters and box-office accountants. . . .
>   This is not to say that the players do not enjoy playing, or the
> spectators do not enjoy watching; but their enjoyment has lost the
> innocence it had for children—which means it has lost precisely
> the healing and redeeming quality that makes it good. (Harris,
> 1975, p. 140)

The 19th-century industrial worker at the ballpark was less active
physically than the farmer or than the athlete on the field, but he was
still there. In the late 20th century McLain's leather-lunged blue col-
larites are still at Tiger Stadium and the Silverdome, but most of the

audience (sometimes as much as 99.9%) is not present. (I take my figure from the 1980 Super Bowl, where a little more than 100,000 fans watched in the Rose Bowl and about 100 million on the tube, and from Snyder and Spreitzer's [1983] report that on a typical fall Sunday about 750,000 fans watch pro football in a stadium and about 22 million watch it on TV). We do not have to have the view seemingly held by Jack Scott, Paul Hoch, Lewis Mumford, and Gregory Stone, that only spontaneous play for fun without an audience is healthy, to see this as unhealthy. Michener argues that athletic stadia should be located downtown rather than in the suburbs because the ballpark crowd is about the only place where the isolated city dweller can get a concrete sense of community and civic pride! (Michener, 1977). By contrast with watching a game from the stands, Michener would see watching it in front of TV as corruption.

Let's look at two examples of medium events as compared with stadium events.

- *Baseball:* The fan does not see the half of what is going on to make baseball the pleasure it has become in 100 years. The televiewer lacks freedom; seeing baseball by television is too confining, for the novelty would not hold up for more than an hour, if it were not for the commentator. . . . What would old timers think of such a turn of affairs—baseball from a sofa! Television is too safe. There is no ducking the foul balls. (Dunlap, 1939)
- *Football:* The networks with their zeppelins and zoom lenses, their dreamlike instant replays of color and violence have changed football from a remote college pastime to something like voyeurism.

No matter how fine his TV reception, no beer and armchair quarterback can hope to see the true games. For all the paraphernalia, the tube rarely shows an overview; pass patterns and geometric variations are lost in a kaleidoscopic of close-ups and crunches. (Kanter, 1973, pp. 54–55)

Do today's fans object? Although it removes them from the true context of the sport situation, Susan Birrell and John Loy comment, "the American spectator seems more than happy to accept the television sport experience. . . . Television has trained America to focus on particular bits of action and ignore, or perhaps never come into meaningful contact with a live event experience. Perhaps this explains why many disgruntled fans leave a live game complaining that they could have seen it better on television" (Birrell & Loy, 1979, p. 13).

Jeffrey Goldstein and Brenda Bredemeier (1977) have made a strong argument that medium sports corrupt spectators by overemphasizing game *outcome* over the *process* of play. Most sports on the media, they remind us, are zero-sum games (see chapter 3). With the exception of diving, figure skating, and gymnastics, the style of the activity itself is subordinated to the question, Who wins? This is all related to the process by which the media have come to pay the bill for college and professional team sports: Winning records get TV contracts, losers do not. Viewers, young and old, take the professional orientation as the model for their own interest and activity. Goldstein and Bredemeier believe that this is to the economic interest of the networks, because if people learned to put process ahead of outcome, they might prefer to play sports themselves rather than watch the pros on TV.

Relating Goldstein and Bredemeier to studies we have previously discussed, medium sports accentuate the process by which Webb found interest in skill and fairness giving way to the need to win. In Ciuciu's language, they socialize their viewers for organized, as against extemporized, games. They promote the lifestyle that Coakley found in organized children's sports and discourage the orientation that he found in informal children's games. As psychologists, Goldstein and Bredemeier judge that emphasis on outcome undermines the personal pleasure that people might get out of the process of participating in sport. (Their view has experimental support in a 1973 study in which Lepper, Greene, and Nesbitt found that a group of elementary school children who were rewarded for performance in a play activity had significantly less interest in performing the activity in free time than did a control group who were not rewarded.) Goldstein and Bredemeier believe that emphasis on outcome spreads the philosophy of the athletic subculture that we discussed in chapter 10: "There is little room in this schema for also-rans, liberals, and females."

Depersonalization, Violence, Quality, and the Media

Another influence of the media that may be regarded as corrupting is the *substitution of another person's perception for the fan's own experience.* How this happens was dramatically illustrated by an experience that Paul Comisky, Jennings Bryant, and Dolf Zillman (1977) had in trying to select "aggressive" and "normal" segments of a hockey game for an experimental study on violence. The researchers made their selection by viewing the segments as one ordinarily watches TV. When they split the video and sound tracks, they discovered to their surprise that the segment they had rated aggressive really had very little rough action but that the announcer had managed to convince them that "we were witnessing rough and tough ice hockey at its best, with the action threatening to turn into fisticuffs at any minute" (p. 151).

The segment that they had labeled normal contained several very rough incidents, but the announcer had let the action carry itself with no dramatic buildup. That experienced sport psychologists were so taken in makes it more impressive than it would have been had it happened to their student subjects.

Two contrasting views of this kind of phenomenon are illustrated by Howard Cosell's statement that the job of ABC announcers is to create entertainment and by NBC's experiment in broadcasting a whole football game without commentary so that the medium fan became, in effect, a stadium fan.

The reverse process, whereby the stadium fan becomes a medium fan, is illustrated very graphically by the fan who brings a transistor radio or even a portable TV to the game so that he can find out from a sportcaster what he really is seeing. The most dramatic example of the invasion of the stadium by the medium is the introduction in stadia in Los Angeles, Kansas City, and New Orleans of huge screens for isolation or slow-motion replays. Is this a corruption or a widening of the spectator's experience? "It appears," says Eldon Snyder and Elmer Spreitzer, "that the live spectator cannot compete with the sensory stimuli experienced by the TV viewer with the multiplicity of camera angles, special effects, and announcers" (1983, p. 224). It boils down to the question of whether it is better to have a superior product or to do one's own thing. This question is pointed up by Frederick Klein's comment about the 1980 Winter Olympics: "Make no mistake . . . ; what we saw wasn't winter sports as they are but only as a rich, efficient and experienced American television network can present them. With but few exceptions . . . the drama of the games stemmed from the application of the broadcaster's art" (Klein, 1980, p. 19). Again, is it a corruption to see the games not as they are but as TV creates them?

The medium event is corrupted in the sense that *the fan and the broadcaster are partners in violence* (Bryant & Zillman, 1983). Fans generally like to see violence, and the media provide the violence deemed necessary to sell their light beer, toothpaste, automobiles, and computers. Research with media sport segments like those previously discussed has shown that males rate violent segments as more enjoyable to a statistically significant degree, and females also prefer violent segments but not significantly so. Hockey segments are also experienced as more enjoyable when they are rougher. Subjects enjoy tennis better when they believe that the opponents hate each other's guts. How do the media satisfy this need? In part by the kind of theatrical tactics employed by the hockey announcer in the aggressive segment that tricked the social psychologists. In part by selecting for isolation and slow motion replay the roughest parts of the action (the good hit, etc.) and their sequels: the ministrations of trainer and team physician, the injured player in pain on the bench. Partly violence is presented in special sport features, apart from actual game coverage. Some of it appears in promotional segments (grabbers) for sporting events soon to be shown.

What are the limits to violence in the medium event? As with humor, say Bryant and Zillman, there is a certain limit beyond which violence becomes unacceptable. Fans—medium as well as stadium—do like to see sportsmen *risk* death. The greatest excitement seems to come when a death-defying hero has a slim but credible chance to survive. Do fans watch dangerous sporting events *hoping* to see someone killed? Bryant and Zillman cite a cartoon in which a promoter is telling a disgruntled stunt driver: "What are you bitching about? After all, 50,000 people have paid to see you jump fourteen cars." The driver's answer is, "My problem is that they've come to see me jump *thirteen* cars." These researchers believe that this involves a lower view of human nature than they find it necessary to accept. They theorize instead that risk-taking violence is desired by sportscasters (who are really cheerleaders in the ritual drama) and by fans because *risk builds drama*. Violence creates what the media call an "establishing shot." What does it establish? That the protagonists who are willing to risk limb or life are really in it for keeps, that this is really "deep play" (in which, we will remember, according to Bentham the risk is so great that no sane person would take it).

Finally, the media may actually *corrupt the quality of play*, as David Halberstam (1981) shows in his discussion of what happened to pro basketball after it was discovered by the television industry, specifically CBS, in the late 1960s. The chain of events ran like this: The arrival of TV money for basketball as an attractive, sometimes prime time entertainment led to a change in the type of people owning basketball teams. Local businessmen for whom a team was an important investment about which, and for which, they cared tended to be bought out by young, often absent multimillionaires for whom the franchise was a low priority investment or, if unprofitable, a tax write-off. Loyal local fans who cheered their team on in the arena gave way to TV viewers who watched a game as one of several entertainment options. Income was accordingly derived not from the box office, but from TV contracts. Players began to see themselves as prime entertainers and to expect to be paid by the standards of the entertainment industy. The number of franchises expanded to accommodate the wide range of TV markets. With more franchises to stock, the average quality of players declined, and with it the general team morale and standard of play. CBS couldn't cover all the teams adequately and so the National Basketball Association was in effect split into leagues—half a dozen well-covered teams and the rest. The number of games increased to keep pace with the increase in franchises, and so of course did the amount of travel. Exhausted and injured players with no-cut contracts began to dog it during the interminable season and save themselves for the playoffs. As the quality of play dropped, so did the Nielsen ratings and the income from sponsors. In turn, TV coverage of even the playoffs deteriorated, to the frustration of real basketball fans. Halberstam attributes the whole descending spiral to the emergence of pro basketball as a medium event.

Even Lasch (1977), who regards the spectator as an involved participant in an agonistic ritual, would have to consider watching on the tube a very diluted substitute for watching from grandstand or bleacher seat. He sees it as a positive source of corruption: "Television has enlarged the audience for sports while lowering the quality of that audience's understandings," and "as spectators become less knowledgeable about the games they watch, they become more sensation-minded and bloodthirsty." When this happens, "ritual drama, and sports all degenerate into spectacle" (p. 26).

Sport is corrupted, Lasch also says, when it ceases to be an end in itself, enjoyed for itself, and becomes a means to some external end—such as profit making, patriotism, moral training, or the pursuit of health. We could add also, the prestige of the institution that sponsors sport. "When the game itself comes to be regarded as incidental to the benefits it supposedly confers on participants, spectators, or promoters, it loses it particular capacity to transport both participant and spectator beyond everyday experience—to provide a glimpse of perfect order uncontaminated by commonplace calculations of advantage" (Lasch, 1977, p. 26). (Here we are back at Sutton-Smith's definition of play as an oasis of self-chosen rules in a world where one is ordinarily subjected to rules imposed from without.) When sport becomes instead the mirror image of a society compulsively fixated on money, status, power, and entertainment, it is corrupt.

A football player turned philosophy professor, John McMurtry of the Canadian University of Guelph, charges that *competing for victory* also corrupts the search for excellence in sport:

The pursuit of victory reduces the chance to work for excellence in the true performance by rendering it subservient to emerging victorious. I suspect that our conventional mistake of presuming the opposite—presuming that the contest for prize framework and excellence of performance are somehow related as a unique cause—and effect—may be the deepest lying prejudice of civilized thought. Keeping score in any game—especially team games—is a substantial indication that the activity in question is not interesting enough in itself to those who keep score. (Cited in Tutko & Tosi, 1976, pp. 201–202)

Of very different opinion is Andrzej Wohl, a sport sociologist from a communist country (Poland):

The fundamental driving force of the development in sport technique is competition in sport. This is a characteristic feature of sport. In all spheres of human creativity, its development takes place through effort to obtain maximum results and through the accumulation on this basis of practical experience and rationalized knowledge. However, only in sport has an automatic mechanism been created, optimizing the aspirations to achieve maximum results in the form of an all-round, public system of sport competition, with precisely worked out rules and regulations and with such institutions as national and international championships and finally the Olympic Games. (Wohl, 1975, p. 32)

The corruption of sport is sweepingly summarized in the position paper sent me by my sociologist father, Arthur Calhoun, in the 89th year of his life, when I taught my first class in sport and culture at the University of Miami (see It's Not Sport, p. 345). He uses the term *sport* in its original sense—disport (play). (Compare the Spanish *deporte*.) In the light of what I have said in this chapter I would seem to disagree with item 17. But not entirely. With all due respect for the important role of sport in dramatizing the agonistic human condition, I am inclined to feel that sport is properly *fun*, that mass ritual drama is not fun, but serious work, and that the agonistic spectacle, like money, status, power, and entertainment, is also a corruption of our profound need for release through play.

Assuming that the sport spectacular is a ritual morality play (good guys triumphing over bad guys), I am inclined to apply James Dow's distinction between the psychology of ritual and the psychology of play (Dow, 1980, pp. 5, 6). The effect of ritual, including the sport spectacular, is hypnotic possession, says Dow, whereas real play involves a symbolic and liberating expression of emotions. Flowing play is self-actualizing, sport ritual is self-stupifying. To translate self-fulfillment or genuine catharsis into hypnotic possession is, I think, to corrupt it. In other words, *sport as ritual drama* is also a corruption of the spirit of play.

Two final notes on where spectator participation in the sport spectacular may be leading us as we approach the 21st century. One verges on absurdity, the other on tragedy.

In late 1985 the NFL was considering the testing in 1986 of helmets with radio receivers that would enable players to hear signal callers without interference by crowd noise. To keep quarterbacks from using the system to signal downfield pass catchers, referees would be provided with a remote control to enable them to cut off reception at the snap of the ball.

It's Not Sport

It's not sport, if it involves anything except fun; for example:

1. *If it is for health.*
2. *If it is for physical development.*
3. *If it is to reduce.*
4. *If it is a "pastime."*
5. *If it is a distraction, an escape.*
6. *If it is to impress someone.*
7. *If it is for social standing.*
8. *If it uses professional trainers or coaches.*
9. *If there is money involved (beyond "costs").*
10. *If competition is featured.*
11. *If a team uses players for elsewhere.*
12. *If it "represents" something.*
13. *If it has arbitrary rules.*
14. *If it keeps records.*
15. *If it appears on "sports pages."*
16. *If it deals in éclat.*
17. *If audiences are welcomed.*
18. *If it has "patrons."*
19. *If it is arbitrarily seasonal.*
20. *If it violates seasons (e.g., ice-skating in summer or swimming in winter).*

Note. From Arthur W. Calhoun, personal communication, November 30, 1973

At about the same time Irving Goldaber told my sport sociology class that, according to the best estimates of crowd management experts, in an Orange Bowl crowd up to 1,200 spectators (0.5 to 2.0%) possess handguns. He predicted that an assassination attempt on a player or official in a major stadium is a real possibility in the near future.

The "twelfth man" has subverted the spirit of fun in ways of which even Colosseum gladiator-watchers never dreamed.

Postscript

As Plato suggested, life is a game, to be played as a game, by agreed-upon rules, within limits of time and space. Because of its limits of time, it is a game we all must lose. But in another sense, it is a game we all must win—if we choose. For, to rephrase Grantland Rice's classic lines:

When the One Great Scorer comes
To write against your name
Whether you won or lost is
How you played the game.

So too it may be—also if we choose—in the games within the Game.

References

Adediji, J.A. (1978). The acceptance of Nigerian women in sport. *International Review of Sport Sociology*, **13**(2), 39–45.

Adediji, J.A. (1979). Social and cultural conflicts in sport and games in developing countries. *International Review of Sport Sociology*, **14**(1), 81–88.

Adorno, T.W., Frenkl-Brunswik, E., Levinson, D.J., & Sanford, R.N. (1950). *The authoritarian personality.* New York: Harper and Row.

Ager, L.P. (1976). The reflection of cultural values in Eskimo children's games. In D.F. Lancy & B.A. Tindall (Eds.), *The study of play: Problems and prospects* (pp. 92–98). Champaign, IL: Leisure Press.

Aguilera, R. (1973). A sociological profile of educational sport in Cuba and its development. *International Review of Sport Sociology*, **8**(2), 119–121.

Allen, F. L. (1950, October). The big change. *Harper's Magazine*, pp. 145–160.

Amdur, N. (1971). *The fifth down: American democracy and the football revolution.* New York: Coward, McCann, and Geoghegan.

Anyanwu, S.U. (1980). Issues in and patterns of women's participation in sports in Nigeria. *International Review of Sport Sociology*, **13**(1), 85–93.

Arens, W. (1975). The great American football ritual. *Natural History*, **84**, 72–80.

Aristotle. (1911). *Nicomachean ethics.* New York: Dutton. (Original work dated 1095 D26)

Arms, R.L., Russell, G.W., & Sandilands, M.E. (1979). Effects of viewing aggressive sports on the hostility of spectators. *Social Psychology Quarterly*, **42**(3), 275–279.

Artemov, V.A. (1981). Athletic activity in the lifestyle of urban and rural residents (Based on time-budget data). *International Review of Sport Sociology*, **16**(1), 53–57.

Ashe, A. (1977, February 6). Send your children to the libraries: An open letter to black parents. *New York Times*, sect. 5, p. 2.

Atkin, R. (1977, May 12). Hockey's shortcoming. *Christian Science Monitor*, p. 11.

Avedon, E., & Sutton-Smith, B. (1971). *The study of games.* New York: Wiley.

Axthelm, P. (1970). *The city game.* New York: Harper's Magazine Press.

Bain, L. (1978). Differences in values implicit in teaching and coaching behaviors. *Research Quarterly,* **49**, 5–11.

Baker, W.J. (1982). *Sports in the Western world.* Totowa, NJ: Rowman and Littlefield.

Bandura, A. (1973). *Aggression: A social learning analysis.* New York: Prentice-Hall.

Barkow, A. (1974). *Golf's golden grind: The history of the tour.* San Diego: Harcourt Brace Jovanovich.

Barnard, C.I. (1946). *The function of the executive.* Cambridge: Harvard.

Bateson, G. (1972). A theory of play and fantasy. In G. Bateson (Ed.), *Steps to an ecology of mind: Collected essays in anthropology, psychiatry, evolution, and epistemology* (pp. 177–193). San Francisco: Chandler.

Benedict, R. (1934). *Patterns of culture.* Boston: Houghton Mifflin.

Bennis, W.G., & Slater, P.E. (1968). *The temporary society.* New York: Harper and Row.

Bentham, J. (1931). *The theory of legislation.* San Diego: Harcourt Brace Jovanovich.

Berkowitz, L. (1965). The concept of aggressive drive: Some additional considerations. In L. Berkowitz (Ed.), *Advances in experimental social psychology* (Vol. 2, pp. 301–329). New York: Academic Press.

Berkowitz, L. (1972). *Sports competition and aggression.* Paper presented at the Canadian Sports Psychology Symposium, Waterloo.

Berndt, R.M. (1940, October). Some aboriginal children's games. *Mankind* [Australia], p. 2.

Betts, J.R., (1953). The technological revolution and the rise of sport. In J.W. Loy, Jr., and G.S. Kenyon (Eds.), *Sport, Culture, and Society* (pp. 145–166). New York: Macmillan.

Betts, J.R. (1974). *America's sporting heritage, 1850–1950.* Reading, MA: Addison-Wesley.

Birrell, S., & Loy, J.W., Jr. (1979). Modern sport: Hot and cool. *International Review of Sport Sociology,* **14**(1), 5–19.

Blalock, J. (1977). *The guts to win.* Norwalk, CT: Golf Digest.

Blanchard, K. (1976). Team sports and violence: An anthropological perspective. In D.F. Lancy & B.A. Tindall (Eds.), *The anthropological study of play: Problems and prospects.* Champaign, IL: Leisure Press.

Bodley, H. (1986, April 25). 'Millionaires club' hardly exclusive. *USA Today*, pp. 1-C, 2-C.

Bonsov, J.B. (1981). Physical culture and sport in the system of cultural values of the rural population. *International Review of Sport Sociology*, **16**(2), 45-53.

Bouton, J. (1971). *Ball four*. New York: Dell.

Bowman, J.R. (1978). The organization of spontaneous adult social play. In M.A. Salter (Ed.), *Play: Anthropological perspectives* (pp. 239-250). Champaign, IL: Leisure Press.

Brailsford, D. (1969). *Sport and society: Elizabeth to Anne*. Toronto: University of Toronto Press.

Bratton, R.D., Kinnear, G., & Koroluk, G. (1979). Why man climbs mountains. *International Review of Sport Sociology*, **14**(2), 23-36.

Brickman, P. (1977). Crime and punishment in sports and society. *Journal of Social issues*, **33**, 140-164.

Brinton, C. (1959). *A history of Western morals*. San Diego: Harcourt Brace Jovanovich.

Brodie, J. (1973). I experience a kind of clarity: Interview with Michael Murphy. *Intellectual Digest*, **3**(5), 19-22.

Brower, J.J. (1973). *The quota system: The white gatekeeper's regulation of professional football's black community*. Paper presented at annual meeting of the American Sociological Association, New York.

Bryant, J., & Zillman, D. (1983). Sports violence and the media. In J.H. Goldstein (Ed.), *Sports violence*. New York: Springer-Verlag.

Bryce, J. (1905, March 25). America revisited: The changes of a quarter-century. *Outlook*, pp. 733-740.

Bury, J.E. (1955). *The idea of progress*. New York: Dover.

Buss, A.H., & Durkee, A. (1957). An inventory for assessing different kinds of hostility. *Journal of Consulting Psychology*, **21**, 343-348.

Cagigal, J. (1970). Social education through sport: A trial. In G.S. Kenyon (Ed.), *Contemporary psychology of sport* (pp. 339-348). Chicago: Athletic Institute.

Caillois, R. (1955). The structure and classification of games. *Diogenes*, **12**, 62-75.

Caillois, R. (1961). *Man, play, and games*. New York: Free Press.

Calhoun, D.W. (1976). *Persons-in-groups: A humanistic social psychology*. New York: Harper and Row.

Cascio, C. (1975). *Soccer, U.S.A.* Washington: Luce.

Cavanaugh, B.M., & Silva, J.M., III. (1979). Spectator perceptions of fan misbehavior: An attitudinal inquiry. In C.H. Nadeau, W.R. Halliwell, K.M. Newell, & G.C. Roberts (Eds.), *Psychology of motor behavior and sport* (pp. 189–198)(2). Champaign, IL: Human Kinetics.

Charnovsky, H. (1968). The major league professional baseball player: Self-conception versus the popular image. *International Review of Sport Sociology,* **3,** 39–55.

Cheska, A.T. (1979). Sport spectacular: A ritual model of power. *International Review of Sport Sociology,* **14**(2), 51–72.

Chi, Y. (1958). Looking at China's leap forward from the point of view of international competition. Cited in J. Riordan (1972), *Sports, politics, and ideology in China.* Middle Village, NY: Jonathan David.

Chinese communists in wartime. (1959). *China Sports,* No. 5.

Chourbagi, Z. (1968). Physical education and sports in Syria. *International Review of Sport Sociology,* **3,** 197–199.

Ciuciu, G. (1979). The socialization process of children by means of extemporized and organized games. *International Review of Sport Sociology,* **9**(1), 7–21.

Coakley, J.J. (1982). *Sport and society: Issues and controversies.* St. Louis, MO: Mosby.

Cochard, L'Abbe. (1889). Le jeu de paume a Orléans. In *Mémoires,* Orléans Société Archéologique et Historique de l'Orléanais, **22,** 297–340.

Comisky, P., Bryant, J., & Zillman, D. (1977). Commentary as a substitute for action. *Journal of Communication,* **27**(3), 150–153.

Commonwealth v. the American Baseball Club of Philadelphia. (1927, July 30). Cited in *Literary Digest,* p. 28.

Cooley, C.H. (1962). *Social organization.* New York: Shocken.

Coulton, G.G. (1974). *Medieval panorama.* New York: W.W. Norton.

Cousy, B. (1975). *The killer instinct.* New York: Random House.

Cozens, F.W., & Stumpf, F. (1953). *Sports in America.* Chicago: University of Chicago Press.

The crime of the anti-party, anti-military, anti-revolutionary, revisionist Ho Lung. (1967, February 9). *Sports Battlefront,* p. 19, No. 8–9.

Csikszentmihalyi, M. (1975). *Beyond boredom and anxiety: The experience of play in work and games.* San Francisco: Jossey-Bass.

Csikszentmihalyi, M. (1980). Letter to Phillips Stevens, Jr., reported in Play and work: A false dichotomy? In H.B. Schwartzmann (Ed.), *Play and culture* (p. 319). Champaign, IL: Leisure Press.

Culin, S. (1907). *Games of the North American Indians.* Washington: Bureau of American Ethnology.

Czarnowski, S. (1956). *Works.* Warsaw: Panstwowe Wydawn, Naukowe.

Delk. (1971, May). Why parachutists jump. *Parachutist,* pp. 12–13.

Donne, J. (1929). Devotions upon emergent occasions. In J. Hayward (Ed.), *Complete poetry and selected prose.* London: Nonesuch.

Dow, J. (1980, Winter). Ritual and play. *Newsletter of the Association for the Anthropological Study of Play,* pp. 5–6.

Dubois, P.E. (1974, Fall). Sport, mobility, and the black athlete. *Sport Society Bulletin,* 40–61.

Dulles, F.R. (1940). *America learns to play: A history of popular recreation, 1607–1940.* New York: Appleton-Century-Crofts.

Dunlap, H.L. (1951). Games, sports, dancing and other vigorous activities and their function in Samoan culture. *Research Quarterly,* **22,** 298–311.

Dunlap, O.E., Jr. (1939, May 21). *New York Times.* Cited in S. Birrell & J.W. Loy, Jr. (1979). Modern sport: Hot and cool. *International Review of Sport Sociology,* **14**(1), 5–19.

Dunning, E. (1983). Social bonding and violence in sport: A theoretical-empirical analysis. In J.H. Goldstein (Ed.), *Sports violence* (pp. 129–146). New York: Springer-Verlag.

Durant. W. (1939). *The life of Greece* (Pt. 2 of *The story of civilization*). New York: Simon and Schuster.

Durant, W. (1944). *Ceasar and Christ* (Pt. 3 of *The story of civilization*). New York: Simon and Schuster.

Durant, W. (1950). *The age of faith* (Pt. 4 of *The story of civilization*). New York: Simon and Schuster.

Durant, W. (1957). *The reformation* (Pt. 6 of *The story of civilization*). New York: Simon and Schuster.

Duthie, J.H. (1980). Athletics, the ritual of a technological society? In H.B. Schwartzman (Ed.), *Play and culture.* Champaign, IL: Leisure Press.

Earle, J. (1628). *Micro-cosmographie.*

Edwards, H. (1973). *Sociology of sport.* Homewood, IL: Dorsey.

Edwards, H. (1979). Sport within the veil: The triumphs, tragedies, and challenges of Afro-American involvement. *Annals of the American Academy of Political and Social Science,* **445,** 116–127.

Eitzen, D.S. (1984). The structure of sport and society. In D.S. Eitzen (Ed.), *Sport in contemporary society: An anthology* (pp. 51–57). New York: St. Martin's.

Eitzen, D.S., & Sanford, D.C. (1975). The segregation of blacks by playing position in football: Accident or design? *Social Science Quarterly,* **55,** 948–959.

Eitzen, D.S., & Tessendorf, I. (1978). Racial segregation by position in sports: The special case of basketball. *Review of Sport and Leisure,* **3**(1), 109–138.

Ekart, A. (1954). *Vanished without a trace.* London: Max Parish.

Eldridge, L. (1978, August 10). Changing values in sports. *Christian Science Monitor.*

Elias, N., & Dunning, E. (1966). Dynamics of group sports with special reference to football. *British Journal of Sociology,* **17,** 388–402.

Eliot, C.W. (1905). The evils of college football. *Woman's Home Companion,* **32,** p. 7.

Ellis, W. (1829). *Polynesian researches* (No. 1). London: Fisher, Son, and Jackson.

Epstein, S., & Taylor, S. (1967). Instigation to aggression as a function of degree of defeat and perceived aggressive intent of the opponent. *Journal of Personality,* **35,** 265–289.

Erikson, E. (1964). Inner and outer space: Reflections on womanhood. *Daedalus,* **93,** 582–606.

Eshkenazi, G. (1972). *A thinking man's guide to pro hockey.* New York: Dutton.

Famaey-Lamon, A., Hebbelinck, M., & Cadron, A.M. (1979). Team-sport and individual sport. *International Review of Sport Sociology,* **14**(2), 37–50.

Farrer, C. (1976). Play and inter-ethnic communication. In D.F. Lancy and B.A. Tindall (Eds.), *The study of play: Problems and prospects* (pp. 98–104). Champaign, IL: Leisure Press.

Feshbach, S. (1961). The stimulating versus cathartic effect of a vicarious aggressive activity. *Journal of Abnormal and Social Psychology,* **53,** 381–385.

Fisher, M. (1983, December 27). Elite, dedicated few make Orange Bowl go. *The Miami Herald,* pp. 1A, 5A.

Fitzgerald, F.S. (1925). *The great Gatsby.* New York: Scribner's.

Flood, C. (1970). *The way it is* (with Richard Carter). New York: Trident.

Fortes, M. (1970). Social and psychological aspects of play in Taleland. In J. Middleton (Ed.), *From child to adult* (pp. 14–74). Austin: University of Texas Press. (Reprinted from *Africa,* 1938, **11**[4])

Frank, J. (1948). Opinion in Gardella v. Chandler, Second Federal Circuit Court of Appeals.

Frederickson, F.S. (1960). Sports and the cultures of man. In W.R. Johnson (Ed.), *Science and medicine of exercises and sport.* New York: Harper and Row.

Frederickson, F.S., & Cozens, F.W. (1947, October). Some aspects of the role of games, sports, and recreational activities in the culture of modern primitive peoples. *Research Quarterly,* **18,** 198–218.

Friedenberg, E.Z. (1967). Introduction. In H.S. Slusher, *Man, sport, and existence.* Philadelphia: Lea and Febiger.

Friedlander, L. (1928). *Roman life and manners under the Roman empire.* London: Finley, Moses.

Furst, R.T. (1971). Social change and the commercialization of professional sports. *International Review of Sport Sociology,* **6,** 153–173.

Gabriel, R.H. (1929). Foreword. In J.A. Krout (Ed.), *Annals of American sport: Vol. 15. The pageant of America: A pictorial history of the United States* (pp. 1–8). New Haven: Yale.

Galbraith, J.K. (1971) *The new industrial state.* Boston. Houghton-Mifflin.

Gallwey, W.T. (1974). *The inner game of tennis.* New York: Random House.

Gardiner, E.N. (1930). *Athletics of the ancient world.* New York: Oxford.

Gardiner, E.N. (1970). *Greek athletic sports and festivals.* Dubuque, IA: Brown.

Garvey, E.R. (1979). From chattel to employee: The athlete's quest for freedom and dignity. *Annals of the American Academy of Political and Social Science,* **445,** 91–101.

Geanakoplos, D.J. (1968). *Western civilization: Paleolithic man to the emergence of economic powers.* New York: Harper and Row and American Heritage.

Geertz, C. (1972). Deep play: Notes on the Balinese cockfight. *Daedalus,* **101,** 1–37.

Geertz, C. (1973). *The interpretation of culture.* New York: Basic Books.

Gilbert, B. (1969, June 23, 30, July 7). Drugs in sport. *Sports Illustrated,* pp. 64–73, pp. 30–42, pp. 30–35..

Gilbert, B. (1974). What counselors need to know about college and pro sports. *Phi Delta Kappan,* **56,** 121–124.

Gilbert, B., & Twyman, L. (1983, January 31). Violence: Out of hand in the stands. *Sports Illustrated*, pp. 62–72.

Gill, D.L., & Perry, J.L. (1979). A case study of leadership in women's intercollegiate softball. *International Review of Sport Sociology*, **14**(2), 83–91.

Goellner, W.A. (1953). The court ball game of the aboriginal Mayas. *Research Quarterly*, **24**, 147–168.

Goldstein, J.H., & Arms, R.L. (1971). Effects of observing athletic contests on hostility. *Sociometry*, **34**, 83–90.

Goldstein, J.H., & Bredemeier, B.J. (1977). Socialization: Some basic issues. *Journal of Communication*, **27**, 154–159.

Goodger, B.C., & Goodger, J.M. (1977). Judo in the light of theory and sociological research. *International Review of Sport Sociology*, **12**(2), 5–34.

Goodhart, P., & Chataway, C. (1968). *War without weapons*. London: Allen.

Goranson, R.E. (1970). Media violence and aggressive behavior: A review of experimental research. In L. Berkowitz (Ed.), *Advances in experimental social psychology* (Vol. 5, pp. 2–31). New York: Academic Press.

Gorky, M. (1928, August 14). *Pravda*, p. 8.

Granet, M. (1930). *Chinese civilization*. London: Routledge.

Grella, G. (1975). Baseball and the American dream. *Massachusetts Review*, **15**, 562–573.

Grusky, O. (1963). The effect of formal structure on managerial recruitment. *Sociometry*, **26**, 345–353.

Gulick, L. (1898, October). Some psychical aspects of muscular exercise. *Popular Science Monthly*, pp. 793–805.

Halberstam, D. (1970, September). Baseball and the national mythology. *Harper's*, pp. 22–25.

Halberstam, D. (1981). *The breaks of the game*. New York: Knopf.

Hall, G.S. (1937). *Adolescence*. New York: Appleton-Century-Crofts.

Hanford, G.H. (1979). Controversies in college sport. *Annals of the American Academy of Political and Social Science*, **445**, 66–79.

Hare, N. (1971). A study of the black fighter. *Black Scholar*, **3**(3), 2–9.

Harris, J.C., & Park, R.J. (1983). *Play, games, and sport in cultural contexts*. Champaign, IL: Human Kinetics.

Harris, S.J. (1975). Pro sport is mercenary combat. In *The Best of Sidney Harris* (pp. 140–141). Boston: Houghton Mifflin. (Original work published in *Chicago Daily News*, February 22, 1971)

Harris, S.J. (1983). The new "profession" of sports. *ETC: A Review of General Semantics*, **40**(1), 53–58.

Harrower, M.R. (1934). Social status and the moral development of the child. *British Journal of Educational Psychology*, **4**, 75–95.

Hartmann, D.P. (1969). Influence of symbolically modeled instrumental aggression and pain cues on aggressive behavior. *Journal of Personality and Social Psychology*, **49**, 129–134.

Hastorf, A.H., & Cantril, H. (1954). They saw a game: A case study. *Journal of Abnormal and Social Psychology*, **49**, 129–134.

Henderson, R.W. (1947). *Ball, bat, and bishop: The origin of ball games.* New York: Rockport Press.

Hennig, M. (1976, April 1). Cited in *Christian Science Monitor*, p. 2.

Henry, J. (1949). The social function of child sexuality in Pilagá Indian culture. In P.H. Hoch & J. Zubin (Eds.), *Psychosexual development in health and disease* (pp. 91–101). New York: Grune and Stratton.

Hermann, H.U. (1978). *Soccer fans.* Schorndorf: Hofmann.

Herodotus. (1862). *History.* (G. Rawlinson, Trans.). London: J. Murray. (Original date unknown).

Hoch, P. (1972). *Rip off the big game: The exploitation of sports by the power elite.* New York: Doubleday.

Holmen, M., & Parkhouse, B. (1981). Trends in the selection of coaches for female athletes: A demographic inquiry. *Research Quarterly*, **52**(1), 9–18.

Holt, J. (1970, September–October). Some thoughts on education. *Edcentric*, **1**. (Available from P.O. Box 185, Eugene, OR)

Homer. (1919). *Odyssey* (A.T. Murray, Trans.). New York: Putnam.

Honig, D. (1975). *Baseball: When the grass was green.* New York: Coward, McCann, McGeoghegan.

Howell, M.L., Dodge, C., & Howell, R.A. (1975). Generalizations on play in "primitive" societies. *Journal of Sport History*, **2**(2), 145–155.

Hughes, R., & Coakley, J.J. (1978). Player violence and the social organization of contact sport. *Journal of Sport Behavior*, **1**(4), 155–168.

Huizinga, J. (1984). *The waning of the Middle Ages.* New York: St. Martin's. (Original work published 1924)

Huizinga, J. (1964). *Homo ludens: A study of the play element in culture* (4th paperback printing). Boston: Beacon.

Hurford, D. (1977, July 25). I'll do anything I can get away with. *Sports Illustrated*, pp. 30–32, 37.

ISSN Newsletter [Institute for the Study of Sport and Society]. (1973). Oberlin, OH.

Izenberg, J. (1972). *How many miles to Camelot? The all-American sport myth.* New York: Holt, Rinehart and Winston.

Jackson, M. (1962, December). College football has become a losing business. *Fortune*, pp. 119–121, 174, 176, 181, 182, 184.

Jameson, Mrs. S. (1930). *The decline of merrie England.* New York: Bobbs-Merrill.

Janowitz, M. (1960). *The professional soldier: A social and political portrait.* New York: Free Press.

Jefferies, S.C. (1984). Sport and education: Theory and practice in the USSR. *Quest*, **36**, 164–176.

Jefferson, T. (1937). Letter to Peter Carr. Cited in D. Wecter, *The saga of American society: A record of social aspirations, 1607–1937.* New York: Scribner's.

Johnson, W. (1971). *Super spectators and the electric Lilliputians.* Boston: Little, Brown.

Johnson, W. (1973a). Faces on a new China scroll. *Sports Illustrated*, **39**(13), pp. 82–100.

Johnson, W. (1973b). An eager people in the swim. *Sports Illustrated*, **39**(14), pp. 42–67.

Johnston, D. (1976, September 8). Study: Sports doesn't boost success. *The Miami Herald.*

Jonosza, W. (1932). It should't be like this. *Start Magazine* (Poland), **19**.

Kanter, S. (1973, October 8). Football: Show business with a kick. *Time*, pp. 54–55.

Keefer, R., Goldstein, J.H., & Kasiarz, D. (1983). Olympic games and participation in war. In J.H. Goldstein (Ed.), *Sports violence* (pp. 183–198). New York: Springer-Verlag.

Keenan, F.W. (1975). The athletic contest as a "tragic" form of art. *International Review of Sport Sociology*, **10**(1), 39–54.

Keller, A.G., & Davie, M.R. (1934). *Essays of William Graham Sumner.* New Haven: Yale.

Kelley, R.F. (1932). *American rowing: Its background and traditions.* New York: Putnam.

Kieran, J., & Daley, A. (1973). *The story of the Olympic games: 776 B.C. to 1972* (rev. ed.). Philadelphia: Lippincott.

The king's majesties declaration to his subjects, concerning lawful sports to be used. (1906). In S.R. Gardiner (Ed.), *The constitutional documents of the Puritan revolution* (3rd ed., pp. 99–103). Oxford: Clarendon. (Original work published 1618)

Klapp, O.E. (1962). *Heroes, villains, and fools.* New York: Prentice-Hall.

Klapp, O.E. (1969). *Collective search for identity.* New York: Holt, Rinehart, and Winston.

Klein, F. (1980, February 2). 52 hours of Olympic highlights. *Wall Street Journal,* p. 13.

Kolatch, J. (1972). *Sports, politics, and ideology in China.* Middle Village, NY: Jonathan David.

Koppett, L. (1973). *The essence of the game is deception: Thinking about basketball.* Boston: Little, Brown.

Kraft, I. (1967, January). Pedagogical futility in fun and games. *NEA Journal,* **56,** 71–72.

Kraus, H., & Hirschland, R.P. (1954). Minimum muscular fitness tests in school children. *Research Quarterly,* **25,** 178–188.

Krawczyk, B. (1965). *Career patterns and professional aspirations of students of the Academy of Physical Education.* Unpublished doctoral dissertation, University of Warsaw.

Krawczyk, B. (1973). The social role and participation in sport. *International Review of Sport Sociology,* **8**(3–4), 47–62.

Kropotkin, P.A. (1955). *Mutual aid: A factor in evolution.* Boston: Porter Sargent. (Reprint)

Krout, J.A. (1929). *Annals of American sport* [Vol. 15 of R.H. Gabriel (Ed.), *The pageant of America: A pictorial history of the United States*]. New Haven: Yale.

Kuyper, A. (1931). *Calvinism.* Grand Rapids, MI: Eerdman.

Lapchick, R. (1984). *Broken promises: Racism in American sports* New York: St. Martin's.

Lasch, C. (1977, April 28). The corruption of sports. *New York Review of Books,* pp. 24–30.

Lenin, V.I. (1932). *State and revolution.* New York: International.

Lenk, H. (1973). *Philosophie des sports* [*Philosophy of sport*]. Schorndorf: Hofmann.

Leonard, G. (1974). *The ultimate athlete.* New York: Viking.

Leonard, W. M., II. (1977). An extension of the black-Latin-white report. *International Review of Sport Sociology,* **12**(3), 75–86.

Lepper, M.R., Greene, D., & Nesbitt, R.E. (1973). Undermining children's intrinsic interest with extrinsic rewards: A test of the overjustification hypothesis. *Journal of Personality and Social Psychology,* **28**, 129-137.

Lever, J. (1969). Soccer: Opium of the Brazilian people. *Trans-action,* 7(2), 36-43.

Lever, J. (1978). Sex differences in the complexity of children's play. *American Sociological Review,* **43**(4), 471-483.

Likert, R. (1967). *The human organization.* New York: McGraw-Hill.

Linton, R.M. (1936). *The study of man.* New York: Appleton-Century-Crofts.

Lipsyte, R. (1975). *Sports world: An American dreamland.* New York: Quadrangle.

Lomax, A. (1974). *Dance in human history* [Film]. Berkeley: University of California Extension Media Center.

Lopiano, D.A. (1981). Affidavit in U.S. District Court for the District of Columbia, Association for Intercollegiate Athletics for Women, Plaintiff v. National Collegiate Athletic Association, Defendant.

Loy, J.W., Jr. (1969). The study of sport and social mobility. In G.S. Kenyon (Ed.), *Sociology of sport* (pp. 101-119). Chicago: Athletic Institute.

Loy, J.W., Jr., & McElvogue, J.F. (1970). Racial segregation in American sport. *International Review of Sport Sociology,* **5**, 5-24.

Lüschen, G. (1967). The interdependence of sport and culture. *International Review of Sport Sociology,* **2**, 127-141.

Lynd, R., & Lynd, H. (1963). *Middletown.* San Diego: Harcourt Brace Jovanovich.

Mac Aloon, J., & Csikszentmihalyi, M. (1983). Deep play and the flow experience in rock climbing. In J.C. Harris & R.J. Park (Eds.), *Play, games, and sport in cultural contexts* (pp. 361-384). Champaign, IL: Human Kinetics.

Macaulay, T.B. (1871). *The history of England from the accession of James the Second.* London: Longmans, Green, Reader, and Dyer.

Mahler, F. (1975). Play and counter-play: On the educational ambivalence of play or its utilization to counter the negative effects of play. *International Review of Sport Sociology,* **10**(2), 115-125.

Mahmood, A. (1981). Direction and planning of sport for children and young people. *International Review of Sport Sociology,* **16**(1), 115-125.

Maksimenko, A.M., & Barushimana, A. (1978). Attitude towards sport activity of top-class athletes of Central Africa. *International Review of Sport Sociology,* **13**(2), 37–50.

Malinowski, B. (1950). *Argonauts of the western Pacific: An account of native enterprise and adventure in the Archipelagos of Melanesian New Guinea.* New York: Dutton.

Mallery, O. (1910). The social significance of play. *Annals of the American Academy of Political and Social Science,* **35**, 152–157.

Mark, M.M., Bryant, F.J., & Lehman, D.R. (1983). Perceived injustice and sports violence. In J.H. Goldstein (Ed.), *Sports violence* (pp. 83–109). New York: Springer-Verlag.

Mauss, M. (1923–1924). Essai sur le don. In *L'Année Sociologique.* Paris: Presses Universitaire de France.

Mayo, E. (1946). *The human problems of an industrial civilization.* Cambridge: Harvard.

McClelland, D.C. (1976). *The achieving society.* New York: Van Nostrand Reinhold.

McGeehan, O. (1925, October 24). *Literary Digest,* p. 42.

McIntosh, P.C. (1971a). An historical view of society and social control. *International Review of Sport Sociology,* **6**, 5–16.

McIntosh, P.C. (1971b). *Sport in society.* London: Watts.

McLain, D. (1975). *Nobody's perfect* (with David Niles). New York: Dell.

McLuhan, M. (1967). *The medium is the message.* New York: Bantam.

Mead, G.H. (1967). *Mind, self, and society from the standpoint of a social behaviorist.* Chicago: University of Chicago Press. (Original work published 1934)

Mead, M. (1980). *Sex and temperament.* New York: Morrow. (Original work published 1935)

Mead, M. (1970). *Culture and commitment: A study of the generation gap.* New York: Doubleday.

Medvedev, Z. (1971). *The Medvedev papers.* London: Macmillan.

Meggyesy, D. (1970). *Out of their league.* Palo Alto, CA: Ramparts.

Meier, K.V. (1981). On the inadequacies of sociological definitions of sport. *International Review of Sport Sociology,* **16**(2), 79–102.

Metheny, E. (1975). The creative process in sport. In E. Metheny (Ed.), *Moving and knowing: Sport, dance, and physical education* (pp. 117–149). Mountain View, CA: Peek.

Mewshaw, M. (1983). *Short circuit: Six months on the men's professional tennis tour.* New York: Atheneum.

Meyer, H. (1973). Puritanism and physical training: Ideological and political accents in the Christian interpretation of sport. *International Review of Sport Sociology,* **8**(1), 37–52.

Michener, J.A. (1977). *Sports in America.* New York: Fawcett.

Miller, S. (1973). Ends, means and galumphing: Some leitmotifs of play. *American Anthropologist,* **75**, 87–98.

Miller, W. (1963). *Russians as people.* New York: Doubleday.

Millett, K. (1970). *Sexual politics.* New York: Doubleday.

Morikawa, S. (1977). Amateurism—Yesterday, today, and tomorrow. *International Review of Sport Sociology,* **12**(2), 61–72.

Morton, H.W. (1963). *Soviet sport, mirror of Soviet society.* New York: Macmillan.

Mulloy, G. (1960). *The will to win: An inside view of the world of tennis.* New York: Barnes.

Mumford, L. (1934). *Technics and civilization.* San Diego: Harcourt Brace Jovanovich. (Reprinted in 1963.)

Murray, H.J.R. (1913). *A history of chess.* Oxford: Clarendon.

Natan, A. (1958). *Sport and society.* London: Bowes and Bowes.

Niwa, T. (1973). The function of sport in society (with special reference to sport in Japanese business enterprise). *International Review of Sport Sociology,* **8**(1), 53–68.

Novak, M. (1976). *The joy of sports: End zones, bases, baskets, balls, and the consecration of the American spirit.* New York: Basic.

Ogilvie, B. (1974). The stimulus-addicts, a psychosocial paradox. In W.C. Schwenk (Ed.), *The winning edge* (pp. 43—50). Washington: American Alliance for Health, Physical Education, and Recreation.

Ogilvie, B., & Tutko, T. (1971, October). Sports—If you want to build character, try something else. *Psychology Today,* pp. 60–63.

Oliver, C. (1971). *High for the game.* New York: Morrow.

Padwe, S. (1970, September 22). Big time football is on the skids. *Look,* pp. 66–69.

Padwe, S. (1971, December 14). Sports and politics must be separate—At least some politics that is. *Philadelphia Inquirer,* p. 35.

Page, C.H. (1973). The mounting interest in sport. In J.T. Talamini & C.H. Page (Eds.), *Sport and society: An anthology* (pp. 3–14). Boston: Little, Brown.

Parrish, B. (1972). *They call it a game*. New York: New American Library.

Pausanias. (1918). In W.H.S. Jones, (Trans.), *Description of Greece*. London: W. Heinemann.

Pearson, K. (1979). The institutionalization of sport forms. *International Review of Sport Sociology*, **14**(1), 50-60.

Pearton, R.E., & Gaskell, G. (1981). Youth and social conflict: Sport and spectator violence. *International Review of Sport Sociology*, **16**, 57-67.

Petrie, B.M. (1971). Achievement orientations in adolescent attitudes toward play. *International Review of Sport Sociology*, **6**(2), 89-101.

Petrie, B.M. (1977). Examination of a stereotype: Athletes as conservatives. *International Review of Sport Sociology*, **12**(3), 51-62.

Petrovic, K. (1976). Effects of social stratification and socialization in various disciplines of sports in Yugoslavia. *International Review of Sport sociology*, **11**(2), 95-113.

Pettavino, P.J. (1982). The politics of sport under communism: A comparative study of athletics in the Soviet Union and Cuba. *Dissertation Abstracts International*, **43**, pp. 2082-2083. (University Microfilms International No. DA. 8225834.)

Piaget, J. (1948). *The moral judgment of the child*. New York: Free Press.

Piaget, J. (1962). *Play, dreams and imitation in childhood* (C. Gattegno & F.M. Hodgson, Trans.). New York: Norton.

Pileggi, S. (1977, March 14). Scorecard. *Sports Illustrated*, p. 10.

Plimpton, G., & Curry, B. (1977, March-April). The Green Bay monster. *Quest*, pp. 32-34, 36, 38, 94.

Polednak, A.C., & Damon, R. (1970). College athletes, longevity, and cause of death. *Human Biology*, **42**, 28-46.

Powel, H., Jr. (1926). *Walter Camp*. Boston: Little, Brown.

Prestage, E. (1928). *Chivalry*. New York: Knopf.

Quirk, J., & El Hodiri, M. (1974). The economic theory of a professional sports league. In R.W. Noll (Ed.), *Government and the sports business* (pp. 33-80). Washington, DC: Brookings.

Ralbovsky, M. (1974). *Destiny's darlings: A world championship Little League team twenty years later*. New York: Hawthorn.

Reisman, D., & Denney, R. (1951). Football in America: A study in cultural diffusion. *American Quarterly*, **3**, 309-325.

Reston, J. (1966, October 11). *Minneapolis Tribune*, p. 6.

Riordan, J. (1977). *Sport in Soviet society: Development of sport and physical education in Russia and the USSR*. New York: Cambridge.

Rivers, J.P. (1965). Honour and social status. In J.G. Peristiany (Ed.), *Honour and shame*. New Haven: Yale.

Roberts, J.M., Arth, M.J., & Bush, R.R. (1959). Games in culture. *American Anthropologist*, **61**, 597–605.

Roberts, J.M., & Sutton-Smith, B. (1962). Child training and game involvement. *Ethnology*, **1**, 166–185.

Roberts, J., & Sutton-Smith, B. (1966). Cross-cultural and psychological study of games. *Behavior Science Notes*, **3**, 131–144.

Roberts, J., & Sutton-Smith, B. (1970). The cross-cultural and psychological study of games. In G. Lüschen (Ed.), *The cross-cultural analysis of games*. Champaign, IL: Stipes.

Robinson, J. (1967). Time expenditure on sports across ten countries. *International Review of Sport Sociology*, **2**, 67–87.

Roethlisberger, F., & Dickson, W.J. (1947). *Management and the worker*. Cambridge: Harvard.

Rooney, J.F. (1974). *A geography of American sports*. Reading, MA: Addison-Wesley.

Rosensteil, A. (1976). The role of traditional games in the process of socialization among the Motu of Papua, New Guinea. In D.F. Lancy & B.A. Tindall (Eds.), *The anthropological study of play: Problems and prospects* (pp. 67–70). Champaign, IL: Leisure Press.

Rostow, W.W. (1962). *The stages of economic growth*. New York: Norton.

Roszak, T. (1969). *The making of a counter culture*. New York: Doubleday.

Rote, K., & Winter, J. (1966). *The language of pro football*. New York: Random House.

Rubin, B. (1980a, March 3). *Miami Herald*, p. D1.

Rubin, B. (1980b, April 1). America's fastest Olympic hero, Jesse Owens, loses fight to cancer. *The Miami Herald*, pp. 1–A, 4–A.

Ryan, E.D. (1974). Sport and aggression. In W.C. Schwank (Ed.), *The winning edge*. Washington: American Alliance for Health, Physical Education, and Recreation.

Ryan, F.J. (1958). An investigation of personality differences associated with competitive ability, and further observations on competitive ability in athletics. In B.M. Wedge (Ed.), *Psychosocial problems of college men* (pp. 113–139). New Haven: Yale.

Ryan, P. (1971, February 1). A grim run to fiscal daylight. *Sports Illustrated*, pp. 18–23.

Sack, A.L. (1973). Yale 29, Harvard 4: The professionalization of American football. *Quest*, pp. 24–34.

Sack, A. (1977). Sport: Play or work? In P. Stevens (Ed.), *Studies in the anthropology of play* (pp. 186-195). Champaign, IL: Leisure Press.

Sage, G.H. (1974a). Machiavellianism among college and high school coaches. In G.H. Sage (Ed.), *Sport and American society* (pp. 187-207). Reading, MA: Addison-Wesley.

Sage, G.H. (1974b). Value orientations of American college coaches compared to those of male college students and businessmen. In G.H. Sage (Ed.), *Sport and American society* (pp. 207-228). Reading, MA: Addison-Wesley.

Salter, M.A. (1980). Play in ritual: An ethnohistorical overview of native North America. In H.B. Schwartzman (Ed.), *Play and culture* (pp. 70-82). Champaign, IL: Leisure Press.

Savage, H.J. (1929). *American college athletics* (with H.W. Bentley, J.T. McGovern, & D.F. Smiley). Princeton: The Carnegie Foundation for the Advancement of Teaching.

Saxon, G. (1953). The fate of the immigrant. In A. Naftalin, B.N. Nelson, M.Q. Sibley, D.W. Calhoun, & A.G. Papandreou (Eds.), *Personality, work, community* (pp. 309-315). Philadelphia: J.B. Lippincott.

Schafer, W.E. (1969). Some social sources and consequences of inter-scholastic athletics: The case of participation and delinquency. In G.S. Kenyon (Ed.), *Aspects of contemporary sport sociology* (pp. 29-44). Chicago: The Athletic Institute.

Schaffer, J. (1927, July 30). Pennsylvania bans Sunday baseball as unholy. Cited in *The Literary Digest*, pp. 28-29.

Scholtz, G.J.L., & Olivier, J.L. (1984). Attitude of urban South Africans toward non-racial sport and their expectations of future race relations—A comparative study. *International Review for the Sociology of Sport*, **19**(2), 129-143.

Schram, S.R. (1962). *Une etude de l'education physique* [A study of physical education]. Paris: Mouton.

Schumacher, E.F. (1975). *Small is beautiful: Economics as if people mattered*. New York: Harper and Row.

Schwartzman, H. (1979, Fall). Children's use of metaphor in imaginative play events. *Newsletter of the Association for the Anthropological Study of Play*, **6**(2).

Scorecard. (1969, September 29). *Sports Illustrated*, p. 11.

Scotch, N.A. (1961). Magic, sorcery, and football among urban Zulu: A case of reinterpretation under acculturation. *Journal of Conflict Resolution*, **5**, 70-74.

Scott, J. (1969). *Athletics for athletes*. Oakland, CA: Other Ways Books.

Scott, J. (1971). *The athletic revolution*. New York: Free Press.

Scott, J., & Sauer, G. (1971). The souring of George Sauer. *Intellectual Digest*, **2**(4), pp. 52–55.

Scully, G.W. (1974). Discrimination: The case of baseball. In R.G. Noll (Ed.), *Government and the sports business* (pp. 221–247). Washington, DC: Brookings.

Seiden, H. (1977, September 9). Winning's only way to preserve civilization, according to Woody. *The Miami News*, pp. 1C, 3C.

Seneca. (1970). *Epistles* (3 vols.). (Richard M. Gummere, Trans.). Cambridge, MA: Harvard.

Seppänen, P. (1981). Olympic success: A cross-national perspective. In R.F. Gunther Luschen & G.H. Sage (Eds.), *Handbook of Social Science of Sport*, (pp. 93–116). Champaign, IL: Stipes.

Seppänen, P. (1984). The Olympics: A sociological perspective. *International Review for the Sociology of Sport*, **19**(2), 113–125.

Shaw, G. (1972). *Meat on the hoof: The hidden world of Texas football*. New York: Dell.

Sheard, K.G., & Dunning, E. (1973). The rugby football club as a type of "male preserve." *International Review of Sport Sociology*, **8**(3–4), 5–24.

Sherif, M., & Sherif, C.W. (1969). *Social psychology*. New York: Harper and Row.

Sherman, S.P. (1924). *Points of view*. New York: Scribner's.

Shneidman, F.N. (1978). *The Soviet road to Olympus: Theory and practice of Soviet physical culture and sport*. Toronto: Ontario Institute for Studies in Education.

Siler, C.A. (1919, October). Physical education in China. *The Chinese students' Christian journal*, **6**(1).

Simmel, G. (1950). *The sociology of Georg Simmel* (K.H. Wolff, Trans.). New York: Free Press.

Simons, B. (1980, February). We shall overcome (eventually). *Professional Sports Journal*, pp. 47–52.

Sipes, R.H. (1973). War, sports, and aggression: An empirical test of two rival theories. *American Anthropologist*, **75**, 64–86.

Slater, P. (1970). *The pursuit of loneliness*. Boston: Beacon.

Slusher, H.S. (1967). *Man, sport, and existence*. Philadelphia: Lea & Febiger.

Smith, G. (1973, January). The sport hero: An endangered species. *Quest*, pp. 59–70.

Smith, M.D. (1975). Sport and collective violence. In D.W. Ball & J.W. Loy (Eds.), *Sport and social order: Contributions to the sociology of sport.* Reading, MA: Addison-Wesley.

Smith, P. (1920). *The history of the reformation.* New York: Harper Brace Jovanovich.

Snyder, E.E., & Spreitzer, E.A. (1983). *Social aspects of sport.* New York: Prentice-Hall.

Sohi, A.H. (1981). Social status of Indian elite sportsmen in perspective of social stratification and mobility. *International Review of Sport Sociology,* **16**(1), 61–74.

Solberg, W.U. (1977). *Redeem the time: The puritan Sabbath in early America.* Cambridge: Harvard.

Solzhenitsyn, A. (1971). *The cancer ward* (N. Bethell & D. Burg, Trans.). London: Penguin.

Soubhi, A.M. (1977). Physical education and sport in the life of Iraqi women. *International Review of Sport Sociology,* **12**(2), 107–109.

Sperling, G., Jr. (1975, October 26). *Louisville Courier-Journal.*

Sports. (1978, Fall). Project on the status and education of women. Washington, DC: Association of American Colleges (No. 21).

Stejskal, M. (1970). Folk-athletic games. *International Review of Sport Sociology,* **5**, 175–184.

Steiner, G. (1974, October 28). Fields of force. *New Yorker,* pp. 185–188.

Stone, A.A. (1950). *The effect of sanctioned overt aggression on total instigation to aggressive responses.* Unpublished honors thesis, Harvard University, Cambridge.

Stone, G.P. (1972). American sports: Play and display. In E. Dunning (Ed.), *The sociology of sport.* London: Cass.

Storr, A. (1968). *Human aggression.* New York: Atheneum.

Stubbes, P. (1972). *The anatomy of abuses.* New York: Da Capo. (Original work published 1583)

Suits, B. (1967). What is a game? *Philosophy of Science,* **34**, 148–156.

Sumner, W.G. (1885). *Essays in political and social science.* New York: Holt.

Sumner, W.G. (1933, June). Bequests of the nineteenth century to the twentieth. *Yale Review,* pp. 732–754.

Sumner, W.G. (1940). *Folkways: A study of the sociological importance of usages, manners, customs, mores, and morals.* Boston: Ginn.

Surface, B. (1974, November). Pro football: Is it getting too dirty? *Reader's Digest,* pp. 151–154.

Survey of the Chinese mainland press. (1963, April 18). No. 2978. Hong Kong: U.S. Consul General.

Sutton-Smith, B. (1959). *The games of New Zealand children.* (Reprinted in Sutton-Smith, 1972.)

Sutton-Smith, B. (1969). Discussion in C.I.C. Symposium on the Sociology of Sport, November 1968. Reported in G.W. Kenyon (Ed.), *Aspects of contemporary sport sociology* (pp. 45-52). Chicago: Athletic Institute.

Sutton-Smith, B. (1972). *The folkgames of children.* Austin: University of Texas Press for the American Folklore Society.

Sutton-Smith, B. (1979, Summer). *Newsletter of the Association for the Anthropological Study of Play,* **6**(1).

Sutton-Smith, B., Roberts, J.M., & Kozelka, R. (1963). Game involvement in adults. *Journal of Social Psychology,* **60**, 15-30.

Sutton-Smith, B., & Savasta, M. (1976, April). *Sex differences in play and power.* Paper presented at annual meeting of Eastern Psychological Association, Boston.

Swados, H. (1957). *On the line.* Boston: Little, Brown.

Swierczewski, R. (1978). The athlete—The country's representatives as a hero. *International Review of Sport Sociology,* **13**(3), 89-100.

Swift, E.M. (1983, November 17). An army man to the core. *Sports Illustrated,* pp. 38-46.

Sykes, G. (1958). *The society of captives.* Princeton: Princeton.

Szot, Z., & Jurkiewicz, B. (1979). An attempt at defining the influence of selected factors exerted on results in sport and gymnastics. *International Review of Sport Sociology,* **14**(2), 73-82.

Talamini, J.T., & Page, C.H. (Eds.). (1973). *Sport and society: An anthology.* Boston: Little, Brown.

Tamásné, F. (1979). Involvement in sport and watching of sport events at a large enterprise in Budapest. *International Review of Sport Sociology,* **14**(1), 61-79.

Taps for 'Matty'—He played the game. *Literary Digest.* (1925). **87**(4), pp. 42, 44.

Tawney, R.H. (1947). *Religion and the rise of capitalism.* Baltimore: Penguin.

Telander, R. (1986, January 27). Just a bear of a bear. *Sports Illustrated,* pp. 38-40, 49.

Terkel, S. (1975). *Working.* New York: Pantheon.

Tiger, L. (1970). *Men in groups.* New York: Vintage.

Tilgher, A. (1965). *Homo faber: Work through the ages* (D. Canfield, Trans.). Chicago: Regnery.

Toynbee, A.J. (1947). *A study of history.* New York: Oxford.

Turner, E.T. (1974). The effects of viewing college football, basketball and wrestling on the elicited aggressive responses of male spectators. Cited by Thomas A. Tutko in Walter C. Schwank (Ed.), *The winning edge* (pp. 325-327). Washington: American Alliance of Health, Physical Education, Recreation and Dance.

Turner, V. (1969). *The ritual process.* Hawthorne, NY: Aldine.

Turner, V. (1983). Liminal to liminoid, in play, flow, and ritual: An essay in comparative symbology. In J.C. Harris & R.J. Park (Eds.), *Play, games, and sport in cultural contexts* (pp. 123-164). Champaign, IL: Human Kinetics.

Tutko, T., & Bruns, W. (1976). *Winning is everything, and other American myths.* New York: Macmillan.

Tutko, T., & Tosi, U. (1976). *Sports psyching: Playing your best game all of the time.* Los Angeles: Tarcher.

Tylor, E.B. (1878). Backgammon among the Aztecs. *Macmillan's Magazine* (London), **39**, pp. 142-150.

Ugwuoke, J.O. (1978). *The extent of participation in intramural sports competition by the female students of the University of Nigeria.* Unpublished research project, Nsukka Campus, University of Nigeria.

Umphlett, W.L. (1974). *The sporting myth and the American experience.* Cranbury, NY: Bucknell University Press.

Underwood, J. (1969, October 1). The desperate coach. *Sports Illustrated,* p. 8.

UNESCO. (1957). *The place of sport in education.* Paris: Author.

Updike, J. (1960, October 26). Hub fans bid kid adieu. *New Yorker,* pp. 109-110, 112, 114-116, 121-122, 124, 126-128, 131.

Upshaw, G., & Garvey, E.R. (1980). Preface. In *Institutional discrimination: A study of managerial recruitment in professional football.* Report prepared for the NFL Players Association.

Van Glascoe, C.A. (1980). The work of playing redlight. In H.B. Schwartzman (Ed.), *Play and culture* (pp. 228-231). Champaign, IL: Leisure Press.

Vaz, E.W. (1974). What price victory? An analysis of minor hockey league players' attitudes towards winning. *International Review of Sport Sociology,* **9**(2), 33-55.

Veblen, T. (1899). *The theory of the leisure class.* New York: Macmillan.

Veeck, B. (1965). *The hustler's handbook.* New York: Putnam.

Virgil. (1932–1934). *Poems,* in *Virgil* (H. Rushton Fairclough, Trans.). Cambridge, MA: Harvard. (Original date unknown)

Voigt, D.Q. (1974, Spring 1979). Reflections on diamonds: American baseball and American culture. *Journal of Sport History,* **1,** 3–25.

Waller, W. (1961), *The sociology of teaching.* New York: Russell and Russell.

Walters, R.H., & Thomas, E.L. (1963). Enhancement of punitiveness by visual and audio visual displays. *Canadian Journal of Psychology,* **17,** 244–255.

Watson, G.G. (1977). Games, socialization, and parental values: Social class differences in parental evaluation of Little League baseball. *International Review of Sport Sociology,* **12**(1), 17–48.

Webb, H. (1969a). Reaction to Loy. In G.S. Kenyon (Ed.), *Sociology of sport* (pp. 120–131). Chicago: The Athletic Institute.

Webb, H. (1969b). Professionalization of attitudes towards play among adolescents. In G.S. Kenyon (Ed.), *Aspects of contemporary sport sociology* (pp. 161–178). Chicago: The Athletic Institute.

Weber, M. (1958). *The Protestant ethic and the spirit of capitalism* (T. Parsons, Trans.). New York: Scribner's.

Weinberg, S.K., & Arond, H. (1952). The occupational culture of the boxer. *American Journal of Sociology,* **57,** 460–469.

Weiss, P. (1969). *Sport: A philosophical inquiry.* Carbondale: Southern Illinois University Press.

Wells, H.G. (1911). *Floor games.* London: Frank Palmer.

Williams, R.L., & Youssef, Z.I. (1975). Division of labor in college football along racial lines. *International Journal of Sport Psychology,* **6**(1), 3–13.

Winder, D. (1976, April 2). Tennis courts: A smashing success. *Christian Science Monitor.*

Wohl, A. (1975). The influence of the scientific-technical revolution on the shape of sport and perspectives of its development. *International Review of Sport Sociology,* **10,** 19–38.

Yeager, R.C. (1979). *Seasons of shame.* New York: McGraw-Hill.

Yetman, N.R., & Eitzen, D.S. (1982). Racial dynamics in American sport: Continuity and change. In N.R. Yetman (Ed.), *Majority and minority: The dynamics of race and ethnicity in American life.* Newton, MA: Allyn and Bacon.

Zillman, D., Katcher, A., & Milavsky, B. (1972). Excitation transfer from physical activity to subsequent aggressive behavior. *Journal of Experimental Social Psychology,* **8,** 247–259.

Zouabi, M. (1973). Physical education and sport in Tunisia. *International Review of Sport Sociology*, **10**(3–4), 109–114.

Zygulski, K. (1973). *Film hero*. Warsaw: Wydawnictwa Artystyczne i filmowe.

Index